Lending and borrowing were commonplace in Athens during the fourth century B.C. and could involve interest rates, security and banks, but the part played by credit was very different from its familiar rôle in capitalist society today. Using a combination of sources, but concentrating on the law-court speeches of the Attic Orators, Dr Millett shows how lending and borrowing were a way of ordering social relations between Athenian citizens. Although debt could be disruptive, it had as its more positive side the strengthening of ties between individuals. That was, in turn, an aspect of the solidarity between citizens which was a part of the Athenian democracy.

LENDING AND BORROWING IN ANCIENT ATHENS

LENDING AND BORROWING IN ANCIENT ATHENS

PAUL MILLETT

University Lecturer in Ancient History and Fellow of Downing College,
Cambridge

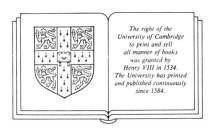

The right of the
University of Cambridge
to print and sell
all manner of books
was granted by
Henry VIII in 1534.
The University has printed
and published continuously
since 1584.

CAMBRIDGE UNIVERSITY PRESS

Cambridge
New York   Port Chester
Melbourne   Sydney

Published by the Press Syndicate of the University of Cambridge
The Pitt Building, Trumpington Street, Cambridge CB2 1RP
40 West 20th Street, New York, NY 10011-4211, USA
10 Stamford Road, Oakleigh, Melbourne 3166, Australia

First published 1991

Printed in Great Britain at the University Press, Cambridge

British Library cataloguing in publication data
Millett, Paul
Lending and borrowing in ancient Athens.
1. Greece. Athens. Government, ancient period
I. Title
332.02400938

Library of Congress cataloguing in publication data applied for

ISBN 0 521 37333 6 hardback

To my parents

Contents

Preface

This book has been a long time in the writing. It started out as a Cambridge doctoral thesis, 'The structure of credit in fourth-century Athens', begun in 1976 and completed in 1983. Although the subsequent seven-year delay in turning the thesis into a book has not been deliberate, the result is probably a better piece of work. I am grateful to my Faculty and College for not putting me under direct pressure to rush into print. The present version is the product of extensive rethinking and rewriting, away from the restrictions engendered by the Ph.D. format, in favour of the broader approach indicated by the change of title.

Concern that this study should be accessible outside the narrow circle of classical scholars has prompted several decisions about presentation. In the first place, I have tried to explain, however briefly, many terms and concepts which will be familiar to ancient historians. To explain everything would be cumbersome, and non-classicists may occasionally want to refer to entries in either the *Oxford Classical Dictionary* or the glossary of legal and associated terms at the back of Cartledge, Millett and Todd (1990). Secondly, I have made extensive use of quotations from ancient texts, all of which are translated into English. Key words and phrases are transliterated, and no Greek script appears in the text or notes. This decision was taken with many misgivings and I am aware of the understandable objections that will be raised by Greek scholars. But the gains in terms of a shorter, cheaper and less forbidding book seemed, on balance, to outweigh the inconvenience to those wanting to look at the Greek.

It should also be explained that the choice of endnotes in place of footnotes was a deliberate decision, which to some readers will seem inconvenient and even perverse. But, with the aim of producing a relatively uncluttered and readable text, detailed and supplementary material has been relegated to the notes, which are therefore longer than usual. A number of technical discussions, of interest to specialists, are included as appendices. In this way, I hope the book may be read on two or more different levels, according to the interest and expertise of the reader.

For all this, the result is still a monograph, with all or most that that entails. I have, for example, tried to be reasonably systematic in the citation of primary sources and in taking account of secondary literature. Such signs of obsession may perhaps be forgiven in what is the first (and possibly the last) full-length study of this aspect of Greek civilization. Although it would be folly to claim or aim at completeness, future researchers should at least find a representative body of material on which to base their investigations. I have, on occasion, adopted a polemical tone in dealing with the earlier literature on credit. This is intended to express as clearly as possible how my views differ from those of my predecessors. Concern for clarity also accounts for the attention to method that I have tried to sustain through the study. What seem to me to be the characteristics of my own approach are set out in the opening chapter.

Those who are familiar with the work of M. I. Finley will recognize in what follows many of the debts I owe to his writings. In particular, his *Studies in Land and Credit in Ancient Athens* (1952) provided the starting-point for many of the ideas developed in this study. But my obligation goes deeper: Finley supervised the thesis on which this book is based and, until his death, continued to act as informal adviser. He is much missed. Other people have been generous with their time and trouble. Professors John Crook and Keith Hopkins, who examined the thesis, made me think hard about the kind of book I wanted to write. Successive drafts have been read by Paul Cartledge, Michael Crawford, Tim Hochstrasser, Iris Hunter, Stephen Oakley, Robin Osborne, Ritchie Robertson and Stephen Todd. Their comments have resulted in changes on almost every page. Although he does not realize it, Mr G. Ponomarenko assisted me in writing Chapter VI by clarifying my ideas about the importance of neighbourly relations.

Over the last decade, personal credit and debt have achieved an unwelcome topicality which hardly seemed possible when I began my researches. A report by the *Money Advice Funding Working Party*, published while this preface was being written, estimates that as many as half a million families in the United Kingdom may be facing more or less serious financial difficulties. In this connexion, I must myself acknowledge many debts (both metaphorical and financial) to a long line of bank managers and their assistants. Deserving special mention is Mr David Whitley of Barclays Bank (Mill Road Branch), a long-standing correspondent, who always had faith that I would (and will) repay the money in the end. Whether my own continuing experience of borrowing and repayment has helped me to a better understanding of indebtedness in the Greek world is difficult to say. Certainly, the range of emotions that owing money gives rise to, ranging from despondency to a kind of reckless bravado, make me unwilling to generalize about the psychology of Athenian debtors.

My feelings towards my wife and children for their support and toleration while I have been writing this book can hardly be set down in writing. I hope they know anyway.

Downing College
Cambridge

CHAPTER I

Approaches to lending and borrowing

AESCHINES AND HIS CREDITORS

Towards the beginning of the fourth century, Aeschines of Sphettos, an Athenian citizen and a former pupil of Socrates, appeared as plaintiff in a court action arising out of an unpaid debt. Why Aeschines should have been the plaintiff is not clear from the fragments of the speech that the orator Lysias wrote for delivery by the unnamed defendant. These few fragments survive through their quotation some six hundred years later by a character in Athenaeus' *Deipnosophistae* (*The Scholars' Banquet*) in support of an argument that philosophers are not automatically the most moral of men. I cite the relevant passages in full, because they provide a convenient introduction to my methodology, and to the chief characteristics of the structure of Athenian credit relations as presented in this study. The opening speaker is Myrtilus, one of the learned guests at the imaginary dinner described by Athenaeus (xiii.611d–12f):[1]

In fact, there is nothing more unphilosophic than the so-called philosophers. For whoever expected that Aeschines, the pupil of Socrates, would prove himself such a character as the orator Lysias describes in his speeches about agreements (*tōn sumbolaiōn*)?... In a defence speech entitled *Against Aeschines the Socratic concerning a debt*...the orator begins as follows:

'I should never have expected Aeschines, men of the jury, to hazard a verdict in a case so scandalous as this, and I do not think that he will easily find another case more tainted with blackmail (*sukophantōdesteran*). For the plaintiff here, men of the jury, owed money with interest at three drachmas per month [3 per cent per month] to the banker Sosinomus and to Aristogiton. He came to me with the appeal that I should not allow him to be parted from his property because of the interest. "I am setting up", he said, "in the trade of making perfumes. I need funds (*aphormēs*), and will pay you interest at nine obols per mina per month [1½ per cent per month]."...'

After this, the speaker again attacks him for the way in which he borrowed the money: he paid up neither interest nor principal; he had let the day of payment lapse, and by a court verdict was judged to be in default; and †a branded slave† of his had been seized in compensation. Finally, after many other accusations against him, the speaker concludes:

> 'But enough of this, men of the jury. He has behaved like this not only towards me, but towards all others who have dealings with him. Is it not the case that shopkeepers who live near him, and from whom he receives advances (*prodoseis*) without making repayments, shut up their shops and go to law with him? Do not his neighbours suffer so terribly at his hands that they abandon their own houses and rent others far away? As for the *eranos*-contributions he has collected, †he does not pay out the sums left over, but they are completely ruined by this pedlar, as if rounding the turning-post†. So many people go to his house at dawn to claim what he owes them, that passers-by imagine he is dead, and that they have come to attend his funeral. What is more, the men in the Piraeus are in such a state of mind, that it seems much safer to sail to the Adriatic than to lend money to him.
>
> In fact, he regards what he borrows as far more his own than what his father bequeathed to him. Has he not acquired the property of Hermaeus the perfume-maker, after seducing his wife, who was seventy years old?'

Lysias goes on to ridicule Aeschines' courtship of Hermaeus' aged wife ('easier to count her teeth than the fingers of one's hand') and, after an invitation for witnesses of the facts to step forward, the fragment breaks off.

On the face of it, this collection of fragments is not particularly revealing about either Aeschines or his opponent. As is almost invariably the case with Athenian law-court speeches, we hear only one side of the story, and we do not even know the verdict reached by the jury.[2] Nonetheless, in the context of this study of Athenian economy and society, the rights and wrongs of the dispute are irrelevant. That is because, ignoring issues of innocence and guilt, it is possible to dig below the surface and use these fragments of Lysias as a quarry of information about contemporary Athenian society. If I dwell on this technique of inference, this is on the grounds that it is fundamental to my analysis of the Attic Orators. It is the published versions of their commissioned speeches that are the essential source of evidence about Athenian credit relations.

This indirect approach is, for the most part, a matter of common sense. The speechwriter was bound to produce the strongest possible arguments in an attempt to convince the jury of his own client's innocence and his opponent's guilt: that was what he was paid for. Even when this meant stopping short of downright lies, the facts of the case could always be twisted in the interests of the client. Once this is acknowledged, the advantage of hindsight often makes it possible to identify the material that is incidental to the speaker's line of argument, and therefore less liable to distortion. As a litigant would avoid telling lies that could be convincingly refuted by his opponent, so he would instinctively shy away from the distortion of details of everyday affairs and behaviour which were within the experience of the jury. To fail to do so would be pointless: arousing the suspicion of the jurors and weakening his overall credibility. So, although the argumentation of a speech might be a complete fabrication, the speaker will paradoxically strive to present a plausible and presumably realistic picture of contemporary social institutions.[3]

Application of this inferential technique to the Lysias fragments prompts some preliminary statements about credit relations in fourth-century Athens. Perhaps the most striking observation is that when Aeschines wanted credit, he turned to a banker only in desperation, from whom he secured a loan at what was indisputably a usurious rate of interest. As is explained below, this notion of bankers as 'lenders of last resort' runs counter to the traditional and prevailing interpretation of Athenian banking and credit. In addition, the fragments conveniently list (with humorous exaggeration) the various sources of credit that Aeschines had already exhausted before turning to the banker Sosinomus. He was no longer able to borrow from local shopkeepers, neighbours (implying friends), fellow-citizens in general through *eranos*-contributions (interest-free 'friendly' loans), or the men in the Piraeus who presumably specialized in high-risk maritime loans. The general impression is of a range or hierarchy of types of credit open to Athenian citizens. When a citizen had, like Aeschines, exhausted one or more of these sources, he moved on to the next available supply. Bankers were only the last in a long line of different species of credit, described in detail in the chapters that follow.

Whether this tentative reconstruction of credit relations based on the Lysias fragments is correct and, if correct, whether it is typical, cannot be settled on the evidence of the fragments alone. This qualification introduces a further, fundamental aspect of my analysis. If it is to have any general value, my treatment of the structure of credit must be all-embracing, incorporating and explaining a wide range of the available evidence. Aggregation of the evidence confirms which elements are typical and therefore potentially significant. In order to make sense of the extensive material on credit from Athens, it seems best to assimilate the information into a model or ideal type (the terms are interchangeable). A model may be described as an attempt to reduce a complex reality to something that is simpler and therefore more readily comprehensible. The process involves the deliberate suppression of detail which appears to be less significant in favour of material that is judged to be crucial – a technique that is applied automatically and often subconsciously in the everyday business of life (see Lockwood, *DSS* s.v. 'ideal type analysis'; Finley 1985a: 60–1). The selection and interpretation of the Lysias fragments given above constitute a rudimentary model of Athenian credit relations, the validity of which can be established only by testing against other evidence.

Ancient historians have tended to fight shy of ideal-type analysis: apparently on the grounds that the process of model-building implies a degree of prejudgement that is at odds with the traditional philological method of 'collecting evidence and interrogating it with an open mind' (Frederiksen 1975: 171). Apart from epistemological problems about the possibility of an 'open mind' (see Finley 1982: 201 and 1985b: 180–3), an uncompromisingly empirical approach could hardly handle the complex mass of data about credit (much of it fragmentary) that survives in Athenian sources. The response to this difficulty has been the adoption of what might be termed the 'anecdotal' method, based on the presentation of isolated and hopefully significant passages. But passages taken out of context cannot be interpreted with confidence; and in the selection of telling examples there is a bias towards what seems superficially familiar. These dangers are appropriately illustrated by the way in which the Lysias fragments have been misread by historians holding anachronistic views of the Athenian economy. They portray Aeschines not as an impoverished spendthrift (for which, incidentally, there is independent evidence), but as an 'entrepreneur', borrowing 'capital' with which to start up an 'industry'. Aeschines will reappear towards the end of this study, where he forms part of an examination of the rôle of Athenian bankers within the complex of credit relations.[4]

THE PERVASIVENESS OF CREDIT

The range of source material to be analysed and incorporated into the model is extensive: the sheer quantity of evidence is itself a crude indicator of the extent to which lending and borrowing permeated Athenian society. A few illustrations may help give an impression of scope and scale.

Well to the fore are the Attic Orators. In the thirty-two speeches attributed to Demosthenes (XXVII–LIX), there are approximately 150 references to credit transactions of one type or another; and in the whole corpus of the Orators there is hardly a speech without some allusion to lending and borrowing. Comedy, in so far as it reflects 'everyday life' also has plenty to say about credit.[5] Both Alexis and Nicostratus wrote plays (now lost) called *Tokistes* (*The Usurer*) (*CAF* fr. 230 ~ *FAC* II p. 484 fr. 230; *CAF* fr. 25 ~ *FAC* II p. 38 fr. 25; see below, p. 186). Several comedies depend on a loan or loans as part of the plot. Notable is the *Clouds* of Aristophanes, where the leading character, head-over-heels in debt, becomes a pupil of Socrates in a bid to defraud his creditors. The slighter parts played by debt in the *Hero* and *Dis Exapaton* (*Twice a Swindler*) of Menander are discussed below (pp. 8, 63 and 77). At least four other plays have passing references to credit implying that owing money was seen as a natural and normal condition for Athenian citizens. A speaker in Aristophanes' *Birds* (ll. 114–16) suggests that a leading characteristic of mankind is to fall into debt and then try to avoid repayment. An unplaced fragment from Menander's *Citharistes* (*The Lyre Player*) (Sandbach fr. 1 ~ Allinson p. 378 fr. 281) expresses envy for wealthy people as not being kept awake at nights worrying about their debts. In another fragment from an unidentified play by Philemon (*CAF* fr. 88 ~ *FAC* IIIa p. 58 fr. 88), 'not owing anyone anything' is cited as a blessing to be ranked fourth to good health, success and happiness. Finally, the heroine in Aristophanes' *Ecclesiazusae* (*Assemblywomen*), responding to a challenge from a sceptical male (ll. 567 and 660–1), singles out an end to distraining for debt as one of the advantages of the new, female regime.[6]

Wherever there is a debtor there must also be a creditor, but Comedy naturally stresses the negative side of the relationship. For a more balanced picture of lending as well as borrowing, there are the *Characters* of Theophrastus, dating from the final decades of the fourth century. This short text, consisting of thirty brief character

sketches or caricatures of people who might be met on the streets of
Athens, has almost thirty references to credit operations. The
Characters themselves, all of whom are unpleasant or foolish types,
repeatedly display their negative qualities by adopting anti-social
attitudes towards lending and borrowing.[7]

Moving away from comedy and caricature, credit also finds a
place in the remoter world of political theory and philosophy. For
Plato and Aristotle, debt was a factor in the political process, helping
to explain the shift from oligarchy to democracy (*Rep.* 555B–56A)
and the rise of tyranny (*Rep.* 566A, 573E; *Politics* 1267a10). Apart
from casual references to lending and borrowing (*Rep.* 459E, 465C,
549E; *Laws* 736C–E), refusal of a request for a loan is the starting-
point for a dialogue on right and wrong behaviour (ps.-Plato,
Demodocus 384B–85C); and the celebrated debate on justice in the
Republic opens with a discussion of the morality of always repaying
what one owes (329D–32B).[8] The philosophical dimension of debt
and obligation overlaps with another type of material: metaphorical
references to borrowing and repayment, emphasizing Athenian
familiarity with the concept of credit. Metaphors drawn from
lending and borrowing are plentiful and scattered through all
branches of literature. I therefore concentrate on two common and
connected images: the idea that life is a loan from the gods, and the
notion of vengeance as the exaction of a debt.[9]

'We are all owed as a debt (*opheilometha*) to death', runs part of an
epitaph attributed to Simonides (Diehl 139 ~ Edmonds II 150). The
sentiment that life was a loan to be repaid by death was an almost
proverbial saying, appearing in many periods and places (Lattimore
1962: 170–1), not least on the Athenian stage (Eur. *Andr.* 1272; *Alc.*
419 and 782). The motif is elaborated by Plato in his *Timaeus*
942E–43A), where, in order to make mortal men, the gods 'borrow'
(*daneizein*) earth, air, fire and water from the *kosmos* – a debt which
has to be repaid (*apodidōmi*).[10] The gods could apparently call in their
loans at will: so did Apollo demand repayment (*ekprattein*) from
Cassandra for his granting her the gift of prophecy (Aesch. *Ag.*
1275–6 with Fraenkel 1950: *ad loc.*). By appropriately pious
behaviour it might be possible to build up a counter-obligation, and
so earn a stay of execution (e.g. Callim. *Epigr.* LV); but false oaths
were a liability (*chreos*) that could not be concealed from the gods
(Theog. 1195–6). The unjust man might pay the penalty himself or
it could be left to his children to discharge the debt (Theog. 197–208).

The presentation of vengeance as the exaction of a debt and the possibility of its transmission between generations have powerful dramatic potential which is exploited to the full in Tragedy. The theme is sustained right through the *Oresteia* of Aeschylus, where conflicting obligations owed to gods and men generate overpowering tensions. The obligation imposed on Agamemnon to exact rec-ompense (*praktor, prattein*: *Ag.* 111, 705, 812 and 823) from the Trojans for the seizure of Helen involves him in the death of his daughter, for which he has to pay (*apotinein*: *Ag.* 1503) with his own life. For the murder of her husband, Clytemnestra owes a debt for which she in turn faces execution (*opheilein, prattein*: *Cho.* 310–11; cf. *Eum.* 624). Finally, the Erinyes unsuccessfully intervene as collectors of the debt (*praktores, chreos*: *Eum.* 319 and 260) that Orestes incurred by killing his mother.[11]

The inclusion in the *Oresteia* of language drawn from the field of finance has not escaped notice (Macleod 1982: 134; Goldhill 1984: 170). But the association of revenge with the concepts of debt and repayment goes beyond a series of striking metaphors to say something substantial about the character of credit in Athens. Behind the imagery lies the idea of reciprocity: the obligation to return like for like. This connexion between reciprocity and credit is crucial to my analysis of lending and borrowing in ancient Athens. It suggests an attitude towards credit relations that is far removed from our own conventional ideology of credit. The links between lending, borrowing and reciprocal gift-giving will be examined in detail in the following chapter. As a preliminary, I cite three further characteristics of Athenian credit operations; all emphasizing the gulf between ancient and modern conceptions of credit institutions.

Tied in with reciprocity is the breadth of the concept of credit in Athenian sources. The range of overlapping meanings of *pistis* – the approximate equivalent of 'credit' – is revealing: trust, faith, belief, confidence, assurance, honesty, proof and pledge (all from LSJ[9]; see Taillardat 1982). Only relatively rarely does *pistis* seem to mean 'credit' in the narrow, economic sense of 'credit-worthyness'. So the banker Phormion is said to enjoy *pistis* with those who know him for a sum of money greater than his own property (Dem. xxxvi.57, with Paley and Sandys 1910: *ad loc.*; cf. Partsch 1909: 359–64). By contrast, modern economists tend to restrict the scope of credit to a precise set of relationships. For Baltensperger (1989: 97), the extension of credit means 'to transfer the property rights on a given object (e.g. a sum of money) in exchange for a claim on specified objects (e.g. certain sums of money) at specified points of time in the future'. That is an unusually broad definition, but the formalism of 'specified objects' and 'specified points in time' is not appropriate to conditions of credit in Athens. Some of the restrictions are made explicit in an older encyclopaedia article by Hawtry (*ESS* s.v. 'credit'), who stipulates that true credit operations must involve a pecuniary obligation. He admits that this condition cuts out both lending of goods with an obligation to return the same goods, and also deposits of goods or money. But as far as the Athenians were concerned, loans of goods were always thought of as credit transactions; and in the case of deposits, *pistis* was paramount.[12]

A second characteristic of Athenian credit operations is the relative simplicity of individual loan transactions, with goods or money being borrowed and repaid in the same way. Obligations arising out of credit sale – deferred payment for goods or services – are rare (see Millett 1990). Also absent from Athenian sources are undisputed examples of credit instruments in the form of promissory notes, cheques and bills of exchange: all transactions were carried out on the basis of cash or kind.[13] One result was the physical transfer of cash and valuables over considerable distances, with all its inconveniences and dangers. The pseudo-Demosthenic speech *Against Phormion* (XXXIV) arose out of the alleged loss by a shipwreck of a sum of money intended for the repayment of a loan; and the plot of Menander's *Dis Exapaton* grows out of a visit by a young Athenian to Ephesus in order to collect a debt owing to his father.[14] From the whole of classical Athens, we hear of only three occasions on which arrangements were made to avoid the actual transference of cash (Lysias XIX.25–6; Isoc. XVII.35–7; [Dem.] L.28; all discussed by Bongenaar 1933: 161–3). In each case, arrangements were *ad hoc* and on an informal basis without any direct involvement of banking institutions. Absence of credit instruments also meant that there could be no *creation* of credit by banking institutions operating on a limited cash base and issuing paper credit. There was, instead, a straight transference of resources or purchasing-power direct from lender to borrower (Bogaert 1968: 336–42; Finley 1985b: 196–8).

My third characteristic of credit picks up this non-involvement of Athenian banks in the creation of credit – one of the major functions of modern commercial banking (Sayers 1967: 218–60). Out of the hundreds of loans known from classical sources, only a tiny number were supplied by banks. The exhaustive study of Greek banking by Bogaert (1968: 370, n. 391) lists only eleven bankers' loans from ancient Athens. This supports my preliminary deduction from the Lysias fragments, that Athenian citizens turned to bankers only as lenders of last resort; but it also calls into question the weight that has been given to banking in the literature on Athenian economy and society. For the last 150 years and more, from Böckh (1817) to Bogaert (1968) and beyond, the bibliography on Athenian credit relations has been heavily biased in favour of banks, to the exclusion of other sources of credit. This is, in a sense, understandable: banks are familiar to everyone, and, for orthodox, neo-classical economists and modern economic historians, banking institutions are the providers of credit *par excellence*.[15] The misleading richness of the evidence for Athenian banking reinforces the expectation that this pattern holds good for the ancient Greek world. Apart from casual references, some six speeches from the corpus of the Orators are directly concerned with a single banking business – that centred around Pasion (Isoc. xvii; Dem. xxxvi, xlv, [xlvi], [xlix] and [lii]). The result is an abundance of coherent, detailed information. By contrast, references to other types of credit, though plentiful, are scattered through the sources and do not make the same immediate impact.[16]

This focussing of attention on banks and bankers' credit has helped to create a picture of Athenian credit relations that is at odds with the ideology of reciprocal gift-giving outlined above. It is also part of a wider-ranging debate on the nature of the economy of ancient Greece. The so-called 'primitivist–modernist' controversy ought to have died a natural death long ago, but it still refuses to lie down. Much of what has been written (and continues to be written) about Athenian economy and society can be appreciated and evaluated only against the background of this debate.

PRIMITIVISTS, MODERNISTS AND WEBERIANS

In view of the surveys of the controversy that already exist, there is no need to rehearse the arguments in full.[17] What follows is intended as a critical survey of the literature only in so far as it is relevant to the question of credit. In order to prevent the discussion degenerating into an unhelpful list of books and articles, related items are grouped together and structured around successive stages of the primitivist–

modernist debate. This gives four more or less distinct categories: 'antiquarian' accounts of credit, antedating the debate; items central to the debate itself; works in what might loosely be termed the Weberian tradition; and specialist studies of particular aspects of credit. In the interests of brevity, less important and uninfluential items are either relegated to the endnotes or ignored. The earlier, detailed bibliography on banking is already covered by Bogaert (1968: 27–34; 1986a), and I have not included purely juristic treatments of credit operations.[18]

Post-classical awareness of Greek writing on credit goes back as far as the medieval schoolmen with their concern over the propriety of taking interest (Noonan 1957). This acquaintance tended, however, to be narrowly focussed on Aristotle's comments about the morality of lending at interest (Langholm 1983, 1984). The whole debate reached a scholarly climax with the publication of two treatises by the seventeenth-century pamphleteer, Claudius Salmasius (de Saumaise): *De modo usurarum* (1639) and *Dissertatio de foenere trapezitico* (1640). These massive and influential compilations broke new ground in drawing on a wide range of Greek, Roman and Hebrew texts in an attempt to prove that there was nothing morally reprehensible about lending money at a moderate rate of interest.

Moving away from the Greek world as providing material for polemical argument, study of Athenian credit for its own sake begins with a short chapter in Böckh's *Staatshaushaltung der Athener* (1817: 123–32).[19] But the ten or so pages that Böckh gives to non-maritime credit are strictly antiquarian in character and something of a disappointment. After six pages on rates of interest, only three are devoted to the possible sources of credit, with a garbled survey of bankers', usurers' and 'friendly' loans. Altogether more impressive is the treatment of lending and borrowing in Büchsenschütz's *Besitz und Erwerb im griechischen Altertum* (1869a: 478–512). In thirty-five pages, Büchsenschütz covers the attitudes of the philosophers towards money and loans, use of written agreements, rates of interest and main types of security. There are also short sections on bankers, maritime loans, public loans and loans offered by temples. Despite Will's emphatic observation (1954: 11, n. 2) that *Besitz und Erwerb* – along with its companion volume *Die Hauptstätten des Gewerbefleisses im klassischen Altertum* – 'n'ont *aucune valeur historique*', it remained the fullest survey of Greek credit until well into the twentieth century.

In 1876, less than ten years after the appearance of *Besitz und Erwerb*, Bücher published the first (and almost unnoticed) version of his controversial theory of economic development. His much more influential *Die Entstehung der Volkswirtschaft* appeared in 1893, and this marks the beginning of what has come to be called the primitivist–modernist debate.[20] Credit was one of the factors discussed by Bücher as part of his three-stage theory of development (summarized by him on p. 147), broadly corresponding to ancient, medieval and modern worlds. In the first stage of 'closed household-economy' (*geschlossene Hauswirtschaft*) such credit transactions as occurred between individual economic units tended to be consumption loans without any proper interest charge; loans at interest were seen as somehow 'unnatural' (p. 114). In the second phase of the 'city-economy' (*Stadtwirtschaft*), Bücher argues that loans were generally concealed as sales, with the borrower 'renting' back his land from the creditor, handing over interest payments disguised as rent (p. 129). Only the final stage of 'national-economy' (*Volkswirtschaft*) saw the appearance of true productive credit in the sphere of trade (pp. 138–9).

As will emerge in the chapters that follow, there is more than a measure of truth in Bücher's characterization of lending between households in ancient Greece as interest-free consumption credit. But as a *complete* picture of credit relations in the ancient world – which it was never meant to be – his presentation is obviously inadequate. Nevertheless, in their modernizing attacks on Bücher's model, neither Meyer (1895) nor Beloch (1902) made much play with credit. It was left to a later generation of scholars, notably Gomme (1937a: 54–6) and Rostovtzeff (1941: II, 1278–9), to indicate, in opposition to the primitivist view, that the banks of fourth-century Athens apparently contradicted the idea of a closed, household economy.[21] And recent years have seen the appearance of a string of anti-primitivist papers from Thompson (1978, 1979a, 1982 and 1988), taking a line on credit that can be best described as 'neo-modernist'. But the concentration in earlier stages of the debate on the issues of manufacturing and long-distance trade may help to explain the imperfect treatment that credit receives in my third group of works, loosely classified as 'Weberian'.

Weber himself introduced the question of credit and debt into his synoptic study of ancient societies, *Agrarverhältnisse im Altertum* (1909).[22] But, because the work is without detailed notation, it is

often difficult or impossible to recover the ancient evidence on which
Weber based his generalizations. In the subsection on pre-classical
Greece (pp. 147–89), he rightly stresses the tendency of peasants to
fall into debt and the importance of debt-bondage. The material on
credit in the section on classical Greece ('especially Athens',
pp. 189–219) is less convincing. Alongside penetrating comments on
the significance of *eranos*-loans (pp. 210–11), and the inability of
metics to lend or borrow on real security (p. 192), are several
questionable statements. I do not know, for example, of any evidence
to support the suggestion that in the fourth century B.C. peasants
were replaced by the landed aristocracy as the leading agitators for
the cancellation of agrarian debts (p. 216). The same objection
applies to Weber's eye-catching association of ancient banking
institutions with those of the thirteenth century (p. 45):

...ancient banking seems to have been in the hands of the tax farmers of
a very few centres of political power, Rome in particular as well as Athens
and a few others. Furthermore different kinds of business...were transacted
with legal instruments essentially similar to those of the early Middle Ages.
Thus the bill of exchange, already known in early mediaeval times, existed
in a rudimentary form; similarly the rates, terms and legal regulation of
interest were all generally comparable to early mediaeval equivalents.

The comparison is reminiscent of Meyer's notorious assimilation of
fifth-century Greece to sixteenth-century Europe (1895: 118–19);
but Weber differs massively from Meyer in labelling this supposed
sophistication of the ancient 'banking industry' as the 'exception
that proves the rule' about the low level of development of the
ancient economy. Its removal only serves to strengthen the general
thrust of his analysis.

Similarly uneven is the treatment that credit receives at the hands
of Hasebroek – the leading disciple of Weber, so far as the ancient
Greek economy is concerned (see Cartledge 1983). His early paper
'Zum griechischen Bankwesen der klassischen Zeit' (1920), though
full of insights into Athenian banking, is distinctly modernist in
outlook. Hasebroek argues here for the existence of giro-transactions
between accounts within individual banks, and a clearing system
between banks to avoid unnecessary transfers of cash. In his later
monograph, *Staat und Handel im alten Griechenland* (1928), Hasebroek
modified his position, withdrawing support for a clearing system and
acknowledging that there was in the classical sources no conclusive

evidence for giro-type transactions.[23] And yet, in spite of these qualifications, Hasebroek's comments on credit are still at odds with the Athenian material. Altogether inadequate is his account of why money-lending was so widespread in classical Greece. He gives as 'the explanation' the desire of affluent individuals to make their wealth 'invisible' in order to dodge public expenditure and as a protection against confiscation (p. 88). Although this may indeed have been a factor in making some people ready to lend money, it was neither the only nor the most important reason.

The probability that Weber and Hasebroek were on shaky ground in their incidental comments on credit does nothing to diminish the appeal of their overall approach to Greek economy and society. Briefly, that is the analysis of institutions and the appreciation of their distinctive features against the broader background of the *polis*. In an earlier paper on maritime loans and the wider structure of credit in Athens (1983), I tried to show how a more realistic model of credit relations could be consistent with Hasebroek's conclusions about the organization of Athenian trade. The value of a Weberian approach to lending and borrowing receives support from two contrasting treatments of credit in Athens. At one extreme are the few pages that Bolkestein devotes to credit in his sketch of the classical Greek economy, *Het economisch leven in Griekenlands bloeitijd* (1923; 135–47).[24] Although no more than an outline account, it comes closer to the core of Athenian credit than any other general work of which I am aware.[25] The contrasting study is Finley's full-length monograph, *Land and Credit in Ancient Athens* (1952), which is also the first item in my final category of specialist studies of particular aspects of credit.

The relationship between Finley's work and Weberian sociology is crucial but complex (Finley 1981: xvii–xviii). That Finley's attitude towards Weber's ideas and method was anything but uncritical can be seen from the final chapter of his last book: 'Max Weber and the Greek city-state' (1985a: 83–103). There may be a hint of this ambivalence in Finley's references to Weber in *Land and Credit*, his first book, where approving citations of Weberian insights are balanced by qualifications (pp. 68–9 and 293, n. 85). Apart from these scattered references, the approach of *Land and Credit* is thoroughly Weberian in the breadth of its treatment. The guaranty aspects of credit, which are the subject of systematic study (p. vii), are integrated into the wider society of the *polis*, raising issues that were to reappear in Finley's later publications, notably his *Ancient Economy* (1985b).[26] There is a striking illustration of the range of *Land and Credit* in the comparison with Fine's *Horoi. Studies in Mortgage, Real Security and Land Tenure in Ancient Athens* (1951). The two books appeared almost simultaneously and both are based on the close analysis of the so-called '*horos* inscriptions' (see my Appendix 1). In contrast to Finley's treatment, the substance of Fine's study is a narrow, juristic analysis of security types, paying minimal attention to the wider ramifications of economy and society.

Much the same could be said of the remaining specialist studies, discussed at greater length in later chapters. A partial exception is Korver's monograph, *De terminologie van het crediet-wezen en het Grieksch* (1934), which is offered, according to the introduction (p. 1), as a contribution towards the resolution of the primitivist–modernist debate. Korver's aim in examining the terminology of credit is twofold: to discover whether the Greeks had a fixed terminology for credit operations, and to see what light the terms themselves throw on the level of economic development. After a painstaking classification of terms wholly or partly associated with lending and borrowing (including those in the papyri), Korver concludes that terminology was not fixed, and that the resulting imprecision suggests a low level of development (pp. 144–6).[27] Korver's book remains an essential tool for the study of credit relations; but, in spite of some impressive insights (see the following chapter), the body of his analysis is overwhelmingly philological in character.[28]

Even more restricted in scope is Billeter's *Geschichte des Zinsfusses im griechisch-römischen Altertum* (1898), which is still cited as the standard guide to ancient interest rates. The work dates from the earliest years of the primitivist–modernist controversy, of which Billeter was apparently aware: his introductory comments point out the rôle of interest rates as a guide to levels of economic development (pp. 1–2). But the remainder of the monograph is exclusively devoted to the analysis of numerical rates of interest. Billeter's methodology and conclusions are examined in detail in Chapter IV. Apart from studies relating to maritime loans (de Ste Croix 1974; Millett 1983; see Chapter VIII, below), the only other aspects of Athenian credit to be covered by specialist monographs are *eranos*- or 'friendly' loans, and banking. Vondeling's extended study *Eranos* (1961) was conceived under the influence of Bolkestein. As might be anticipated, Vondeling is aware of the broader social implications of *eranos* institutions, but his approach is uncomprisingly mechanical. All known examples of the word *eranos* from Homer down to A.D. 325 are catalogued and classified. The result is a strait-jacketed analysis that is only intermittently helpful in the study of the structure of credit (see my Chapter VI).

Finally, there are the detailed studies of Athenian banking; and it was the preoccupation of ancient historians with banks and bankers that provided the starting-point for this survey of modern literature on credit. All previous research on Athenian banks is summarized, and in large part superseded, by Bogaert's two books on Greek banking: *Les Origines antiques de la banque de dépôt* (1966) and *Banques et banquiers dans les cités grecques* (1968).[29] If Bogaert's work is here singled out for special mention, it is because it marks the most important contribution to the study of Athenian credit since the appearance of Finley's *Land and Credit* in 1952. As in the penultimate chapter of this study I make a series of critical observations about Bogaert's methodology and conclusions, it needs to be stressed at the outset that his work is a monument of careful and thorough scholarship. Both books are impeccably researched and suggest many promising lines of investigation. Nevertheless, Bogaert's approach to the rôle of banks in Athenian economy and society is flawed. He is, in brief, hampered by a narrow, almost neo-classical conception of the function of banks in the Greek world, and this necessarily restricts his analysis. Towards the end of his examination of credit banking (1968: 373–4), Bogaert concludes that bank loans were quantitatively less important than the combination of maritime loans and loans from private lenders. That could almost be taken as the point of departure for my own analysis of Athenian credit relations.

PRIMITIVE, PRE-CAPITALIST AND NON-CAPITALIST SOCIETY

What is striking about the debate over the ancient economy is the persistence of the modernist point of view; all the more so, given the existence of the Weberian alternative (Austin and Vidal-Naquet 1977: 7). In this section are examined some of the reasons for this durability: not in order to refight old battles, but because they have implications for my own approach.

At the heart of the primitivist–modernist controversy are a pair of assumptions, both having a bearing on the idea of economic change.

Fundamental is the assumption that economic change is a linear process. Although there may be occasional checks and even doublings-back, development follows a uniform path towards a predictable goal, advancing from pre-capitalist to capitalist society. Out of this arises the supposition that, once enough data have been gathered about an economy, it may be located at the appropriate point along the curve of capitalist development. This in turn suggests the existence of 'middle ground' between the extremes of primitivism and modernism that sensible scholars will naturally want to occupy. Such is, for example, the position that Bogaert claims to hold in his view of Greek banking (1986b: 25–7). The misapprehensions inherent in this idea of continuum and compromise will emerge in due course; preliminary objections are raised by Finley (1965c: 11–13).

Closely associated with the concept of linear development is the second assumption that economic evolution is natural, involves progress and improvement, and is therefore desirable. In the capitalist economy, this positive outlook is typically expressed as the quest for continuing economic growth. The broadly progressivist view of history and society, of which economic development is a part, is too familiar to need detailed comment; much the same can be said of its implausibility.[30] The fallacy of automatically linking evolution to progress is sharply stated by Diamond in the opening chapter of his book *In Search of the Primitive* (1987: 1–48), the theme of which supplies the connexion back to the primitivist–modernist debate.

'Primitive' is a complex term with a cluster of meanings: 'early, ancient, old-fashioned, simple, rude, uncivilized or of rudimentary civilization, original, primary', says a standard dictionary. In the hands of anthropologists, the word is used as a label for societies that are outside the tradition of Western (or Eastern) civilization. In theory, this sense of 'primitive' need have no pejorative overtones (Diamond 1987: 123–5), but almost all its associations are at odds with deep-seated and commonly held attitudes towards the Greeks. The ancient Greeks owe their prominence in Western culture to their supposed excellence as models: 'the legacy of Greece' and 'our debt to the Greeks' are familiar phrases. Emphasis is on intellectual continuity and the high level of Greek sophistication. Seen in this light, it seems almost heretical to portray the Greeks as in any way 'backward', which is apparently implied by the terminology of the primitivist–modernist debate. Even anthropologists have conventionally excluded Greeks and Romans from their category of primitive peoples. Diamond actually offers Plato's *Republic* as his exemplar of a 'civilized' society (1987: 176–202). More usual is the construction of primitive society as the ever-changing mirror-image of contemporary culture (Kuper 1988: 1–14). That, then, would seem to be the motive behind the recurring impulse to present the Greeks as economically sophisticated, which is assumed to mean 'capitalist' or 'proto-capitalist'. The list of works is long and continues to grow: a recent and explicit addition is Lowry's study of *The Archaeology of Economic Ideas* (1987). Intrigued by the analogy of 'our ancient debts in areas from physics to city planning, politics and philosophy to mathematics and exact sciences' (p. xiv), Lowry attempts to trace the ancient Greek origins of modern economic theory. The effort is heroic but misguided.[31]

Apart from the misleading terminology of primitivism, anthropologists are also divided over its validity as an analytical category (Kuper 1988; briefly, Leach 1982: 140–5). So-called 'primitive' societies, when viewed (so far as is possible) in their own terms, turn out to be as complex and sophisticated as their Western counterparts. This can certainly be the case with non-capitalist economies, as noted by Firth in his introduction to a collection of essays on credit in peasant societies:

It may be difficult, however, to relate the amount of credit in existence at a given time to the productive organization of the community. Observers of credit operations in primitive or peasant economic systems have sometimes been struck by the great proliferation of credit relationships. (Firth and Yamey 1964: 32)

The remark is borne out by many essays in the collection, which reveal complex networks of lending and borrowing that could hardly be classed as 'economic' in the conventional, neo-classical sense (see the example of Rossel Island, below, p. 18). That is why economies and their institutions cannot necessarily be ranged along a continuum of development. The same discontinuity marks the non-capitalist economy of Athens and its credit relations. One of the main conclusions to emerge from this study should be the way in which a refined and extensive structure of credit can exist apart from developed or developing capitalist institutions.[32]

The comparative material I have found helpful in framing my model is accordingly not drawn from the credit institutions familiar from the developed world; except, that is, where they highlight differences. Far more illuminating are studies of 'submerged' credit structures within capitalist societies: the consumption loans supplied by pawnbrokers, usurers and other small-scale lenders who barely figure in textbooks of economics.[33] Not surprisingly, the most fruitful sources of analogies are the non-capitalist economies of either the past or the Third World. I have tried to deploy this material, taken from many periods and places, with care, being only too aware of the pitfalls of the comparative method. Simply pointing out an apparent parallel proves nothing; ideally, the parallelism between the two sets of data needs to be sustained, or at least to recur at critical points. Where comparative material is not central to the argument it may still be used as a control, indicating what is or is not likely or possible. To take as an illustration an admittedly extreme example, awareness of the evidence available from other societies could have saved Heichelheim from his extravagant claims about the impact of coinage and interest in early archaic Greece:

Coin economy and interest combined formed a novel economic basis and were responsible for an economic revolution, the beginnings of the Greek *polis* as an economic entity, initiating the glorious centuries of Greek efflorescence ... The striking of coin money and the use of capital for interest are economically unthinkable without a suitable background for profitable capital transactions which the early Greek *polis* had to create both by laws and by attracting enterprising settlers, if its founders wanted to succeed and endure. (Heichelheim 1938: 1, 221)

There are a number of independent reasons for rejecting this theory, but parallel evidence from non-capitalist societies in general – and, in particular, Rossel Island – provides a sharp antidote to Heichelheim's dogmatic linking of coinage and interest with capital and profit. In the early decades of this century, Rossel Island was one of the few 'primitive' societies that remained almost completely isolated. Situated to the south-east of Papua, the island was difficult of access; rumours of cannibalism discouraged visitors and kept outside interference to a minimum. Even so, the anthropologist W. E. Armstrong, who visited Rossel Island in the 1920s, found a highly sophisticated system of credit based on shell money (Lancaster 1962). The system involved a network of interest payments many times more complex than anything encountered in a Greek *polis*, archaic or otherwise.[34]

SCOPE AND LIMITATIONS OF THE ANCIENT EVIDENCE

Although comparative evidence is an integral part of this study, I have tried to ensure that major conclusions are based securely on the testimony of the ancient sources. Even there, the range of Greek material is (with the exception of the following chapter) effectively limited to Athens in the fourth century. That is not a matter of choice: the 'Atheno-centricity' of the surviving literature is notorious, and the primacy of the fourth-century Orators as a source of detailed information about Athenian credit operations has already been noted (above, p. 2). From the so-called 'Golden Age' of Athenian history, the quantity of evidence for credit relations is negligible. The passages from Tragedy cited earlier in this chapter (p. 7) are, in fact, the earliest direct references to lending and borrowing to have survived from Athens. Old Comedy is a partial exception (p. 5) and the handful of references to lending and borrowing by Herodotus and Thucydides confirm the connexion with reciprocity (see Gould 1989: 42–7 and 82–5). But so far as the recovery of the detailed structure of credit is concerned, as in so many areas of her socio-economic history, fifth-century Athens remains a virtual desert (Millett 1984b).[35]

At the other end of the chronological scale, the sequence of private speeches ends abruptly in *c.* 320. This cut-off date lends apparent weight to the idea that the conquests and death of Alexander, conventionally seen as ushering in the Hellenistic age, also mark a clear break in the economic organization of Athens and the other *poleis*. But the links that relate the ending of forensic oratory to the changes associated with the Hellenistic period are at best indirect. The private speeches of the Orators owe their survival, not to the inherent interest of their subject-matter, but to their standing in antiquity as masterpieces of rhetoric. They were also, almost without exception, attributable to speakers who had made their reputations through involvement in democratic politics. Demosthenes is only the outstanding example of a tradition that begins with Antiphon (Thuc. viii.68). Macedonian domination of Athens from 321 and the dismantling of the democracy meant the end of great political oratory. There is a brutal symbol of the death of oratory in the way Demosthenes and Hyperides were proscribed and hunted down by the victorious Macedonians (Ps.-Plut. *Moralia* 846E–47B, 849A–D). It is entirely fitting that Dinarchus, the last of the recognized Orators, who made his mark after the destruction of the democracy, should have been a non-citizen and a Macedonian sympathizer. According to Dionysius of Halicarnassus (*Dinarchus* 2), he owed his reputation to the fact that all the other orators of real merit had been banished or executed.[36]

Concerning possible changes in the economy of Hellenistic Athens, replacement of the democratic *politeia* inevitably had repercussions on the socio-economic institutions that were integral to the *polis*. I will suggest in Chapter VI that the structuring of credit relations peculiar to Athenian economy and society was bound up with the democratic ideology. But any such shift would be gradual; the suppression of the democratic constitution was, after all, intermittently opposed by the *dēmos* for almost half a century (Ferguson 1911: 1–187). As evidence against instantaneous change, it is sufficient to point to the plays of Menander and the *Characters* of Theophrastus – all dating from the later fourth and early third centuries. In spite of attempts to argue to the contrary, they reflect a society which in its essentials is identical to that of the Orators, or even the Old Comedy of Aristophanes.[37]

Outside the fourth century and the testimony of the Orators, information about Athenian credit becomes discontinuous and of uncertain independent value. For the rest of the Greek world, this is the picture that holds good for all periods, including the fourth century. There are isolated islands of evidence that cannot be combined to produce a detailed map of credit relations. Next to Athens, the mainland state about which we are generally best informed is Sparta. The scatter of evidence surviving about Spartan lending and borrowing is typical of other *poleis*. Aristotle has in his *Politics* an ambiguous allusion to court hearings arising out of 'agreements' (*sumbolaia*), which may include loans. The Byzantine scholar Photius cites Dioscurides, an author who may be dated from the fourth century B.C. to the first century A.D., describing the Spartans' use of 'tally-sticks' in the recording of loans (*Lexicon* s.v. '*skutalē*').[38] The list is hardly impressive, yet the broad existence of debt in Sparta is confirmed by Herodotus (VI.59), who describes a mechanism built into the Spartan system for the remission of quasi-public debts. And for the later third century, programmes of debt-cancellation are attributed to Agis IV in 243–242 (Plut. *Agis* 8–13; Asheri 1969: 51–3) and Cleomenes III in 227 (Plut. *Cleom.* 10; Asheri 1969: 55–7).[39]

It is ironic that the strongest evidence for the existence of debt in Sparta should involve its abolition. Both Plato (*Laws* 684E and 736C–37B) and Isocrates (XII.259) heap praise on the Spartans for being unique amongst the Greeks in never having cancelled debts. That is an obvious exaggeration, but the historical record outside Sparta is peppered with laws relating to the abolition or remission of debt. From the early sixth to the first century B.C. the standard collection by Asheri (1969) lists forty examples, to which other items may be added.[40] Agitation for the abolition of debt (*chreōn apokopē*), in association with redistribution of land (*gēs anadasmos*), were familiar factors in the generation of *stasis* or political conflict (Asheri 1969: 73–104; Finley 1983: 107–13): such were the grounds of Plato's and Isocrates' admiration for Sparta. In his paradigmatic account of extreme *stasis* on the island of Corcyra, Thucydides identifies the murderous hatred of debtors for their creditors as increasing the bitterness of the conflict (III.81). Aeneas Tacticus, a fourth-century writer on military matters, appropriately advises that in cities under siege, interest and even the principal owed between inhabitants should be reduced or cancelled altogether, thereby reducing the risk of betrayal of the city by disgruntled debtors (XIV.1). Precautionary measures include the Athenian jurors' oath (as preserved by Demosthenes XXIV.149), which prohibits the cancellation of debts and the redistribution of private property; while one of the stipulated aims of the so-called 'League of Corinth' of 338 was to ensure that no member state abolished debts ([Dem.] XVII.15).[41]

All this, in conjunction with certain modern attitudes to debt, has helped to create an image of ancient Greek credit that is predominantly negative (see Chapter IX). Debt had (and still has) the potential to be damaging; but the all-too-common association of borrowing with the breakdown of the *polis* calls for qualification. The nature of the surviving non-Athenian sources tends to over-stress the part played by debt in time of crisis. Indebtedness typically finds its way into the historical record when the *politeai* was somehow disrupted, resulting in an inscription or occasional entry in a literary source. The bias is exemplified by the appearance of debt in the second book of the *Oeconomica* attributed to Aristotle (and probably by one of his Peripatetic pupils). This section of the work consists of a collection of anecdotes, supposedly drawn from the past, suggesting ways in which states in tight financial corners might raise additional revenue.[42] On at least five occasions, the problems facing a *polis* involve borrowing (Byzantium, 1347a1; Chios, 1347b35; Abydos, 1349a3; Rhegium, 1349b18; Syracuse, 1349b27). At Byzantium, for example, we are told how, during a grain shortage, metics had irregularly lent money to citizens on the security of real property (see my Appendix II); while at Rhegium, poor citizens borrowed from the rich in order to pay off a war indemnity.

Even in the crisis-prone world of the *Oeconomica* there is evidence for the neutral function of credit. At Chios, shortage of public funds led to a decree that private debtors should pay over what they owed to the *polis*, with interest being paid out of the revenues. What made this forced loan feasible was an existing law that debts had to be entered in public records (*eis to dēmosion*). The allusion is presumably to some mechanism ensuring the publicity of credit and other operations involving the transfer or encumbrance of real property. Dareste (1882a; 1902: 105–8) was able to find evidence for a public repository for loan and other agreements (*chrēophulakion, archeion*) in thirty-eight cities from classical and Hellenistic Greece; the list could probably be extended. A sample of the type of record preserved in such an archive survives as the so-called 'Mortgage Register' from Tenos (*IG* XII 5.872 ~ *IJG* I no. VII 64–106). This inscription, recently redated to the late fourth century, records from a period of one-and-a-half years some forty-seven transactions involving real property, many of which include an element of credit (e.g. §§ 2, 30, 34, 37 and 46; see Finley 1952: 226, n. 21; Etienne 1985). Other methods of publicity are hinted at by Theophrastus in his *Laws*: at Cyzicus it was the rule that any offer of property as security had to be announced at frequent intervals for several days before the agreement was finalized (Szegedy-Maszak 1981: fr. 21.1).

Arrangements for publicity are probably the clearest evidence for day-to-day credit operations outside Athens.[43] In Attica itself (and several islands under Athenian influence) publicity was provided by *horos*-inscriptions, of which more than 250 examples survive (see Finley 1952: 3–9, with my Appendix I). And Athens supplies my second, major qualification to the close association of debt with crisis in the Greek world. Credit in ancient Athens was not merely neutral, but had a positive rôle, ordering and strengthening relationships within the citizen body. The main theme of my study is the part played by lending and borrowing in the broad structure of the Athenian *polis*.[44]

The remaining chapters may be summarized as follows. The second chapter deals with the ideology of Athenian credit, and its possible origins in the practice of reciprocal gift-giving. In contrast to the remaining six chapters, which present an analysis that is broadly static, an attempt is here made to trace the development of ethical attitudes towards credit from the earlier archaic period down to the fourth century B.C. Within the fourth century, the relatively abundant evidence from Athens and the Orators makes practicable a detailed reconstitution of the structure of credit. My third and fourth chapters look at some of the more important structural features of fourth-century credit relations, including the purposes for which loans were sought, possible political implications of indebtedness, the problem of repayment, and the rôle of interest in the credit mechanism. Remaining chapters analyse the sources of credit open to Athenian citizens and their varying implications. Chapters v and vi treat the 'purest' form of credit relations, with a strong sense of reciprocal obligation combined with absence of interest and security. This category includes loans between *philoi*: family, neighbours and other associates. The institution of *eranos*-loans extended this pure form of credit more widely, theoretically involving the citizen body as a whole. The closing chapters cover deviations from this ideal of reciprocal, interest-free lending. At its simplest level, this involved unsystematic lending at interest between citizens, without any intention to make a living through money-lending. That, together with lending-at-interest by corporate institutions, is the subject of the seventh chapter. The eighth chapter treats the three main subdivisions of professional money-lending; namely, usurious lending on a petty level, professional lenders operating with their own capital, and bankers lending out a mixture of their own and other people's money. In the final section of the chapter, I try to show how banks played a peripheral (though still significant) part in the overall structure of credit relations. A short, concluding chapter brings the study to an end.

CHAPTER II

The ideology of lending and borrowing

THE CASE AGAINST STEPHANUS

In the previous chapter (p. 9), it was explained how our exceptionally detailed knowledge of the bank of Pasion derived from a series of law-court speeches. Half of these speeches (Dem. XXXVI, XLV and [XLVI]) were the fruit of litigation by Pasion's son, Apollodorus, trying to recover monies which he claimed had been embezzled by his father's associate, Phormion. Our immediate concern is with a passage from one of these speeches; but, as both Phormion and Apollodorus will reappear throughout this study, some detail about their relationship may prove helpful.[1]

Pasion began his career in the later fifth century as the slave of Antisthenes and Archestratus, who ran one of the earliest banks known in Athens. At some date around 400 Pasion was given his freedom and, by a process not clear to us, gained control of the bank. The business flourished and Pasion deployed his wealth wisely, so that some time after *c.* 390 he became an Athenian citizen. Shortly before his death in 370/69, he retired from active involvement in banking; the bank, and also a workshop making shields, were rented to Phormion, his former slave and assistant. The career of Phormion turned out to be no less remarkable than that of Pasion. Not only did he receive his freedom: according to the terms of Pasion's will he was to marry his master's widow, receiving a dowry of five talents. He was also to act as guardian to Pasion's younger son Pasicles; the elder son, Apollodorus, had already come of age. In this capacity, Phormion retained control of both bank and shield manufactory for approximately eight years, paying over an annual rent. In 362, Pasicles came of age and the assets were returned to Pasion's estate, the spoils being divided between the two sons. Phormion went on from strength to strength, and in 361/0 emulated Pasion by receiving a grant of citizenship – probably a result of his public benefactions during the 360s. Ten years later, he appeared as defendant in a court case against his stepson Apollodorus, who accused him of having embezzled a portion of the funds entrusted to him as part of the banking business.[2] The speech for the defence survives, being written by Demosthenes for delivery by one of Phormion's friends: hence its title: *On Behalf of Phormion* (XXXVI).[3]

The case is exceptional among Athenian law suits in that we know its outcome. Apollodorus spoke second, and in another place he describes how, as soon as he stood up to deliver the opposing speech, he was howled down (Dem. XLV.6; see Millett 1990: 179). Such was the impression made by the speech on Phormion's behalf, that the jurors refused to hear a single word from Apollodorus and found heavily against him. As he failed to receive even a fifth of the votes cast, he was forced to pay up the *epōbolia* – one sixth of the twenty talents he was claiming from Phormion. The Athenian judicial system made no formal provision for appeals. Apollodorus therefore sought to reopen the case by bringing an accusation of perjury against Stephanus, one of Phormion's witnesses. From this second suit there survive two speeches, both delivered by Apollodorus *Against Stephanus*. Again, both speeches are attributed to Demosthenes (XLV and [XLVI]).[4] The line of argument taken by Apollodorus was that on the previous occasion the jury had been thoroughly misled by the false testimony given by Stephanus. It was therefore appropriate that he should make vigorous character-attacks on his opponent, of which the following passage forms only a small part (XLV.69–70):[5]

You have been far better off than you deserved, yet to whom among the mass of the Athenians have you ever made a contribution (*eisenegkas*)? To whom have you ever given help? To whom have you done a kindness? You could not mention a single one. But, while lending out money at interest (*tokizōn*) and regarding the misfortune and necessities of others as your good fortune, you ejected your own uncle Nicias from his ancestral home, you have deprived your mother-in-law of the resources on which she lived, and so far as it was in your power, you made the son of Archedemus homeless. No one has ever exacted payment from a man defaulting on the principal as harshly as you exact interest from your debtors. A man, then, whom you find to be so brutal and savage on all occasions, are you not going to punish when you have caught him in the very act of wrongdoing? That is a terrible thing you will be doing, men of the jury, and not in any sense just.

It goes almost without saying that no confidence can be placed in the accuracy of Apollodorus' charges, and it may be significant that no supporting depositions are offered.

Accusations of this general type – stigmatizing the failure of a rich opponent to help out his poorer fellow-citizens – are a commonplace of Greek forensic oratory. There can, for example, be no more than a handful of speeches in the entire corpus of the Orators which fail to mention the speaker's scrupulous performance (or over-performance) of his liturgies. These were items of public expenditure imposed on the wealthiest citizens, the willing performance of which brought distinction. It was also in order to accuse one's opponent of dodging his liturgy obligations. This is what happens in the speech under discussion: Apollodorus attacks Stephanus as the worst sort of liturgy-dodger (§§66–7), while stressing not only his own public generosity (§78), but also that of his father (§85). There are also close connexions between the obligation of the wealthy to help out fellow-citizens directly by gifts and interest-free loans, and indirectly through the performance of liturgies.[6] Apollodorus' attack on Stephanus is characteristically overdrawn, but the message is plain. It was presumably the sort of theme to appeal to an Athenian jury, and have them nodding in sympathy with Apollodorus.[7]

The attack on Stephanus as made by Apollodorus is valuable evidence for what might be called the ideology of credit relations in fourth-century Athens. According to the scale of values to which an Athenian jury collectively subscribed, the good citizen should be willing to come to the aid of his needy fellows with gifts, interest-free loans in the form of *eranos*-contributions (implied in the passage above by the semi-technical term *eisēnegkas*, from *eispherein*), and other non-monetary kindnesses. By contrast, only a villain like Stephanus lent money at interest, so taking advantage of other people's ill-fortune. All this seems straightforward enough and might pass without comment, were it not for an apparent contradiction in the testimony of the Orators. Against the conventional morality of credit, as expressed by Apollodorus, there are plenty of other occasions in law-court speeches where loans at interest are freely admitted without any sense of embarrassment or shame. To give but one example, there is the *First Speech Against Aphobus* (xxvii.9), in which Demosthenes openly tells the jury that one item of his father's estate was 'about a talent of silver, lent out at the rate of a drachma per month (= one per cent); the interest on this amounted to more than seven minas per year.' Other instances of these unashamed loans at interest appear in similar breakdowns of assets making up estates (e.g. Isaeus VIII.35 and XI.42–3).

The problem here is not a simple one of deciding which side to believe. An obvious way out of the difficulty would be to see the conflict as being between conventional and actual morality – the outcome of hypocrisy. Citizens freely lent money to one another at interest, and pretended this was morally reprehensible only when it suited their purpose (typically, in the law courts). Although there is an element of truth in all this, a closer examination of the evidence suggests that the position is more complex. It is as if there were in Athens two distinct sets of credit relations that could be presented as either complementary or contradictory according to the circumstances. The shifting relationship between these two systems can best be approached by an examination of the possible origins and early evolution of the ancient concept of credit.

LOANS AND GIFTS

In his classic essay on forms of exchange in archaic societies, Marcel Mauss argued that credit had its beginnings in the institution of gift-giving:

Now a gift necessarily implies the notion of credit. Economic evolution has not gone from barter to sale and from cash to credit. Barter arose from the system of gifts given and received on credit, simplified by drawing together the moments of time which had previously been distinct. Likewise purchase and sale – both direct sale and credit sale – and the loan derive from the same source. There is nothing to suggest that any economic system which has passed through the phase we are describing was ignorant of the idea of credit, of which all archaic societies around us are aware. (Mauss 1925: 35)

By offering this theory, Mauss was consciously opposing contemporary views of economic development, which saw credit as characteristic of the final, sophisticated phase in the evolutionary sequence of barter, sale and credit (Gras 1930).[8] Mauss's counterargument, that the concept of credit was equally familiar to 'primitive' societies, is corroborated by empirical studies including those mentioned in the previous chapter (pp. 15–18), and also by the testimony of early Greek society introduced below. Moreover, immediate support for the association of credit with reciprocal gift-giving comes from the Greek terminology of lending and borrowing.

In brief, the various Greek words for 'give' and 'lend' are inextricably interlinked. On the one side, the common words for 'to give' and 'gift' also have the sense of 'to lend' and 'loan'; on the other, the words for 'to lend' all have the subsidiary meaning of 'to give'. Thanks to the exhaustive analysis of the Greek terminology of credit by Korver (1934), the evidence may be presented in summary form.[9]

Conspicuous are words meaning 'give' with the subsidiary sense of 'lend'. This meaning of *didōmi* – the commonest word for 'give' – can be traced back to Homer, where all loans are 'gifts' (see n.8). I note only three examples, all taken from the *Iliad*. When Patroclus made his appeal to Achilles to lend him his armour, he said (xvi.40), 'Give (*dos*) me your armour to put on my shoulders.' And when Odysseus and Diomedes set out on their night raid, their friends lent them various items of equipment. Diomedes had left his sword by the ships, so Thrasymedes 'gave' him his sword along with a shield and helmet (x.255); Meriones 'gave' to Odysseus a bow, quiver, shield and helmet (x.260). It is clear from the context that these were intended as temporary loans and not outright gifts, but the words used are respectively *dōke* and *didou*. From the early archaic period, Hesiod in his *Works and Days* (l. 453) speaks with contempt about the improvident neighbour who says, 'Give me (*dos*) a yoke of oxen and a wagon.' And for the classical and Hellenistic periods, Korver (pp. 94–7) cites cases of *didōmi*, *ekdidōmi* and *ekdosis*, all having the sense of 'loan'.[10]

What is striking here is the complete identification in the earliest Greek literature of 'to lend' with 'to give'. Even more impressive is the way in which virtually all words for 'lend' in classical usage have the original or wider sense of 'give' or 'help'. The commonest word for 'to lend' is *daneizein* (Korver, pp. 79–84), a term always identified by modern lexicographers as having the specific sense of lending *at interest* (so says Chantraine 1968–80: s.v. '*danos*': 'prêter à intérêt, pratiquer l'usure'). As a broad generalization, that is fair enough, but there is reason to think that *daneizein* and the associated noun *daneion* ('loan') were originally connected with the idea of giving. The evidence is almost entirely derived from the ancient lexicographers, who are notoriously erratic and enigmatic (see Whitehead 1986: 53–5); but on this occasion they do present a picture that is at least consistent. Under the heading *daneion*, the *Etymologicum Magnum* has the entry: '*daneion* derived from *danos*, which signifies "gift" (*dōron*)'. Offered in support is a quotation from the third-century poet Euphorion (fr. 90): 'whom Hector gave (*ōpasen*) the *danos*' – presumably a reference to the sword that Hector gave to Ajax. According to Tryphon, a grammarian of the first century B.C., *daneion* originally had the sense of 'a gift not to be returned' (*anaphaireton dōron*). Obscurer still is a garbled entry in the lexicon of Hesychius under *danēs*. After some juggling with the text, the entry seems to read: '*danos*: either "gift" (*dōron*), or "parts" (*merida*), or "privilege" (*geras*), or "loan" (*daneion*)'. Korver (pp. 79–80) tentatively interprets this sequence as indicating the changing sense of *danos*: from the part of the sacrifice (*meris*) given to the priest as a gift of honour (*geras*) to a gift in general, and thence to a loan. Whatever the reality behind this particular piece of speculation, the lexicographers as a whole confirm the connexion between *daneizein* and giving; Chantraine links *danos* with the root of *didōmi* – 'to give'.

Modern lexica, including LSJ[9] (s.v. '*chraō*'), contrast *daneizein* (lending at interest) with *kichranai* (lending on a 'friendly' basis); Chantraine (1968–80: s.v. '*danos*') identifies *kichranai* with 'prêt à usage'. The root sense of the word seems to be 'to supply what is needed'. Frequently, *kichranai* does indeed refer to the loan of an object for the temporary use of another person: often the borrowers are friends and neighbours, for whom – as will be indicated below – interest was not appropriate. So there is some practical justification for the observation made in the lexicon called the *Souda* (s.v. '*daneisai*') that: 'The word *chrēsai* [*from kichranai*] is to be ranked above *daneisai*; for *chrēsai* refers to friends (*epi philōn*), *daneisai* to chance acquaintances (*pros tous tuchontas*).' But this simple distinction between charging interest and lending interest-free, loaning either cash or objects, to either acquaintances or friends, is not rigidly maintained in classical texts. Korver (pp. 74–9) cites several passages in which *kichranai* refers to monetary loans, some of which even bear interest (see also Bogaert 1986a: 22, n. 22).

Remaining words used in connexion with loan transactions may be dealt with more briefly. Korver points out that, whereas both *daneizein* and *kichranai* lost the sense of 'give' before the classical period, this underlying meaning is generally preserved by other terms used to describe credit operations. So *proiesthai* (Korver, pp. 89–93) has the broad sense of 'to send forth', with the subsidiary meaning of 'to spend one's money', without any formal expectation of an equivalent financial return. According to Demosthenes (XVIII.114), the *stratēgos* Nausicles was often awarded crowns by the people in recognition for money which he 'spent out of his own pocket (*apo tōn idiōn proeito*)'. Similarly, Aristotle in his *Rhetoric* (1366b7) states that 'generous men (*eleutheroi*)' are those who 'spend money (*proientai*) and do not vie with each other in accumulating possessions'. But, elsewhere in the classical sources, *proiesthai* commonly has the sense of lending, and sometimes with interest; according to Korver (p. 92) it is so used at least eight times in the Demosthenic corpus.

Parallel to the development of *proiesthai* is that of *sumballein*. The word has the general sense of 'bring together', narrowing down to 'make a contribution' – again, without any expectation of a specific financial return (Korver, pp. 93–4). In his *Anabasis* (1.1.19), Xenophon writes that certain towns made contributions (*suneballonto*) to maintain a band of mercenaries who were protecting them against the Thracians. With reference to this passage, the *Souda* glosses *suneballonto* with *pareichonto* ('supply'). Again from Xenophon (*Hell.* VI.5.5), when the Mantineians were under pressure from the Spartans, their allies made contributions (*sunebalonto*) of three talents towards the cost of a defensive wall. But, like *proiesthai*, *sumballein* is commonly used in classical texts to describe interest-bearing loan transactions.[11]

In each of the examples presented above, the process of transformation is essentially the same. A word originally signifying some species of gift-giving is modified to represent loan transactions. This typically involves the creation of a supplementary meaning so that the word continues to have associations with giving. Only in the case of *daneizein* is the transition from gift to loan complete.[12] Also, there is only one classical Greek word for 'lend' where a transition from giving to lending is not apparent, and in this case the exception does help confirm the rule. Perhaps because of the ambiguity of all other terms associated with credit, the Greeks invented a special word to describe lending at interest: *tokizein* (Korver, pp. 97–9). As the verb is apparently not found in any surviving source earlier than the fourth century, it *may* be a relatively late coinage. The rôle of interest (*tokos*) in the development of credit relations is discussed in detail in the sections that follow.[13]

Terminology is a strong argument in support of Mauss's association of credit with gift-giving, but by itself it is not enough. For further confirmation there is an early Greek text presenting patterns of exchange which prove to be consistent with the model suggested by Mauss. The text in question is Hesiod's *Works and Days*, almost certainly a piece of oral poetry, and generally agreed to date from *c.* 700. As I have dealt elsewhere with the historical interpretation of the world of Hesiod, the discussion that follows is restricted to those aspects of the poem relevant to the ideology and development of credit.[14]

A coherent account of the small-scale peasant community described in the *Works and Days* must draw on the poem as a whole; but the material with a bearing on gift-giving, reciprocity and credit is concentrated in a passage of some twenty lines towards the middle of the poem (ll. 342–63). If the *Works and Days* has a single theme, it is how to preserve intact the individual peasant's *oikos* or household, and even increase its prosperity. The passage in question encapsulates Hesiod's recipe for success. Although it forms a continuous whole, for the sake of clarity I divide it into three unequal sections with the following headings: Reciprocity of services between neighbours (ll. 342–8); Reciprocity of credit operations between neighbours (ll. 349–51); Reciprocity and gift-exchange (ll. 352–63). Some general comments on the first section serve as an introduction to the passage as a whole.

Call your friend to a feast, but leave your enemy alone; and especially call him who lives near you: for if any misfortune happen in the place, neighbours come without making preparations, but relations stay to prepare themselves. A bad neighbour is as great a plague as a good one is a great blessing; he who enjoys a good neighbour has something precious. Not even an ox would die but for a bad neighbour.

These verses, with their emphasis on neighbourly co-operation, at first appear as a marked contrast to the stress that Hesiod lays on self-sufficiency and rivalry between neighbours in the rest of the poem. Close to the beginning of the work, he praises strife between neighbouring *oikoi* as an incentive to hard work (ll. 11–26). Later, he promotes self-sufficiency as an essential element of success (ll. 364–7):

What a man has by him in the *oikos* does not trouble him: it is better to have everything at home, for whatever is abroad (*thurēphin*) may mean loss. It is a good thing to draw on what you have; but it grieves the heart to need something and not to have it, and I bid you mark this.

It will not always be possible to borrow what is needed (ll. 407–9 and 453–7):

Make everything ready in the *oikos*, so that you may not have to ask of another and he refuse you, and so, because you are short, the season pass you by, and your work come to nothing.

...it is easy to say: 'Give me a yoke of oxen and a wagon', and it is easy to refuse: 'I have work for my oxen'. The man who is rich in fancy thinks his wagon as good as built already – the fool! He does not know that there are a hundred timbers to a wagon. Take care to lay these up beforehand in the *oikos*.

With this possibility of a refusal in mind, Hesiod advises the well-prepared farmer to keep in reserve a prefabricated plough (ll. 432–4): 'For if you should break one of them, you can put the oxen to the other.' The point behind all these elaborate and time-consuming precautions is to be independent of, and therefore have the advantage over, one's neighbour (ll. 471–8). And in light of all these expressions of individualism and self-sufficiency, it is hardly surprising that Austin and Vidal-Naquet should preface their translation of the 'neighbourly reciprocity' passage (ll. 342–8, quoted above), with the comment that (1977: 204): 'The poet seems to waver between the ideal of good neighbourliness...and the invitation to self-sufficiency.' There is, in fact, no need to diagnose wavering or inconsistency here, because in the context of the Hesiodic *oikos*, the two concepts of co-operation and self-sufficiency are complementary. Clarification of this apparent paradox in the *Works and Days* comes from the comparative study of other peasant societies. In an influential paper on what he terms the 'dyadic contract', Foster examines some aspects of the social relations between Mexican peasants. He concludes that for these people, the ideal of success is:

to be able to live *sin compromisos*, to be strong, masculine, independent, able to meet life's continuing challenges without help from others, to be able to avoid entangling alliances. Yet, paradoxically, the struggle to reach this goal can only be made by saddling oneself with a wide variety of obligations. Strength and independence in fact always depend on the number and quality of the ties one maintains. (Foster 1967: 214)

This seems to parallel precisely the position in the *Works and Days*, where the ideal is also complete independence and self-sufficiency. But, as this is impossible, it is essential that relationships between neighbours are of the right quality: that is, you are the equal or superior of your neighbour, and do not end up in a position of dependence. 'And so', says Hesiod (ll. 477–8), 'you will have plenty till you come to bright springtime, and will not look wistfully to others, but another shall be in need of your help.'[15]

The importance of ending up on the right side in the process of gift-giving is the theme of the second, short section of the passage under discussion (ll. 349–51):

Take fair measure from your neighbour and pay him back fairly with the same measure, or better, if you can; so that if you are in need afterwards, you may find him sure.

The aim, then, is not merely to wipe out the original obligation, but, if at all possible, to create a counter-obligation, thereby converting one's former creditor into a debtor. This mechanism seems to be a recurrent feature of reciprocity in peasant and other non-capitalist societies. According to Foster (1967: 217–19), a strict requirement of the reciprocal relationships between modern Mexican peasants is that an exactly even balance between partners should never be struck. This ensures that exchanges between pairs of individuals will continue into the future. Only when a relationship is to be deliberately wound up is the debt settled with any precision. Identical mechanisms are described by Sahlins (1965: 222–3); and also by Mauss (1925: 35, cf. 40), attributing to the Indians of North-West America 'the duty of returning with interest gifts received in such a way that the creditor becomes the debtor'.

The third and final section of the passage from the *Works and Days* gives more detailed instructions for the conduct of reciprocal gift-giving (ll. 352–63):

Do not get base gain: base gain is bad as ruin. Be friends with the friendly, and visit him who visits you. Give to one who gives, but do not give to one who does not give. A man gives to the open-handed, but does not give to the tight-fisted. Give is a good girl, but Take is bad and she brings death. For the man who gives willingly, even though he gives a great thing, rejoices in his heart; but whoever gives way to shamelessness and takes something for himself, even though it be a small thing, it freezes his heart; for if you add only a little to a little and do this often, soon that little will become great. But he who adds to what he already has, will keep off bright-eyed hunger.

These verses have often been misunderstood by commentators, both ancient and modern, who have been unaware of the institution of gift-giving and its implications. Even in antiquity, according to the Byzantine commentators Proclus and Tzetzes, the verses dealing with the reciprocal basis of gift -giving (ll. 353–5) were rejected as spurious by Plutarch. This was apparently on the grounds that the attitude towards giving implicit in the passage was based on selfishness and obligation, to the exclusion of generosity (Paley 1861: *ad loc.*). More recent commentators have been misled by the last few lines of the passage. The antithesis built into these verses seems to involve a contrast between the unhappiness of the man who takes (ll. 359–60) with the happiness of the man who gives (ll. 357–8). But commentators tend to shy away from this reading; presumably on the grounds that it goes against the grasping mentality that Hesiod seems to show elsewhere. They take instead ll. 359–60 as referring, not to the misery of the man who takes, but the misery of the man from whom something is taken. So the person having his heart frozen is not the robber but the person being robbed (Paley 1861: *ad loc.*, following Moschopoulos; cf. West 1978 and Verdenius 1985). Even so, the straightforward interpretation of these lines is consistent with the practice of gift-giving as described by Mauss. To be on the receiving end of a gift is to be put at an immediate disadvantage: it freezes the heart and places the taker in a posture of dependence. The giver, by contrast, is placed in a superior position. Such is the process Hesiod warns against when he explains how the frequent receipt of gifts – however small – soon adds up to a big debt of obligation. This is in contrast to the man who does not take, but concentrates instead on adding to what he already has, presumably by hard work. This notion then flows naturally into a short section in praise of self-sufficiency (ll. 364–7), and there is no need to adjust the order of the verses as proposed by Evelyn-White (1914: with 363 immediately after 360).

Discussing the passage as a whole (ll. 342–63), commentators tend to remark on its lack of coherence. For Paley (1861: *ad loc.*), it is 'a collection of ancient maxims, somewhat after the manner of Theognis, and strung together without any nearer connexion than the general relations between neighbours'. No doubt the passage can be read as a sequence of unconnected aphorisms; but it is a distinctive part of Hesiod's poetic technique to combine these aphoristic elements as building blocks to make a coherent whole (see Havelock 1966; Beye 1972). As I have tried to show, the passage does have the strong connecting theme of reciprocity and, with its blurring of gifts and loans, is in full agreement with Mauss's account of reciprocal gift-giving and credit in other societies.

The *Works and Days* is exceptionally valuable to the ancient historian as offering a self-contained account of the working of a peasant community. This is something that exists nowhere else in the literature from archaic and classical Greece. Even for fourth-century Attica, the period and place with by far the richest documentation, direct information about the peasantry is conspicuous by its absence.[16] There is therefore the temptation to let the *Works and Days* stand as proxy for everything we do not know about the peasant communities of classical Attica. I have argued elsewhere for the long-term stability of peasant society in pre-capitalist economies (Millett 1984a: 106–7). But in the case of Athens, major developments over the centuries make close comparisons dangerous. The similarities are certainly there: some four hundred years after the *Works and Days* the 'Rustic' (*agroikos*) out of Theophrastus' *Characters* conforms to the Hesiodic pattern by lending out a basket, sickle, bag, and even his plough (IV.11). Ranged against this are conflicting rural attitudes towards the city: the result of the integration of city and countryside that was the achievement of the classical *polis*. For Hesiod, in his village of Ascra, the nearby city or town of Thespiae was a place to be avoided if possible (Millett 1984a: 90–1 with n. 16). Theophrastus' 'Rustic' is, by contrast, described in terms of his relationship with the city. He is twice connected with attending the assembly (§§1 and 3), and goes up to the city to make purchases, have a bath and get his hair cut (§§12–14).[17]

Towards the end of the previous section (p. 27) it was suggested that there were in fourth-century Athens two different sides to the structure of credit. The hypothesis offered above about the possible origins of lending and borrowing within the framework of reciprocal gift-giving goes some way to clarify the relationship between the two components. As illustrated by the behaviour and status of Theophrastus' 'Rustic', out of the reciprocal relationships of the *Works and Days* emerge elements of both continuity and change. There is, as already hinted, continuation of the Hesiodic principle in the reciprocal lending between neighbouring *oikoi* in fourth-century Athens. Discontinuity occurs with the extension of this ideology of reciprocity to the wider world of the *polis*. The network of obligation envisaged in the *Works and Days* is local, not extending beyond the village. But the development of the concept of citizenship and citizen-solidarity provided (at least in Athens) the rationale for the extension of the ideal to the *polis* as a whole – or, at least, to its citizen members. This ideology of mutual support is apparent in the accusation against Stephanus: Apollodorus taunts his opponent with having failed to help citizens who were worse off than himself.

It was probably inevitable that the extension of such an ideal to include the whole *polis* would result in its dilution. Distance between citizens, both physical and metaphorical, gave the scope for a contrasting type of lending and borrowing – the other side of the structure of credit. Here, the relationship between creditor and debtor was more 'impersonal', calling for formal safeguards to prevent or compensate for default by the borrower. As there was no expectation of reciprocal help at some future date, the place of the return loan or gift was taken by the payment of interest. This is again clear from the Stephanus passage, with Apollodorus deliberately harping on the way in which Stephanus exacts interest from his debtors. If a single item can be said to differentiate between the two sets of credit relations, it is the charging of interest. In the remainder of this chapter, the ideology of the two types of credit and the key rôle of interest are explored in greater detail.

RECIPROCITY AND INTEREST

The almost complete absence of information about the peasantry of fourth-century Attica has already been noted. This near-silence extends to peasant debt, about which the literary sources give not the merest hint.[18] And yet it seems incredible that Athenian peasants *never* got into difficulties and were forced to borrow. High mortality rates, life-cycle crises and interannual variability in crop yield are just a few of the factors that conspire to make indebtedness (or its shadow) a feature of peasant society (Millett 1984a: 112, n. 33). The Orators occasionally include the kind of scenario that could have driven those operating close to the margin into debt. Apollodorus reminds the jurors of a recent year, 'when the water even dried up in the wells, so that not even a vegetable grew in the gardens' ([Dem.] L.61). At the opposite extreme, the unnamed speaker in Demosthenes' speech *Against Callicles* (LV.28) tells the jury 'how many people in the countryside have suffered from floods in Eleusis and in other places'.

Those who could not meet these and similar difficulties from their own resources presumably borrowed in the way of the *Works and Days*. It is conceivable that a few might have got deeply into debt and been forced to sell up. But sporadic failures are normal in agrarian societies – probably in any society – and need not be restricted to peasants. The world of Xenophon's *Oeconomicus* is that of the wealthy landowner, but success is far from guaranteed. Socrates is made to remark how, of those cultivating similar land (III.5), 'some complain that they are completely ruined and in want through their farming, while others, again through their farming, have everything they need in plentiful supply'. And again (xx.1), how 'some live in plenty and have more than enough, while others cannot even procure the necessities of life, but are also in debt (*prosopheilousin*)'. His companions reply in true Hesiodic vein that what makes all the difference is good management of resources and the willingness to do the right thing at the right time. In any event, the turnover of plots in fourth-century Attica, peasant or otherwise, was not on a scale to attract the attention of contemporaries.[19]

Historians (ancient and modern) notice debt when it reaches crisis proportions, but not all peasant borrowing is to be associated with hard times or improvidence. Alongside loans of grain to needy neighbours, Hesiod also envisages the day-to-day lending of draught animals and farm equipment. The distinction is made explicit when he warns his feckless brother that if he comes cadging (ll. 396–7), he will not 'loan out any item or lend any grain in the future'.[20] Although Hesiod only once names the actual equipment being borrowed (ll. 453–4, wagon and oxen), the context of other references shows that farm implements are intended (ll. 364–7 and 407–8). Loans of tools, utensils and labour services are a recurring feature of peasant societies. In contrast to credit-crises, they constitute a type of borrowing that is so mundane as rarely to find its way into the literary sources in any detail.[21] To extend Hesiod's list of borrowable items, we may turn to the French village of Montaillou in the early fourteenth century, the subject of a celebrated study by Le Roy Ladurie (1975).

Circumstances have preserved a wealth of detail about the 'structures of everyday life' of the villagers. The picture of Montaillou presented by Le Roy Ladurie parallels that of the *Works and Days* at several significant points. The village itself was a collection of peasant households, and this basic social unit was called an *ostal* by the peasants themselves, and a *domus* by the Latin-speaking Church authorities. So far as can be ascertained, this *ostal* or *domus* was almost the exact equivalent of the peasant *oikos* of Hesiod's Ascra. Describing the collective structure of the households, Le Roy Ladurie stresses the Hesiodic motif mentioned above (p. 31) – the rivalry between individual peasant families (p. 354):

But the *domus* had marked tendencies towards autarchy and subsistence economy. The lack of co-operation between the cellular economies of individual houses in Montaillou is striking. This tendency produced a loyalty to a house rather than a parish, and thus militated against the growth of a civic sense of community.

And yet collaboration did occur between the households of Montaillou, taking the form of loans of tools and utensils, along with other minor acts of co-operation. Apart from loans of grain, grass and hay, we hear of neighbours lending one another wood, fire, mules, axes, pots, cabbages, turnips, sieves, wine-measures and hemp-combs (pp. 5, 42, 37 and 198). A similar list of borrowings can be drawn up from fourth-century Athens through the *Characters* of Theophrastus. Apart from the plough, basket, sickle and bag lent out by the 'Rustic' (IV.11), we hear about barley, bran (IX.7), salt, a lamp-wick, cumin, marjoram, garlands, cakes (X.13), a silver cup (XVIII.7), a horse (XXVII.10), and a cloak (XXX.10). That this kind of lending was commonplace in classical Athenian society may be inferred from the anti-social behaviour of the 'Penurious Man' (*mikrologos*), who forbids his wife to make these petty loans with the words (X.13): 'These things mount up over the year.'

With the exception of the 'Rustic', the setting of the *Characters* is essentially urban. The practice of reciprocal borrowing apparently extended beyond the small-scale, rural communities of the *Works and Days* to the city. But here, too, the people involved – when we hear anything about them – tend to be members of close-knit groups: typically family, friends or neighbours. In Menander's *Dyscolus* the plaguing of neighbours with requests for loans of household utensils is a comic motif of some importance. Cnemon, the 'bad-tempered man' of the title, tries to live the life of a recluse in the countryside. Even so, he finds himself being badgered for the loan of a stew pot (ll. 456–9), a cooking pot (l. 505), a stewing pot and basins (l. 914), seven tripods and twelve small tables (l. 916), nine rugs (l. 922), a curtain one hundred feet long (ll. 923–4), and a large, bronze mixing bowl (l. 928). Appropriately, the cook Sicon boasts of his technique in cadging from neighbours (ll. 487–93):

> ...He told
> You off? Perhaps you asked him with the finesse
> Of a pig! Some folk don't know how to do a thing
> Like that. There's a technique to it that I've
> Discovered. I help millions in the town (*polis*)
> Pestering their neighbours, borrowing pans from all
> Of them. A borrower must use soft soap.

He goes on to describe a part of his technique, addressing potential lenders as 'Dad', 'Mother', 'Madam' or 'Good chap', according to age, sex and status (ll. 493–7).[22]

A list of loans like this could be drawn up at considerable length.

Examples are commonest in Comedy, but they occur in almost all types of literature, including the Orators.[23] A feature they have in common is the absence of interest, witnesses and security: such precautions were neither practical nor necessary. That is the point behind a joke in Aristophanes' *Ecclesiazusae* (ll. 446–50), where claims are being made for the superiority of women over men. It is argued that when women lend items to one another – things like dresses, jewellery, cash and drinking bowls – even though they do not insist on witnesses being present, the loans are still returned. This is supposed to be amusing because there was obviously no need for witnesses in such trivial transactions. A similar sort of joke is made at the expense of Theophrastus' 'Distrustful Man' (*apistos*, XVIII.7). If it is merely a neighbour who wants to borrow some drinking cups, he refuses outright; if it is a close relation (*oikeios kai anagkaios*), he will agree, but only after taking every precaution short of testing the weight and quality of the metal beforehand and appointing a guarantor. The rationale behind the mutual trust that ought to exist in this type of lending is summed up by Firth with reference to modern peasant society:

Household loans of implements and utensils are common. They are normally not interest-bearing since the frequency and duration of service between the same sets of persons obviates the need for any incremental attitude. The services in the long run tend to cancel out. The security is personal knowledge plus the potential need for reciprocal borrowing. (Firth and Yamey 1964: 30)

Extension of this concept of mutual assistance to the citizen-body as a whole brought complications as well as benefits. In theory, the *polis* was, as Aristotle observes in the opening sentence of his *Politics*, a *koinōnia*. The word has no exact equivalent in English, but incorporates the ideas of sharing and holding in common – a veritable 'community of interests' (see Mulgan 1977: 13–17). Allied to *koinōnia* is the quality of *homonoia*: concord or consensus based on the common outlook of citizens about an appropriate pattern of civic behaviour (Kerferd 1981: 149–50). The notion is linked explicitly to lending between citizens in a fragment of Democritus, dating from the later fifth century (DK fr. 255):[24]

When the powerful (*hoi dunamenoi*) take it upon themselves to make advances (*protelein*) to the needy, and to aid them and grant them favours (*charizesthai*), then there is pity and no isolation but companionship and mutual protection and concord among the citizens (*homonous*) and other good things too many to catalogue.

Approximately a century later, the identical ideology was deployed by Apollodorus in his attack on Stephanus for allegedly failing to help out his fellow-citizens in need.

So much for the theory; reality was naturally different. The sheer size of a *polis* like Athens meant that with the best of intentions it was impossible for any citizen to have even a fleeting acquaintance with his thousands of fellow-citizens (Thuc. vIII.66; see Osborne 1985a: 64–5). Unless he was intent on creating a public impression of generosity or extravagance, an ordinary citizen would limit the range of his reciprocal lending. That is why Theophrastus characterizes his 'Boastful Man' (*alazōn*, xxIII.5–6) as claiming to have made *eranos*-contributions to needy citizens totalling more than five talents. Common sense suggests the ways in which people with cash to spare would normally focus their lending on to fellow-citizens with whom they were directly acquainted. Such personal knowledge would typically depend on ties of kinship, locality and friendship – or a combination of all three. The influence of these factors is examined in detail in Chapters v–vi. In general terms, the greater the 'social distance' between two citizens, the less likely it became that they would be willing to lend to one another without appropriate precautions. As relationships became increasingly tenuous, a position would eventually be reached at which the 'personal knowledge' referred to by Firth in the quotation above ceased to exist. Beyond that point it became legitimate for the lender to require some formal sanction to guarantee repayment. Along with absence of personal knowledge went the improbability of a reciprocal loan or similar service. This opened the way for the payment of interest by way of a substitute for the return favour. In theory, repayment of principal with the addition of an interest charge constituted a final settlement of the obligation with no expectation that the relationship between borrower and lender would continue into the future.[25]

The concept of non-reciprocal lending is presumably as old as reciprocity itself. What marked a new departure was its formal acceptance within the world of the *polis*. Such a major step, a potential threat to the ideal of citizen solidarity, attracted the attention of both contemporaries and later theorists. Apart from traces surviving in archaic customs and laws, the recognition of formal, interest-bearing loan transactions caught the concern of conservative thinkers like Plato and Aristotle. The fullest discussion of the characteristics of the two types of relationship comes in a long passage from the *Nicomachean Ethics* (1162b21–63a6), where it forms part of Aristotle's analysis of friendship (*philia*):

There are two ways of being just, one unwritten (*agraphon*), and one governed by rules of law (*kata nomon*). And similarly, one type of friendship of utility (*to chrēsimon philias*) would seem to depend on character (*ēthikē*) and the other on rules (*nomikē*) ... Friendship dependent on rules is the type that is on explicit conditions (*epi rhētois*). One type of this is entirely mercenary (*pampan agoraia*) and requires immediate payment (*ek cheiros eis cheira*), the other is more generous and postpones the time (of repayment), but conforms to an agreement (requiring) one thing in return for another. In this kind of friendship it is clear and unambiguous what is owed (*to opheilēma*), but the postponement is a friendly aspect of it. That is why some cities do not allow legal actions (*dikai*) in these cases, but think that people who have formed an arrangement on the basis of trust (*kata pistin*) must put up with the outcome.
Friendship (for utility) that depends on character (*ēthikē*) is not on explicit conditions (*ouk epi rhētois*). Someone makes a present or whatever it is, as to a friend, but expects to get back as much or more, since he assumes that it is not a free gift but a loan (*ou dedōkōs alla chrēsas*). And if he does not dissolve the friendship on the terms on which he formed it, he will accuse the other... We should, if we can, make a return worthy of what we have received, (if the other has undertaken the friendship) willingly. For we should never make a friend of someone who is unwilling, but must suppose that we were in error at the beginning, and received a benefit from the wrong person; for since it was not from a friend, and this was not why he was doing it, we must dissolve the arrangement as though we had received a good turn on explicit conditions (*epi rhētois*).

There are difficulties about the detailed interpretation of this passage, not the least of which is the extreme compression of Aristotle's Greek, making translation impossible without expansion and paraphrase. Also problematical is use of the word *philos* ('friend') to cover a disconcertingly wide range of relationships.[26] Setting aside these obstacles, Aristotle seems to be giving guidance for the conduct of two sets of relations: those which are according to rules (*nomikē*), on explicit conditions (*epi rhētois*) and usually 'one-off'; and those which depend on character (*ēthikē*), where nothing is settled and there is the expectation that reciprocity will continue into the future. Rules for the *ēthikē* relationship are strongly reminiscent of the advice from Hesiod about giving only to one who gives in return (above, p. 33). Where a relationship starts out as *ēthikē*, but one of the partners refuses to reciprocate, it must be transformed into a *nomikē* association and terminated.

Aristotle's parenthetical observation, that in certain states legal backing was refused to loan and other agreements, is borne out by a law, not from Athens, but from Italian Locri. According to Zenobius (*Prov.* v.4), Zaleucus – the early seventh-century lawgiver of Locri – established a law forbidding the use of written agreements in loan transactions. Although Zenobius was writing in the second century A.D. and the tradition is necessarily suspect, this may reflect an attempt to preserve the gift element in loans and prevent their development into formal obligations enforceable at law.[27] Viewed against this background of informal gifts and formal loans, an otherwise obscure custom from Cnossus makes better sense. In the fifty-third of his 'Greek Questions' (*Moralia* 303c), Plutarch asks: 'Why was it the custom among the Cnossians for those who borrowed money to snatch the cash?' And he offers the tentative solution: 'Was it in order that if they defaulted (*aposterountes*) they might be liable to the charge of violence and so punished the more?' Halliday (1928: *ad loc.*) admits to being baffled by this, while McCartney (1931) ingeniously, but unconvincingly, explains the snatching as a means of avoiding the evil eye. In fact, Plutarch's original suggestion may point in the right direction. Snatching could have been a legal fiction designed, in the absence of laws relating to the breaking of agreements, to differentiate between a loan and an outright gift. By symbolically assimilating loan to theft, a legal sanction could be established against defaulting debtors.

In the passage from the *Ethics* quoted above, Aristotle apparently accepts the *status quo* regarding formal and informal transactions. Plato, however, was unwilling to compromise. In his second-best society, described in the *Laws*, loans at interest were not to be recoverable by process of law (742c; cf. 921c): 'It will be in order for the borrower to refuse absolutely to return both interest and principal.' By contrast, the raising of *eranos*-loans is explicitly allowed (915E); after all, *eranos*-credit was symptomatic of, and served to strengthen, citizen-solidarity. That is presumably the explanation behind Plato's reservation that *eranos*-contributions should not be recoverable at law. They were, as he says, raised by and from friends (*philoi*), between whom court actions were inappropriate (Millett 1990: 186–7).

Part of the detailed thinking behind Plato's objections to formal credit transactions is made explicit in the *Republic* (555E–56B), where Socrates identifies interest-bearing loans as a piece of the process responsible for subverting the stability of oligarchy, leading to democracy. In brief, the wealthiest citizens are presented as abusing their positions of power by encouraging the less well-off to spend heavily and run into debt. This is done deliberately, so that the wealthy may lend them money (*eisdaneizontes*) as a prelude to buying them out, so becoming still richer and more powerful. The outcome is a large body of disaffected people 'burdened with debt', but the danger they pose is ignored by the wealthy (555E):

> These money-makers (*chrēmatistai*) with bent-down heads, pretending not to see them, but inserting the sting of their money into any of the remainder who do not resist, and harvesting from them in interest as it were manifold offspring of the parent sum, foster the drone and pauper element in the state.[28]

Indebtedness also has its part to play in the shift from democracy to tyranny, at least as envisaged by Plato (556A). The popular leader (and potential tyrant) is seen as winning the support of the mob by hinting at the redistribution of land and cancellation of debts (see above, p. 21). As in the *Laws*, the solution offered by the *Republic* to the destructive rôle of debt is a law that 'voluntary agreements' (*ta hekousia sumbolaia*) should be at the risk of the person on the giving and not the receiving end (556A–B).[29]

Plato's broad preoccupation with interest-bearing loans arose out of the threat he perceived that they posed to the unity of the *polis* – the rich get richer and the poor are disfranchised. There is an analogous sense of the inappropriateness of interest in the *Nicomachean Ethics* (1121b34), where Aristotle contrasts 'generosity' (*eleutheria*) with 'mean-spiritedness' (*aneleutheria*). As an extreme illustration of the latter, he cites 'usurers (*tokistai*) lending small sums at high interest (*epi pollōi*)'. This is because they 'take more than they ought and from the wrong sources' (1122a1–3), by which Aristotle presumably means poor citizens. At the opposite end of the scale, the generous man gets his wealth from proper sources (his own private means, 1120b1), and gives it in the right amounts at the right time to the right people (1120a24–6). Again, it is to be presumed that Aristotle has in mind the deserving poor, which brings us back to the sentiments expressed a century earlier by Democritus (above, p. 39).

In a valuable digression on money and interest in the Greek world, George Grote – himself a banker – contrasts the absence of 'all public antipathy against lenders at interest' with the outmoded views of the philosophers (1846–56: II, 476–83 = ch. XI). 'But the feeling against lending money', he writes, 'remained in the bosoms of philosophical men long after it had ceased to be justified by the appearances of the case as at first it had really been' (pp. 481–2). The impression given (and not only by Grote) is that Plato and Aristotle were badly out of touch with reality, defending an unpopular and untenable position on interest-bearing versus interest-free credit. And yet Apollodorus' attack on Stephanus, with which this chapter opened, shows how 'public antipathy against lenders at interest' could still appear as a part of conventional morality.[30] Where the ideology of Plato and Aristotle departed from current practice was in its assumption that the two systems of formal and reciprocative credit were necessarily incompatible. Different kinds of relationship were appropriate to the varying degrees of social distance between the people who made up the *polis*. Alongside his talent loaned out at interest (above, pp. 26–7), the elder Demosthenes had also at the time of his death a further talent lent out in *eranos*-loans of between 200 and 300 dr. apiece (Dem. XXVII.11). In the remainder of this study, I hope to demonstrate the scope for integration between the two systems of lending and borrowing. As a preliminary, the final section of this chapter traces, so far as is possible, the intrusion of formal elements into the early structure of credit.

INTEREST AND THE EARLY CREDIT MECHANISM

A history of Greek credit relations through time cannot be written, not even for Athens. As explained in the opening chapter (pp. 19–20), only for the fourth century is it possible to recover the structure of credit in any detail, resulting in an analysis that is therefore essentially static. It is, of course, unrealistic to suggest that credit relationships stood completely still, even within the fourth century; but I would argue that changes were minimal and warrant the assumption of a static structure (see Ober 1989: 36–8). The same assumption cannot, however, be made about the three centuries or so before 400 B.C. So far in this chapter I have suggested ways in which fourth-century credit relations reflect the origins and early development of credit as a species of reciprocal gift-giving. The picture that has emerged is one of comparative statics, with models being compared across three hundred and more years of archaic and classical history. Ideally, the gap should be filled with a sequence of models: each one representing the credit structure at some significant point along its line of development down to the late classical period and beyond. In practice, the ancient sources are hopelessly inadequate for anything on this scale. The only partial exception involves the payment of interest, where it may be possible to build some kind of bridge between the two models. That said, it has to be emphasized that much of the reconstruction that follows is necessarily hypothetical.

Perhaps the most speculative part of the process concerns the origin of interest payments. Conventional theories argue along etymological lines from the word *tokos*, the commonest Greek term for 'interest', which in this context is connected with the offspring of cattle. It is explained how in primitive, pastoral societies, cattle were commonly lent and borrowed. If the loan were for any length of time, the cattle would naturally increase in number and therefore be returned with *tokos* (see, for example, Appleton 1919: 469–76). Pausanias tells a story which, however unhistorical, seems to fit the bill. It concerns a Messenian called Polychares, allegedly a victor in the Olympic Games of 764 (IV.5):

This man, possessing cattle without land of his own to provide them with sufficient grazing, gave them to Euaephnus the Spartan to feed on his land, Euaephnus to have a share of the produce of the cattle (*tou karpou tōn boōn*).

That arrangement finds no parallel from the later Greek world, where the importance of cattle in food production is disputed (see Hodkinson 1988; Skydsgaard 1988). In fact, none of the passages connecting *tokos* as interest back to 'offspring' mention cattle. According to Aristotle, in a celebrated observation (*Politics* 1258b5), interest is called *tokos* because 'the offspring is of the same kind as the parent; *tokos* begets coin out of other coin.[31] Similarly neutral are the punning passages from Plato's *Republic* cited above (p. 43 with n. 28). According to LSJ[9] (s.v. '*tokos*'), the word has the general sense of the offspring of any living creature, or the act of parturition itself. Also in evidence is *tokos* with the metaphorical meaning of the increase of seed sown in the earth (Xen. *Cyr.* VIII.3.38; Philemon, *CAF* fr. 88 ~ *FAC* IIIa 58 fr. 88). I therefore prefer to take *tokos* with the sense of interest as referring back to a general sense of increase, rather than to the specific case of cattle. It may be that the concept of interest payments was already established before the parallel with parturition was appreciated and *tokos* applied to interest.[32]

As an alternative to etymological explanations of interest, it may help to think along institutional lines, harking back to a detail in the gift-giving process as described by Hesiod (ll. 349–51). When repaying a gift to a neighbour, Hesiod advises repayment of the same amount, 'or better if you can; so that if you are in need afterwards, you may find him sure' (see above, pp. 32–3). Commentators on the *Works and Days* have instinctively interpreted this additional payment as 'interest' (so Paley 1861: *ad loc.*); and interest is the term used by Mauss to describe an analogous aspect of gift-giving in modern non-capitalist societies (1925: 35). Korver alone seems to grasp the significance of these verses as a possible indication of the origin of interest (1934: 63). He suggests that the obligation to pay interest on loans was originally a moral liability and not, as later, a formal commitment enforceable at law. Of course, the material collected by Mauss shows how moral obligations can be even more binding than legal commitments; but the testimony of the *Works and Days* implies that the return of a loan without interest was at least an acceptable alternative. The problem lies in identifying the phase in the development of credit during which the shift took place, with interest emerging as a formal obligation legitimately imposed by the lender.[33]

The earliest appearance of *tokos* as interest in a source with a secure date is in one of Pindar's *Olympian Odes* (x.5–9), composed *c.* 475. The poet apologizes for having forgotten that he was 'owing' (*opheilōn*) a poem to his patron: 'But *tokos* is able to do away with a bitter rebuke.' If anything, Pindar endows interest with the Hesiodic quality of something extra and unexpected, putting the borrower back on an equal footing with the lender. But this is a piece of poetry, and the point cannot be pressed. The chief interest of the passage is in showing how, already in the earlier fifth century, the terminology of interest and credit could provide material for a high-flown poetic metaphor.[34] What seems to be certain is that the formalizing of interest was complete by the later fifth century, where the plays of Aristophanes supply a *terminus ante quem*. So far as Aristophanic comedy is concerned, interest is an accepted feature of life; notably in the *Clouds* (ll. 1286–97), where the payment of interest is the subject of an elaborate joke. In the absence of specific evidence, the most we can do is to draw guarded conclusions about the circumstances likely to favour such a decisive adjustment in the character of interest.

It is difficult to imagine a formal system of interest payments within the close-knit community described in the *Works and Days*. The whole system of generalized reciprocity detailed by Hesiod depended on the preservation of good relations between neighbours who were apparently on a more or less equal footing. Any person who tried to insist on interest payments would quickly find himself excluded from communal activities. Imposition of interest is possible only for people who are in some way outside the community – either in terms of physical distance, or because a higher level of prosperity (or breeding) puts them on a different social plane. As it stands, the model derived from the *Works and Days* has no opening for people like this; it shows a closed, self-contained system, with simple mechanisms for maintaining short- and medium-term equilibrium.[35]

In the short run, equilibrium could be preserved by temporary transfers of commodities (typically grain) between *oikoi*. There is an excellent, though fictitious, description of the process in a letter of Alciphron (II.3):

The violent hailstorm has sheared off our standing grain, and there is nothing to save us from famine. For lack of cash we cannot buy imported wheat. But you, so I hear, have something left over from last year's good harvest. So please lend me (*daneison*) twenty measures, to give me the means of saving my own life and the lives of my wife and children. And when a year of good harvest comes, we will repay the same measure, or better if the crop is abundant. Do not allow good neighbours to go down in straitened times.

Although this is a late, literary composition, the Hesiodic echo is unmistakable (cf. II.12); and the letter spells out in realistic detail one of the several 'survival strategies' adopted by peasants to tide themselves over short-term difficulties.[36] The worst that could happen would be a habitual borrower being turned away empty-handed. Hesiod warns his brother that he may be able to cadge from his neighbours two or three times, but beyond that he will be wasting his time (ll. 394–404). In the medium run, more significant adjustments could be made by transfers of real property. Again, the process is described in the *Works and Days* (ll. 334–41), with less efficient farmers – including persistent borrowers – having their holdings absorbed by the more successful *oikoi*.

In the short and medium term, the system could cope with disturbances on a limited scale; but in the long term, the position was more precarious. In the first place, dependence on internal adjustments to preserve stability broke down when crises affected whole sections of the community. If a majority of smallholders were in difficulty, there could be no temporary redistribution between neighbours as envisaged in the letter quoted above. Secondly, tensions would build up as extra land accumulated in the hands of the more prosperous *oikoi*, and communities ceased to be collections of peasant proprietors of even approximately equal status. The process may be seen in action in a range of agrarian societies, including the Punjab in the early twentieth century (Darling 1947: 197–9), and Russia before the Revolution (Dobb 1966: 43–4).

One or both of these difficulties may have faced the peasantry of Attica in the period before the legislation of Solon (traditionally dated to 594/3; see *AO* xi). Although the roots of the Solonic crisis are not recoverable with any precision, they are largely irrelevant to my purpose here.[37] As indicated above (p. 36), indebtedness and obligation are recurring characteristics of peasant society. It would need only a succession of bad harvests (unusual, but by no means unprecedented: see Hdt. iv.151) to push marginal cultivators into debt or dependence. However unusual the political outcome, there is no need to hunt for special economic factors behind the Solonic crisis.[38] As conventional reciprocal agreements could not cope with generalized disturbances, hungry peasants would be forced to look outside their immediate community, attaching themselves to some person of substance as a protector. Although patrons are typically identified with aristocrats, a wealthy local landowner would do equally well (Garnsey 1988: 58–63). That may have been the origin of the categories (peculiar to Attica) called *hektēmoroi* and *pelatai*, who probably represented groups of dependent peasants rather than debt-bondsmen (Finley 1965a: 156; cf. Andrewes in *CAH*[2] iii part 3 337–81). A characteristic of this type of relationship is the exploitation of the inferior partner. According to the Aristotelian *Athenaion Politeia* (*Constitution of Athens* II), such was the position in Attica immediately before the archonship of Solon.

The purpose behind the debt-dependence mechanism is identified by Finley (1965a: 155–6) as the securing of a labour force rather than adding to income through interest payments (cf. Gallant 1982: 122–4). That may well be right, as the ancient *testimonia* emphasize enslavement as the consequence of debt; interest is not so much as mentioned in the *Constitution of Athens*.[39] In marked contrast is an intriguing passage from Plutarch's *Greek Questions* (xviii), purporting to give an account of affairs at Megara after the expulsion of the tyrant Theagenes:

What is 'return interest' (*palintokia*)?

When the Megarians had expelled Theagenes their tyrant, for a short time they were well disciplined in their government. But later, when the demagogues had poured a full and heady draught of freedom for them, as Plato says, they were utterly corrupted. Among the shocking acts of misconduct towards the wealthy, the poor would enter their homes and insist on being entertained and banqueted sumptuously. But if they did not receive what they demanded, they would treat all the household with violence and insult. Finally, they enacted a decree (*dogma*) whereby they took back from the lenders (*para tōn daneistōn*) the interest they happened to have given. They referred to the affair as 'return interest'.

If the traditional datings can be believed, the association of Theagenes with Cylon, the would-be tyrant of Athens, places these events in the early sixth century. That would make them roughly contemporary with the Solonic crisis in the neighbouring state of Attica.[40] Odd statements by Aristotle (*Politics* 1305a24–6) and Thucydides (1.126) suggest that Theagenes was a popular tyrant who came to power by supporting the poor against the rich. According to Plutarch's source, even after the expulsion of the tyrant the poor were able to keep or regain the upper hand. Compelling the wealthy to offer hospitality to the poor looks like a deliberate distortion of the patron–client relationship, reversing the rôles of exploiters and exploited. This is presumably to be understood as the context of the *dogma*, forced on the rich by the poor, revising the terms of loan transactions.

Whatever the historicity of this passage, it preserves the tradition of a limited restitution of interest, as opposed to the *seisachtheia* or wholesale cancellation of debts, attributed to Solon. The implication is that payment of interest, not repayment of the principal, was resented as unjust and exploitative. The concept of *palintokia* therefore represents a return to the system described in the *Works and Days*, where interest was not imposed by the creditor as a condition of his agreement.

On the face of it, the case of Megara after Theagenes is comparable to Attica before Solon: the rich and powerful took advantage of their position to exploit or oppress those in difficulties. Even so, the Athenian evidence does have a different slant. For Megara, there is no information about the domination of the poor by the rich: that has to be inferred from the subsequent revolt against interest. At Athens, there is evidence about the exploitation of the poor, but nothing reliable about interest payments. And yet, the one fragment of evidence that does link interest with Solon also ties in with the Megarian material. There is a law, attributed to Solon, quoted by the speaker in Lysias' speech *Against Theomnestus* (x.18):

'Money is to be placed out (*to argurion stasimon*) at whatever rate the lender (*ho daneizōn*) may want.'

'Placed out', my fine fellow, is here not a case of placing in the balance, but of exacting as much interest as one wishes.

As to whether the law is genuinely Solonic, use of the term *stasimon* with the sense of 'lent' does at least guarantee that it is archaic. *Stasimon* with this precise meaning occurs only in this passage (Billeter 1898: 5; Korver 1934: 114).

It is a reasonable assumption that the law dates from some disturbance over debt during the archaic period. Given our knowledge of early Athenian history, the natural place to locate this law would be alongside the legislation of Solon: removal of the power to enslave debtors was compensated by confirmation of the lender's right to exact interest. Granted the antiquity of the law, that it cannot with any certainty be linked with Solon does not matter much. It is to be interpreted as the reverse of the Megarian *palintokia*; that is, a victory for creditors over their debtors, giving them complete control over the charging of interest.

Whether or not the law on interest is genuinely Solonic, the *seisachtheia* itself may have given the peasantry of Attica only a temporary breathing-space. So far as can be told, the legislation of Solon did nothing to get at the root of the agrarian crisis that was threatening the peasant proprietors. This is perhaps reflected in the three decades of disorder that led up to the tyranny of Pisistratus, with its popular support.[41] Absence of any reference to agrarian problems in the period after the tyranny seems to imply that Pisistratus was able to get to grips with the problem. Possible pressure on the land may have been relieved by settlements at Sigeum and in the Thracian Chersonese (Hdt. v.94; vi.35–6). For the peasants left behind, Pisistratus provided direct financial help in the form of loans (Aristotle? *Ath. Pol.* xvi.2–4):

Among other things, he [Pisistratus] was benevolent, mild and forgiving to those who did wrong. What is more, he made advances of cash (*proedaneize chrēmata*) to those who were without the means to further their work, and to support themselves by farming. He had two motives for this: he did not want them to live in the city, but scattered in the country; and if they had enough to live on and were busy with their own affairs, they would neither want to meddle with affairs of state, nor have the time to do so. At the same time, the working of the land increased his revenues, for he took a tenth of the produce.

We are not obliged to accept the motives behind Pisistratus' loans as supplied by the *Constitution of Athens*. It is a recurring theme in Aristotelian ideology that farmers ought to be too busy with their work to meddle in politics (*Politics* 1292b25–9, 1318b9–16 and 1319a26–33; see Day and Chambers 1962: 93–4). A more promising way of approaching the loans is in relation to Pisistratus' overall conception of the government of Attica. There are two linked themes here: reduction of the power of the local aristocracy, and strengthening of the authority of the state as embodied in the tyrant himself. These are reflected in measures intended to increase centralization in the state, and to encourage individuals to identify with the state as citizens.[42] Both themes are present in the mechanism of Pisistratus' loans to needy peasants. The peasantry would no longer be dependent on aristocratic or other powerful creditors; instead, they would owe their allegiance direct to Pisistratus as patron (see Finley 1983: 46–7; Millett 1989a: 22–3). The loans were probably without interest, which would place the recipients under an additional debt of obligation to Pisistratus.[43] It is a reasonable assumption that the loan-fund was financed by the levy on produce mentioned in the same section of the *Constitution of Athens* (*Ath. Pol.* xvi.4, with Rhodes 1981: *ad loc.*). This way, the peasant loans could have a redistributive function, with the tax in kind falling most heavily on larger landowners. The anecdote that follows (*Ath. Pol.* xvi.6) about Pisistratus' grant of exemption to a struggling hill-farmer as the origin of the term 'tax-free land' (*chōrion ateles*) could imply that the poorest peasants were free from the levy.[44]

After Pisistratus' loans, information about credit in Athens disappears for almost a century until the reappearance of lending and borrowing in the plays of Aristophanes.[45] I therefore close this chapter with a brief restatement of how the structure and ideology of credit may have developed from the archaic period to the fourth century.

In the early archaic model derived from the *Works and Days*, the reciprocal basis of credit transactions originated in a community of peasants who were very approximately equal in terms of wealth and status. Such a system presumably continued in the countryside, and is detectable in the town in loans of household goods between neighbours and friends. But by the fourth century, a weakened concept of co-operative reciprocity was being applied on a much larger scale to the citizen body as a whole. In theory, membership of the *koinōnia* of the *polis* placed all Athenians under a common obligation to help each other out. The development of this ideal depended on the growth of a sense of community and solidarity among Athenian citizens. In reality, people would naturally restrict their support to those closest to them in terms of kinship, friendship, or physical proximity. As a result, there grew up a complementary set of credit relations, characterized by formal loan agreements and exaction of interest. This alternative type of credit can be tentatively traced from its possible origins in the voluntary 'interest' payments advised by Hesiod, through the apparent insistence of the Megarian *demos* on *palintokia*, to the guaranteeing of the lender's right to exact interest by the law attributed to Solon. Thereafter, the relationship between informal, interest-free credit and formalized, interest-bearing loans is effectively lost until the fourth century with the detailed testimony of the Attic Orators.

The great gap in our knowledge is the part played by fifth-century developments in general, and the Peloponnesian War in particular, in transforming the structure of credit. It could plausibly be argued that the stresses imposed by the war would tend to increase the demand for loans, while weakening the idea of reciprocal support between citizens.[46] The effect could have been to make more respectable the charging of interest, accounting for the conflicting attitudes presented by the Orators, as described in the opening section of this chapter. All this would be in line with the orthodox view of the fifth century as the great age of Athenian achievement – the 'Golden Age' of Athens – with the fourth century characterized as in almost every way a sad falling-away from former greatness. But such an unrelievedly negative picture of Athens' fourth-century fortunes is overdrawn. In the chapters that follow, I hope to show the continuing vitality of the ideology of reciprocity more than holding its own against the impersonal ethos of formalized credit relations.

CHAPTER III

Borrowing and repayment

THE INGRATITUDE OF NICOSTRATUS

A few years before his brush with Stephanus, as described in the previous chapter (see above, pp. 24–7), Apollodorus had involved himself in a law suit against his neighbour Nicostratus. The speech he delivered on that occasion is preserved as the fifty-third oration in the Demosthenic corpus.[1] The ostensible purpose of Apollodorus' accusation was to establish that two slaves, whom Nicostratus and his brother Deinon were claiming as their own property, were in reality the property of a third brother, Arethusius. Because Arethusius was a state debtor – the result of a previous legal encounter with Apollodorus – his property was liable to seizure. According to Athenian practice, a successful prosecution against Nicostratus would have brought Apollodorus a reward of one third of the value of the slaves; but in his introduction to the speech (§§1–3), he renounces all rights to any reward.[2] He claims instead that his true motive for bringing a charge against Nicostratus is a desire to be revenged on the brothers for the repeated injustices he has suffered at their hands. Apollodorus' recital of these wrongs (§§4–13) provides a convenient introduction to the main characteristics of credit in fourth-century Athens as set out in this and the following chapters.

Apollodorus begins his account of the origins of the dispute by underlining the good relationship that had previously prevailed between himself and Nicostratus (§4):

Nicostratus, whom you see here in court, men of the jury, was a neighbour of mine in the country, and a man of my own age. We had long known each other, but after my father's death, when I went to live in the country, where I still live, we had much more to do with one another (*mallon allēlois ēdē echrōmetha*), since we were neighbours and men of the same age. As time

53

went on, we became very intimate (*oikeiōs*); indeed, I came to feel on such intimate terms with him that he never failed to win any favour he asked of me; and he, on his part, was useful to me in looking after my affairs and managing them. Whenever I was abroad on public business as trierarch, or on any private business of my own, I used to leave him in charge of everything on my farm.

Here is a fourth-century instance of the type of reciprocal relationship between neighbours so strenuously recommended by Hesiod, with a return of services appropriate to citizens from the upper end of society. The terms *echrōmetha* (from *chraomai*, 'to make use of') and *oikeiōs* (from *oikeios*, lit. 'belonging to one's household') are often associated with this kind of shared connexion, and we will meet them again. But Apollodorus goes on to explain how, in this case, his goodwill was the cause of his downfall.

On the occasion in question, Apollodorus was sent on a voyage round the Peloponnese as trierarch; as usual, he asked Nicostratus to look after his domestic affairs. But while he was away, three of Nicostratus' agricultural slaves ran away – an incidental indication of Nicostratus' relative wealth. Nicostratus went after them, but was captured by pirates and himself sold as a slave at Aegina. When Apollodorus returned from his voyage, Deinon told him of his brother's misfortunes (§§ 6–7):

... stating that although Nicostratus had sent him letters, he had not gone to fetch him because he was short of funds for the journey; and he also told me he heard his brother was in a dreadful state. When I heard this, I was touched with compassion for Nicostratus on account of his ill-fortune, and at once sent his brother Deinon to fetch him, giving him (*dous*) three hundred drachmas for his journey. When Nicostratus got home, he at once came to me, embraced me, and thanked me for providing (*pareschon*) his brother with money for the journey. He then bewailed his own unhappy lot and, while complaining of his own relatives, he begged me to help him, just as in past time I had been a good friend (*philos*) to him. Then he wept and told me he had been ransomed for twenty-six minas, and urged me to make some contribution (*eisenegkein*) towards the cost of his redemption.

The word *eisenegkein* (from *eispherein*, 'to contribute') makes it clear that Nicostratus was asking for an *eranos*–loan from his friend. To be noted here is the non-productive purpose for which he makes his request. That is entirely typical of credit transactions in classical Athens, and can be paralleled many times over in the fourth-century sources (see the next section). The passage also contains a hint of the 'hierarchy' of sources of credit to which I briefly alluded in the opening chapter (p. 3). For reasons which become clearer later in the speech, Nicostratus was unable to get the help he needed from his relatives; he therefore turned instead to his friend and neighbour, Apollodorus.

Apollodorus was moved by Nicostratus' tale of woe, and agreed to help him (§§ 8–9):

I answered that in time past I had been a true friend to him, and that I would help him now in his distress. I said I forgave him the three hundred drachmas which I had given (*edōka*) his brother for the expenses of the journey to fetch him, and I would also make a contribution (*eranon*) of one thousand drachmas towards his ransom. Nor did I make this promise in words only, and fail to perform it in fact. But since I was not well-provided with funds in consequence of my quarrel with Phormion and of his depriving me of the estate which my father left me, I took to Theocles – who was at that time carrying on a banking business – some cups and a gold crown, which I happened to have in my house as a part of my ancestral inheritance. I told him to give to Nicostratus a thousand drachmas; that sum I gave him as an outright gift (*edōka dōreian*), and I acknowledge that it was a gift (*homologō dedōkenai*).

Of interest here is the ease with which loans could be converted into gifts, reinforcing the testimony of terminology and of the *Works and Days* (ll. 33–42), where the dividing line between gifts and loans is blurred. In the Nicostratus passage, two loans are transformed into gifts: Deinon's *viaticum* of 300 dr., and the *eranos*-contribution of 1,000 dr.[3] Also significant is the way in which Apollodorus raised this contribution. Whatever the truth behind Apollodorus' protestations of financial embarrassment – the direct result of Phormion's dishonesty (see above, pp. 24–5) – one thousand drachmas was a substantial sum. It is the median value for loans secured by real property as recorded on *horos* inscriptions (Millett 1982: 222–3); or, expressed another way, the equivalent of a skilled artisan's pay for approximately two years (Markle 1985: 293). In this case, Apollodorus raised the sum by offering pledges to a banker. Although a direct approach to a banker, without any preliminary tapping of relatives and friends, is untypical of Athenian credit relations, it is not inexplicable. By Apollodorus' own admission (§ 14), his relatives were the last people in Athens who would help him out with loans. In any case, as the son of a former slave, the number and quality of kinship connexions open to Apollodorus might be limited. It is also possible that Apollodorus' relationship with the banker Theocles was more informal than impersonal. In a slightly later speech ([Dem.] L.56), he tells the jury that as the son of the banker Pasion, he is able to borrow money wherever and whenever he wants, by making use of his father's contacts. The Athenian banker Theocles may be just such a contact, and his loan of a thousand drachmas to Apollodorus an act of friendship rather than a pure business transaction.[4]

A few days after this operation had taken place, Nicostratus came back to Apollodorus and begged him for more money to pay off the strangers (*xenoi*) who had lent him the ransom sum. This was because his agreement with them stipulated that he settle up within thirty days, or be indebted for double the amount. Unlike relatives and friends, complete strangers – possibly non-Athenians – felt no compunction about taking advantage of a person's ill-fortune in order to make money.[5] Nicostratus went on to complain that he could raise no cash through his farm, either by sale or by offering it as security: brother Arethusius alleged that he himself was already owed money on it (§10).[6] As a way out of the difficulty, Nicostratus made the following proposal to Apollodorus (§11):

He said, 'Please will you provide me with the amount by which I am short [sixteen minas] before the time limit is passed, in order that what you have already paid, the thousand drachmas, shall not be lost, and that I myself shall not be liable to seizure (*agōgimos*)? I shall make a collection (*eranon*),' he said, 'and when I have got rid of the strangers, I shall pay you in full whatever you lent me (*chrēseis*). You know,' he said, 'that the laws enact that a person ransomed from the enemy shall be the property of the ransomer, if he fail to pay the ransom money.'

Nicostratus' proposition adds a further level to the relative–friend–neighbour hierarchy of credit. Theoretically, an *eranos*-collection extended beyond one's immediate circle of friends to include chance acquaintances and, under ideal circumstances, the citizen-body as a whole. In the case in question, the practical consideration of the thirty-day limit caused Nicostratus to regard an *eranos*-collection as second-best to a temporary, direct loan from his friend and neighbour.

Apollodorus was apparently impressed by Nicostratus' appeal.[7] According to his reported version of the conversation, he replied in the following terms (§12):

'Nicostratus, in past times I was a true friend to you, and now in your misfortune, I have helped you to the full extent of my power. But since at the moment you are unable to find the whole amount due, and because I have no funds to hand myself, any more than you have, I loan you (*kichrēmi*) whichever part of my property you wish. You can offer this property as security for the balance of the sum you need, have the use of the money for a year without interest (*atokōi*), and pay off the strangers. When you have made your collection (*eranon*), as you propose, then you can settle my debt.'

Nicostratus naturally jumped at this generous offer, and went on his way rejoicing. Apollodorus closes this section of the speech by detailing the resulting financial transaction, and Nicostratus' subsequent black ingratitude (§13):

Accordingly, I offered my tenement house (*sunoikian*) as security for a loan of sixteen minas from Arcesas of Pambotadae, whom Nicostratus himself introduced to me (*prouxenēsen*). He lent me the money (*daneisanti*) at the rate of $1\frac{1}{3}$ per cent per month. But when Nicostratus had got the money, so far from showing gratitude (*charin*) for what I had done for him, he immediately began to lay a plot against me, to rob me of my money, and become my enemy...

As can be seen from this passage, Apollodorus' help did not take precisely the form of his original proposal. He had suggested a loan of the property itself to Nicostratus, who would then offer it up as security in a loan transaction that he would negotiate himself. The implication was that Nicostratus would himself bear the burden of any interest payments that might be necessary. As the borrower normally remained in possession of real security (Finley 1952: 10–13), such an arrangement would have had no significant effect on Apollodorus' circumstances – provided that Nicostratus did not default on the loan. But in the event, Apollodorus seems to have contracted the loan himself, and was therefore liable to pay the interest incurred. I see no real difficulty in this discrepancy between proposed and actual transactions: law-court speeches are notorious for their imprecision in matters of technical detail (see Millett 1990: 178–9). As things turned out, Apollodorus presumably intended to collect the interest charge from Nicostratus either every month or at the end of the year. Moreover, from the point of view of the lender, direct dealing with Apollodorus would sidestep any awkwardness arising out of the title to the property that was originally going to be 'lent' to Nicostratus as security.

What cannot be satisfactorily explained on the basis of the

surviving detail is the relatively high rate of $1\frac{1}{3}$ per cent per month that Apollodorus contracted to pay on behalf of his friend. As argued in the following chapter, the 'conventional' rate in Athens was 1 per cent per month, and the additional $1\frac{1}{3}$ per cent is all the more surprising in that creditor and debtor were introduced to each other by Nicostratus himself. Arcesas is not known from any other source and cannot be identified as a professional money-lender. As an occasional lender at interest, he can be paralleled by many of the creditors appearing in the Orators and on the *horos* inscriptions.[8]

Apollodorus rounds off his narrative with the complaint that Nicostratus has shown no gratitude (*charis*) for the sacrifices made on his behalf. This use of *charis* comes as no surprise, as the word was almost a technical term, representing what a donor expected to receive in return in a reciprocal exchange (see below, Chapter v). But Nicostratus' failure to show an appropriate return of *charis* was only the beginning of Apollodorus' troubles. He goes on to describe how Nicostratus formed a conspiracy against him, and had him falsely listed as a public debtor. There followed sundry acts of robbery and vandalism against Apollodorus, culminating in an alleged attempt on his life (§§ 14–17). Apollodorus eventually got some satisfaction by bringing a successful action against Arethusius, who was fined a talent. It was in connexion with this unpaid one-talent fine that Apollodorus delivered his speech against Nicostratus, accusing him of conspiring to conceal the property of Arethusius.

How much of this actually happened cannot now be recovered. As Apollodorus himself says in the introduction to his narrative (§3), it is his intention to inform the jury of the 'greatest and most flagrant' of his opponents' wrongdoings. The whole speech is constructed with that end in view, and it may be noted that out of its twenty-nine sections, only seven are given over to proving the point nominally at issue – Arethusius' ownership of the slaves.[9]

In my account of the antecedents to the case, I have made free use of Apollodorus' own words. This is partly to give some impression of his forensic technique, but mainly to highlight the complexity of the credit relations contained in the speech. Nicostratus' capture and sale by pirates set up a chain of seven separate credit operations, and there are in the speech incidental references to two further loan transactions.[10] Although the case may be unusual in the complexity of its network of credit relations, every element can be paralleled elsewhere in the fourth-century literature. There are obvious points of contact between the outlines of credit as they appear in the Nicostratus speech, the Lysias fragment *Against Aeschines the Socratic*, and Hesiod's *Works and Days*. Taken together, they constitute a rudimentary model of the fourth-century structure of credit. In the remainder of this chapter, and in the following chapter, key aspects of that model are analysed in detail, with particular attention to broader social and economic implications. Elements under examination are the reasons for which loans were sought, problems of repayment and possible political implications, and the determinants of interest.

THE DEMAND FOR CREDIT: PRESSURE OF CIRCUMSTANCE

Credit in Athens was overwhelmingly sought for non-productive purposes. Only exceptionally, if ever, did a borrower take out a loan with the intention of increasing his wealth (Millett 1983: 42–7). The most liberal-minded reading of the source material can produce only eight credit transactions that might conceivably be termed 'productive', and they remain the exceptions that prove the non-productive rule. And yet, scholars persist in their efforts to inject a productive element into Athenian credit relations. As some readers will be justifiably weary of this long-running debate, details of arguments and counter-arguments are banished to Appendix III. In the following section, one of the eight loans, which has the best claim to be called 'productive', is examined in detail in an attempt to bring out its near-unique nature. For the rest, I concentrate on the more positive evidence for the various branches of non-productive credit.[11]

A straightforward classification of loan-types from Athens is bound to be arbitrary and imperfect, but there is a broad (if blurred) dividing line between 'emergency' loans arising out of unforeseen circumstances, and those loans which were deliberately and voluntarily contracted for 'prestige' purposes. Loans in the first category – to pay for ransoms, funerals, dowries, fines and like – could be sought by citizens from all social levels. But loans required for considerations of prestige – conspicuous expenditure, liturgies and military commands – are typically (though not inevitably) associated with citizens at the upper end of the social scale.

Loans of the first type involved an element of compulsion, and often misfortune. They therefore placed an obligation on those in

more fortunate circumstances to help out. Stephanus, it will be
recalled, was accused by Apollodorus of exploiting the ill-luck of his
fellow-citizens by lending at interest rather than coming to their
assistance (above, pp. 25–6). The approved response may be seen
in the debt for ransom in the Nicostratus case, where it is taken for
granted that relatives, friends and neighbours will help out with
loans, if not with outright gifts. In the *Nicomachean Ethics* (1164b30–
65a2), Aristotle cites as an illustrative example a man's duty to
ransom his friends and close relatives. There is a clear case of this in
Isaeus' speech *On the Estate of Apollodorus* (VII.8), where the speaker
seeks to establish the existence of close friendship between
Apollodorus (not the son of Pasion) and his grandfather. As part of
his proof, he points out that when his grandfather was made a
prisoner-of-war, Apollodorus 'consented to contribute money
(*chrēmata eisenegkein*) for his ransom, and to act as hostage until he
could raise the necessary sum of money'.

The regularity with which the ransoming of prisoners-of-war
appears in the sources suggests redemption rather than long-term
enslavement as the norm; the same might be said of people captured
by pirates (references in Ducrey 1968: 238–46; McKechnie 1989:
117–19). This is understandable as, apart from the inconvenience
and danger of accommodating large numbers of male prisoners,
ransoming was potentially more profitable. Although Nicostratus
seems to have been relatively prosperous, he was not a particularly
eminent citizen. Even so, he was ransomed for the substantial sum of
twenty-six minas. Plato, on the occasion of his sale into slavery and
subsequent redemption, is reputed to have fetched either twenty or
thirty minas (Diod. XV.7.1; Diog. Laert. III.20). Aeschines suggests
that a really well-connected prisoner-of-war might have to pay
more than a talent to secure his release (II.100). Simple comparisons
are liable to mislead, but Plato ransomed was probably worth
approximately ten times his price as a slave (provided a purchaser
could be found).[12]

The circumstances surrounding the enslavement and ransoming
of Plato closely parallel those involving Nicostratus. Both were
offered for sale in the market at Aegina, and in both cases they were
bought by people who effectively functioned as creditors, lending the
victims their own purchase price until they could arrange to pay it.
In Plato's case, the purchaser was reputedly a character from Cyrene
called Annikeris (Diog. Laert. III.19–20). He sent Plato back to his

companions (*pros tous hetairous*) in Athens, who immediately dispatched to him the purchase price. This Annikeris is supposed to have refused, saying that the Athenians were not the only people worthy of the privilege of helping out Plato. Once again, a loan is transformed into a gift. The experience of Nicostratus was less touching and presumably more typical, with the purchasers/ creditors reinforcing their right to repayment with a formal agreement (*sungraphai*), complete with penalty clause.[13]

The ransoming of prisoners was evidently seen as a civic duty, extending beyond relatives and friends to include the citizen-body as a whole – analogous to the ideal of reciprocal lending described in the previous chapter (pp. 37–8). Aristotle in his *Rhetoric* (1400a21) uses as an illustration of forensic technique the sentiment that 'he (my opponent) has never yet lent anything, but I have ransomed many of you'. That is precisely the line taken by Lysias (XII.20), who puts forward the paradox that he and his brother (though metics) had ransomed many citizens, while his opponent and the rest of the Thirty Tyrants (though citizens themselves), had committed many outrages against their fellow-Athenians (cf. Isaeus v.43). The possible pay-off for this unwonted generosity is made explicit in another speech of Lysias, *On Behalf of Eryximachus*, where the speaker defends himself against an accusation of oligarchic sympathies. He tells the jury how, after doing his bit and more at the Battle of Aegospotami, he not only brought his trireme safely home, but also 'ransomed one of the other trierarchs' (§§100–8). This is part of the speaker's declared intention of basing his defence on his previous good character. As he himself explains (§§64–76), 'My object in exposing my person to so many hazards on your behalf and in spending ungrudgingly so much of my inheritance in your interests was that...were I ever brought into court on a false charge, I might with confidence render an account of my career.'[14] Demosthenes was presumably hoping for a similarly sympathetic hearing when, in his speech *On the False Embassy* (XIX.169–70), he reminded the jury about the many prisoners he had personally ransomed from Philip. As in the cases of Nicostratus and Plato, Demosthenes' loan of the necessary sums was eventually converted into an outright gift.[15]

Other occasions on which relatives, friends and fellow-citizens were expected to help out with loans and gifts are set out in Lysias' speech *On the Property of Aristophanes* (XIX.59).[16] The speaker describes the generosity of his father; how, in addition to his numerous and costly public services,

...he also joined in privately providing dowries for daughters and sisters of certain needy citizens; there were men whom he ransomed from the enemy, and others for whose funerals he provided money.

A handful of texts record individuals being forced to borrow in order to pay the costs of funerals – in each case, the funeral of a parent. In the Demosthenic *Second Speech Against Boeotus* (XL.52), the speaker claims to have borrowed one thousand drachmas to pay for the expenses of his father's funeral. A similar sort of operation, though on a humbler scale, may lie behind part of an inscription from the Athenian *agora*, dating from 367/6 (*SEG* XII.100; translated with discussion by Finley 1953b). The text records the confiscation and sale by the state of a house belonging to one Theosebes, son of Theophilus, of the deme Xypete. Theosebes (whose name ironically means 'god-fearing') had been accused of *hierosulia* or sacrilege, and was found guilty by default. When the house came to be sold, it was found to be encumbered with four prior charges. One of the claims, which was for thirty drachmas, was made by one Isarchus of Xypete, whose own words are quoted in the inscription (28–9), 'because I buried Theophilus, whose house this was, and the wife of Theophilus'. The debt was allowed by the authorities. As Theosebes and Isarchus share the same demotic, they may have been neighbours (see Osborne 1985a: 5, Whitehead 1986: 234, n. 9, and below, p. 146). A third, fictitious example of a loan to bury a parent, from Menander's *Hero*, is described towards the end of this section.[17]

Rather more material survives concerning the obligation of relatives and friends to help dower the sisters and daughters of impoverished citizens. Although there was no strict legal requirement that a father supply his daughter with a dowry, the moral and social pressures were considerable; at least, towards the upper end of Athenian society (Finley 1952: 79–80; Lacey, 1968: 109–10; Schaps 1979: 74–88). The strength of these pressures may be deduced from the ways in which litigants introduce the giving of dowries into their speeches. Absence of a dowry could be used as an argument that no marriage took place (Isaeus III.8 and 28). A small dowry was used as evidence that the prospective husband was not a wealthy man (Isaeus XI.40): 'such a dowry (of twenty minas) would not be given to a husband with a large fortune.' Speakers occasionally use the existence of a daughter needing a dowry as the basis of an emotional appeal to the jury. The plaintiff in the Demosthenic *Second Speech Against Boeotus* (XL.4) describes how he has 'a daughter who is already of marriageable age', adding (§5): 'It is therefore just on many accounts that you should aid me who am being wronged.' Towards the end of the speech, he warns the jury (§56): 'If you leave me in the lurch... I shall have no means of giving a dowry to my daughter' (cf. Dem. XLV.74). He cannot have been as fortunate in his relatives as Epilycus, son of Tisander, who appears briefly in Andocides' speech *On the Mysteries* (1.117–23). He died in Sicily, leaving property worth two talents, debts adding up to five, and two unmarried daughters. His nephew Andocides makes much forensic capital out of his alleged willingness to marry one of the daughters, despite the absence of any dowry. The lady in question unfortunately died before the marriage could take place (see *APF* 8429 IV).

Hard-up fathers and brothers naturally felt able to call on relatives and friends for help in finding dowries. The speaker in Isaeus' *On the Estate of Hagnias* (XI.38–9) finds it necessary to defend himself against an accusation of base conduct (*kakia*), inasmuch as he has failed to dower any of the four daughters of his dead brother. Demosthenes in *On the Crown* (XVIII.268) indirectly reminds the jury not only about the prisoners he has ransomed, but also the dowries he has helped to provide. And in an earlier speech (XXVII.69), he rounds off his accusation by contrasting his opponent with 'those of our fellow-citizens who, out of their own funds, have dowered the daughters of impoverished relatives and even friends'. In Isaeus' *On the Estate of Apollodorus* (VII.9), referred to above (p. 60), Apollodorus is depicted as responding to kindnesses shown by the speaker's grandfather with reciprocal acts of generosity, including the dowering of his benefactor's daughter (additional examples in Schaps 1979: 79–81). Although the sources give the impression that much of this assistance took the form of outright gifts, loans are not to be ruled out. In the *First Speech Against Onetor* (XXX.12), Demosthenes assumes the jury will agree with his proposition that a man will automatically prefer to borrow rather than fail to pay over a dowry.[18]

The types of non-productive borrowing described above, to pay for ransoms, burials and dowries, could apply to citizens from all social levels. Modern peasant communities provide plenty of parallels (Darling 1947: XXVI and 52–9; Firth 1966: 176–82). But because our material is necessarily drawn from the Orators, it tends to involve people from the upper ranges of Athenian society. This lop-sided testimony in part explains the absence of examples of the most urgent type of non-productive credit: borrowing in order to buy food and other necessities needed to stay alive. The sole surviving example from classical Athens is imaginary, occurring in a passage of wider interest from Menander's *Hero* (ll. 28–36).

The setting of the play is the Attic deme of Ptelea. In the only scene to survive, the slave Getas interrogates his fellow-slave Davus about two further 'slaves', a brother and sister called Gorgias and Plangon. Davus explains how their father, Tibeius, had once been a slave in their master's household. Having gained his freedom, he worked as a shepherd. Davus continues

Tibeius their father was an old man, and in order to provide food he took a mina from my master. Then he took a second mina – there was a famine (*limos*), you see – and faded away.

GETAS. Because your master would not give him a third mina?

DAVUS. Perhaps. When he died, Gorgias borrowed a little more and buried him. After performing the rites, he came here to us, bringing his sister with him. And here he stays until the debt is worked off (*to chreos apergazomenos*).

GETAS. But what about Plangon?

DAVUS. She's with my mistress. She works the wool and waits on her.

This passage is remarkable for its implication that Gorgias and his sister were subject to a form of debt bondage (see further below, pp. 77–8). Menander presumably describes here a type of non-productive borrowing that was common when times were hard. It may be significant that he makes Davus talk about *limos* ('famine') rather than the milder *sitodeia* or 'food shortage' (see Garnsey 1988: 18–20). As with ransoms and dowries, the provision of help for needy citizens in difficult times could be seen as a civic duty. Theophrastus' 'Boastful Man' (*alazōn*, XXIII.5) brags that in the recent food shortage (*sitodeia*) he gave contributions totalling more than five talents to destitute citizens. To make donations may have been estimable; to boast about them was not.[19]

THE DEMAND FOR CREDIT: PRESTIGE EXPENDITURE

In a valuable article on 'Personal loans' (in *ESS*), Sieveking points out that non-productive credit has often been sought 'to cover the conventional needs of a social class accustomed to elaborate expenditures'. The relevance of this generalization to the élite of ancient Athens is well brought out by Davies in his introduction to *APF*. After detailing the various ways in which the Athenians promoted political equality amongst the citizen-body, Davies explains (p. xvii) how at least some of the wealthy and well-born Athenians 'counter-attacked' by

> deploying their assets in the active and artful build-up of a political investment in goodwill. The channels of this investment included public service and the discharge of office, conspicuous consumption on horses, houses, gastronomy, or mistresses, ready willingness in paying levies and subscriptions, but above all ostentatious generosity in the performance of the liturgies which sustained Athens' navy and adorned her innumerable religious festivals. The motive was *philotimia*, the objective *lamprotēs*, and the reward a steady income of *charis* from one's fellow citizens, to be exploited as a lever to office and as a refuge in times of trouble.[20]

Politics were well to the fore in this deliberately lavish expenditure; and in the remainder of this chapter the political implications of non-productive borrowing by the élite will become increasingly prominent.

The types of expenditure summarized by Davies can be divided into two broad categories: outlay aimed at conspicuous consumption to achieve a glamorous and luxurious life style worthy of admiration, and lavish expenditure on liturgies and other public services to win a reciprocal return of gratitude. The first of these categories is brilliantly exemplified by the career of Alcibiades and in turn encapsulated in words placed in Alcibiades' mouth by Thucydides (VI.16.1–4). Alcibiades here presses his claim before the Athenian assembly to lead the naval expedition of 415 to Sicily:[21]

> Athenians, I have a better right to command than others...and at the same time I believe myself to be worthy of it. The things for which I am abused bring fame to my ancestors and to myself, and to the country profit besides. The Hellenes, after expecting to see our city ruined by the war, concluded it to be even greater than it really is, by reason of the magnificence with which I presented it at the Olympic Games [of 416], when I sent into the lists seven chariots, a number never before entered by any private person, and won the first prize, and was second and fourth, and took care to have everything else in a style worthy of my victory. Custom regards such displays as honourable, and they cannot be made without leaving behind them an impression of power...And this is not useless folly, when a man at his own private cost benefits not himself but the city: nor is it unfair that

he who prides himself on his position should refuse to be on an equality with the rest.

In the light of Alcibiades' excessive expenditure on prestige goods and pastimes, attested both anecdotally and epigraphically (see *APF* 600 IX), it is surprising that no explicit statement about his indebtedness has survived. But the precariousness of his finances may be inferred from the comment of Thucydides that (VI.15.3) 'he indulged his desires beyond his actual means, in keeping horses as well as in his other expenses'. This is said by way of introduction to the speech by Alcibiades quoted above; and Thucydides gives as a motive for Alcibiades' sponsorship of the Sicilian expedition his desire to replenish his personal fortune (VI.15.2; cf. VI.12.2). In the event, the campaign had barely begun when Alcibiades, recalled to Athens to stand trial, escaped into exile.[22]

The outstanding Athenian example of a 'consumption loan', taken up in order to finance conspicuous expenditure, is actually fictitious, though there are still tenuous political links. In Aristophanes' *Clouds*, Phidippides, the spendthrift son of the prosperous peasant Strepsiades, causes his father sleepless nights by running up debts in connexion with his chariot-racing. As Strepsiades goes through his household accounts, he lists loans of 1,200 drachmas for a racehorse, and 300 dr. for a racing chariot (ll. 12–31). His subsequent comments (ll. 41–55) present him as a classic case of a moderately well-off individual being forced to live beyond his means. He blames his financial difficulties on a marriage into the aristocracy, to a niece of Megacles with appropriately expensive tastes, inherited by her son (see the comments of Dover 1968a: *ad loc.*).

One of our few indications of debts arising out of conspicuous consumption involves a Megacles. In his *Acharnians* (ll.614–17), Aristophanes has one of his characters mention

the son of Coesura and Lamachus who, but the other day, were so involved in *eranoi* and debts that their friends called 'look out', just as people do when emptying slops at night.

Davies (*APF* 9688 x) plausibly identifies 'the son of Coesura' with a Megacles (*APF* 9697) who was known to have expensive tastes; in 436 he won the four-horse chariot-race at Olympia. Davies further conjectures (*APF* 9688 xIV) that Megacles may have been forced to meet his obligations by hypothecating real property, and draws a comparison with Callias III (*APF* 7826). Rather more is known about the spectacular decline in the wealth of Callias, who was reputed to have frittered away a family fortune larger than that of any contemporary (Lysias XIX.48). Old Comedy supplies the evidence for Callias' extravagant expenditure (Eupolis, *Autolycus CAF* fr. 44 ~ *FAC* I 326 fr. 44; *Colaces CAF* fr. 143–5 ~ *FAC* I 386 fr. 143–5); and also for his permanent state of indebtedness (Cratinus *CAF* fr. 12 ~ *FAC* I 27 fr. 12, with Fine 1951: 170).

As a final illustration of the link-up between politics, conspicuous consumption and debt, there is the case of Pericles' son Xanthippus, as told by Plutarch (*Pericles* XXXVI). Whereas Pericles himself had a reputation amongst contemporaries for his austere lifestyle, his son was supposed to be a spendthrift. Moreover, he had married an aristocratic wife with expensive tastes – a daughter of Tisander of the Philaid *genos* (*APF* 8429 IV). As his father gave him only a small allowance, says Plutarch, 'he therefore approached one of Pericles' friends and borrowed money from him, pretending that this was on the instructions of Pericles'. When the friend asked Pericles for repayment, he found himself being taken to court for having lent the money in the first place. The broad parallel with Strepsiades' woes, arising out of an extravagant son, spurred on by a wife with aristocratic pretensions, is striking but certainly fortuitous.[23]

The evidence for conspicuous consumption driving politicians into debt is apparently confined to the last thirty years or so of the fifth century. Whether that has any wider historical significance will be discussed towards the end of this chapter. Characteristic of the fourth-century sources is the theme of over-expenditure and indebtedness through public service. The competitive *ethos* of liturgy-performance, combined with the peculiar mechanism of payment, encouraged people to indulge in expenditure far beyond their means.

Some of this is reflected in the commonly encountered paradox that the burdens imposed by wealth are greater than those following on poverty. Xenophon in his *Oeconomicus* shows Socrates as arguing that with a fortune of only five minas he is better off than Critobulus with an estate worth perhaps a hundred times as much (rather more than eight talents). When Critobulus demurs, Socrates offers a detailed explanation (II.5–6). In the first place, Critobulus is obliged to regulate his personal relationships in a manner appropriate to a wealthy man: expensive sacrifices, lavish entertainment of both strangers and citizens, and general open-handedness. As for public responsibilities:

I also observe that the *polis* is already laying on you heavy expenses, in keeping horses, acting as *choregos*, gymnasiarch, or *prostatēs*. If a war should break out, I know that they will impose on you the trierarchy, and *eisphora*-payments so great that you will not find it easy to bear them. And if ever you are thought to have fallen short in your performance of these duties, I know that the Athenians will punish you just as much as if they had caught you stealing their property.

To be sure, Xenophon has an axe to grind on behalf of the wealthy man; but the *topos* – that wealth brought with it crippling financial burdens – seems too pervasive to be a complete fabrication. Also impressive is the range of associated references to liturgy-dodging and concealment of wealth (collected by Davies 1981: 83, n. 10 and 88–9, nn. 3–6). A few figures may help to give some idea of scale and confirm that these complaints are not merely bad-tempered bellyaching on the part of the élite.

General discussion of liturgies and *eisphorai* is hampered by successive changes in their administration, details of which remain obscure (see Rhodes 1982; MacDowell 1986a; Gabrielsen 1989). But the need for change may itself indicate dissatisfaction with the way the systems spread (or failed to spread) their burdens. That is the natural inference to be drawn from the gradual increase in the number of individuals needed to support a single trierarchy: as many as sixteen by the later fourth century (Dem. XVIII.104, with Davies 1981: 22–3). The trierarchy was the most expensive liturgy, costing as much as one talent; the cheapest (providing a chorus for the Panathenaea) came to 300 dr. In the middle range, the 'average' festival liturgy cost between 1,200 and 3,000 dr. (*APF* xxi–xxii). The collected evidence from fourth-century sources suggests that liturgical burdens fell on persons with property worth three talents or more (*APF* xxiii–xxiv). It needs to be stressed that the figure of three talents represents assets and not income. Expectations that the heaviest obligations would be carried by the wealthiest individuals were not always fulfilled (Jones 1957: 56–7). In any case, the resources of even the richest Athenians were far from boundless. The largest landed estates can hardly have exceeded a couple of hundred acres (de Ste Croix 1966; Burford-Cooper 1977–8: 168–70).[24]

The incidence of *eisphora*-payments was also uneven and unpredictable. Individuals could apparently be called on at short notice to find relatively large sums, perhaps as much as 3,000 or 4,000 dr (Lysias XXI.3; cf. Davies 1981 : 82). The timing of payments could be awkward. Apollodorus, in his speech *Against Polycles* (L.8–9), tells the jury how, on the departure of the fleet in 362, he was appointed trierarch and simultaneously made responsible for the advance payment of his own and other people's *eisphora*. He claims never to have recovered the monies he advanced on others' behalf, 'because at the time I was abroad in your service as trierarch; and afterwards, when I returned, I found that the money from those who had resources had already been gathered in by others, and that those who were left had nothing'. Although this is obviously meant as a ploy to win the jurors' sympathy, Apollodorus' complaint about the uncollectability of his debts is at least plausible. A few years later, if Demosthenes can be believed (XXI.53), defaulting *eisphora*-payers escaped the official collector by clambering over roofs and hiding under beds.[25]

Implicit in all this is the idea that only the very wealthiest citizens were capable of meeting substantial public expenditure without dipping into reserves or running into debt. In his speech *On the Estate of Philoctemon* (VI.38), Isaeus highlights the wealth of a family by claiming they could afford to undertake the most expensive liturgies without having to sell off any of their property (*archaia*). There is a similar idea behind an attack on Apollodorus in Demosthenes' speech *For Phormion* (XXXVI.41). The speaker insists that his expenditure on choruses and trierarchies is so insignificant as to be funded out of income (*prosodos*), leaving his capital (*archaia*) untouched. Earlier in the speech (§39) he claims that Apollodorus' spending on public services amounts to less than the interest on twenty minas (perhaps 240 dr.). The accusation is grossly unfair, as Apollodorus' expenditure on liturgies was, if anything, well above the average for a wealthy Athenian. The speech *For Phormion* was delivered *c.* 350, and for the twenty years or so down to that date, at least seven liturgies can be attributed to Apollodorus – a figure to be regarded as a minimum (*APF* 11672 XII). One of these liturgies repays closer study as revealing in detail how public service could result in private debt.

The Demosthenic speech *Against Polycles* (L) arose out of Polycles' alleged refusal to take over from Apollodorus as trierarch on the appointed day in 461, causing him to remain in service for an extra six months (§1). Throughout the speech, Apollodorus depicts his opponent as being both offensive to him personally, and careless of his obligation to the state (§§26, 31 and 66). Moreover, he insinuates that the *stratēgos* Timomachus, who was commanding the fleet and might have been expected to enforce the exchange, had been 'bought off' by Polycles with the promise of a thirty-mina loan (§44). But a careful reading of the speech by Ballin (1977: 216–21) suggests that Polycles' reluctance was entirely understandable in light of Apollodorus' extravagant expenditure on ship's equipment and wages for the crew. He repeatedly reminds the jury that the ship's tackle was not, as was usual, drawn from the public store (§§7, 26, 27 and 34), and he stresses his own payment to the crew of bonuses and exceptionally high wages (§§7, 11, 12, 16 and 35). If Apollodorus can be believed – and he is emphatic about the detail and accuracy of his accounts (§§10, 30 and 65) – this was easily the most expensive trierarchy on record, with pay alone totalling almost ten talents. There is a sharp contrast here with all other figures for trierarchic expenses, which never exceed one talent. It is hardly surprising that Polycles was unwilling to fall heir to such an unnecessarily heavy obligation. By all accounts, Apollodorus was a wealthy man, with property in three demes (*APF* 11672 xi). But even he could finance this *de luxe* trierarchy (combined, as it was, with the payment of *proeisphora*) only by heavy borrowing. Five such loans are detailed in the body of the speech: two secured on real property, and the other three contracted away from Athens. The figures given for three of the loans add up to a little less than one talent (5,700 dr).[26]

Apollodorus was exceptional in that as the son of a former slave he felt it doubly necessary to ingratiate himself with the *dēmos* through heavy public expenditure. That is presumably the explanation behind his over-performance of liturgies and their extraordinary lavishness.[27] But other citizens with smaller fortunes and less need to justify themselves were also forced to support their slighter public services by borrowing. In the pseudo-Demosthenic speech *Against Euergus and Mnesibulus* (XVLII.54), the speaker makes a bid for the sympathy of the jury by telling them that, 'because of my liturgies and *eisphorai* and ambition (*philotimias*) towards you, some of my furniture has been pledged as security (*enechura*) and some has been sold'. A similar claim is made by the anonymous speaker in a fragment of Isaeus, preserved by Dionysius of Halicarnassus (*On*

Isaeus 13 ∼ Forster 1927: fr. 34). He tells how all that he owned, except property which was already pledged as security, had been consumed by liturgies, with the result that he was unable to borrow any more money. These are, of course, sob-stories, designed to win over the jury; but other allusions to debts arising out of liturgies are too explicit to be dismissed as rhetorical inventions. Demosthenes, in his *Second Speech Against Aphobus* (XXVIII.17–18, cf. XXI.78–80), describes how he was forced by his opponents to assume the expense of a trierarchy at short notice. He claims to have discharged this obligation, amounting to twenty minas, by hypothecating all his property – including the family home (see MacDowell 1990: *ad loc.*).

The cash shortages experienced by Apollodorus while campaigning as trierarch were by no means unique. Periodic financial embarrassment seems to have been an occupational hazard for Athenian commanders in the fourth century.[28] We hear of even the austere Phocion refusing to contribute to a public sacrifice because he was already owing money (Plutarch, *Phocion* IX; cf. Trittle 1988: 39). But the best documented case is that of the *stratēgos* Timotheus, described in detail in Chapter VIII (see below, pp. 213–15). In short, if the testimony of the forty-ninth speech in the Demosthenic corpus can be believed, in order to finance his campaign of 373 to Corcyra, Timotheus borrowed more than seven talents. Small wonder that Isocrates lavishes praise on the strict economy of Timotheus' campaigning (XV.108–12). Right through the Greek world, the division was blurred between public and private resources deployed in warfare. Financing wars is an expensive business, and the scope for initiative was regularly extended by borrowing. In Lysias' *On the Property of Aristophanes* (XIX.22–6), the speaker lists the substantial sums – totalling approximately six talents – that Aristophanes, his friends and his relatives lent to Evagoras, king of Salamis on Cyprus, in his struggle against the Persians.[29]

THE PREDICAMENT OF ARISTARCHUS

The preceding classification of non-productive loans is far from exhaustive, but it does establish a pattern. There is nothing strange about the almost complete absence of productive borrowing from the Athenian scene: in non-capitalist societies non-productive credit is the norm (see Yang 1952: 5). The best modern comparisons relate to the 'mixed' economies of the Third World. Figures for India for the first half of this century suggest that somewhere between 60 and 70 per cent of rural debt may have been contracted for non-productive purposes (U Tun Wai 1957–8: 81, n. 2; cf. Darling 1947: 19–20).[30]

In the case of classical Athens, it is possible to dig deeper and explore the background to this absence of productive credit. Standard explanations along the lines of neo-classical theory invoke the apparently high rates of interest prevailing in fourth-century Athens. Rates of one per cent and more per month are presumed to have made the profitable re-investment of borrowed funds a near-impossibility (Bogaert 1968: 356–7). But rates of interest and profit are relative, as revealed by the frequent and successful financing of maritime trade with borrowed money costing anything up to 30 per cent per voyage. There was, in any case, plenty of interest-free credit potentially available for productive investment, if required. Yet a survey of the known motives behind *eranos*- or 'friendly' loans reveals no instance of a productive use (Vondeling 1961: 72). The explanation of so deep-seated a phenomenon as non-productive borrowing necessarily involves the probing of Athenian mentality. This is a wide-ranging issue, reaching to the heart of ancient economy and society. My concern here is with the limited field of lending and borrowing.

The reasons for which Athenians typically sought loans were almost inevitably associated with the unpleasant necessities of life – ransoms, fines, burials, food-shortages, tax-payments and public service. The contrast between the climate of borrowing in fourth-century Athens and credit as perceived in the modern, capitalist world, is starkly summarized by Finley:

Psychologically, their approach was one of grief and despair, the atmosphere that is associated with 'mortgaging the old homestead'. To be compelled to hypothecate one's property was a calamity to be rectified as quickly as possible. Today, in complete contrast, the objective of the owner of an income-producing property is, under ordinary circumstances, to encumber it as much as he can because the interest he will have to pay will be less than the interest he can obtain by re-investing the borrowed money. (Finley 1952: 87)

It would require a substantial leap of imagination on the part of an ancient Athenian to grasp the idea of debt as something beneficial, to be actively sought. Accordingly, in Demosthenes' speech *For Phormion* (XXXVI.5), the speaker felt it necessary to explain in detail the apparent paradox that Pasion was entered as a debtor to the bank rented out to Phormion, not out of poverty (*aporia*), but out of a desire for action (*philergia*).[31] By the same token, the element of compulsion in non-productive credit helps to explain why interest-free loans were not mobilized for productive purposes. Interest-free, informal credit was typically granted by relatives and friends to citizens who were in difficulties, their motive being a mixture of duty, generosity and reciprocal self-interest. They would naturally look askance at the recipient of a friendly loan who took advantage of their open-handedness for his own financial profit.

The absence of a productive or entrepreneurial mentality in Athens is highlighted by the single unequivocal case of productive credit that does survive in the sources. It forms a part of Socrates' advice to his impoverished friend Aristarchus, as recounted by Xenophon (*Mem.* II.7). Aristarchus, a once-wealthy Athenian, complains to Socrates about his domestic and financial difficulties. The civil disorders of 404–403 have resulted in the loss of his farm and the abandonment of his town properties by their tenants. What is more, as a result of the troubles, hordes of female relatives have come to live with him, making a total of fourteen free persons under the one roof. Apart from their quarrelling all the time, feeding them is becoming a problem, and Aristarchus tells Socrates about the impossibility of raising ready money (§2):

No one will buy furniture, and there is no money to be borrowed (*daneisasthai*) anywhere. It seems to me you would sooner find money by looking in the street than by borrowing.

After several pages of sustained argument, Socrates manages to persuade Aristarchus that he ought to put his female relatives to work making cloth. Aristarchus explains (§11):

By the gods...you seem to me to give good advice, Socrates. Before now, I have not wanted to borrow money because I knew that when I had spent the loan, I would not be able to pay it back. Now I think I can do it, I will obtain what is necessary for the work.

Using borrowed money, wool was purchased, the women were set to work, and the whole scheme turned out to be a roaring success.

It is only to be expected that this anecdote should be seized on as a 'typical' case of productive credit (see Oertel in von Pöhlmann 1925: 515). And yet the context implies that Aristarchus' behaviour was utterly uncharacteristic of his fellow-citizens. It is significant that Xenophon includes the story in a work intended to show up the remarkable and individual qualities of his friend Socrates. Were there nothing out of the ordinary about Aristarchus' solution to his problem, the anecdote would have no point. More specifically, there is the length and intricacy of the argument introduced by Socrates in order to educate Aristarchus about the feasibility of a productive loan – the bulk of the dialogue (§§3–10). The tailpiece to the story is also instructive. Some time later, Aristarchus reports back to Socrates that he is being criticized by the hard-working women as the only person in the house doing nothing towards his keep. Socrates does not reassure Aristarchus by telling him that as the entrepreneur, bearing the risk of the enterprise, he is entitled to the reward of his initiative. Socrates suggests instead that he should compare himself to a watch-dog, enabling the women to work in safety (§§12–14). So it would seem that not even Socrates had developed a coherent theory of capitalist investment, and his advice to Aristarchus was no more than a novelty.[32]

POVERTY AND THE PROBLEM OF REPAYMENT

In the anecdote retold above, Aristarchus confessed to Socrates that, until he had been enlightened about the possibility of productive borrowing, he was unwilling to borrow what he knew could not be paid back. Taking out a loan to buy the food his family needed would have merely prolonged the agony. The initial reluctance of Aristarchus raises one of the major paradoxes about non-productive credit: assuming the borrower's resources remain static, it is difficult to see how repayment would be possible, or even the point of borrowing in the first place. Precisely that point is made by Plutarch in one of his *Moral Essays* entitled 'That people ought not to borrow' (827D–832A). This is an exhortatory tract, warning the reader about the danger – and the avoidability – of getting into debt.[33] 'Do you have any possessions?' Plutarch asks his audience (829F). 'Then do not borrow, for you are not without resources. Do you have no possessions? Then do not borrow, for you will not be able to pay up.'

Ironically, it was indeed those persons most in need of emergency loans to keep body and soul together who found credit hardest to come by. The phenomenon is, of course, universal. Demonstration of the paradox that those least in need of credit are generally the most credit-worthy was a major theme of Darling's brilliant study, *The Punjab Peasant in Prosperity and Debt* (1947) – the paradox being implicit in the title. Darling discovered that the Punjab, probably the most prosperous of all the Indian provinces, was also the most heavily indebted. Moreover, within the several districts of the Punjab itself, there was a direct correlation between the fertility of the land and the depth of indebtedness (pp. 212–13). There is no mystery about this relationship between debt and relative prosperity. For persons living at, or close to, subsistence level, borrowing was only a short step from complete ruin. The most poverty-stricken of Darling's Indian villagers complained of being too poor to have a debt (p. 13).

Darling's study serves as a reminder that a high level of indebtedness need not be socially disruptive or morally reprehensible. 'Millions of cultivators,' he says (p. xx), 'are born in debt, live in debt, and die in debt.' A recent, forceful statement by Hill (1986: 83–94) underlines the positive rôle of debt in the rural communities of the Third World. What matters here is what might be termed the 'Micawber effect' – the long-term relationship between level of borrowing and ability to repay. If the equilibrium is disturbed in a way unfavourable to the borrowers, and if the disturbance continues, debt may eventually cease to be a socio-economic phenomenon, and turn instead into a political problem. Looking back to the ancient world, such a transition seems to have occurred in late Republican Rome, where debt was a key factor in generating the tensions that are characteristic of the last years of the Republic. Apart from general statements and complaints (Royer 1967: *passim*), indebtedness appears as a powerful stimulus behind the rebellion of Catiline, involving both impoverished peasants and high-spending members of the élite (references in Yavetz 1963). The subsequent measures of Caesar's dictatorship go some way to confirm the severity of the problem (Frederiksen 1966). The Roman experience will reappear in the remainder of this chapter as I examine the contrasting relationship between debt, repayment and politics in ancient Athens.[34]

The ideal would be a spread of material across Athenian society, tracing the variations in patterns of borrowing and repayment between different groups of people. In practice, all that is possible is the drawing of a crude distinction of the behaviour of the rich and the poor: precisely the division made by Plutarch in the passage cited above.

If you are poor, says Plutarch, do not borrow. You will not be able to repay the loan, and there is the likelihood that you will end up even deeper in debt. This apparently common-sense statement seems to be borne out by two episodes already encountered: the crises affecting pre-Solonic Attica and post-Theagenic Megara (above, pp. 48–9). In both places, either indebtedness of the poor or their dependence on the rich appear to have reached and passed over the critical threshold. But these are only the earliest examples surviving from a long line of debtors' and dependents' rebellions in the Greek world. From the sixth to the first century B.C., Asheri (1969) details forty examples of laws relating to the problem of debt, and that by no means exhausts the relevant material (above, pp. 48–9 with n. 40).[35] It is against this background of agitation over debt that the experience of fourth-century Athens seems striking. Of the forty references in Asheri's catalogue, sixteen are to be dated to the fourth century; but from Athens, where we are relatively well-informed, there is not even a whisper of debt causing problems for the poor.[36]

The tentative conclusion I would draw from this is that the poorer citizens of Athens were somehow better off than many of their counterparts elsewhere in the Greek world, and therefore able to resist the pressures that might otherwise have driven them into dependence and debt. Scholars seem to have sensed this, though without giving explanations that are necessarily convincing. Jones comments on what he perceives to be the even distribution of wealth in Athens, with a gentle gradation from affluent to needy (1957: 90). De Ste Croix provides a possible mechanism with his suggestion that Athenian inheritance laws helped preserve property within the family, which would otherwise have accumulated in the hands of the rich (1981: 102). But one wonders how far the poorest citizens were bound by rules and regulations about the transfer of property (for their avoidance elsewhere, see Lane Fox 1985). In any case, Jones's opinion about the equitable distribution of property is open to question. Working from almost identical material, Davies (1981: 34–7) arrives at the opposite conclusion. The graph he produces, even allowing for massive margins of error, implies a thoroughly uneven distribution of property for fourth-century Athens.

A possible solution may lie, not so much in the distribution of property, as in the redistribution of income. What distinguished classical Athens from virtually all other Greek *poleis* was the institution of public pay: for holding minor state office, serving on juries, rowing in the fleet, and (from *c.* 400) attending the assembly. Taken together, these payments represent a continuous redirection of wealth from those at the upper end of society to citizens lower down the scale. This was apparently enough to maintain a majority of those towards the bottom of the pile either at or just above the minimum level of subsistence (Finley 1983: 46–7, with Millett 1989a: 37–43). Although public pay might not, in the first instance, go where it was most needed to alleviate want, a secondary redistribution could be carried through by the citizens themselves, via the network of reciprocal loans mentioned above (pp. 37–9), and described in detail in later chapters. Although most of our surviving examples of *eranos*-credit involve wealthier citizens (see Chapter VI), there are hints that the institution operated at all stages of Athenian society, right down to the level of slaves ([Dem.] LIX.30–1; cf. Rädle 1970, on Delphic manumission). In the *Oeconomicus* of Xenophon (II.3), Socrates presents himself as a poor man, with property worth approximately five minas. In the course of his demonstration that the poor are in reality better off than wealthy citizens (see above, p. 67), he describes what is evidently an *eranos*-type loan. 'As for myself,' he explains (§8), 'even if I were in want, I am sure you are aware that there are persons who would assist me, to the extent that even if each contributed a little, they would drown my modest means in a flood.' That prophecy is made to come true in Plato's account of the trial of Socrates (*Ap.* 38B), where four of his followers offer to club together to guarantee payment of a thirty-five mina fine, in place of the single mina proposed by Socrates himself.

In spite of this generally optimistic picture, it should not be presumed that poorer citizens never needed to borrow, nor got into difficulties by borrowing more than they could hope to repay. The Greek conception of 'poverty' (*penia*) implies the need to work for one's living rather than utter destitution (*ptōcheia*).[37] A person who possessed no land to offer as security for a loan could offer pledges (*enechura*) in the form of movable property. Pledges were occasionally high-value items (jewellery, Dem. XLI.11; mass of copper, [Dem.] XLIX.50–2; gold crown, [Dem.] LIII.9); but ordinary household objects also appear (see Chapter II, n. 18). When a character in Aristophanes' *Ecclesiazusae* wishes to make an inventory of his movable property, which he lines up outside his house (sieve, pots, cock, oil flask, tripods), a passer-by naturally assumes he is intending to offer everything as pledges (ll. 746–55; cf. Athen. XIII.585c).[38]

What of the would-be borrower who was not merely poor (*penēs*), but destitute (*ptōchos*)? On the face of it, such a person would not be

able to borrow at all; having no property, no one would take the risk
of lending to him, save out of charity. But in the Greek world at
large, even the most poverty-stricken borrower had something to
offer to a potential creditor. He could offer security in the shape of
his own person. Although only scattered evidence survives, de Ste
Croix is surely correct in his suggestion that debt-bondage was
always widespread in ancient Greece (1981: 162–5).[39] Post-Solonic
Athens is conventionally viewed as the great exception to this rule,
as a result of Solon's celebrated law prohibiting loans on the person
(Arist. *Ath. Pol.* VI.1). But the position in Athens need not have been
as clear-cut as is usually assumed, and clouding the issue is the scene
from Menander's *Hero* cited above (pp. 63–4).

The play, it will be recalled, is set firmly in Attica, with Gorgias
and Plangon working in Laches' house until the money they and
their father borrowed has been paid off. This looks suspiciously like
debt-bondage, and de Ste Croix points to the date of the play, after
the destruction of the democracy in 322, when 'forms of debt-
bondage could well have crept in and even received at least tacit
legal recognition' (1981: 163). Although that is a possible
explanation, the answer may be simpler. The father of Gorgias and
Plangon was originally a slave of Laches, who gave him his freedom.
As a freed slave of metic status, Tibeius would be obliged by law to
adopt his former master as his *prostatēs* (Harrison 1968–71: 1, 184–5).
It was to his *prostatēs* or patron that Tibeius would naturally turn for
protection in time of famine, as would his orphaned children. They
were themselves non-citizens, and presumably fell outside the scope
of Solon's law. In any event, they were probably to be thought of as
voluntarily discharging a 'debt of honour' on behalf of their dead
father. This would explain Davus' response when asked if Plangon is
a slave (*doulē*): 'Yes, sort of, in a kind of way' (l. 20).

Abolition of debt-bondage by law and its actual disappearance
are two different things. Although debt-bondage has repeatedly
been outlawed in the modern world, it continues to flourish under
other names and through the use of legal fictions (see Ennew 1981:
a report of the Anti-Slavery Society). Provided people are
superficially willing – perhaps in the face of starvation – to assign
their own or their family's labour to another person, there is little
that the law can do to prevent it. The possibility should not be ruled
out that even Athenian citizens who were at the end of their tether
might enter into some sort of voluntary contract. Provided that they
were few in number and not subject to outrageously bad treatment,

there was no reason why this practice needed to give rise to political agitation along pre-Solonic lines.[40]

It will be apparent that all too little is known about the detailed indebtedness of the Athenian *dēmos*. About the wealthier citizens, we are better placed; it is here that the patterns of borrowing and repayment, referred to at the beginning of this section, are most illuminating.

BORROWING BY THE ATHENIAN ELITE

It was Plutarch's opinion that those rich in property had no need to borrow in the first place (827F): 'A man produces a witness and a guarantor (*bebaiotēn*) to confirm that, since he has property, he deserves credit; whereas, since he has it, he ought not to be borrowing.' Plutarch's solution is to sell off all property that is surplus to requirements and make do with less. Cicero, it may be noted, gave similar advice to the followers of Catiline (*Against Catiline* II.17). But this kind of 'common sense' approach ignores the practicalities of societies in which status is inseparable from the possession of property (Xen. *Oec.* IV.4–V.20, for an idealized view; cf. Cicero, *de Off.* II.150–1). The evidence of the Attic Orators seems to suggest that specific obligations were only occasionally met by sale of land and houses. In fact, sale of property is regularly presented as involving some species of fraud. On several occasions it is tied in with the avoidance of liturgy obligations (Isaeus VI.3, VII.71 and XI.48; Dem. V.8; Aeschin. I.101).

It may be significant that in giving examples of what ought to be sold off to raise cash, Plutarch does not mention real property (828A–B). He talks instead about disposing of silver plate and other unnecessary items of precious metal. But it is unclear whether even wealthy Athenians possessed much in the way of movable property, apart from slaves and perhaps a few items of gold or silver, which might be heirlooms or part of a dowry ([Dem.] LIII.9; Dem. XXVII.10). This is certainly the impression to be gained from a reading of the so-called 'Attic Stelae' from 414, recording the sale of the property of persons, including Alcibiades, convicted of sacrilege (*SGHI*² 79 ~ Fornara no. 147, for excerpts and full references). Alongside extensive holdings of land and slaves is a pitiful collection of odds and ends of personal property. Even Alcibiades, notorious for his extravagant lifestyle (Plut. *Alc.* XVII) can muster only a motley collection of beds, blankets, cloaks and pots (*APF* 600 IX, with Pippin

1956). Doubts remain regarding the completeness of the Attic Stelae as inventories (see Lewis 1966). But the impression of meagre holdings of movable property is strengthened by the speaker in Lysias' *On the Property of Aristophanes* (XIX.29–31). He explains to the jury how Aristophanes, with all his financial commitments – five liturgies and numerous *eisphorai*, together with the purchase of a house and more than three hundred *plethra* (*c.* 70 acres) of land, all within the space of five years – was not in a position to acquire many personal effects. He adds (§30):

Even people credited with long-established wealth may fail to produce any effects that are of value: for at times, however much one may desire it, one cannot buy things of the sort that, once acquired, will be a permanent source of pleasure.

The speaker goes on to claim that, in spite of this, the personal effects of Aristophanes realized more than 1,000 dr. – more than had ever been made before at a sale of confiscated property. If there is anything like truth in this statement, it helps to show why sale of movable property could not be relied on to raise the substantial sums needed to finance expensive liturgies and the like. The use of property, real or otherwise, as security in a loan transaction at least offered the *possibility* of subsequent repayment.[41]

The same mentality can be seen writ large in the field of *polis* finance. When Isocrates (II.19) advises Nicocles, the young king of Salamis on Cyprus, to manage his *polis* as if it were his ancestral estate, he reflects current Greek practice. Socrates is shown as telling his friend Nicomachides that the difference between care of public and private affairs is merely one of degree (Xen. *Mem.* III.4.12). After the fashion of domestic finances, state 'budgets' were organized on a hand-to-mouth basis. Regular sources of revenue were generally adequate to balance anticipated outgoings, and reserve funds were the exception. Unforeseen expenses were therefore met by extra-ordinary, *ad hoc* measures, with loans as a regular stand-by.[42] All this is apparent from the second book of the Aristotelian *Oeconomica*, with its string of schoolboy dodges for raising cash to meet unforeseen expenses (see above, pp. 21–2). Typically, these emergency funds are needed in time of food-shortage or war; examples are given from all over the Greek world, and the tricks usually add up to straight-forward extortion or forced loans.[43] Epigraphical evidence confirms this anecdotal material. Setting aside the elements of trickery and fraud, *poleis*, like individuals, commonly resorted to loans to meet extraordinary expenditure. The most compact collection of evidence comes from Delos, where the so-called 'Sandwich Marble' (*GHI* II 125) shows that between 377/6 and 374/3 the Temple of Apollo lent money to no fewer than thirteen *poleis* in the Cyclades. The loans ranged from 400 to 6,000 dr., with an arithmetic mean of 2,800 dr. (Bogaert 1968: 127–34). From 314 to 166 the temple lent chiefly to the city of Delos itself, and the purpose of the loans, where preserved, serves to strengthen impressions given by the *Oeconomica*. Loans were secured in order to purchase grain (9,950 dr.), guard against pirates (5,000 dr.), and provide crowns as tokens of honour (numerous examples). The testimony of inscriptions from elsewhere in Greece supports and extends the Delian material (Migeotte 361).

In both the public and the private spheres, the meeting of unpredicted expenditure by the raising of loans, as opposed to sale of property or dipping into non-existent reserves, could only be a temporary solution. And yet the process was not necessarily so pointless or damaging as common sense seems to suggest, or Plutarch would have his audience believe. In the remainder of this section, I will explore systematically the *rationale* behind borrowing and repayment by wealthy Athenians, from which it should emerge that taking out a loan was not merely a postponement of the evil day.

In the first place, borrowing money gave time. That was presumably one reason why loans were favoured by *poleis* which, with their primitive fiscal machinery, were not easily able to raise funds at short notice. This is strikingly illustrated by the fourth-century Pharsalians' appropriation of the personal fortune of their leading citizen as a revolving loan fund with which to balance their budget. According to Xenophon (*Hell.* VI.1.2–3), the task of collecting and administering the city's revenues was entrusted to one Polydamas, who 'gave a yearly account and, whenever there was a deficit, made it good out of his own fortune, paying himself back whenever there was a surplus of revenue'. Even Athens, with its more sophisticated financial arrangements, depended on the fortunes of its wealthier citizens as reserves of ready cash. From the later fourth century, it is recorded that private individuals deposited with Lycurgus the politician sums totalling 650 talents, 'from which he made advances (*prodaneisas*) to meet crises (*kairous*) of the *polis* and *dēmos*' (Plut. *Mor.* 852B, cf. 841D; detailed discussion by Migeotte no. 3). These deposits were presumably voluntary, and Migeotte (*ibid.*) speculates that they might have borne interest. But that seems unlikely, given the system of forced loans built into the mechanism for *proeisphora*-payments. Certain wealthy individuals were made responsible for paying large amounts of *eisphora* in advance, on behalf of their fellow *eisphora*-payers. In this way, the required sum could be handed over to the public treasury with a minimum of delay and without the need for a complex system of collection; whether *proeisphora*-payers were easily able to claim repayment for their public loans is another matter (see above, pp. 68–9).[44]

Borrowing by private individuals gave a breathing-space. Even if the day of reckoning could not be put off indefinitely, it could at least be postponed by securing a second loan to pay off the original creditor (e.g. [Dem.] XXXIII.6–7, [Dem.] XXXIV.23, Dem. XXXVII *passim* – see below, pp. 193–7). Plutarch, in a striking series of images, mocks those debtors who try to discharge their obligations by taking out further loans (830E–31B):

> But the man who is once involved remains a debtor all his life, exchanging, like a horse that has once been bridled, one rider for another ... For just as a man who has fallen in the mud must either get up or stay where he is, but who turns and rolls over covers his wet and drenched person with more dirt; so in their transfers and changes of loans, by assuming additional interest payments and plastering themselves with them, they weight themselves down more and more. They are like persons ill with cholera, who do not accept the treatment, but vomit up the prescribed medicine, and then continue constantly to collect more disease.

Although Plutarch's warnings are real enough – the three examples from the Demosthenic *corpus* noted above ended in court cases – he ignores the practice of replacing interest-bearing loans with loans at either a lower rate of interest or none at all. The technique is well attested in the surviving sources. Aeschines, in the Lysias fragment with which this study opened, ended up paying interest at $1\frac{1}{2}$ per cent per month in place of the original 3 per cent. In the Demosthenic speech from the beginning of this chapter, Nicostratus replaced a loan from *xenoi*, carrying a stiff penalty clause, with a less pressing loan from a friend and neighbour. This was, in turn, to be replaced with a series of *eranos*-contributions (cf. Isaeus VII.8; above, p. 60). Provided interest-bearing credit could be converted into an interest-free loan or, even better, a series of small *eranos*-loans, it could be paid off piecemeal and over an extended period. The device of splitting large loans between different creditors is familiar from other times and places (Firth and Yamey 1964: 31).[45]

Even if a creditor demanded repayment before funds were

available, an unscrupulous borrower stood a reasonable chance of brazening things out so as to delay or even avoid repaying. The lengths to which a lender might have to go in order to recover a bad debt were considerable, involving self-help at virtually every stage (Lintott 1982: 26–8; Ober 1989: 293, n. 1). Long before the dispute reached the courts the disgruntled creditor would be expected to bring extra-legal pressure to bear. In Aristophanes' *Clouds* (ll. 1214–302), Strepsiades is visited by two of his creditors who demand repayment and threaten formal proceedings. If personal appeals to the debtor failed to have the desired effect, pressure could be increased by mobilizing public opinion, shaming him in front of his neighbours. Gernet cites in connexion with the early development of law in Greece the Indian practice of *dhārna*, or laying siege to a defaulting debtor's door (1948–9: 181–4; cf. Barton 1949: 130–3). This may be the trace of reality behind Lysias' humorous description of the crowds of irate creditors who swarm outside Aeschines' house at dawn (above, pp. 1–2).[46]

If informal actions had no effect – and they seem to have left Strepsiades and Aeschines relatively unmoved – the creditor was faced with the dilemma of whether to take his debtor to court. This was not an easy or automatic choice, especially if the sum involved was small. A series of obstacles, almost all stemming from the rôle of self-help in the legal process, discouraged court action. In the first place, there was the relative complexity of procedure in setting a prosecution in train, with the danger of being non-suited or otherwise placed at a disadvantage (Harrison 1968–71: 1, 206–27; MacDowell 1978: 145–54). The speaker in Lysias' *On the Property of Eraton* (XVII.5) complains how his opponents, from whom he was seeking the repayment of a debt, had an earlier case quashed on the grounds that he brought it before the wrong court. Secondly, there was apparently a large element of risk inherent in appearing before an Athenian jury. Our knowledge of behaviour in the courts (and the fears repeatedly expressed by litigants) suggest that a plausible speaker could hope to carry the day – all the more so, if he employed a professional speechwriter. In the suit between Phormion and Apollodorus, the speech on Phormion's behalf (allegedly by Demosthenes), made such an impression on the jury that Apollodorus never got as far as opening his mouth (above, p. 25). A creditor could, of course, hedge his bets by hiring his own speechwriter, but any improvement in the chance of gaining a verdict had to be balanced against the expense. Costs were not recoverable, and the maximum sum for which a debtor could be liable was twice the amount outstanding.[47]

Even if a creditor were successful in winning over the jury, he faced a third, formidable difficulty in executing the judgement (Harrison 1968–71: II, 185–90). It was here that the concept of self-help was strongest, and a determined debtor might meet force with force. The Demosthenic speech *Against Euergus and Mnesibulus* (XLVII) is a catalogue of violent acts allegedly perpetrated against the unfortunate plaintiff, who had been designated by a decree of the people as the person responsible for levying execution on Mnesibulus, a public debtor. And there are other cases in which violence appears as an integral part of the process of execution (Dem. XXII.50–8, Dem. XXIV.197 and [Dem.] LIII.15).[48] Small wonder that Plato in his *Republic* (549E) presents the man who wants a quiet life as failing to prosecute a person who owes him money.

In view of the risks and uncertainties consequent on being a creditor, it seems difficult to understand how anyone in their right mind could be persuaded to lend money to anyone other than relatives and the closest of friends.[49] But it must be borne in mind that a picture of borrowing and repayment based on the testimony of the Orators will necessarily exaggerate fraud and default. At least thirteen of the cases in the corpus sprang from the non-repayment of a debt. Omitting maritime loans, the speeches of Lysias, Isaeus and Demosthenes contain references to more than twenty-five occasions on which the debtor either defaulted or tried to embezzle the loan. This compares with only a dozen or so cases in which there is unambiguous evidence of repayment.[50] These figures cannot be representative of the mass of loan transactions. Although quantification is impossible, it has to be presumed that, in a majority of cases, loans were repaid or the lender otherwise squared. Where default did occur, it is a reasonable assumption that settlement was regularly made more-or-less amicably by retention of pledge, transference of security or decision of an arbitrator.[51]

POLITICS AND THE POSSIBILITY OF REPAYMENT

The discussion so far has been based on the assumption that the resources of those borrowing remain static, or even decline (above, p. 74). After all, the impulse behind non-productive borrowing springs from inadequacy of means. But the possibility has to be considered that, in the medium or longer term, the borrower's resources might increase, diminishing the tendency to default. That this was thought of as feasible is indicated by a comment of Apollodorus in the Demosthenic speech *Against Timotheus* (XLIX; see above, p. 71). He explains to the jury how his father lent money to the impoverished Timotheus, because he thought that (§3)

> if Timotheus got safely out of these dangers and returned home from the service of the King of Persia, when the defendant was in better circumstances than at the time, he would not only recover his money, but would be in a position to obtain whatever else he might want from Timotheus.

The idea that Timotheus would be able to pay up when again in funds is twice repeated in the speech (§§24 and 64).

As the leading *stratēgos* of his day, Timotheus was uniquely well placed to bring about a dramatic improvement in his fortunes; his eventual success is described below. But Pasion's reported faith in his borrower has a wider significance, hinting at a possible parallel with credit relations in late Republican Rome. The high level of indebtedness of the Roman élite is firmly linked to political ambition. To have even a chance of competing successfully in the race to hold high office, it was vital to lavish large sums on public games, conspicuous consumption, electoral bribery and the like (Frederiksen 1966: 129; Hopkins 1978: 48–9). What made creditors willing to lend massively to men in the early stages of their senatorial careers was the expectation of eventual repayment. It was appreciated that the profits of a provincial or similar command would enable an indebted aristocrat to meet his creditors, and still have plenty to spare: a cycle of borrowing and repayment that was informally recognized by the Romans themselves (Frederiksen 1966: 128, n. 6).

Concerning classical Athens, attention has hitherto been focussed on the non-material benefits conferred by expenditure on public service; rightly so, as these were undoubtedly the most pressing considerations in making citizens willing to part with their wealth and even run up debts. And yet there is evidence that the conventional return of *charis* could occasionally be complemented by a direct financial profit. Accusations that leading politicians mobilized their influence in order to amass wealth are a commonplace in the literature (Harvey 1985). According to the oligarchic Critias, as quoted by Aelian (*Varia Historia* x.17 = DK fr. B45), when Cleon entered political life, none of his possessions were free from encumbrance; when he died, he left an estate worth fifty talents. Davies finds this figure credible, in light of Cleon's inheritance of his father's tannery, and 'the widespread stories of his peculation and political monies'(*APF* 8674). A tale of rags to riches is told of Aeschines by Demosthenes (XVIII.131), how he became 'wealthy in place of destitute' (his alleged bribes are listed in *APF* 14627). Counter-accusations against Demosthenes are common. In a famous passage, Aeschines accuses him of having squandered his inheritance and, 'having vaulted onto the speaker's platform', making massive profits out of politics (III.173). The various financial gains that Demosthenes is supposed to have made as a politician are catalogued and classified by Davies (*APF* 3597 XXI), who presumes that the information conveys a general reflection of reality.

The problem of precisely how much of all this to believe is insoluble, and Wankel (1982) rightly warns against accepting at face value what are stock charges of corruption. But the very frequency with which the accusations were made may itself be significant, and there are other hints that corruption (at least, as we understand it) was widespread in Athens (Harvey 1985: 89–102). For the Greeks, 'corruption' was a flexible concept. The normal word for 'bribe' was 'gift' (*dōron*), and provided any monies received did not result in actions against the interests of the *polis*, the practice was tolerated (Hyp. *Dem.* VI cols. 24–5, with Harvey 1985: 108–13). Also blurred was the distinction between public and private interests; much more so than would be considered legitimate in our own political system (Wankel 1982: 47). This overlapping of private with public appears in the realization that performances of liturgies could be profitable in a narrow, financial sense.

The distinction between material and non-material gain is made explicit by the unnamed speaker in Lysias' *Against a Charge of Taking Bribes* (XXI). The account of his expenditure on public services with which the speech opens (§§ 1–5) records a sequence of liturgies 'of an intensity and expensiveness unparalleled in Athenian history' (Davies in *APF* D7, under 'Broken and lost names'). In a ten-year span (411–401), the defendant spent rather more than ten talents – four times the sum he claims as the legal minimum (§5). This excessive zeal was apparently to compensate for the oligarchic sympathies of which the family was suspected. Although the speaker plainly expects to receive from the jury the *charis* due for his services, he firmly rebuts the anticipated allegation that he *profited* from his numerous liturgies (§18). That kind of accusation is actually made in another speech of Lysias (XIX.57), where the litigant reminds the jury: 'There are, indeed, persons who spend money in advance...in order to obtain a return of twice the amount from appointments for which you consider them worthy' (cf. Lys. XXV.30). In Demosthenes' speech *On the Trierarchic Crown* (LI.13), the unknown speaker is more specific about the ways in which liturgies could be turned to private advantage:

When a man who has taken the trierarchy for hire (*misthōmenos*) sets sail, he plunders and pillages everybody; the profits he reaps for himself...and you alone of all people are unable to travel anywhere without a herald's staff of truce because of the acts of these men in seizing hostages and provoking reprisals...

This is admittedly overdrawn, but Demosthenes hints at less drastic ways in which public service could be combined with private profit. In the midst of his accusations against Midias (XXI.167), he tells the jury how his opponent, while serving as trierarch, shirked convoy duty to load up with a cargo of fences, cattle, door-posts and pit-props for his personal use. Whatever the truth behind this accusation (and triremes were short of cargo space), it seems inconceivable that trierarchs would not occasionally benefit from their service away from Athens.

It was absence from Athens that made the trierarchy potentially the most lucrative of all the liturgies. For the same reason, opportunities for profit open to *stratēgoi* were potentially even greater. There are numerous cases of individual commanders making profits out of their campaigns, and sometimes facing recriminations as a result (Davies 1981: 67). Diotimus was accused of having pocketed forty talents received from traders while on convoy duty (Lysias XIX.50); Ergocles was put to death on the grounds that he misappropriated more than thirty talents while commanding a naval expedition in Asia Minor (Lysias XXVIII; cf. XXIX.2 and 14). It is against this background that the large-scale loans by Pasion to Timotheus begin to make financial sense. In fact, Pasion's estimation of Timotheus' ability to restore his fortunes was probably justified. As a result of a successful campaign in Egypt on behalf of the Persians, Timotheus was apparently able to recover his former prosperity (*APF* 13700).

Although the financial rewards reaped by some Athenians in public service seem to suggest similarities with the Roman élite, the

parallel should not be pressed. If anything, it is the differences
between the two systems that are illuminating. At Rome, there was
the institution of the *cursus honorum* which, however often it was
disregarded, served to blend in a single career the three elements of
public benefaction, political activity, and military command – all
culminating in a provincial or other profitable command. In fourth-
century Athens, there were obvious overlaps between public service,
politics, and military activity; but the three strands were not
formally intertwined. On the contrary, as the fourth century
progressed, the distinction between politicians and commanders
(*rhētores kai stratēgoi*) became increasingly clear-cut (Hansen 1983;
cf. 1987: 50–4). Unlike the Romans of the late Republic, the fourth-
century Athenians had no subject empire fit for exploitation. The so-
called 'Second Athenian Confederacy' was a poor substitute for an
empire, and its 'Foundation Charter' of 377 goes to considerable
lengths to limit the scope for exploitation of the allies by individual
Athenians (*GHI* II 123 ∼ Harding 35).[52]

Without parallel in Rome were the popular Athenian juries,
with their suspicious attitude towards private gain through public
service. It is presumably not a coincidence that approving references
to profits made through military command tend to involve service
on behalf of some other state. It was through serving the king of
Persia that Pasion allegedly looked forward to Timotheus' renewal
of his fortunes. Similarly, Aristophanes is reported to have supplied
the king of Salamis on Cyprus with everything in his power, 'with a
view towards recovering more' (Lysias XIX.23; cf. p. 71, above, with
Herman 1987: 96–7). The implication is that personal gains by those
holding public office were somehow at the expense of the *polis*.
Accordingly, ambitious citizens vied for high office chiefly out of
considerations of power and prestige. If there were financial gains
which went some way to cover costs incurred, that was a welcome
bonus. Rewards were never guaranteed, and fear of reprisals
through the courts would have inhibited those who might otherwise
have created opportunities for profit.

Support for the inadequacy of financial gain from public life may
be found in patterns of property distribution among the Athenian
élite. If taken at face value, the Attic Orators state unambiguously
that large landed fortunes tend to dwindle over time (see Andreyev
1974: 25). The speaker in Lysias' *On the Property of Aristophanes*
(XIX.45–9) reports how people thought to be wealthy have often

turned out to be in much poorer circumstances. As evidence, he cites
five examples of leading Athenians whose fortunes, on their deaths,
were worth only a fraction of their value in popular imagination.
The plaintiff in the Demosthenic speech *Against Phaenippus* (XLII.4)
similarly reminds the jury that 'to enjoy unbroken prosperity is not
customarily the permanent fortune of any large number of our
citizens'. To be sure, both litigants are trying to buttress their own
arguments; but the underlying truth of their observations seems to
be supported by statistical evidence collected by Davies (1981:
85-7). After a systematic study of property-holdings through
generations, he can find only one family in which members possessed
liturgical status in all five generations for which evidence exists. This
may be contrasted with the figure of 357 families which are known
to have been wealthy enough to perform liturgies in only one
generation. As Davies would be the first to admit, our knowledge
through time of the Athenian élite is lop-sided (*APF* xxvii–xxxi). But
the high degree of impermanence among families making up the
'liturgical class' may in part be explained by the practical problems
involved in repaying non-productive loans out of inadequate estates
(above, pp. 67–70).

This chronic instability of wealth among leading Athenians invites
a further comparison with the Roman experience: why it was that
such an apparently high rate of failure amongst the Athenian élite
failed to generate the tensions and revolutionary tendencies present
in late Republican Rome. 'The heavily indebted aristocrat turned
lightly to thoughts of revolution', writes Frederiksen (1966: 130),
with Catiline and his debt-ridden companions as only the outstanding example. By contrast, Athens in the fourth century, right
down to the destruction of the democracy in 322, seems singularly
free from any serious or effective oligarchic opposition. Resisting the
temptation to fall back on vague statements of 'commitment to the
democratic ideal' on the part of the élite, it may be that the very
principle of political equality they wished to circumvent made loss of
property less of a disaster than at Rome. In the late Republic, status
was formally geared to wealth, so that falling below the appropriate
census-rating meant loss of access to political and military office
(Beard and Crawford 1985: 40–7). Even a man who retained
ownership of his property might be expelled from the senate, were it
thought that too much of it had been encumbered by borrowing
(Asconius 84c, with Frederiksen 1966: 128–9). In fourth-century

Athens, it was possible for a man of limited wealth to continue to play an active part in the political process. As for military commands, the law alluded to by Dinarchus (1.71), that *stratēgoi* were obliged to own land within the boundaries of Attica, effectively excluded nobody.[53]

If we move away from the fourth century, back in time, beyond Athens' defeat in the Peloponnesian War, the picture looks subtly different. In so far as the uneven distribution of evidence allows comparisons to be made, there are several hints that some politicians in the later fifth century approached more closely their Roman counterparts. It has been plausibly suggested that the disruptive level of competition that characterized politics in the late Republic was a response to Rome's acquisition of an empire: increased rewards for success stimulated greater rivalry (Beard and Crawford 1985: 68–71). For the second half of the fifth century, Athens also had an empire which individuals were able to exploit to their own advantage. There was, in particular, the practice of acquiring substantial holdings of property in the territory of subject states (Gauthier 1973). Also broadly contemporary with possession of the empire is the evidence, however slight, for politicians running into debt through conspicuous expenditure and consumption. As noted above (p. 67), this appears to be a fifth-century phenomenon, with no examples surviving from after the Peloponnesian War. Along similar lines, Davies has detected a dramatic decline in the number of Athenians competing in chariot races at the various Panhellenic games held after 400 (1981: 98–103 and 167–8). He draws from this the tentative conclusion that conspicuous expenditure of this type lost in importance during the fourth century.

The thread running through this presentation is the career of Alcibiades – not, it must be said, the most typical of Athenian politicians. We have already seen how his financial difficulties arose in part out of chariot-racing and other kinds of lavish expenditure, which he then manipulated as a claim to political power (p. 65). Whether or not he aimed at tyranny, his flirtation with oligarchic politics and active promotion of the oligarchic revolution of 411 are not in doubt. My tentative conclusion is that loss of the empire lowered the stakes in political competition in Athens; and that was one of the factors making for the greater political stability of the democracy in the fourth century.[54]

CHAPTER IV

The rôle of interest

MOEROCLES AND THE METAPHOR OF INTEREST

Amongst the topics covered in Aristotle's *Art of Rhetoric* is the use of metaphor. Embedded in a long list of illustrations, most of them *bons mots* by Athenian politicians, is the following example (1411a16–18):

Moerocles said that he was no more of a villain than one of the respectable people (*tina tōn epieikōn*), whom he named; for that man played the villain at 33⅓ per cent (*epitritōn tokōn*); but he himself at only 10 per cent (*epidekatōn*).

The context of the comment is unknown, but Moerocles can be identified as a contemporary of Demosthenes.[1] Although earlier commentators failed to appreciate the point of the metaphor (see Billeter 1898: 12), the allusion is presumably to the exaction of interest from borrowers (not profits; see Freese 1926: *ad loc.*). The figures quoted seem to represent the highest and lowest rates commonly found in Athens. In what follows, I will try to show how the moralizing aspect of the metaphor gives a clue to the fixing of Athenian interest rates.

Ancient interest rates come second only to banks in the attention they have received from historians, but an approach along moral lines is at odds with earlier suggestions. Superficial similarities invite arbitrary comparisons between ancient and modern rates, frequently combined with attempts to determine interest trends over time (see *OCD*[2] s.v. 'interest, rate of'). Interpretation of the evidence tends to be based on the assumption that the level of interest is itself a significant indicator of the condition of society. Böckh cites with approval a remark he attributes to Hume (see below), to the effect that (1842: 59) 'a high rate of interest and profit is an infallible sign that industry and trade are still in their infancy'; and the idea is repeated by Billeter (1898) on the first page of his standard history of ancient interest rates. But common sense suggests that the level of interest, when taken in complete isolation, cannot be even a general guide to the economic condition of a community. To give a modern example, the record interest rates experienced in the 1980s by Western capitalist economies were associated with a prolonged economic depression; by contrast, the severe slump of the 1930s was accompanied by rates of interest that were historically low.[2]

Interest rates have meaning only when viewed as part of the overall credit structure, and comparisons are valid only if like can be compared with like. There is literally a world of difference between the rate of interest extorted by a usurer from a desperate client in fourth-century Athens, and the minimum lending rate as regulated by the Bank of England. Historians who describe the rates of interest prevailing in the Greek world as 'high' have apparently been misled by contemporary experience (Büchsenschütz 1869a: 496; Michell 1957: 30–1; Davies 1981: 64). A comparison with rates from other non-capitalist societies actually suggests that the 'customary' Athenian rate of 1 per cent per month (see below) was relatively modest. The annual rates charged by Mesopotamian temples varied from 20 to 50 per cent (Bogaert 1966: 51–63). The maximal annual rates from early medieval India, as given in legal sources (Sharma 1965–6: 59–66), extend from 10 to at least 60 per cent; and maximum rates have a habit of becoming the minimum. Appleton (1919: 491–8) presents a selection of nineteenth-century material drawn from 'populations pauvres, pastorales ou agricoles', with no rates lower than 10 per cent and many higher than 100 per cent per annum. For borrowing in rural areas of modern underdeveloped countries, U Tun Wai (1957–8: 123) gives an estimated annual average of 30 per cent. No conclusion should be drawn from the way in which all the rates in this list are higher than their Athenian equivalents.

Confusion of ancient historians over interest rates in part reflects the uncertainty of modern economists. Interest theory must be one of the most abstruse aspects of economic analysis, with a discouragingly wide range of overlapping and contradictory theories. Most economists would accept the definition of interest given by Marshall as (1890: 73) 'The payment made by a borrower for the use of a loan...expressed as the ratio which the payment bears to the loan', but there is much less agreement over the rationale or justification for interest payments. The debate, which spills over into the area of ethics, has been continuous from early medieval times down to the present day. The treatment of the problem offered here is necessarily simplified and selective, restricted to those elements of interest theory which have been singled out by historians as having some bearing on interest rates in the ancient world.[3]

INTEREST THEORY AND THE DETERMINANTS OF INTEREST

To be rejected at the outset are present-day processes of interest-formation, whereby central banks manipulate the short-run market rate of interest by adjustments in the minimum lending rate and the selling of bonds. Also to be disregarded is the bulk of neo-classical interest theory, which has no bearing whatsoever on the ancient Greek world, and dubious relevance to the developed capitalist economy it is supposed to explain (see the comments by Robinson 1971: 25–51).

Amongst older theories of interest, the so-called 'quantity theory' has proved popular with ancient historians over the years. According to the simplest version of this hypothesis, the rate of interest is inversely proportional to the quantity of money in circulation. An increase in the money supply – and in the Greek world that means precious metals – will result in a corresponding fall in interest levels. Among the most recent ancient historians to favour this mechanism is Bogaert (1968: 328), who explains the 'high' rates of interest prevailing in Athens as a consequence of the shortage of coined money (compare Tod in *CAH*[1] V 26). The more complex, dynamic analyses by Bury and Meiggs (1975: 363) and Glotz (1920: 241) are essentially identical. Both envisage growth in the 'money supply' as being counter-balanced by an increasing demand for commercial credit. And yet, for all its plausibility, the fallacy behind the crude quantity theory of interest was exposed as long ago as the eighteenth century by David Hume in his essay *Of Interest* (1752). Hume pointed out the error in treating money as a commodity and interest as its price, with an increase in supply relative to demand necessarily resulting in a fall in the price level. He explained how the rate of interest was not a price but a ratio; other things being equal, a doubling of the quantity of money in circulation will result in a doubling of prices, so that in order to achieve a given end, a borrower will need to take up twice as much money. In this way, an equilibrium will be preserved between supply of and demand for loans at the original rate of interest.[4]

The discussion of the quantity theory given above refers several times to *the* rate of interest; but the phrase involves an abstraction that may not be appropriate to the ancient world. Apart from geographical and chronological variations in rates of interest, in any given time and place there will typically be not one rate, but a whole complex of interest rates. The bundle of rates corresponds to different types of credit operation, depending on factors which include relative risk, duration and liquidity. In order to simplify the building of models involving interest, economists postulate the existence of a single rate – the 'pure' or 'net' rate of interest – which represents the whole complex of rates. This pure rate is commonly conceived as the interest on a perfectly safe, near-liquid loan, and is therefore often associated with the return on government bonds. It is assumed that all other rates move in step with the pure rate of interest (see Ingersoll in Palgrave, s.v. 'interest rates').

The concept of a pure rate of interest plays a central rôle in theories of the determination of interest. At least as early as Adam Smith in his *Wealth of Nations* (1776), it was assumed that, at a given time and place, the rate of profit on capital (that is, production goods) would approximate to the rate of interest on loans (see Panico in Palgrave s.v. 'interest and profit'). In his chapter 'Of the profits of stock' (pp. 133–50), Smith laments the difficulty of ascertaining the average rate of profit, but consoles himself with the thought that interest on money acts as a general guide. 'It can be laid down as a maxim', he says (pp. 134–5), 'that wherever a great deal can be made by the use of money, a great deal will commonly be given for the use of it; and that wherever little can be made by it, less will commonly be given for it... The progress of interest, therefore, may lead us to form some notion of the progress of profit.' And in the pages that follow, Smith manipulates the market rate of interest as a guide to rates of profit in various parts of the world. Although historians of economic theory have tended to stress the incoherence of Smith's account of interest formation (e.g. Blaug 1968: 42), he does appear to have envisaged that interest was determined by the rate of profit. In an earlier passage, he describes interest as (p. 79), 'always a derivative revenue'.

The link established by Smith between 'the usual market rate of interest' and 'the ordinary profits of stock' was refined by later classical economists until it approached the form in which it is commonly found today: the pure rate of interest equals, and is determined by, the marginal productivity of capital (see Conard

1963: 11–13). The derivation of the pure rate of interest – and with it the whole complex of rates – from the rate of return on real capital, lies at the heart of most text-book accounts of the determinants of interest. Several ancient historians have been attracted by the apparent simplicity of the mechanism, and have applied it to the problem of interest formation in the Greek world. The trend began with Böckh (1842: 126), and finds a more recent supporter in French, who argues that (1964: 155) 'evidence for the high returns available from commerce is afforded by the level of interest charged; the rate never falls below 12 per cent except for personal accommodation...' (for French's hedging of bets on interest formation, see his further comment, p. 197, n. 43). But a brief examination of the various elements in the mechanism linking interest to the return on capital only serves to show its inappropriateness to the economic structure of the Greek world.

In its simplest form, ignoring complications such as administrative costs and risk premiums, the interest–profit mechanisms may be thought to work as follows. Should the pure rate of interest be below the rate of return on capital, money will be borrowed and invested in real capital. The effect will be simultaneously to lower the rate of return on real capital and bid up the rate of interest until equilibrium is achieved – theoretically, when the two rates are identical. Similarly, if the rate of interest is above the rate of return on capital, the low level of demand for loans will cause the interest rate to fall until an equilibrium is reached. The functioning of the mechanism therefore requires that potential borrowers/investors remain keenly aware of the relationship between pure rate of interest and marginal productivity of capital. A moment's thought shows the inappropriateness of this condition to the ancient Greek world.

It is argued below that the Athenians had no notion of the 'usual market rate of interest' as conceived by Smith; still less the 'pure rate of interest' of modern economists. There was, in the same way, only the crudest conception of relative rates of profitability in Athens. This is apparent from repeated failures to make 'rational' economic sense of Demosthenes' detailed account of his father's manufacturing interests (xxvii–xxix). Demosthenes supplies for the benefit of the jury crude figures for net annual profits which, despite an abundance of prices and values, cannot be re-calculated and expressed as a percentage of total costs. That this was not merely forensic fudging but the usual state of affairs may be inferred from the interpretation of Greco-Roman accounting methods offered by Mickwitz (1937 and 1939: 20–1) and de Ste Croix (1956: 32). Even at their most sophisticated, ancient Greek accounts were intended as checks on embezzlement, not as guides to profit and loss. It would be foolish to argue that the Greeks had no concept of, or desire for, increased profitability; Demosthenes' father was, after all, a wealthy man. But the rudimentary nature of accounting techniques reflects the Athenians' inability to balance overall profitability against a rate of interest.[5]

A third and final difficulty distances the interest–profit mechanism even further from the Greek world. An essential part of the relationship is the process whereby borrowed funds are invested in real capital; it is, in other words, *productive* borrowing that links the rate of interest to the rate of return on real capital. Economists from Adam Smith onwards (1776: II, 33–4) have noted the existence of non-productive credit, but gone on to argue that its insignificant volume prevents it from having any measurable impact on the conditions governing productive borrowing. In this way, rates of interest on non-productive loans will be determined by the rates prevailing for productive credit (see Patinkin, *IESS* s.v. 'interest'). But, as detailed in the previous chapter, the position in classical Athens was precisely the opposite, with possible productive loans mentioned in the sources barely reaching into double figures (p. 59). It is therefore perverse to argue as if Athenian interest rates for landside loans bore any relation to rates of profit. All the more so, as economists have regularly pointed out this critical distinction between the credit structures of capitalist and non-capitalist societies.[6]

It was appreciated by the early classical economists that there were short-run shifts in market rates of interest which could not be explained in terms of changes in the rate of return on capital. In a passage that is mildly critical of Smith's use of interest as a guide to profit, Ricardo remarks how (1817: 297) 'the rate of interest, though ultimately and permanently governed by the rate of profit, is however subject to temporary variations from other causes'. To account for these variations, Ricardo devised what has come to be called the 'loanable funds' theory of interest, reaching its classic formulation in the hands of Mill (1848: II, 647–59). According to the loanable funds theory, the market rate of interest is determined by the demand for loans for investment purposes (itself determined by the rate of profit on capital), and the supply of loanable funds (as determined by the volume of savings). The rate of interest therefore acts as a regulator, bringing supply and demand for funds into equilibrium.

The loanable funds theory has the attraction for ancient historians of operating independently of the rate of return on capital. Demand for loans could be determined by the kind of external factors that are regularly associated with non-productive credit – food shortages, warfare and the like. As a result, loose formulations of the loanable funds model are probably the most popular explanation of interest formation amongst Greek historians (Beauchet 1897: III, 250; Bury and Meiggs 1975: 363; Michell 1957: 30–3; Davies 1981: 64). And yet, the assumptions on which the loanable funds theory is based are as alien to Athenian economy and society as those of the interest–profit mechanism.

Take the hypothetical case in which an excessive demand for loans puts the model out of equilibrium. Theory suggests that competing borrowers will bid up the rate of interest until sufficient of them have dropped out, and enough new borrowers have been tempted to enter the market, to establish a new equilibrium. The critical term here is 'market', as the loanable funds theory presupposes the existence of a money market, with its host of attendant assumptions – none of which is appropriate to fourth-century Athens. Whereas the theory assumes fully flexible rates of interest, I argue below that Athenian interest rates were fixed by custom and tradition. Moreover, the presumption that the demand for credit will be elastic, able to respond to shifts in the rate of interest, may not apply to those who borrow out of necessity rather than voluntarily, for productive purposes. Finally, the forces that fix the equilibrium rate of interest within the market structure depend on near-perfect and instantaneous knowledge on the part of both borrowers and creditors, combined with perfect access to all parts of the market. Such ideal conditions barely exist in the organized money market of modern capitalist economies; to attribute them to the economy of the fourth-century Athens is to perpetrate a gross anachronism.[7]

The gulf between the supply of credit in classical Athens and in a modern money market may be gauged by drawing comparisons with systems of rural credit in under-developed economies. Development economists stress the poor knowledge of borrowers about alternative sources of credit, their limited access to lenders outside their immediate vicinity, and the scope for monopoly profits on the part of lenders (Bottomley 1963a, 1963b and 1964). In a valuable study of credit in rural Chile, Nisbet (1967) presents a picture which parallels the Athenian system at several points, with its emphasis on non-productive borrowing, the large proportion of borrowers (70 per cent) making use of informal sources of credit, and the wide range of lenders (friends, neighbours, relatives, *patrones*, village stores, itinerant traders, and local money-lenders). Where interest is charged, the near-monopolistic position of lenders combines with inelasticity of demand on the part of borrowers to produce usurious rates of interest: anywhere from 18 to 360 per cent per annum (p. 77). The imperfections of these 'unorganized money markets' are summed up by U Tun Wai (1957–8), in a passage which deserves quoting in full (pp. 81–2):

... it is questionable whether the existing arrangements should be referred to as 'markets'. They are much less homogeneous than the organized markets and are generally scattered over the rural sector. There is very little contact between the lenders and borrowers in different localities. The usual textbook conditions for a perfect market are completely non-existent: lenders and borrowers do not know the rates at which loans are being contracted in other parts of the country; the relationship between borrower and lender is not only that of debtor and creditor but is also an integral part of a much wider socio-economic pattern of village life and rural conditions.

The final sentence provides a clue to the process of interest formation in fourth-century Athens. In the section that follows, the taking of interest is viewed against the wider background of Athenian social relations.

INTEREST IN THE ATHENIAN MODEL

The preceding pages have shown the inadequacy of conventional economic theory as a guide to the realities of Athenian economy and society. The Athenian moral code made it difficult for citizens to behave like the rational economic men of neo-classical theory. Perhaps the single most important observation to emerge from my study so far is the *personal* character of loan transactions. A simple list of the loans recorded in the Orators shows that the majority were interest-free: a tendency not always appreciated by historians, misled by modern experience. As the dominant form of lending, interest-free credit set the moral tone for credit relations in general.

A case in point is the situation in the speech *Against Nicostratus*, described in the previous chapter (pp. 53–9). Apollodorus claims that he not only obliged his friend with interest-free loans, but also implies that he himself paid out interest in order to raise a part of the cash required. Behaviour like this is at odds with attempts to explain interest as 'the reward for waiting' or 'compensation for the sacrifice of liquidity' – respectively the neo-classical and Keynesian interpretations of interest (Marshall 1890: 232; Keynes 1936: 165–74). Interest in the Athenian model has instead an overtly ethical function, distinguishing between loans which were personal, and those which were on a more formal basis. In personal transactions between relatives, friends, neighbours and the like, there was an almost automatic expectation of a reciprocal favour at some future date: the loan was part of a wider relationship. In impersonal credit operations, where there was no existing bond between lender and borrower, or desire that a bond should be established, repayment of the loan terminated the association, and interest took the place of the return favour.

The hypothesis has already been advanced that interest in the Greek world may have originated as a voluntary, additional payment on the part of the borrower, which was in due course converted into an obligatory charge, imposed at the discretion of the lender (pp. 44–52). The distinction between repayment of the principal as a moral duty, and exaction of interest as unethical exploitation, survived into the fourth century, reflected in the opposition of Plato and Aristotle to the taking of interest (pp. 40–4). In addition to the passages already cited, there is a less familiar, but enlightening statement in the *Problems* attributed to Aristotle, and presumed to be the work of one or more of his Peripatetic followers. Because of the apparent contradictions the passage contains, it is translated in full (950a28–b4):

Why is it more terrible to embezzle a deposit (*parakatathēkēn*) than a loan (*daneion*)? Is it because it is shameful to act unjustly towards a friend (*philon*)? The man who embezzles a deposit wrongs a friend; for no man makes a deposit with a man he does not trust. But where there is a debt (*chreos*), there is no friend; for if a man is a friend, he does not lend (*daneizei*) but gives (*didōsin*). Or is it because the injustice done is greater? For in addition to the loss, he has betrayed a trust (*pistin*), for which – if for no other reason – he must abstain from wrongdoing. Besides, it is mean-minded not to return like for like (*tois isois*); for the depositor gave it (*edōken*) as a friend, but the other made away with it like an enemy; but the lender (*daneizōn*) did not give it as a friend. And what is more, in the former case, the gift (*dosis*) was made with a view towards safekeeping and return, but in the latter it was for gain (*ōpheleias*). We are less indignant at losing if we are pursuing gain (*kerdos*), like fishermen losing their bait, for the risk is readily apparent. Yet again, men mostly make a deposit when they are conspired against and unfortunate, but it is the well-to-do (*hoi euporountes*) who lend (*daneizousi*); and it is more terrible to wrong the unfortunate than the fortunate.

The author seems at first sight to be saying that all loans are 'impersonal': 'If a man is a friend, he does not lend but gives.' Nevertheless, it is clear from the context that interest-free, reciprocal loans are here being assimilated to gifts (above, p. 55). The contrast is with loans bearing interest. This is implied by repeated use of *daneizein* for 'lend', and confirmed by the allusion to going after gain (*kerdos*) – presumably a reference to interest payments. The final point about lenders being 'fortunate' and 'well-to-do' ties in with objections to professional money-lenders registered in non-philosophical sources. It will be recalled how Apollodorus attacked Stephanus on the grounds that he lent out money at interest, and therefore regarded the misfortunes of others as his own good fortune (p. 25, above). Along similar lines is a passage from Demosthenes' speech *Against Pantaenetus* (XXXVII.53), in which the speaker agrees that the jury are right to hate those lending money who 'make a trade (*technēn*) of the business, with no thought of fellow-feeling (*sungnōmēs*), or anything else other than gain'.[8]

This interpretation of Athenian attitudes towards interest finds support in the analogous ideology of early Jewish society, as depicted in the Old Testament. In spite of obvious differences, the structure of the two societies was in some ways similar. The kinship morality of the Hebrew tribes was built on the solidarity of the clan, to the exclusion of the stranger or foreigner (de Vaux 1958–60: 3–17; Neufeld 1955; 383–99). This sense of community, and the commitment to preserving it, are reflected in several laws designed to protect the poor. For example, gleanings were left for the poor to pick up (Leviticus, XIX.9–10; Deuteronomy XXIV.19–21), and the produce of fallow land could be reaped by the poor (Exodus XIII.10–11); the tradition of the seventh- and fiftieth-year releases is noted elsewhere (Chapter III, n. 35, with de Vaux 1958–60: 173–7). This is the close-knit society that forms the background to the familiar biblical laws against interest, here cited in their probable chronological order (Exodus XXII.25–7; Leviticus XXV.35–7; Deuteronomy XXIII.19–20):[9]

If you advance money to any poor man amongst my people, you shall not act like a money-lender: you must not exact interest in advance from him. If you take your neighbour's cloak in pawn, you shall return it to him by sunset, because it is his only covering...

When your brother-Israelite is reduced to poverty and cannot support himself in the community, you shall assist him as you would an alien or stranger, and he shall live with you. You shall not charge him interest on a loan, either by deducting it in advance from the capital sum, or by adding it on repayment. You shall fear your God, and your brother shall live with you; you shall not deduct interest when advancing him money nor add interest to the payment due for food supplied on credit.

You shall not charge interest on anything you lend to a fellow-countryman, money or food or anything else on which interest can be charged. You may charge interest on a loan to a foreigner but not to a fellow-countryman.

The general sense and purpose of the prohibitions is clear: no interest was to be exacted from fellow-Jews as this could be a threat to communal solidarity. Only the wicked man lends at interest (Proverbs xxviii.8). The laws naturally apply to non-productive loans to the poor (Chapter iii, n. 30), and can be matched in other close-knit societies. From the ancient world, it is necessary to look no further than Tacitus' description of the Germans, who are said to have no knowledge of lending at interest (*Germania* xxvi.1; compare the Islamic prohibition of interest: Neufeld 1955: 408–9).[10]

The biblical banning of interest was double-edged as, according to the Deuteronomic version, lending at interest was still permitted between Jew and non-Jew. This parallels, though in an exaggerated form, the rôle of interest in the Athenian model, where the lender was at least free to reach his own decision about the nature of his relationship with the borrower. In fact, the distinction between debtors as insiders or outsiders could be drawn even more sharply. The *Siphre* or ancient commentary on Deuteronomy (§263) insisted that a definite command was laid on Jews to exact interest from foreigners (Maloney 1971: 102). Use of interest as a weapon against those outside the community is found elsewhere. Ironically, biblical texts permitting the taking of interest from non-Jews were taken up by the early Christian Church, and turned against the Jews themselves. That is the interpretation placed on the brother/stranger dichotomy by St Ambrose (cited from Nelson 1969: 4), who identifies as strangers, '... the notorious foes of God's people... From him demand usury, whom you rightly desire to harm, against whom weapons are lawfully carried. Upon him usury is legally imposed. On him whom you cannot easily conquer in war, you can quickly take vengeance with the hundredth. From him exact usury whom it would not be a crime to kill.'[11]

The extent to which later Jews adhered to their laws forbidding the taking of interest among themselves is problematical (see de Vaux 1958–60: 170–1; Gamoran 1971: 133–4; Maloney 1971: 96–109). By contrast, the decay of the Deuteronomic doctrine in the Christian West has been brilliantly traced by Nelson (1969). The book's cumbersome subtitle: 'From tribal brotherhood to universal otherhood' is intended to convey the gradual weakening of interest as an ethical concept, serving to differentiate between insiders and outsiders. This is analogous to the process already identified for early Athens, with the extension of the ideal of reciprocity to a crowded community necessarily resulting in dilution. As was argued in an earlier chapter (p. 40, above), decreasing intimacy between borrower and lender lessened the likelihood of reciprocal assistance and made more legitimate the charging of interest. Even though classical Athens, with its tens of thousands of citizens, did not recognize the brother/other cleavage with the same rigidity as Judaic law, or even early Christian teaching, it is only in this ethical context that Athenian interest can be explained.

Although the critical distinction in both Deuteronomic and Athenian models is between interest-bearing and interest-free loans, the mechanism may be extended to account for the differing sizes of interest payments. As the charging of interest is characteristic of impersonal loan transactions, so the size of interest payment is proportionate to the degree of impersonality between lender and borrower. The broad concept of an inverse relationship between remoteness of relationship and favourable conditions of exchange has been fully documented, with special reference to reciprocity, by Sahlins (1965; see Chapter II, n. 25). Included among his illustrations is the Deuteronomic division between strangers and brothers (p. 191). The distinction is taken several stages further by a scheme of interest payments developed in early India (Sharma 1965–6: 60–1). Indian lawgivers are said to have devised a complex system of interest rates which varied according to the relative castes of lender and borrower. Loans between members of the same caste were at a flat rate of 24 per cent per annum, with an additional 10 per cent being added for each gradation between people of different castes. The extent to which this formalized system was applied may be doubted, but it presumably reflected prevailing practices and attitudes. A simpler and more workable system of payments was found by Barton among the Ifugao tribe in the Philippines (1919: 56–7) – close relatives pay no interest and remote kin make low payments.

The evidence on interest payments from Athens, though consistent with the social-distance model, is admittedly not decisive. The appropriateness of the hypothesis has to be assessed by an examination of the overall structure of interest rates. There is a preliminary difficulty here, as the pattern of Athenian interest rates is complicated by two separate systems of computation. The more common method expresses the rate in terms of the number of obols or drachmas charged for each mina (= 100 drachmas) borrowed over a period of a month. Hence 'at five obols' (*epi pente obolois*) corresponds to 10 per cent per annum. 'At a drachma' (*epi drachmēi*) to 12 per cent per annum, 'at eight obols' (*ep' ektō obolois*) to 16 per cent annum, and so on, up to 'at three drachmas' (*epi trisi drachmais*) equalling 36 per cent per annum.[12] The alternative method expresses interest paid as a fraction of the principal: 'one-tenth interest' (*tokoi epidekatoi*) corresponds to 10 per cent, with similar expressions for one-eighth (*epogdooi* = $12\frac{1}{2}$ per cent), one-sixth (*ephektoi* = $16\frac{2}{3}$ per cent), one-fifth (*epipemptoi* = 20 per cent) and one-third (*epitritoi* = $33\frac{1}{3}$ per cent).

The preference the sources show for reckoning interest by the month implies that interest-bearing loans tended to be short-term. The impression is strengthened by incidental references to monthly settlements of accounts. Strepsiades in Aristophanes' *Clouds* (ll. 746–56) devises a lunatic scheme to evade the payment of interest by using magic to draw down the moon: 'money is borrowed by the month', he says (l. 735; see Dover 1968: on l. 17). The plaintiff in Hyperides' *Against Athenogenes* (§ 19) tells the jury that his perfume-selling opponent received his accounts monthly; and Theophrastus represents his 'Penurious Man' (*mikrologos*) as pestering his debtor for a half-obol interest payment before the end of the month (x.2). Lending at short-term like this, limiting the lender's risk, seems to be a characteristic of non-institutional credit in underdeveloped economies (Harper 1961: 170–1; Karkal 1967: 85; Nisbet 1967: 79). For the ancient world, there was the additional attraction that monthly reckoning of interest would avoid complications when months were intercalated (Bickerman 1980: 31; Caillemer 1870: 14).

Taken together, the systems of monthly and fractional interest are capable of expressing a wide range of rates. For the sake of convenience, I present the collected evidence in tabular form, recalculating monthly rates (indicated by an asterisk) on an annual basis.[13]

10%   *Dem. xxx.7: dowry retained after divorce, transformed into loan (see below)
Arist. *Rhet.* 1411a16: rate alone mentioned (see above, p. 91)
Finley 1952: no. 102: rent/interest inscribed on *horos* from Amorgos

12%   *Dem. xxvii.9: interest on a talent of money
*Dem. xxxvii.5: rent/interest for purchase of crushing mill (see Chapter viii)
*Aeschin. iii.104: interest on alleged bribe (see Chapter iii, n. 43)

12½%   [Dem.] l.17: maritime loan? (See Chapter iii, n. 26)
Lexica Segueriana (= *Anecdota Bekker*) i 252, 19: 'loan on a shipment of cargoes'

16%   *[Dem.] liii.13: loan of 16 minas, real security (see Chapter iii, n. 8)

16⅔%   [Dem.] xxxiv.23: landside loan, secured at Cyzicus

18%   *Lys. fr. 38 (see above, pp. 1–2)
*Isaeus xi.42: interest on sum of 4,000 dr. (see below)
*Aeschin. i.107: interest on loan of 30 minas to 'buy' public office (see Chapter iii, n. 32)
*Dem. xxvii.17: interest owed on retained dowry (see below)
*[Dem.] lix.52: interest owed on retained dowry (see below)

20%   Xen. *Poroi* iii.9: rate of return on proposed *rentier* scheme (see Chapter vii)

22½%   [Dem.] xxxv.10: maritime loan

25%   Lys. xix.25: payment of 20 minas for loan of 16 minas (see Chapter iii, n. 29)

30%   [Dem.] xxxv.10: maritime loan

$33\frac{1}{3}\%$ Isaeus fr. 23 in Forster 1927: rate only mentioned
Arist. *Rhet.* 1411a16: rate only mentioned (see above, p. 91)
Xen. *Poroi* III.9: rate of return on proposed rentier scheme (see Chapter VII)

36%   Lys. fr. 38 (see above, pp. 1–2)

Removal of maritime loans from the list leaves a narrow range of rates which broadly supports the social-distance theory of interest. There is the impression that the 'normal' or 'prevailing' rate for impersonal, interest-bearing loans was one drachma on the mina, or one per cent per month. To the three examples listed above may be added a handful of general references, identifying the rate as some kind of norm. When Demosthenes was trying to claim compensation from his guardians, he added to the value of his father's estate an 'interest charge', reckoned *epi drachmēi* (XXVII.17, 23 and 35; XXVIII.13).[14] The same figure is mentioned in an inscription, dated to 345/4, detailing the procedures to be followed when the deme of Halai Aixonides rented out some land (*IG* II² 2492 ~ Epigraphica I 42 ~ *IJG* I XIII *bis* 238–41). It was proposed that certain olive trees on the land to be leased should be cut down and the timber sold off; the cash resulting from the sale was to be loaned out *epi drachmēi* (ll. 31–41). It may be presumed that, in both these cases, I per cent per month was chosen as a 'normal' and 'reasonable' rate of interest, appropriate to an impersonal loan transaction.[15] That presumption is borne out by the list of 'monthly suits' (*dikai emmēnoi*) supplied by the Aristotelian *Constitution of Athens* (*Ath. Pol.* LII; see Chapter III, n. 50). The catalogue includes cases which occur 'if anyone embezzles money borrowed *epi drachmēi*'. The appearance of the figure in this legal context seems decisive: anyone charging more than I per cent per month for a loan disqualified themselves from taking advantage of the speedy procedure of a monthly suit.

The slender evidence for other rates of interest gives qualified support to the idea of I per cent per month as the norm for impersonal loans. The only example from Athens of an actual loan below I per cent per month involves a monthly rate of five obols (= 10 per cent per annum) in Demosthenes' *First Speech Against Onetor* (XXX.7). The debtor, Timocrates, incurred an obligation by divorcing his wife, but agreeing to retain her dowry as a loan at five obols per month, in place of the nine-obol rate prescribed by law (see below). Although the background to the transaction cannot be recovered, Demosthenes hints at collusion between former husband (Timocrates), new husband (Aphobus) and guardian (Onetor). Concerning loans above 1 per cent per month, there are the merest hints that the rates are to be regarded as on the high side. About the sole example of a loan at eight obols per month (= $1\frac{1}{3}$ per cent, [Dem.] LIII.13), nothing can be said (see Chapter III, n. 8); but the background to loans at nine obols per month (= $1\frac{1}{2}$ per cent) is more promising. The $1\frac{1}{2}$ per cent demanded from Aeschines the Socratic is discussed below. The nine-obol rate in a speech by Isaeus (XI.42) is supplied by a litigant who wants to maximize the size of an estate, of which money out on loan is a component. The rate of $1\frac{1}{2}$ per cent could therefore be his own inflated estimate. Firmer evidence again comes from a legal context: the presumed penal element in the $1\frac{1}{2}$ per cent monthly charge on non-returned dowries, which supports the idea of 1 per cent as the norm.[16]

The concept of a conventional rate of interest, from which deviations had moral overtones, brings us back to the passage from Aristotle's *Rhetoric* with which this chapter opened. Seen against the pattern of rates presented above, Moerocles' contrast between his lending at only 10 per cent with another person's $33\frac{1}{3}$ per cent looks like a deliberate straddling of the 12 per cent norm. Moerocles' interest charge is the lowest found in Athens, and that of his opponent almost the highest.

A theory of interest determination based on social distance has the advantage of flexibility. Earlier explanations of differential rates of interest have tended to concentrate on the risk faced by the lender (Hicks 1969: 72–7). The more likely that the borrower will default, and the less satisfactory the security offered, the higher the rate of interest charged. This is the thinking that dominates the influential study of ancient interest by Billeter (1898), where everything is staked on risk as the determinant of interest rates. No doubt risk had its part to play in determining the appropriate level of interest. That was undeniably the case in maritime loans, where the danger varied from one voyage to the next (e.g. [Dem.] XXXV.10). But the exceptional nature of maritime credit will be brought out in Chapter VIII. Concerning landside loans, risk of non-repayment was only one of a complex of factors influencing the relationship between lenders and borrowers. By way of illustration, there is the case of Aeschines and his creditors, with which the study opened.

Aeschines originally took out a loan at the usurious rate of 3 per cent per month: its impersonal quality is revealed by the involvement of a banker. He was able to refinance his borrowing by contracting a fresh loan at half the former rate; but there is no reason to believe that his circumstances had changed, making him less of a risk. Aeschines' new creditor was a person who either knew him, or knew of him. He assures the jury that he never imagined a pupil of Socrates would behave in such a disgraceful way (612b). Although this is so much rhetoric, it does imply that personal knowledge stemming from a closer relationship made appropriate a lower level of interest. Although it would be unwarrantable to identify the speaker as a 'friend' of Aeschines, his behaviour corresponds to a comment in Bentham's *Defence of Usury* (1787: 24): 'Persons who either feel, or find reasons for pretending to feel, a friendship for the borrower, cannot take of him more than the ordinary rate of interest.' In the chapters that follow, the ramifications of friendship (*philia*) in Athens will be explored in detail.

The conventional or customary rates of interest proposed above for Athens appear in other societies at low levels of conventional economic development. U Tun Wai associates customary rates with static conditions in modern underdeveloped countries (1957–8: 107): and Leemans (1950) traces stable rates for loans of barley and silver through several centuries of Babylonian history. Attempts to identify trends in ancient Greek interest levels should therefore be viewed with deep suspicion. The conventional belief that, after the end of the fourth century, interest rates began to fall, is well summarized in the following passage from Tarn and Griffith:

In Alexander's reign the usual rate was 12 per cent... By about 300 the rate had fallen to 10 per cent... reflecting the fall in the drachma consequent upon the circulation of the Persian treasure, and 10 per cent... remained usual throughout the third century, though $8\frac{1}{3}$ and 6... also occur; in the first half of the second century we meet 6 and 7, both business transactions. After the middle of the century, the rate rises again and by Sulla's time it has got back to the old 12 per cent. (1952: 115)

Ignoring the 'quantity fallacy' in the first part of the passage, the figures supplied by Tarn and Griffith (taken from Billeter) form a series that, in geographical terms, is highly discontinuous: Ilium, Amorgos, Corcyra, Oropus, Peria, Thera, Delphi, Ephesus, Olymos-Mylasa. Not one figure, it should be noted, is drawn from Attica – the source of the original rate of 12 per cent.[17] Turning to the modern world, statistical evidence compiled from underdeveloped economies shows the extent to which interest rates may vary instantaneously from region to region within a single country (U Tun Wai 1957–8: 99–100). Regional variation could explain at least a part of the diversity of rates from different periods and places in the Greek world. It is unlikely to be a coincidence that the only connected sequence of rates to have survived from ancient Greece shows complete stability. From the fifth to the second century B.C., the rate of interest charged by the Temple of Apollo on Delos remained unchanged at ten per cent (Billeter 1898: 9–10 and 58–61).[18]

CHAPTER V

Philia *and friendship*

ARISTOTLE ON FRIENDSHIP

At the heart of Aristotle's analysis of *philia* or 'friendship' in his *Nicomachean Ethics* is an extended discussion of the differing obligations owed to the different varieties of *philoi* (1165a14–35):[1]

Clearly, then, we should not make the same return (*apodoteon*) to everyone, and we should not give our fathers everything, just as we should not make all sacrifices to Zeus. And since different things should be assigned (*aponemēteon*) to parents, brothers, comrades (*hetairois*) and benefactors (*euergetais*), we should accord to each what is appropriate and fitting (*ta oikeia kai ta harmottonta*). This is what actually appears to be done: blood relations (*tous sungeneis*) are the people invited to a wedding, since they share the same family (*koinon to genos*), and hence share in actions that concern it; and for the same reason, it is thought that relations more than anyone must come to funerals.

It seems that we must supply the means of support (*trophēs*) to parents more than anyone. For we suppose that we owe them this (*hōs opheilontas*), and that it is finer to supply those who are the cause of our being than to supply ourselves in this way. And we should accord honour to our parents, just as we should to the gods, but not every sort of honour; for we should not accord the same honour to a father and to a mother, nor accord them the honour due to a wise person or a commander. We should accord a father's honour to a father, and likewise a mother's to a mother.

We should accord to every older person the honour befitting his age, by standing up, giving up seats and so on. With comrades and brothers, we should speak freely, and have everything in common (*hapantōn koinotēta*). To relations, fellow-tribesmen (*phuletais*), fellow-citizens (*politais*) and all the rest, we should always try to assign what is fitting (*to oikeion*), and should compare what belongs to each, as befits closeness of relation, virtue or utility (*kat' oikeiotēta kai aretēn ē chrēsin*). Comparison is easier with people of the same kind, and more difficult with people of different kinds, but the difficulty is no reason for giving up the comparison; rather we should define as far as we can.

109

Several aspects of this passage invite comment: the broadly empirical approach, with an appeal to concrete examples; the unusually wide application of 'friendship' to include parents at one extreme and fellow-citizens at the other; and the association of friendship with giving a return (*apodidōmi*) or rendering what is owed (*opheilō*). All these characteristics are explored later in this chapter. But what is immediately striking is the correspondence between Aristotle's formulation of the varying obligations of friendship and the model of reciprocal credit based on social distance, introduced in earlier chapters (pp. 39–40 and 102–3, above). It was suggested there that decreasing familiarity between lender and borrower increased the chances of a formal or impersonal loan transaction, with interest charge and security requirement. The model, it will be recalled, was based in turn on Sahlins' concept of 'kinship distance' (Chapter II, n. 25), here described in greater detail.

Sahlins visualizes a 'spectrum of reciprocities', defined by the extremes of 'generalized' and 'negative reciprocity', with 'balanced reciprocity' midway between the two poles (1965: 191–6). 'Generalized reciprocity' he defines as 'the solidarity extreme', akin to Malinowski's notion of the 'pure gift', with an overwhelming but unspecified obligation to reciprocate. He cites as an illustration the extreme case of a mother suckling her child. 'Negative reciprocity' (an apparent contradiction in terms) is the 'unsociable extreme', whereby parties aim to gain as much as possible from the encounter, leading to exploitation and even trickery or theft. 'Balanced reciprocity' refers to exchange operations which assume an equal or equivalent return within a finite period of time. Transactions in this category often resemble conventional ideas of trade or barter. According to Sahlins (pp. 196–204), the location of an individual transaction along the spectrum will typically be determined by the degree of kinship between the parties concerned. Moving from generalized to balanced reciprocity, he identifies a sequence of more or less separate sectors: household, lineage, village and tribal; between balanced reciprocity and the pole of negative reciprocity lies the zone of inter-tribal relationships.

Sahlins' diagrammatic representation of his reciprocity spectrum takes the shape of a series of concentric circles, with household at the core and inter-tribal sector at the periphery (p. 199). There is, in fact, nothing new about this broad configuration, which long ago suggested itself as a way of envisaging personal relationships in ancient Greece.[2] The break with Sahlins comes over his concentration on kinship as the decisive factor in ordering relationships. In the case of credit relations, kinship is only one of several possible connexions between lender and borrower. In the following chapter, the hypothesis is put forward that the pervasiveness of family ties in Athenian society may have been over-estimated. The passage from the *Ethics* already quoted lists a few of the possible links: brotherhood, comradeship, tribe-membership, citizenship. Although in our eyes these relationships have little, if anything, in common, they were in the Greek consciousness all covered by the over-arching quality of *philia*. It is therefore *philia* (only inadequately rendered as 'friendship') that emerges as the Athenian equivalent of Sahlins' kinship, extending along the spectrum of reciprocity as far as the zone in which balanced merges into negative reciprocity. As Aristotle says elsewhere in the *Nicomachean Ethics* (1165b32): 'We think we must show gratitude (*charizesthai*) to *philoi* rather than to strangers (*othneiois*).'[3]

Greek literature from Homer onwards is peppered with pronouncements on *philia*: its pleasures, problems, advantages and obligations.[4] The frequency and extravagance of the references give a fair impression of the diffusion of *philia* through Greek society. As well as being universal, *philia* was conceived as a semi-formal institution. There were recognized codes of conduct for *philoi*, occasionally extending as far as the swearing of sacred oaths (Antiphon VI.39, with Fisher 1976: 18–19). A popular conception of justice, with which the *Republic* opens (332A), consists of owing (*opheilein*) good to one's *philoi* and evil to one's *echthroi* or enemies (cf. Dover 1974: 180–1; Blundell 1989: 26–59). Like material debts, the obligations owed by *philoi* could be passed on from father to son (Lysias XVIII.26–7; Isoc. II.19; [Dem.] L.56). All this helps to explain why *philia* looms so large in the ethical writings of Aristotle.[5] The *Nicomachean Ethics* has the fullest discussion of friendship to have survived by any Greek author, taking two books out of ten (VIII and IX), and making up a major theme of the work. It is no coincidence that *philia* is the concept chosen by Aristotle to link the discussion of personal ethics in the *Nicomachean Ethics* with the treatment of the *polis*-community in the *Politics* (Hutter 1978: 106). *Philia* was obviously a key component in Aristotle's perception of contemporary society. Less apparent is whether his presentation can be read as a practical guide to the realities of friendship in fourth-century Athens.

First signs are promising. Close to the beginning of the *Ethics* (1095a28), Aristotle is explicit about the need to commence ethical enquiry by examining those beliefs that are 'most common or seem reasonable'. And part way through the work, in connexion with his analysis of virtue and vice, he restates his method of enquiry (1145b2–8):

> As in the other cases, we must set out the appearances (*tithentas ta phainomena*), and first of all go through the puzzles. In this way, we must prove the common beliefs (*endoxa*) about these ways of being affected – ideally, all the common beliefs, but if not all, then most of them and the most important (*ta pleista kai kuriōtata*). For if the objections are solved and the common beliefs are left, it will be an adequate proof.

The contrast with Plato's deep suspicion of popular opinion could hardly be more marked. Scholars habitually comment on Aristotle's willingness to take serious account of commonly held views (Hardie 1980: 37–8; Lloyd 1968: 204–8); at least, in the field of ethics (Owen 1961). But Aristotle's writings are much more than a mirror of popular morality, and there are limits beyond which an empiricist reading of his work should not be pressed. He will typically take popular opinion as the starting-point for his examination of a problem, subject it to scrutiny, and, if necessary, modify or reject it. This is his way with the question of the nature of happiness, where (1095a20), 'the many (*hoi polloi*) do not give the same answer as the wise'. Right through his ethical writings, Aristotle conducts sporadic and often unacknowledged debates with the doctrines of other thinkers. In the case of *philia*, the form and direction of the Aristotelian analysis have been tacitly but unmistakably influenced by Plato's earlier treatment of friendship in the *Lysis* and the *Symposium* (Annas 1977; Price 1989: 9–12).

Although the exploration of *philia* that follows takes Aristotle as its guide, this is in conjunction with other, non-philosophical texts. Modern bibliography on Greek friendship is heavily weighted towards the theoretical side, away from the functioning of *philia* in Athenian society.[6] That is the warrant for this chapter, preparing the way for a detailed examination of the part played by *philoi* and *philia* in credit relations.

THE SCOPE OF *PHILIA*

'Most other important social relationships exclude friendship. Even highly compatible and close brothers are brothers rather than friends, and friendship tends to be incompatible with such relationships as those of mother and child, lovers, and employer and employee.' So writes Odd Ramsøy, introducing the article on 'Friendship' in the *International Encyclopaedia of the Social Sciences*.[7] And it is true that from the viewpoint of comparative sociology, to say nothing of our own experience, the all-inclusive quality of Greek friendship is anomalous. In the passages from Aristotle quoted above, we have already met *philoi* in the form of fathers, parents, brothers, comrades, benefactors, fellow-tribesmen and fellow-citizens; to which might be added, husbands and wives, fellow-voyagers (*sumplooi*), comrades-in-arms (*sustratiōtai*), guest-friends (*xenoi*) and cousins (all from the *Nicomachean Ethics*: 1158b11ff., 1159b25ff. and 1161b10ff.). Hundreds of passages could be assembled to support the breadth of *philia* as conceived by Aristotle; but perhaps the clearest illustration comes from the *Memorabilia* of Xenophon, plotting the extension of *philia* both inside and outside the family circle.

The *Memorabilia* as a whole is intended as a defence of Socrates' reputation, showing up the error of the Athenians in putting him to death. In a series of some twenty vignettes, Socrates is depicted as the model citizen, unstinting in his advantageous advice to those around him.[8] In the second book are ten dialogues, which are meant as a response to the accusation, reported by Xenophon (1.2.49–55), that Socrates taught vicious habits to those around him. After a lengthy introductory discussion, advising one of his followers about the need for greater self-control (II.1), a sequence of sketches show Socrates offering words of wisdom intended to improve and regulate personal relationships. Socrates is first portrayed as telling off his son for getting angry with his mother (II.2). He argues that as a mother is a son's best *philos* (§13), so she is the last person to whom ingratitude (*acharistia*) should be shown. If we try to please neighbours, says Socrates (§12), and make friends with casual acquaintances like fellow-wayfarers or fellow-voyagers, how much more consideration is to be shown towards one's mother? In the dialogues that follow, the range of relationships is extended within the family to include estranged brothers (II.3). Socrates suggests that if people take the trouble to make friends with fellow citizens and even slaves (§3), they certainly ought to be on friendly terms with their own brothers. The remaining dialogues in Book II deal with the proper regulation of *philia* between persons outside the family circle, and are looked at in greater detail in the following section.

Every modern writer on *philia* recognizes that 'friendship' (or *Freundschaft* or *amitié*) is inadequate as a translation; but views differ about a possible definition or characterization.[9] Possibly the clearest and most persuasive statement is by Goldhill (1986: 79–83), who stresses the *relational* force of *philia*, concluding that it represents (p. 82) 'a way of marking a person's position in society by his relationships. The appellation or categorization *philos* is used to mark not just affection but overridingly a series of complex obligations, duties and claims.' Homer and Tragedy naturally dominate the discussion, which receives fourth-century support from Aristotle, with a blunt statement that (*Eth. Nic.* 1171b32) '*philia* is *koinōnia*, and one is related to a *philos* as to oneself'. *Koinōnia* is almost as untranslatable as *philia* – 'community', 'communality', 'association', 'society' and 'partnership' are all possible renderings – but a passage earlier in the *Nicomachean Ethics* gives some clarification. In view of the importance of this passage in my analysis, I transcribe it almost in full (1159b25–1160a20) :[10]

As we have said at the beginning, *philia* and justice (*to dikaion*) would seem to have the same area of concern and to be found in the same people. For in every *koinōnia* there seems to be some justice, and some kind of *philia* also. At any rate, fellow-voyagers and comrades-in-arms are called *philoi*, and so are members of other *koinōniai*. And the extent of their *koinōnia* is the extent of their *philia*, since it is also the extent of the justice found there. The proverb 'Between *philoi* everything is common (*koina ta philōn*)' is correct, since *philia* involves *koinōnia*. But while brothers and companions have everything in common (*panta koina*), what people have in common in other types of *koinōnia* is limited, more in some *koinōniai* and less in others since some *philiai* are more and some are less ... All *koinōniai* would seem to be part of the political *koinōnia* (*tēs politikēs*). For people keep company for some advantage and to supply something contributing to their life. Moreover, the political *koinōnia* seems both to have been originally formed and to endure for advantage; for legislators also aim for advantage, and the common advantage is said to be just. The other types of the *koinōnia* aim at partial advantage. Voyagers (*plōtēres*), for example, seek the advantage proper to a journey, in making money or something like that, while comrades-in-arms seek the advantage proper to war, desiring either money or victory or a city; and the same is true of fellow-tribesmen and fellow-demesmen (*demōtai*). Some *koinōniai* – religious societies (*thiasōtōn*) and *eranistai* – seem to arise for pleasure, since these are respectively for religious worship and companionship (*sunousias*). All these *koinōniai* seem to be subordinate to the political *koinōnia*, since it aims not at some advantage close at hand, but at advantage for the whole of life.

The testimony of non-philosophical texts supports Aristotle's wide-ranging conception of *koinōnia*, incorporating associations of all kinds.[11] The appropriate conclusion seems to be that *philia* joins the members of any group or *koinōnia* – voluntary, involuntary or incidental – which aims at mutual advantage.

The implied idea of reciprocal obligation, binding *philoi* together, has often been identified as a characteristic of *philia* (e.g. Goldhill 1986: 80–3). Aristotle himself acknowledged the existence of *philia* for the sake of 'utility' (*to chrēsimon*), where people show *philia* towards another person (1156a10), 'not for himself, but in so far as they gain some good for themselves from him'. This is, however, only one of three types of *philia* identified by Aristotle in his *Ethics*. The others are *philia* for the sake of 'pleasure' (*hēdonē*), in which a person becomes a *philos* because he is good company (1156a11); and 'complete' *philia* (*teleia philia*), which is the *philia* of 'good people similar in virtue' (1156b5). This appears to be one of the areas in which Aristotelian analysis leaves behind popular morality, engaging instead in a more detached, philosophical debate. The tripartite division of *philia* is apparently Aristotle's own. As he says by way of introduction (1155b15): 'Some people think there is only one type (of *philia*) because *philia* allows more and less. But here their confidence rests on an inadequate sign; for things of different types also allow more or less.'[12]

In philosophical terms, the connexion between the three types of *philia* is not immediately obvious (Fortenbaugh 1975; Price 1989: 131–61). Aristotle seems to envisage a hierarchy, the top position being occupied by *philia* between the good and equally virtuous. This brand of *philia* is praised as being complete (or perfect), enduring and altruistic (1156b6–32); whereas *philia* solely for the sake of utility, or solely for pleasure, is inferior as being incomplete, aiming at personal advantage, and potentially short-lived (1156a21–b5). Of the two incomplete types, *philia* for pleasure is less inferior, as showing in greater degree the qualities of *philia* between the good and virtuous (1158a1–35). Aristotle's analysis is dominated by the superior type of *philia*, and this is mirrored in modern discussions of his theory of friendship (e.g. Price 1989: 103–30). But whatever its importance in the history of ethical theory, this is not the kind of *philia* that is decisive in understanding Athenian social relations. As Aristotle himself admits (*Eth. Nic.* 1156b24), the best *philia* is likely to be rare (*spania*), for people who are good and equally virtuous are few and far between. By contrast, easily the commonest kind of *philia* is that existing for the sake of utility and mutual advantage (*Eth. Eud.* 1236a34–6): the subject of the following section.

RECIPROCITY AND FRIENDSHIP

For clarification of the rôle of reciprocity in *philia* we turn again to the second book of Xenophon's *Memorabilia*. In the dialogues already discussed, the idea of reciprocal obligation between family-*philoi* is explicit enough; but our concern here is with four dialogues dealing with *philia* outside the family circle (II.4–6 and 10).

The sequence begins with a considered statement by Socrates on the subject of the 'acquisition' (*ktēsis*) and 'use' (*chreia*) of *philoi* (II.4.1). He is made to contrast conventional sentiments about the inestimable value of good friends with the casual way in which they are acquired and cared for. Even slaves, protests Socrates (§§2–4), are chosen with care and diligently looked after. The disquisition closes with a rhetorical flourish, full of commonplaces about the services rendered by a true friend (§§5–7). There follows a short dialogue (II.5) in which Socrates obliquely reproves one of his companions for neglecting a friend who was in material need (*penia*). As part of the process, another of his associates is made to agree with Socrates that, as slaves have a specific monetary value, so friends have a precise cash equivalent. 'I would want to have this man as my *philos* rather than have two minas; that man I would value at less than half a mina. Another I would prefer to ten minas; for yet another I would expend all my money and effort if I could make him my *philos*' (§3). The lesson is that we must strive to make ourselves as valuable as possible to our friends (§§4–5).

In the next dialogue (II.6), Socrates leads Critobulus through an extended discussion of the qualities that are to be sought in friends, and how they are to be identified. The list of qualities to be avoided is instructive. A man who lacks self-control will not be able to help his friends effectively (§1). A man who recklessly spends everything and can give nothing back in return (*mē dunatai apodidonai*) is to be kept at arm's length (§2). A man who is too fond of making money will be so busy looking after his own interests that knowing him will be unprofitable (*anōphelēs*). Similarly, there is no profit in knowing a man who willingly receives benefits, but has no thought of ever returning them (*anteuergetein*). The conclusion reached by Critobulus is that the ideal friend will possess the reverse of all these negative qualities (§5). Finally, Socrates chides one Diodorus with missing out on an opportunity to put an impoverished friend in his debt with some timely assistance (II.10). He points out that the friend in question is a sensitive person, who would be 'ashamed to take a favour from you without making a return' (§3). The parallel is drawn with a householder (*oikonomos*) who thriftily buys a commodity while it is cheap. Diodorus accordingly sets out to visit this person, 'and in return for a small sum, he acquired a *philos* who made a point of thinking how he could help or please him by word or deed'.

Well to the fore in all these anecdotes is the double obligation imposed by *philia*: the duty to help one's friends is balanced by the clear expectation of help in return. To list from the fourth-century literature the endless examples of friends helping out other friends would be a pointless exercise, but a few of the general references give an impression of the strength of the ideology.[13]

It is a commonplace that one of the reasons for wanting to acquire wealth is in order to win and retain friends. So Aristotle asks (*Eth. Nic.* 1155a7–9); 'How would one benefit from such prosperity if one had no opportunity for beneficence (*euergesias*), which is most often displayed, and most highly praised, in relation to friends?' And a character in Xenophon's *Oeconomicus* (XI.9) lists as follows the pleasures of possessing wealth: making rich offerings to the gods, supplying the wants of the *polis*, and helping friends in need. The theme of the obligation to help *philoi* is regularly manipulated by the Orators as part of a character-attack. Apollodorus accuses Stephanus of making friends with the banker Aristolochus, only to desert him and his family in their hour of greatest need, when they had lost all their property (XLV.63–4; above, pp. 23–6). Theophrastus similarly depicts his 'Avaricious Man' (*aischrokerdēs*) as forever cheating and taking advantage of his friends (XXX).[14]

All this is not so far removed from our own ideas about friendship; what, after all, are friends for? Much more alien to our way of thinking, often influenced by the Judaeo-Christian doctrine of giving without any hope of return, is the clear expectation of a counter-obligation.[15] Both sides of the coin are conveniently on display in complementary anecdotes about Diogenes the Cynic (Diog.Laert.

VI.29, 46): how he used to say that we ought to stretch out our hands to *philoi* with the fingers open, not closed; how, on one occasion when short of money, he told his *philoi* that he was not asking for it, but asking for it *back* (*apaitein...ouk aitein*). The near-inevitability of a return is also implicit in the fuss made by Xenophon about the behaviour of his hero Agesilaus, king of Sparta, in giving without any formal expectation of a counter-gift (*Agesilaus* IV.1–4).[16]

The management of obligations between *philoi* had its own etiquette. In a shameless piece of *praeteritio* from his law-court speech *On the Crown* (XVIII.268–9), Demosthenes warns the jurors that he will not defend his reputation by mentioning all the occasions on which he has been accessible (*koinos*), benevolent (*philanthrōpos*), and helpful to those in need (*tois deomenois eparkōn*). He continues:

I will never say a word, or tender any evidence about such matters as the prisoners I have ransomed, or the dowries I have helped to provide, or anything of that kind. It is a matter of principle with me. My view is that the recipient of a benefit ought to remember it for all time, but that the benefactor ought to forget it at once, if the one is to behave decently, and the other is not to be mean-minded. To remind a man of the private kindnesses you have done him is little short of a reproach. Nothing shall induce me to do anything of the sort.

But beneath the surface politeness was the calculating attitude that comes across in the scenes from the *Memorabilia* summarized above. In choosing friends, primary considerations were willingness and ability to repay services in full. One of the vignettes deserves closer study in this respect (above, p. 113). As part of his attempt to reconcile the two estranged brothers (II.3), Socrates urges one of them to take the initiative in re-establishing friendly relations. At first the brother denies that he knows how to do this, but Socrates soon draws him out (§§ 10–14). It turns out that in order to stimulate another person into inviting him to attend a sacrificial feast, he would first extend a similar invitation; in order to encourage a person to look after his affairs while away, he would get in first with an identical offer; and as a way of getting a *xenos* to entertain him while visiting his city, he would offer him hospitality in Athens. The implication is that, by taking the initiative, potentially useful people could be enmeshed in a *philia*-type relationship. Towards the end of the dialogue (§ 15), Socrates actually describes the offering of service and counter-service between *philoi* in competitive terms, appropriate to the games: 'For I think that he (your brother), as soon as he is aware of your challenge in this contest (*eis ton agōna touton*), will strive eagerly (*philoneikēsein*) in order to overtake you in helping out, in both word and deed.'

Concerning this question of getting a good return from one's *philoi*, even Aristotle tempers his high moral stance and lets reality break in. As an exception to his general rule of reciprocating favours, he cites the case of a good person (*spoudaios*) who has received and repaid a loan from a dishonest person (*mochthēros*). If the dishonest man now asks for a loan in return (*antidaneizein*), it should not be given (*Eth. Nic.* 1165a7–12). 'For he expected repayment when he lent to a decent person, whereas you have no hope of it from a bad person. If that is really so, then the demand is not fair; and even if it is not so, but you think it so, your refusal of the demand seems not at all absurd.' Popular attitudes towards friendship and reciprocity may perhaps be summed up by two philosophical fragments from the fifth century. According to Democritus (DK 93): 'When you do a favour, study the recipient first, in case he prove a scoundrel and repay evil for good'; and even more pithily from Epicharmus (DK 30): 'The hand washes the hand: give something and you may get something.'

From the prominence of reciprocity in *philia*, in conjunction with the apparent absence of sentiment, it may be predicted that relationships between *philoi* were easily formed and broken. That is, in fact, the burden of Aristotle's criticism of *philia* for the sake of utility: when a person stops being useful, the other party ceases to be his *philos* (1156a20). In addition, the calculating basis of the relationship gives plenty of scope for disagreement about the adequacy of the return offered (1162b15–20; cf. 1163a10–20):

Friendship for utility, however, is liable to accusations. For these people deal with each other in the expectation of gaining benefits (*ep' ōpheleiai*). Hence they always require more, thinking they have got less than is fitting; and they reproach the other because they get less than they require and deserve. And those who confer benefits cannot supply as much as the recipients require.

This is all the more likely where, as is appropriate between *philoi*, there has been no formal agreement about the return to be made (1162b31–4; quoted above, pp. 40–1). In some states (though not Athens), the laws actually forbade prosecutions arising out of transactions between *philoi* (*Eth. Eud.* 1243a9).

Aristotle's misgivings about the instability of everyday forms of *philia* appear to be no more than the truth. 'While the Greeks idealized friendship to an extent unparalleled in other cultures and produced deep and beautiful analyses of friendship, nevertheless in practice they seem to have suffered from a considerable lack of friendship.' So says Hutter (1978: 81), in a penetrating study of the political ramifications of *philia*. The many moralizing statements about the ease with which *philia* is transformed into *echthra* (hatred) can be matched with actual instances – real or alleged (Fisher 1976: 19; Blundell 1979: 38).[17] The litigant in a speech by Isaeus (i. 9) gives an exchange of words as the event which converted friendship between two relations by marriage into enmity. In a second speech (v.40), failure to repay a loan is said to have transmuted friends from youth into the bitterest enemies. An earlier chapter traced in detail the deteriorating relationship between Apollodorus and Nicostratus, when the latter allegedly refused to repay what he owed (pp. 53–9).[18]

The unabashed openness with which the Greeks accepted the utilitarian quality of much of their friendship makes sense against the broader background of their society. A clue is provided by Aristotle, who introduces the whole subject of *philia* in the *Nicomachean Ethics* with the rhetorical question (1155a9): 'How would one guard and protect prosperity without *philoi*, when it is all the more precarious the greater it is?' And so friendship appears as a form of insurance in a world of capricious fortune. The insurance idea is spelt out in a passage from Menander's *Dyscolus*, where a son advises his father to spread his money around (ll. 805–11):

> So, as long as you
> Control it, father, you yourself, I say,
> Should act generously, aid everyone,
> And by your acts enrich all whom you can.
> Such conduct never dies. If you by chance
> Should ever stumble, it will yield to you like
> Repayment. Better far than hidden wealth (*ploutos aphanēs*)
> Kept buried is a visible true friend (*emphanēs philos*).[19]

The cultural context of *philia* is further explored in an important paper by Adkins (1963), comparing friendship in Homer and Aristotle. Adkins seeks to show how a proper appreciation of *philia* in Homer can help elucidate an otherwise obscure passage in the *Nicomachean Ethics* (1155b17–56b32). This involves consideration of the scope of *philos* in the *Iliad* and *Odyssey*, where it is associated not only with people, but also with inanimate objects, including limbs, beds and native lands. Adkins argues that this broad usage is comprehensible only in the light of the overall structure of Homeric society and values. He accordingly concludes that *philos* was applied to those persons and things on which the Homeric chief (*agathos*) was dependent for his survival in a hostile world. In this way, Homeric 'friendship' appears as a system of calculated co-operation, not necessarily accompanied by any feelings of affection. Adkins applies this concept of *philia* to the presentation of *philia* in the *Nicomachean Ethics*, showing how the Aristotelian account parallels the Homeric view at almost every point. He ascribes this close correspondence to continuity in the underlying conditions of life facing both Homeric *agathos* and head of a fourth-century *oikos*.[20]

This is a bald summary of a complex and suggestive study, but the value here of Adkins' reconciliation of Homer and Aristotle lies in its compatibility with my own conclusions, based on material from the Attic Orators and Hesiod's *Works and Days* (above, pp. 31–6). In every case, there is the overriding importance of reciprocal action, serving as a form of insurance; in both Homeric and fourth-century society, these reciprocal obligations can be transferred from father to son. Also common to all four testimonies is a coolly calculating attitude to the dispensing of favours, with no need for what are conventionally thought of as 'friendly feelings'. Particularly striking is the agreement that the drive for self-sufficiency must be tempered by the formation of co-operative links. Both Hesiod and Aristotle (*Eth. Nic.* 1124b10) approve of the strengthening of reciprocal bonds by returning more than was originally received. Towards the end of his paper (p. 44), Adkins expresses views of reciprocity and self-sufficiency that are almost identical with Foster's formulation of the 'dyadic contract' (above, p. 32).

Agreement between these different texts strengthens the idea of continuity between archaic community and classical *polis* in terms of mutual support through reciprocal exchange (above, pp. 35–6). More specifically, it supports the identification of loans between *philoi* as a type of gift-giving. It has to be said that Aristotle does argue against the assimilation of those giving and receiving favours to lenders and borrowers in credit operations (*Eth. Nic.* 1167b16–24):

Now benefactors (*euergetai*) seem to show *philia* to their beneficiaries more than their beneficiaries do to them, and this is discussed as though it were an unreasonable thing to happen. Here is how it appears to most people (*tois pleistois*). It is because the beneficiaries are debtors and the benefactors creditors (*hoi men opheilousi tois de opheiletai*): the debtor in a loan wishes the creditor did not exist, while the creditor even attends to the safety of the debtor. So also, then, a benefactor wants the beneficiary to exist because he expects gratitude in return (*tas charitas*), while the beneficiary is not insensitive about making the return (*to antapodounai*).

Aristotle goes on to criticize this popular analogy on the grounds that the benefactor, unlike the creditor, actually shows *philia* to the person he has assisted (1167b25–68a5). As an alternative, he draws a comparison with a craftsman, arguing that 'each likes his own product more than it would like him if it acquired a soul'. But this is one occasion on which it seems appropriate to ignore Aristotle's 'aesthetic' interpretation of the donor–recipient relationship, in favour of the view shared by 'most people'. Elsewhere in his examination of relationships between *philoi*, Aristotle slides easily into the terminology of loan transactions (*Eth. Nic.* 1162b31–4, 1163b19–22 and 1165a7–12; *Eth. Eud.* 1243b14–33).

The correctness of the popular identification of loans between *philoi* with gifts is apparently confirmed by a concept common to both. It might be imagined that full repayment of an interest-free loan would cancel completely the original obligation, leaving the recipient clear of the need to make a further return. But even after formal repayment in full, the borrower remained under a debt of obligation to his former creditor. The expectation of a continuing obligation may be inferred from the exception made in the *Nicomachean Ethics* about making a return loan to a dishonest man (1165a7–12; quoted above, p. 119). It finds perfect expression in Theophrastus' portrait of the 'Querulous Man' (*mempsimoiros*, XVII.9):

When his friends (*philōn*) have collected an *eranos*-loan for him and one of them says, 'Now you can be cheerful', he replies, 'How can that be, when I've got to pay every person his money back and, on top of that, owe gratitude (*charin opheilein*), on the grounds that I've been done a favour (*hōs euergetēmenon*).'

Which, of course, he had. The crucial term here is *charis*, having in this context the sense of 'favour' or 'gratitude', and acting as the equivalent of the interest-payment in an interest-bearing loan. The 'Querulous Man' unreasonably resents having to show *charis* to the *philoi* who have lent him money without interest. *Charis* is also the term used in the passage from the *Nicomachean Ethics* quoted above to describe the reciprocal return that benefactors expect from their recipients; and it will be recalled how Apollodorus complained that *charis* was not forthcoming in his dealings with Nicostratus (above, p. 58). The final section of this chapter is given over to an exploration of this important concept.

THE RETURN OF *CHARIS*

Something of the significance of *charis* is conveyed by its appearance in the Funeral Speech of Thucydides, often taken as a paradigm of classical Athenian values (II.40.4):[21]

'When it comes to acting for others, we [Athenians] are different from most people, for we acquire *philoi* not in consequence of what others do for us, but by doing it for them. He who confers the benefit (*charin*) is in a stronger position... whereas he who owes it is slower to act, since he knows he returns the kindness not as a favour (*es charin*), but as a debt (*hōs opheilēma*).'

The physical prominence (and personification) of *charis* in the fourth-century *polis* is underlined in a passage by Aristotle from a part of the *Nicomachean Ethics* which emphasizes the rôle of reciprocity in knitting the community together (1133a2–4):[22]

That is why they give a prominent place to the temple of the Graces (*Charitōn*), so that there will be a return of benefits received (*antapodoseis*). For this is what is special to *charis*: when someone has shown *charis* to us, we must do a service for him in return, and also ourselves take the lead in showing *charis* again.

Both passages develop a meaning of *charis* which is already present in Homer: gratitude in return for a service (other meanings include 'attractiveness', 'gracefulness' and 'kindness'; see Franzmann 1972: 1–2). At the heart of the *Iliad* is Achilles' complaint against Agamemnon that he will not return to the battle because there is no appropriate *charis* for those who bear the brunt of the fighting (IX.315–7; cf. XVII.147). In the *Odyssey* (IV.694–5), Penelope is discontented because the good deeds of the absent Odysseus are not receiving their proper *charis* (for further examples, see Hewitt 1927: 143–7). *Charis* as 'gratitude' is common in archaic poetry (Franzmann 1972), as may be illustrated by two elegies of Theognis, warning against the futility of performing favours (*charis*) for the low-born (*deiloi*). Unlike *agathoi*, they will never return your services (ll. 105–12), so that lending to a *deilos* means loss of both loan and *charis* (ll. 955–6).[23]

With its strong moral overtones of obligation, the concept of *charis* looms large in the Orators. Probably the commonest of all

commonplaces in law-court speeches is what might be called the
'public-service theme': the speaker appeals to the jury to favour his
cause on the grounds that he has benefited the *polis* through his
liturgies and other expenditures or services on behalf of the *dēmos*.
Examples could be drawn from almost every speech, but the
following selection is limited to cases in which *charis* is explicitly
mentioned; other passages are cited and discussed by Davies (1981:
92–5) and Ober (1989: 226–30).

Especially informative is the manipulation of *charis* in Demosthenes' speech *On the Trierarchic Crown* (LI), where the unnamed
speaker puts forward his claim to the crown awarded to the first of
the trierarchs to have his ship ready for service. With heavy irony,
he points out the error of his opponents' ways, in imagining that the
jury would show *charis* not only to those who do their duty to the
polis, but to those who merely say that they do it (§2); they also
dishonestly ask the jury to make a return of *charis* for having done a
good job. Finally, the speaker accuses his opponents of asking the
jurors to show *charis* as if the argument were about a straight gift
(*dōreia*) and not a prize in a competition. They behave as if it were
the job of the jurors to win the favour (*charis*) of men who neglect
their interests, instead of it being their duty to show gratitude (*charis*)
to those who serve them well (§§7 and 17). By playing on the dual
meaning of *charis* as a service both offered and returned, the speaker
highlights the unethical behaviour of his opponents.[24]

In other speeches, the exploitation of *charis* is less intricate. The
speaker in a speech of Lysias (xx.31) is blatant in his efforts to win
the goodwill of the jury. Having detailed his own and his family's
services to the state, he bluntly explains: 'It was not for the sake of
money we might get that we did you good; our purpose was that if
ever we found ourselves in trouble, we might be saved by this plea,
and obtain due *charis* from you.' The defendant in another speech of
Lysias, *On a Charge of Taking Bribes* (xxi), closes with an emotional
appeal to the jury, based on the services he has rendered the *polis*,
which deserve an appropriate *charis* (§25). In a forensic speech by
Isocrates (xviii), the speaker makes a point of warning the jurors
that he is reversing the appeal that litigants usually make. Whereas
everybody else reminds the jury of the gifts (*dōrea*) they have made
to the *polis*, on this occasion he wants the jurors to bear in mind
what they have already given the defendants in return, as evidence
of their previous good conduct (§66–7). A similar line of argument

is advanced by the speaker in Lysias' fragmentary speech *Against Hippotherses* (fr. 1.6.iii in Gernet and Bizos 1954–9: III) – actually delivered on behalf of the author – where the jury are told that Lysias deserves to be acquitted on account of the *charis* that the people have already shown him in return for his acts of goodwill. After all this, it comes as something of a relief to find the plaintiff in another speech of Lysias (XIV.22) actually warning the jury that to allow appeals for *charis* to override the laws is to encourage wrongdoing.[25]

These appeals to the public service theme help to clarify the part played by *charis* in interest-free credit, of which the clearest examples come in the Demosthenic speech *Against Timotheus*. The loan transactions described in this speech are discussed in Chapter VIII; for the present, it is enough to know that the case arose out of Timotheus' substantial borrowings from the banker Pasion (above, pp. 70–1 and 84–5). After Pasion's death, Apollodorus took Timotheus to court on the grounds that he had failed to repay any of the debts owed to his father. Not surprisingly, Apollodorus harps on the theme of Timotheus' lack of *charis* in attempting to rob Pasion of his due return. He opens the speech by assuring the jury that, when they have heard the details of the case, they will agree that Pasion behaved impeccably towards Timotheus, who (§§ 1–2)

…is not only without *charis*, but is the most dishonest of mankind; for he got from my father all that he asked, and received from the bank money at a time when he was in great need and when he was in serious danger of losing his life. Yet he has not only made no return of *charis*, but also robs me (*aposterei*) of what was given.[26]

As in Theophrastus' description of the 'Querulous Man', *charis* here appears as a moral obligation owed over and above the formal repayment of the money borrowed. Apollodorus goes on to complain that although Timotheus took money from the bank 'with *charis*' (§4), he will, by contrast, now pay it back only if forced to do so 'by hostile legal proceedings' (*di' echthras kai dikēs*). Later in the speech (§27), Timotheus is made to compound the offence by being portrayed as solemnly assuring Pasion that even if he were not granted his request for a further loan, 'he would not be angry as another might who failed to obtain what he wanted; but he would show *charis*, if he should ever find himself able to do so, for the services which he had rendered at his request'. Finally (§54),

Apollodorus returns to the theme that, far from showing the *charis* due to his creditor, Timotheus wanted to rob him of the sum loaned. As in the opening section, *charis* is presented as a reciprocal obligation, additional to the cash payment.[27]

This selective study of *philia* began by considering the infinitely wide range of people who might be described as *philoi*; in brief, any individuals associated in a *koinōnia* for the sake of mutual advantage (pp. 113–16). In the following chapter are examined in greater detail those categories of *koinōniai* within which *philoi* were likely to lend and borrow. The headings chosen – relatives, neighbours (including fellow-demesmen) and fellow-citizens – only inadequately represent the range of possibilities, many of which overlap. The characters in Aristophanes' comedies variously appeal to: 'neighbours and demesmen' (*Eccl.* 1115), 'neighbours, relatives and demesmen' (*Clouds* 1322), and 'demesmen and friends' (*Knights* 320 and *Plutus* 254). There is, nevertheless, consolation in the quotation from the *Nicomachean Ethics* with which this chapter began. Although comparison of *philia* is more difficult in relationships of different kinds, that is no reason for giving up the attempt. We should try, concludes Aristotle, to carry the investigation as far as we can.

CHAPTER VI

Non-professional lending: loans without interest

THE TYRANT'S LAMENT

Among Xenophon's slighter works is the *Hiero*, his entirely imaginary account of a conversation between Hiero, tyrant of Syracuse in the earlier fifth century, and Simonides of Ceos, a poet at his court. The dialogue is contrived to show how, contrary to popular belief, tyrants lead a miserable existence. After some introductory comments, the conversation turns in the direction of *philia*. Says Hiero (III.7):

> The firmest *philiai*, I take it, are supposed to be those that unite parents to children, children to parents, brothers to brothers, wives to husbands, and comrades to comrades (*hetairois pros hetairous*). Now you will find, if you look around, that it is for these private persons (*tous idiōtas*) most *philia* is shown (*malista philoumenos*).

Hiero goes on to complain that tyrants, by contrast, run a considerable risk of being murdered by their nearest and dearest. Whether this really was the case is immaterial. What matters here is Hiero's presentation of his list of 'firmest *philiai*' as a hierarchy, with family connexions taking precedence even over *hetairoi* – the closest of companions.[1]

Three related features distinguish intra-family *philia* from *philia* extending outside the family circle. In the first place, *philia* existed automatically between members of a family and was not generated by performance of a specific action. Secondly, there was no careful calculation of relative advantage in the giving or receiving of goods and services; either this was thought to be inappropriate (or impossible), or there was the assumption that a balance would be struck over time. Finally, family *philia* was enduring. Conventional friendships between non-kin could be broken off by mutual agreement, a hostile act, or simple inertia, but bonds within the immediate family were largely (though not entirely) independent of exchange relations.[2] These characteristics identify *philia* within the family circle with the segment of Sahlins' reciprocity spectrum representing 'generalized reciprocity' (above, p. 110–11). It may be recalled that, as his extreme example, Sahlins cites a mother suckling her child – perhaps the most intimate of all family relationships involving an exchange.

Generalized reciprocity is defined by Sahlins as the 'solidarity extreme'. The concept of 'family solidarity' has long been familiar to Greek historians, reaching back, via the work of Gustave Glotz (1904), to Fustel de Coulanges' influential study of *La Cité antique* of 1864. In archaic and classical Athens, kinship connexions have conventionally been seen as extending beyond the nuclear family (*oikia*) to include other descent groups, notably the *genos*. Usually (and probably misleadingly) translated as 'clan', the *genos* consisted of a group of families who claimed descent from a common and often mythical ancestor. The ties that supposedly bound the group together included religious ceremonies, a common burial place, rights and duties relating to marriage, and obligations of mutual support (Connor 1971: 11–14). Combined with other descent groups and extended by links of marriage, the *genos* can be projected as the basis of an imposing web of relationships. A recent study by Littman (1979: 6) talks about 'the mesh of kinship that was the foundation of the social structure of the state'.[3]

This kinship-based model of Athenian society seems to receive indirect support from the dominant position of kinship in anthropological theory, backed up by a seemingly endless parade of empirical studies.[4] But the rôle of kinship within social anthropology is not so clear as is sometimes assumed. 'A thoroughly misleading term and a false criterion in the comparison of social facts' is how the editor ends his introduction to a collection of essays on *Rethinking Kinship and Marriage* (Needham 1971b: cviii).[5] Some of this uncertainty is echoed in the tentative reassessment of the part played by kinship in the ancient Greek world. Already the traditional picture of the *genos* has come under shattering attack, and other parts of the structure are undergoing revaluation.[6] My aim in this chapter is to identify the stage within Athenian kinship relations at which generalized shaded off into balanced reciprocity, indicating the alternatives to family support through lending and borrowing within the community.

THE LIMITS OF FAMILY SOLIDARITY

In 399 Andocides, an Athenian aristocrat, appeared in court to give an account of his part in the events known to us as the 'Mutilation of the Herms' and the 'Profanation of the Mysteries', which had taken place some fifteen years earlier (Andoc. 1). The detailed background to the case may be ignored here (see MacDowell 1962: 1–15), but amongst the accusations made by Andocides' opponents was the denunciation of his own father as one of the culprits. He responds angrily (§§19–20):

According to the prosecution, I myself gave information in the matter of the Mysteries and included my own father in the list: yes, turned informer against my own father! I cannot imagine a more outrageous, a more abominable suggestion. My father was denounced by Pherecles' slave Lydus: it was I who persuaded him to remain in Athens instead of escaping into exile – and it was only after numberless entreaties and by clinging to his knees that I did so. What, pray, was I about in informing against my father, as we are asked to believe that I did, when at the same time I was begging him to remain in Athens – begging him, that is, to let me be guilty of the consequences to himself?

Whatever the logic of the argument, Andocides' defence of his conduct towards his father was meant to strike a sympathetic chord with the jury. The same can be said of his justification later in the speech for having turned informer at all (§§56–8): it was in order to save from almost certain death his father, brother and 'any number of relatives and cousins'.[7]

The obligation to support the members of one's family through thick and thin was a deep-seated duty for an Athenian citizen (Dover 1974: 275–6). Although the motif regularly appears in literature (where the dilemma facing Antigone is only the outstanding example; see Goldhill 1986: 88–106), in the courts it was a commonplace. 'We must help our friends and relatives (*philois kai oikeiois*) as far as possible without perjuring ourselves', says one litigant (Lycurg. fr. E3 in Burtt 1954); 'Is it not right that men on trial should be supported by their relatives and friends?' rhetorically asks another (Hyperides, *Lycophron* 10). And in Lycurgus' speech *Against Leocrates* (§138), the defendant is attacked on the grounds that he is assisted by 'men who have no ties of blood or friendship with him (*mēte genei mēte philiai*), but who always champion defendants for a fee'.

As family support was the expected norm, litigants appearing against their own relatives (almost inevitable in inheritance disputes) felt they had some explaining to do. The speaker in the Demosthenic *Against Olympiodorus* (XLVIII) repeatedly assures the jury of his reluctance to proceed against his brother-in-law, and his attempts to settle the disagreement out of court (§§1, 2 and 8). A common technique was to turn the hostility of one's relatives to good rhetorical effect by stressing their unnatural behaviour. The plaintiff in a speech by Isaeus (1.6–7), after apologising for being forced to appear against his relatives, describes their behaviour as appropriate to people avenging themselves on enemies (*echthroi*). In Lysias' *Against Diogiton* (XXXII), there are several attempts to raise prejudice against an allegedly crooked guardian on the grounds that he was related to those he cheated (§§3, 5 and 12). And in another speech of Isaeus (IX), the speaker complains that his uncle is siding with someone outside the family (§25), 'for he considers that to make money is much more important than being my relation (*tēn emēn sungeneian*)'. The mirror-image of that argument appears in yet another of Isaeus' speeches, where the litigant makes the (to us) surprising claim that he and his associate made a gift of a house to their opponent (v.30), 'not because of his honesty, but as a proof that we have more regard for our relatives (*tōn oikeiōn*), even though they may be utter villains, than for money'.[8]

Even where there was no family connexion between the litigants, a popular device was to blacken an opponent's character by accusing him of ill-treating his relatives. We have already seen, at the beginning of the second chapter, how Apollodorus accused Stephanus of making his uncle homeless and his mother-in-law destitute (cf. Aeschines 1.101–4). Comparable is Demosthenes' attack on the behaviour of Midias (XXI.130), where harm done to relatives (*peri tous oikeious kakourgēmata*) is coupled with outrage (*hubris*) and sacrilege. Demosthenes was himself not immune to this kind of charge. In two speeches (II.93; III.51) Aeschines alludes to an occasion when Demosthenes is supposed to have summoned his own cousin to appear before the Areopagus on a charge of wounding him in the head – a wound which Aeschines claims was self-inflicted.

Law-court speeches are the last place to look for unblemished good conduct (see Chapter I, n. 3); but in the passages collected above (and there are many more) there is apparent tension between the ideology of kinship support and the reality of disputes between relatives. Helping to resolve the conflict are two important studies by

Humphreys of sources of support in the Athenian courts. The earlier study (1985) shows how kin were only one from a range of possible supporters, which included friends, neighbours, cult-associates, opponents' enemies, and even politicians. In her second study (1986), Humphreys examines in detail kinship patterns in the courts. After meticulously logging those relations identified as helping litigants, she concludes that the range of kin specifically identified was narrow (pp. 87–8): 'Frequency of attested interaction falls off rapidly outside the limits of trust based on co-residence at some stage in a nuclear family unit.' Outside that limit, the ideology of family solidarity became increasingly marginal, and liable to be swamped by other considerations. In extreme cases, this could result in disputes which ended in the courts.[9]

The empirical evidence for gradations in kinship solidarity bears out Aristotle's conception of proportional *philia* between relatives (*Eth. Nic.* 1161b16–62a15):

> *philia* in families (*sungenikē*) also seems to have many species, but they all seem to depend on ancestral *philia* (*ek tēs patrikēs*). For a parent is fond of his children because he regards them as something of himself; and the children are fond of a parent because they regard themselves as coming from him...Brothers have *philia* for one another because they have come from the same parents. For the same relationship to the parents makes the same thing for both of them; hence we speak of the same blood, the same stock and so on...Cousins and other relatives are akin (*sunōikeiōntai*) by being related to brothers, since that makes them descendants of the same parents. Some are more akin (*oikeioteroi*), others less, by the ancestors being near to or far from them...Among other relatives, too, the features of *philia* (*ta philika*) are proportional.

This sense of more and less remote kinship, with variable features of *philia*, is reflected in the ambiguous status of more distant relatives. The speaker in Demosthenes' speech *Against Eubulides* (LVII) defends his status as an Athenian citizen. He introduces as evidence the testimony of an assortment of witnesses (§§ 20–3), whom he identifies as relatives (*sungeneis*; see Humphreys 1986: 60–2). His opponent had apparently tried to discredit some of these witnesses by claiming that the defendant had bribed them to pose as relatives. By way of response, he implies that the witnesses received not bribes, but financial help (§§ 52–4); and, elsewhere (§ 25), he adduces as proof of family relationship that certain of the witnesses had shared their property with his father when he was badly off. Whoever is telling the truth, the connexion between the defendant and at least some of his witnesses had to be tenuous for it to be a matter of dispute. The same sort of ambiguity appears in an aside by one of the characters in Xenophon's *Symposium* (IV.51). Niceratus, a man of considerable wealth (*APF* 10808), complains that when *philoi* are in difficulties, 'they draw up genealogies of our relationship (*genealogousi tēn sungeneian*) and never leave my side'. For the opposing point of view there is the complaint of the poor man in a fragment of Menander's play *The Brothers* (Körte fr. 4 ~ Allinson 1921: 312, fr. 4): 'It is a difficult job for a poor person (*penēs*) to find a relation (*sungenēs*). For if he needs help, not a single one admits that he belongs to him. This is because he expects him to be asking for something.'

Any attempt to trace in detail through reciprocal exchange all the fine gradations in the hierarchy of family *philia* is bound to fail. Implicit in the idea of generalized reciprocity is the absence of any formal reckoning or recording of giving and taking. We have already seen how certain relatives were under an obligation to ransom, dower and bury one another (pp. 59–63); and it was here, if anywhere, that loans merged into gifts. The ambivalent status of transactions between close relatives is exploited (by one side or the other) in the dispute over the estate of Cleonymus, as preserved in the first speech of Isaeus. The speaker, who lays claim to the estate, explains how he and his brother were left as orphans (§9). When their guardian also died, and they found themselves in financial difficulties, beset by creditors, they were helped out by their uncle Cleonymus (§12). The speaker portrays this help as a gift; but his opponents, who are also claiming the inheritance, represent all or part of it as a loan, and have set down the two orphans as debtors to the dead man's estate (§2, with Wyse 1904: *ad loc.*). Making due allowance for the imprecision of the evidence, what follows is a broad attempt to distinguish between the varying degrees of reciprocal obligation owed by different sets of relatives.

LENDING AND BORROWING WITHIN THE FAMILY

The setting of Plato's *Laws* is an imaginary conversation between three elderly gentlemen, one of whom has been delegated to compose a law code for a new colony or community. As a preliminary, the assembled colonists are pictured as receiving an exhortatory address on the importance of piety. After listing in order of precedence the various gods to whom honour is due, the speaker arrives at 'living parents' – dead ones count as deities (717A–C):

> It is right that a person in debt (*opheilonta*) should repay his first and greatest debt (*opheilēmata*), the oldest of all obligations (*chreōn pantōn*). He must consider that all he has and holds belongs to those who bore him and brought him up, and he is meant to use it in their service to the limit of his powers. He must serve them first with his property, second with his body, and third with his mind, in order to repay the loan (*daneismata*) of attention and anxious care lent out long ago (*daneistheisas*) on the security of his youth (*epi neois*), now to be discharged (*apodidonta*) to his elders by reason of their age and severe need.

Plato here elaborates on a theme found elsewhere in the *Laws* (869A–C and 930E–32D): how the most binding of all family obligations is owed by children to parents. In these passages, Plato gives prominence to what was already part of popular morality (Dover 1974: 273–4). Eye-catching is the way in which the obligation is expressed as a loan transaction, complete with security and repayment. The idea of debt-repayment is developed by Aristotle in his treatment of *philia* towards parents (*Eth. Nic.* 1163b12–28). There are certain cases, he says, where it is impossible for *philoi* to make adequate returns for favours received; such is the position regarding gods, parents and teachers of philosophy (1164b2). The relationship between father and son is therefore asymmetrical (1163b19–22):

> That is why it seems that a son is not free to disavow his father, but a father is free to disavow his son. For a debtor (*opheilonta*) should return (*apodoteon*) what he owes, and since no matter what a son has done he has not made a worthy return for what his father has done for him, he is always the debtor (*aei ophelei*). But the creditor (*hois d'opheiletai*) is free to remit the debt, and hence the father is free to remit.

Aristotle goes on to say that a father would, in fact, withhold his favour only from a son who was unnaturally vicious; no case of disinheritance is known from Athens (Chase 1933: 147). A few pages further on (1164b27–65a2), Aristotle argues that as a general rule people should return favours (*euergesias antapodoteon*) before taking the initiative in doing good turns for their comrades (*charisteon hetairois*) 'just as we should pay back a loan (*daneion*) to a creditor rather than give to a comrade'. But, even here, the primacy of a son's duty to his father makes an exception possible. What, asks Aristotle, if someone has ransomed you from pirates? Should you not ransom him in return, no matter who he is? The unspoken answer is presumably 'yes'. But what if your benefactor (*euergetēs*) does not need ransoming and merely wants his money back, while your own father needs to be ransomed? Assuming you cannot do both, should you make due return to your *euergetēs*, or extend *charis* to your father? Aristotles' resolution of his rather hypothetical problem is uncompromising: 'It seems you should ransom your father, rather than yourself.'[10]

The identification of respect for parents with repayment of a loan is not limited to philosophers. Expressions of the debt that children owe their parents are commonplace in Comedy, Tragedy and Oratory.[11] The thinking behind the analogy is clear enough. All the trouble and expense bestowed on children in bringing them up is to be repaid by showing parents proper respect and caring for them in their old age (Raepsaet 1971: 87–92). Some aspects of the exchange are spelt out in Socrates' heart-to-heart talk with his son about behaviour towards his mother (Xen. *Mem.* II.2; above, pp. 113). Right through the dialogue, emphasis is on showing a proper degree of *charis* towards one's parents (see Gigon 1956: 86–7). The son is made to agree that failure to return adequate *charis* for benefits bestowed is unjust, and that ingratitude (*acharistia*) is injustice (*adikia*); also, that the greatest obligation imaginable is that owed by children to their parents (§§ 1–4). There follows a vivid presentation of the trials and tribulations endured by a mother in bringing up her child (§5). After further discussion, Socrates closes the conversation by pointing out that the only manifestation of *acharistia* formally recognized and punished by the laws of the *polis* is that shown by children towards parents (§ 13, supported by Arist. *Ath. Pol.* LV.3, with Rhodes 1981: *ad loc.*). He adds the awful warning that a person who is notorious for his lack of *charis* towards parents will soon be without friends (§ 14), 'for no one would expect you to be grateful for any kindness he might show you'.

Part of the interest in this dialogue lies in the prominence it gives to the mother as the giver and receiver of *charis*. In almost every other mention of the motif, the parties named are either parents and children or fathers and sons, to the exclusion of mothers and daughters. This is presumably a reflection of the superior position of the father as *kurios* or head of the household (Lacey 1968: 21–2). When Aristotle wants to account for the differing degrees of *philia* within the family, he does so in terms of closeness of relationship to the father (above, p. 131). And in the *Eudemian Ethics* (1244a10), he says that although there are things one must do for a father and things one must do for a mother, 'the father, nevertheless, is best' (*kaitoi beltiōn ho patēr*). Whereas we might instinctively place the bond between husband and wife at the head of reciprocal relationships within the family (and Aristotle does have some common-sense remarks on *philia* within marriage: *Eth. Nic.* 1162a16–27), Xenophon's Hiero ranks the relationship between husband and wife below that of brothers. Dover (1974: 273) is surely right about the difficulty of fitting wives into the hierarchy of a citizen's personal obligations.[12]

Relationships between parents and children, and possibly between husbands and wives, represent the extreme of solidarity and generalized reciprocity. Within this context, the identification of individual transfers, whether as gifts or loans, would be inappropriate. The next step down the hierarchy to *philia* between brothers allows for greater flexibility in terms of the range of reciprocity. Aristotle gives sound reasons for the close relationship between brothers (*Eth. Nic.* 1161b34–62a1 and 1162a10–15):

Being brought up together and being of an age contributes largely to *philia*; for 'two of an age' get on well, and those with the same character are comrades (*hetairoi*). That is why the *philia* of brothers and comrades is similar.

Philia between brothers has the features of *philia* between comrades, especially when comrades are decent, or in general similar. For brothers are that much more akin to one another (*oikeioteroi*), and are fond of each other from birth; they are that much more similar in character when they are from the same parents, nurtured together and educated similarly; and the proof of their reliability over time is fullest and firmest.

It is fitting that Aristotle should equate *philia* between brothers with that of comrades or *hetairoi*. Although the *philia* of *hetairoi* was the closest commonly encountered outside the family circle, being between non-relatives it could be (and was) broken off. On this analogy, Aristotle's formulation of brotherly *philia* represents a shift along the reciprocity spectrum in the direction of balanced reciprocity.

Other evidence seems to support this reading of Aristotle. 'When brothers agree', Antisthenes is supposed to have said (Diog. Laert. vi.6), 'no walls are so strong as the life they have in common.' The literature is dotted with similarly gnomic expressions of the duties brothers owe to one another (Bolkestein 1939: 80–2). On the practical side, there are plenty of cases of brothers helping each other out. The speaker in Lysias' *On the Property of Aristophanes* (XIX.22) tells how his brother-in-law, urgently in need of funds for a military expedition, 'borrowed' forty minas that his brother had left with him for safe keeping (see Chapter III, n. 29). And the statistics gathered by Humphreys (1986: 73–4) suggest that brothers were the most frequent source of family support in the courts. All this confirms the positive side of Aristotle's analysis of brotherly love. But mutual affection and support were not the universal rule. Xenophon moulded one of his Socratic dialogues around the theme of two estranged brothers (above, p. 113), and the enmity of brothers is a familiar theme in Greek literature (Gigon 1956: 103–5). In the courts, too, brothers could occasionally appear on opposing sides (Dem. XXXVI.22); and there were presumably many more disputes which never got as far as the law-courts (Isaeus II.28–33; Lysias X.5; details in Humphreys 1986: 74–5).

The death of the head of a household was usually, though not inevitably (see Bolkestein 1939: 81, n. 5), the occasion for the division of the property of the *oikos* between the surviving sons (Lacey 1968: 125–30). In a pattern that can be traced back as far as Hesiod's *Works and Days* (ll. 27–41), virtually all the instances in the Orators of bad blood between brothers originated in disputes over the division of the family property. The bitterness of these conflicts should not be underestimated: a quarrel reported in a speech by Isaeus (IX.17) is alleged to have ended in the death of one of the brothers. This fragmenting of estates to create separate *oikoi* seems to be crucial in the shift from fully generalized to a more balanced form of reciprocity between brothers. Hesiod's advice from early archaic Boeotia is blunt: trust and mistrust can be equally damaging, so smile at your brother, but make sure you have a witness.

Traces of this more formal exchange relationship between brothers heading independent households are correspondingly clearer between more distant relatives. Two sets of transactions, both involving in-laws, provide most of the evidence.

Demosthenes' speech *Against Spudias* (XLI) concerns a dispute over the division of the estate of Polyeuctus, deceased. Taken as a whole the case gives an insight into the possible ramifications of credit relations between branches of the same family. Polyeuctus had two daughters, the elder of whom he married to the unnamed speaker, the younger to the Spudias of the title. Along with his elder daughter, Polyeuctus promised a dowry of forty minas, of which only thirty were paid in ready cash; the remaining ten minas were to be handed over on Polyeuctus' death. In order to guarantee payment, a few days before his death, Polyeuctus made over his house to the speaker, by way of security (§5).[13] As Polyeuctus had no surviving son, the estate was to be shared equally between his two daughters, and the court-case arose out of the division of the spoils.

The speaker claimed that, before the division was made, he had the right to deduct the ten minas still owed as part of the dowry. He also accused Spudias of owing to the estate certain items and sums of money that had to be refunded before the share-out took place. The speaker claims that Polyeuctus, when on his death-bed, told a third party that Spudias owed him two minas with interest. This was the cost of a slave that Spudias had bought from him, without paying over the purchase price (§8). A further eighteen minas were owed by Spudias to his mother-in-law, the wife of Polyeuctus (§8), who had also lent him a bowl (*phialē*) and some jewellery (*chrusia*). These items Spudias and his wife had pledged as security to one Demophilus (otherwise unknown) in order to raise cash. The pledges, it is said, were never redeemed (§11). There are also vague and unsubstantiated allusions to 'hangings' (*skēnē*) and 'other similar items' that Spudias was supposed to owe the estate (§11).[14]

With the exception of the loan from Demophilus to Spudias and his wife, all these credit operations were between in-laws, and were accompanied by precautions to protect the interests of the creditors. For the transactions involving the sale of the slave and the eighteen-mina loan, written records were kept by the creditor. The speaker refers to *grammata* (§§9 and 21–2), which were not bilateral contracts, but private accounts kept by the lender (Finley 1952: 214, n. 59). Strepsiades in Aristophanes' *Clouds* (ll. 19–20) similarly kept a *grammateion* in which were recorded details of his borrowings. In addition, the loan of eighteen minas was witnessed by the brothers of Polyeuctus' wife who, says the speaker (§9), 'were present at all times and questioned her on every point, that there might be no awkwardness (*duscheres*) between us'. Both sets of precautions were semi-formal, as presumably befitted exchanges between individuals who were linked by marriage, but also members of independent *oikoi*.

What is to be made of the charging of interest by Polyeuctus in the credit operation that arose out of the purchase of the slave by Spudias? As we have seen, the taking of interest in loan transactions is intimately associated with the notion of *negative* reciprocity – which hardly seems appropriate, even between parties connected only by marriage. The explanation probably lies in the status of the transaction: not a loan, but a credit sale (purchase with deferred payment; see Millett 1990: 175–8). Spudias' motive behind the exchange (the acquisition of a slave) seems to set the process apart from the majority of loan operations, which resulted from some misfortune on the part of the borrower (see Chapter III). Although the ownership of slaves was hardly a luxury in classical Athens, it is hard to see how Spudias' purchase could be bound up with hardship or adversity. This absence of compulsion could account for Polyeuctus' readiness to charge his son-in-law interest on delayed payment of the purchase price.

The plausibility of this reading of the evidence is strengthened by a second transaction combining virtually all the elements of the Spudias affair: relations by marriage, slaves, credit-sale, interest-charge and written record. It appears in the speech *Against Leocrates*, where Lycurgus describes how his opponent abandoned Athens after the defeat at Chaeronea in 338 and, fearing the worst, fled via Rhodes to Megara. The case arose out of the accusation that Leocrates had betrayed the city and was guilty of treason. As evidence that his absence from Athens was meant to be permanent, Lycurgus tells how Leocrates made arrangements to realize his assets and transfer the proceeds out of Athens (§22). Having sent for his brother-in-law Amyntas, he prevailed upon him to buy his house and slaves in Athens for a talent. He further arranged that this sum should be used to satisfy his creditors and contributors in *eranos*-loans, and the balance remitted to him in Megara.[15] Lycurgus continues (§23):

After concluding all this business, Amyntas himself resold the slaves for thirty-five minas to Timochares of Acharnae, who was married to Leocrates' younger sister. Timochares had no money to hand over and so drew up an agreement (*sunthēkas*) which he deposited with Lysicles and paid Amyntas interest of one mina.

The family relationship between Amyntas and Timochares was even slighter than that of Polyeuctus and Spudias: they shared a common relative by marriage in Leocrates, whose sisters were their wives. The remoteness of the connexion may be reflected in the formality of the transaction. Apart from the interest-charge, there was a proper written contract, deposited with a third party. In view of Lycurgus' later identification of Leocrates' trade as that of bronze-smith (§58), it has been realistically suggested that the slaves were his work-force. That being so, Timochares' acquisition of a substantial income-earning asset could only add to Amyntas' readiness to take interest on the deferred payment.[16]

With this exchange operation between Amyntas and his brother-in-law's brother-in-law, we enter a sphere of relationships so attenuated as to barely count in terms of generalized reciprocity. One wonders whether the family connexion had any part to play beyond initiating the transaction. Not so with Theophrastus' 'Mistrustful Man' (*apistos*) when he goes to lend a silver cup (xviii.7). He shows up his obsessively suspicious nature by adopting all the paraphernalia of an impersonal transaction (weighing and testing the metal, appointing a guarantor), even though the borrower is the closest of relatives (*oikeios kai anagkaios*).

NEIGHBOURS AS LENDERS AND BORROWERS

There really is nothing more tiresome (*chalepōteron*), men of Athens, than to have a neighbour (*geitonos*) who is both villainous and greedy; the very thing that has happened to me.

With these words an unnamed speaker opens his defence, as preserved in Demosthenes' speech *Against Callicles* (LV), and sets the tone for what follows. The whole speech bears eloquent witness to the bitterness that can be generated when relationships between neighbours become soured. The case ostensibly arose out of a dispute over a wall which Tisias, the defendant's father, built around his property in the country. The plaintiff, Callicles, claims damages on the grounds that this wall caused flood water to run onto his neighbouring land, damaging his property. But if the son of Tisias can be believed, the conflict cut deeper. He claims that Callicles had designs on his land (§1). In order to force him towards either sale or exchange (§32), Callicles had resorted to blackmail (*sukophantia*) and, in conjunction with his relatives (§§1-2 and 31-4), had brought a series of suits against the defendant, culminating in the case in question.[17]

As part of his defence, the speaker juxtaposes the dastardly behaviour of Callicles with the kind of relations that should (and, he says, did) prevail between neighbours (§23):

Before my opponents set their hand to blackmailing me, my mother and theirs were on intimate terms (*chrōmenēs*) and used to visit one another, as was natural, since both lived in the country and were neighbours (*geitniōsōn*); and since, moreover, their husbands were on intimate terms with one another (*chrōmenōn allēlois*) while they lived.

The sentiment and even the phraseology (*chrōmenos* from *chraomai*) of neighbourly intimacy in the countryside are familiar from the episode of Apollodorus and Nicostratus (above, p. 54; cf. Menander, *Samia* 36–8). The implication is that, in sharp contrast to the conduct of Callicles, neighbours would normally offer each other mutual support. According to Aristotle (*Eth. Nic.* 1166a1), they count as *philoi*.

In the analysis of exchange relations involving *philoi*, neighbours occupy an intermediate position – both physical and metaphorical – between the household and the wider community of the *polis*. In the previous section, I tried to show how relationships between the closest members of a family were characterized by general reciprocity, shading off into a more balanced and formal exchange as family connexions became more remote. In exchange operations between neighbours, the emphasis is firmly on balanced reciprocity, representing a further shift along the spectrum of reciprocity. This intermediate position corresponds to the physical location of neighbours around the *oikos*, installed between the inner circle of the family and the outer ring of the citizen body. Proximity of place is, of course, what makes a neighbour; though varied, the Greek terminology is consistent and explicit.[18] For practical purposes, the 'neighbourhood' of an Athenian citizen may be equated with his 'deme'. Briefly, the deme may be thought of as a local centre of population or nucleated settlement; in the countryside, the great majority were villages or townships (see Osborne 1985a: 192–5). By the so-called 'Reform Bill' of Clisthenes (Andrewes 1977), dating from the end of the sixth century, these natural groupings gained formal recognition and were adapted to form the basis of a comprehensive system of local administration for Attica. Demes (at least five of them) were also created in the built-up area of the City, and were apparently based on pre-existing localities (Whitehead 1986: 26–7). The conventional English equivalent of 'deme' is 'parish', which gives only a weak impression of the part played by the demes within the wider structures of the *polis*.[19]

The best modern estimate puts the number of demes in classical

Attica at close to 140 (Whitehead 1986: 16–22). Assuming for the fourth century a male citizen population of approximately 35,000, a crude calculation suggests that each deme would contain on average some 200 citizens. In reality, some demes were large in terms of population, while others were correspondingly tiny (Whitehead 1986: 22–4); but the inescapable conclusion is that the majority of demes numbered their citizen population at somewhere between one and two hundred.[20] The relatively small scale of these units suggests that the deme-neighbourhood may have constituted a 'face-to-face society': a community in which all or most individuals share a high degree of familiarity (Finley 1985c). The extension of this idea of social intimacy to embrace the whole Athenian *polis* has been rightly ridiculed by Osborne (above, p. 40), who goes on to argue that what is absurd for an entire state may be realistic for smaller units like the demes (1985: 89). Confirmation comes from Whitehead (1986: 69 and 226–7), who provides detailed documentation that demesmen would be expected to know each other personally, and not merely as names. In fact, both books bear repeated witness to the reality and strength of deme solidarity (esp. Osborne 1985a: 21–2; Whitehead 1986: 223–52). Aristotle includes fellow-demesmen in his selection of natural *koinōniai* (above, pp. 114–15), and demesmen are often associated with *philoi* in non-philosophical texts (Whitehead *ibid.* pp. 231–2).

In modern eyes there is nothing strange about the idea that neighbours might have friendly feelings towards one another. But the sense of obligation between neighbours in contemporary British society tends to be negative: not doing anything that might annoy or inconvenience people living nearby. Active co-operation tends to be limited in scope to real emergencies, or restricted to a few close neighbours who have achieved the status of 'friend' (Allan 1979: 87).[21] Athenian expectations were different. The speaker in Lysias' *On the Olive Stump* (VII.18) talks about, 'the neighbours, who not only know from each other what is open for all to see, but even get information of what we try to keep hidden from anyone's knowledge'. But the other side of this enforced intimacy was the positive obligation placed on neighbours to help each other out at all levels.

It has been thought that this strong sense of solidarity in local communities derived ultimately from a sense of common ancestry. The inhabitants of a locality had ties of kinship – real or imagined –

by virtue of being members of the same *genos*. This approach found its fullest expression in Glotz's classic study of family solidarity in ancient Greece (1904). In support of the existence of 'la famille fictive' amongst neighbours, he cites Aristotle's theory (*Pol.* 1252b16-19) about the origins of each village community in a 'colony' (*apoikia*) from a household (*oikos*), 'formed of those whom some persons speak of as *homogalaktes* (lit. 'people suckled with the same milk')'. The process (and the term) remain obscure, and Glotz concedes that, by the time of the Homeric poems, neighbours were no longer identical with kin. He points, nevertheless, to the survival in some states of family-style solidarity in matters relating to the acquisition and alienation of property, where (p. 194), 'la famille fictive suit les principes de la famille naturelle' (see below, n. 24).

The assimilation of neighbourly to family relationships is appealing in its simplicity; but doubts have already been expressed about the indiscriminate application of kinship-based theories of mutual support. The retreat from kinship as the overwhelming *rationale* of ancient personal relationships finds support from a brief study by Wrightson (1982: 39–45) of connexions in the local communities of pre-industrial England. Basing his discussion on the kinds of statistical data not available from the Greek world, Wrightson questions the prevailing view that local social organizations in sixteenth- and seventeenth-century England were aggregates of kinship groups. On the contrary, he argues, the norm was the nuclear family, not attached to any extensive kinship network (p. 45): 'Our current working hypothesis must be that kinship ties beyond those of the nuclear family were of limited significance in the social structure of village communities.' And concerning duties towards relations (pp. 46–7): 'It may be observed that few binding formal obligations were recognized to kin other than members of the individual's own nuclear family and to grandparents and grandchildren.' Although kinsmen were preferred for assistance in family matters (p. 49): 'When seeking aid and support of other kinds they turned above all to their neighbours, even when kin were available.' His section on 'Kinship' ends (p. 51): 'More vital social bonds were those which they individually established and maintained not with an extended kinship group but with another social grouping: the neighbourhood.'

Wrightson's words are quoted at some length here, as the analogies with the ancient Greek material are arresting.[22] From the early archaic period, Hesiod draws a sharp distinction between neighbours and relatives as a source of help in time of trouble, with a clear preference for the former (above, p. 31). Relationships between neighbours are based on a system of balanced reciprocity: 'Give to one who gives, but do not give to one who does not give.' The notion that no concessions are to be made for neighbours who fail to reciprocate is echoed in the evidence from classical Athens. Unworthy of acceptance as a *philos* is the man who 'is always begging something from his neighbours (*tōn plesiōn*) and, if he gets it, cannot give it back; and, if he does not get it, holds a grudge against the person who refused it' (Xen. *Mem.* II.6.2). Neighbours who were less specific in their anti-social behaviour could also find themselves at a disadvantage. In a speech of Isaeus (III.13), the litigant is able to produce neighbours who give evidence of 'quarrels, serenades, and frequent scenes of disorder which the defendant's sister occasioned whenever she was at his house'. Plato, in his *Laws* (843B-c), has stern words about the need to avoid 'those numerous petty injuries done by neighbour to neighbour' which can so embitter relationships.

The disclosure that balanced reciprocity was the norm between neighbours weakens the theory about neighbourly co-operation as an extension of family solidarity. The motive for mutual assistance between neighbours would be the desire for protection and support in a potentially hostile world, as described in the previous chapter (pp. 120–1). Some neighbours need help more than others, and this may partly explain the variations in Athenian marriage patterns detected by Osborne (1985a: 128–38). Whether families choose to forge kinship links through marriage inside or outside the deme depends on particular circumstances (*ibid.* 135–6). Osborne's evidence suggests that the major (and most powerful) families of Athens sought wives and husbands from outside their own deme. Not needing to bother over-much about local connexions, they could build up contacts on a wider front, bringing advantages of increased choice and enhanced prestige. On the other hand, the inhabitants of the deme of Sounion seem to tend in the opposite direction. Osborne's sampling of inscriptions suggests that intra-deme marriage (or, at least, the recording of these marriages) was five times as frequent as in other demes (*ibid.* 140). Osborne tentatively (but plausibly) identifies the practice as reflecting the peculiar character of Sounion as a deme. Silver-mining attracted outsiders to such an extent that demesmen resorted to marrying within the locality (and publicizing those marriages) in order to reassert their identity.

As part of a valuable study of choosing and using kinsmen and neighbours (*ibid.* 127–35), Osborne argues that kin were used in matters involving the integrity of the *oikos* (birth, death, adoption, marriage and burial), but neighbours were preferred for support in the economic sphere. Wrightson saw a similar pattern with respect to the villages of seventeenth-century England. In particular, Osborne makes out a persuasive case for the reciprocal sharing of agricultural labour by neighbours too poor to afford a slave or hired help (*ibid.* 142–6). Direct evidence is meagre (a few hints in New Comedy: Menander, *Dyscolus* 326–35); but, apart from the indirect testimony of Hesiod's *Works and Days*, there is the close co-operation between Apollodorus and Nicostratus, friends and neighbours in the countryside.

Osborne is cautious in his citation of Apollodorus' dealings with Nicostratus as coming from the upper end of the social scale. But everything we know about neighbours in Athens implies that the ideology of co-operation extended right across society. The comedians provide vivid, if fictional appeals for help from neighbours in emergencies. Strepsiades in Aristophanes' *Clouds* (l. 1322), when being beaten up by his own son, calls to his neighbours for assistance, as does Mnesilochus in *Thesmophoriazusae* (l. 241) while having his pubic hair singed off (part of his disguise as a woman). The slave in *Peace* (l. 79) calls out in alarm to the neighbours when his master takes off on a dung-beetle; and when a bucket is lost down the well in Menander's *Dyscolus* (l. 594), the slave's immediate reaction is to get help from next door. In each case, the word used is some part of *geitōn*. In crises involving conflicts in the courts, neighbours and demesmen regularly appear offering support. The speaker in Lysias' *Against Epicrates* (XXVII.12) complains that the demesmen of his opponents will appear in tears to beg them off (for other examples, see Whitehead 1986: 227–30; Humphreys 1985: 340–1 and 343–5).[23]

More tangible support between neighbours extends across the whole range to include substantial cash loans. At its lowest level, neighbourly co-operation would amount to no more than 'borrowing' a light. In Lysias' *On the Murder of Eratosthenes* (1.14), the adulterous wife allegedly used the excuse of re-lighting a lamp at a neighbour's house to explain away the noise of the opening door as she let out her lover. Xenophon's Socrates (*Mem.* II.2.12) rhetorically asks his son whether or not he ought to be pleasant to his neighbour, 'so that he may give you a light for your fire when you need it, and both contribute to your success, and give you prompt and kindly help if you meet with any misfortune'. To be refused fire by a neighbour was the social equivalent of ostracism. The opponent of Dinarchus in his speech *Against Aristogiton* (II.9) is pilloried as an outcast twice over. When in prison as a public debtor, he is supposed to have made himself so disagreeable that the other inmates took a vote that no one should give him a light.

The majority of material exchanges between neighbours would have involved household goods or equipment. Details of these loans from the classical period have already been given in connexion with reciprocal exchange in the *Works and Days* (see pp. 37–9, above, with n. 23). Two examples from Theophrastus' *Characters* will serve as illustrations. We have already met the 'Penurious Man' who forbids his wife to lend out household items on the grounds that they add up over the course of a year. From the other side of the fence, the 'Shameless Man' (*anaischuntos*) 'will go to another house to borrow barley or perhaps bran, and then get the person who has lent it to carry it over to his house' (IX.7). Although small-scale loans of cash are more difficult to pin down in the sources, comparative material argues for their existence. Virtually every study of personal relations in pre-industrial communities comments on the complex networks of cash-credit between neighbours (Wrightson 1982: 52–3, with Holderness 1976, Spufford 1974 and 1976, and Dewindt 1972). Some of the loans contracted by Theophrastus' *Characters* may qualify (e.g. IX.2, XIV.8, XXI.5 and XXX.13); and Strepsiades in the *Clouds* is portrayed as having borrowed cash from a fellow-demesman who complains about the awkward position in which he finds himself, having to press for repayment (ll. 1214–21). According to his opponent-at-law, Aeschines the Socratic is such an inveterate borrower from his neighbours that he forces them to shut up their houses, and rent others far away (above, pp. 1–2).

The relative absence of small-scale money-loans from Athens may be attributed partly to the existence of *eranos*-credit (see the final section, below), and partly to the bias of the surviving sources, away from the lower end of society. From the opposite end of the scale, evidence for sizeable loans between neighbours and near-neighbours is more plentiful. We have already considered in detail the substantial sums lent or given by Apollodorus to his friend and neighbour (pp. 53–9). There are also in the *corpus* of the Orators examples of lenders and borrowers sharing the same demotic, some of whom were presumably neighbours. A litigant from the deme of Thoricus tells of a one-thousand drachma loan from a fellow-demesman in order to bury his father ([Dem.] XL.52). And, in an inscription already noted (p. 62), one Isarchus of Xypete claims a thirty-drachma share in the estate confiscated from Theosebes, also of Xypete. The encumbrance is explained as a debt due to him for having buried the parents of Theosebes. On other occasions, neighbours might act as middlemen, bringing together potential lenders and borrowers. Androcles of Sphettus, the plaintiff in the Demosthenic speech *Against Lacritus* (XXXV.10), apparently had spare cash to lend in a maritime loan. He was introduced to two non-Athenian (and allegedly fraudulent) borrowers by Thrasymedes, also of Sphettus, whom he describes as follows (§6): 'Thrasymedes the son of Diophantus, that well-known Sphettian, and Melanopus, his brother, are close associates (*epitēdeioi*) of mine, and we are on the most intimate terms possible (*chraomai*) with one another.' Like *chraomai* (above, p. 140), *epitēdeios* has the underlying sense of 'useful' or 'helpful'. Thrasymedes seems to have come from a family of some importance (*PA* 4438, with Dem. XIX.297), and Androcles takes care to assure the jury that he was not in any way to blame for the subsequent behaviour of the borrowers (§§ 7–8).

A full prosopographical study would presumably bring to light other groups of borrowers, lenders and middlemen sharing the same deme. By way of a substitute, there are those *horos* inscriptions which have findspots within the deme of the creditor inscribed on them. In his important survey of patterns of land tenure in Attica, Andreyev (1974) found that approximately half the *horoi* mentioning land were found in or near the creditor's deme. In at least some of these cases, the lender, the property acting as security, and therefore the borrower shared the same deme. Caution is called for, because the findspot of a *horos*-stone may not be its original location; the property offered as security need not be anywhere near the residence of the borrower; and the demotic is no guarantee that the lender actually lived in that deme. Notwithstanding these obstacles, Osborne (1985a) has been able to identify and explain various patterns in the representation of local creditors on the *horoi*: strong where the transaction involved house(s), or land and house(s), and weak where only land was offered (pp. 59–60, with Table 5; see my

Appendix 1). There also appear to be several demes in which the number of local creditors is unusually high (*ibid.* n. 43 and 248, n. 53).

The value of the *horoi* as evidence for neighbourly co-operation is doubly uncertain inasmuch as the need for real security may be taken as a sign of mistrust rather than solidarity. It is also probable that some (possibly a majority) of the transactions behind our *horoi* carried an interest charge, indicating exploitation rather than support. On the other hand, a simple request for security need not rule out the co-operative motive. It is a feature of *horos* inscriptions that they bear witness to exchanges involving substantial sums of money (Millett 1982: xi), and: 'Where large sums were concerned that could not easily be forgone in the case of default, formal financial transactions came in to replace casual neighbourliness.' So says Wrightson (1982: 53), drawing on the extensive documentation available to him. By contrast, Theophrastus portrays his 'Avaricious Man' (xxx.20) as deliberately borrowing from his acquaintances the kinds of odds and ends that no one would dream of asking to have back, and would hardly accept, even if they were offered.

Throughout this discussion of co-operation between neighbours, no distinction has been drawn between city and countryside. And yet the comparative studies on which I have drawn are concerned with small-scale village communities, the closeness of which is conventionally contrasted with the anonymity of the city. But in the case of Athens the contrast may be misplaced: the extension of the co-operative outlook from village to the wider community has already been mentioned (above, p. 35). Although Athens was easily the largest city in the classical Greek world, it was not necessarily an undifferentiated conglomeration of buildings and people. The probability was mentioned above (p. 140) that the Clisthenic demes in the city followed existing divisions into localities, which preserved their character and sense of identity. It is even likely that the various quarters of the city continued to be called *kōmai* or 'villages' (Whitehead 1986: 27, n. 98). Support again comes from Wrightson (1982: 56; cf. Johnson 1985: 225), who introduces into his own analysis the concept of the 'urban village', based on the community of the parish within English towns and cities. These local communities might be supplemented by still smaller 'street communities', based perhaps on the 'occupational solidarity' of clusters of craftsmen in particular districts; the Kerameikos or

'Potters' Quarter' is the obvious Athenian parallel. There were, in
addition, other groupings peculiar to the city that cut across local
associations, extending the scope for co-operation. Wrightson singles
out urban guilds, and although these have no precise equivalent in
Athens, there were analogous organizations of which the members
would offer mutual support. Some of these are explored in the
following sections.[24]

KOINŌNIA AND CITIZENSHIP

Some time before his death in 286, the polymath Theophrastus drew
up a will. Of the three copies, one survived to be read and preserved
for posterity by Diogenes Laertius (v.51–7).[25] Theophrastus had
succeeded Aristotle as head of the group of philosophers we now call
'Peripatetic', and most of his instructions are concerned with the
smooth running of the school after his death. A series of specific
injunctions are followed by general directions regarding the
disposition of the whole property (§§52–3):

The garden and the walk (*peripaton*) and all the houses adjoining the
garden, I give to the *philoi* whose names are written below who wish to pass
the time together there and study philosophy (*suscholazein kai sumphilo-
sophein*) ... This is on condition that no one alienates the property or devotes
it to his private use, but they should hold it in common (*koinēi*) like a
temple, and be intimate with one another on terms that are familiar and
friendly (*pros allēlois oikeiōs kai philikēs chrōmenois*) as is right and fitting.
Those sharing in the *koinōnia* (*hoi koinōnountes*) are to be Hipparchus, Neleus,
Strato, Callinus, Demotimus, Callisthenes, Melantes, Pancreon, Nicippus.

The vocabulary of this extract is rich in its associations (above,
pp. 114–15 and 146). The Peripatetics constitute a *koinōnia* consisting of *philoi* who aim to be *chrōmenoi* to one another. Nor were
their services to be entirely intellectual in character. Later in the
will (§§55–6), Theophrastus makes clear his reasons for singling out
Hipparchus as chief executor and beneficiary. He explains how it
had originally been his intention to appoint Melantes, Pancreon and
Hipparchus as joint executors; but he has since seen how Hipparchus
has been of great service to the other two and to Theophrastus
himself, so that his private affairs are now 'badly shipwrecked'.
Theophrastus therefore decided that Melantes and Pancreon should
each receive a talent from the estate, with Hipparchus receiving the
residue once all other commitments had been met. In fact, the

majority of the *philoi* received some substantial bequest in cash or kind.[26]

This *koinōnia* of philosophers is a rather superior version of the kind of association in which all Athenians would participate to a greater or lesser extent. Aristotle's list of specimen *koinōniai* has already been quoted in context (above, p. 113) – fellow-voyagers, comrades-in-arms, fellow-tribesmen and demesmen, religious groups and *eranistai* – but this only hints at the range of possibilities. All citizens would be members of a variety of overlapping groups, temporary and permanent, arising out of family, neighbourhood, work, leisure, military service, civic duties and religious ritual – again, the list is far from complete (Finley 1983: 82). The selection of groups to which a citizen belonged would depend on social status, but all citizens (and even non-citizens) had access to some of them, and all *koinōniai* had the potential to extend mutual assistance to their members. The most pervasive of these associations – family and neighbours – have already been discussed. From the range remaining, I select three, leading to a consideration in the final section of the potential for reciprocal obligation within the citizen-body as a whole.

Towards the casual end of the scale are the *ad hoc* associations of travelling companions singled out by Aristotle as a type of *koinōnia*. Xenophon has Socrates, in conversation with his son (*Mem.* II.2.12, above, p. 113), contrast the deep bond of *philia* between mother and child with the short-lived relationship between fellow-travellers. Socrates asks his son whether it isn't worth one's while to cultivate goodwill (*eunoia*) with travellers on land and sea (*sunodoiporoi, sumplooi*) and other casual acquaintances. An example of this deliberate fostering of *eunoia* between travellers is supplied by Aeschines' jaundiced report of Demosthenes' behaviour on the embassy to negotiate with Philip of Macedon (Aeschin. II). On the way out to Macedon, says Aeschines (§21), Demosthenes made himself thoroughly disagreeable with his arrogant boasting; but, on the way back, he changed his tune and tried to ingratiate himself with his fellow-envoys (§41). 'To one he would promise to organize an *eranos*-collection (*eranon sustēsein*) and to help him in his personal affairs, and to another that he would get him made *stratēgos*.' At the opposite extreme is the behaviour of Theophrastus' 'Avaricious Man' (xxx). When travelling on public business, he leaves behind the allowance provided by the state (*ephodion*) and borrows from his fellow-envoys (*para de sumpresbeutōn daneizesthai*). And when he is travelling on his own account, he leaves behind his slaves to be hired out, and makes use instead of the slaves of his companions (§§ 7 and 17).[27]

Aeschines' antipathy towards Demosthenes was politically motivated; by the same token, political views that were shared could form the focus of a *koinōnia*. One's political allies were *philoi*, and the bond of mutual support is clearest between those *philoi* who were also members of the same *hetaireia*. The verbal connexion with *hetairos* (comrade) is obvious, and the qualities expected of *hetairoi* as the closest of companions (above, pp. 127 and 135) give an inkling of the character of the *hetaireiai*. They were potentially close-knit groups of congenial companions, usually sharing the same approximate age and high status (Connor 1971: 25–9). Their function was primarily social (that is, drinking together), but with political undertones, varying in strength from *hetaireia* to *hetaireia*, and member to member. In their political capacity, the *hetaireiai* are particularly associated in our sources with the anti-democratic movements of the later fifth century. Thucydides describes them as (VIII.54.4) 'existing in the *polis* for mutual support in court cases and elections to office' (Calhoun 1913: 1–19).[28]

Whether or not politics were directly involved, one element in the assistance *hetairoi* offered each other would be financial support, including loans (so assumed by Humphreys 1977–8: 28). Literary evidence for this kind of help, consisting largely of accusations in law-court speeches, is loaded with the innuendo of conspiracy (examples in Calhoun 1913: 43–6). The evidence of inscriptions is less explicit, but in some ways more revealing. In 326/5 one Neoptolemus of Melite, a minor political figure associated with Lycurgus, contributed sums totalling 2,000 dr. towards the liquidation of public (naval) debts owed by five other individuals (*IG* II[2] 1628 384ff. 418; 1629 904ff. 938ff.). There is no evidence that these people were in any way connected by family ties, and Davies plausibly suggests some 'community of outlook' which he tentatively identifies as the 'conservative, but non-oligarchic, Right Wing' (*APF* 10652). Neoptolemus was not the only contributor towards the debts of these people; at least three others appear in the pages of *APF*, giving between them a total of well over a talent (7545, 11234 and 12478). 'The payments look like modified *eranos*-loans', says Davies (*ibid.*); members, perhaps, of a *hetaireia* or more broadly based political *koinōnia* rallying around their *philoi*.[29]

However durable and close-knit the support within *hetaireiai*, so far as the administration of the *polis* was concerned, they were informal groupings. By contrast, formal recognition was extended to the religious associations that make up the third type of *koinōnia* under examination here. Religion impinged upon Athenian life at all levels: its communal aspect is to the fore in the ceremony of sacrifice, perhaps the commonest of all religious rituals (Mikalson 1983: 88–90). Even people in prison held sacrifices; the inmates who denied a light to Aristogiton (above, p. 145) also banned him from their sacrifices. The wider social rôle of public sacrifice was keenly appreciated by Plato. In his *Laws* (771A-D) there are detailed instructions for the organization of religious festivals, with each citizen attending two sacrifices every month. All sacrifices are to be performed in the appropriate public place, with no private shrines allowed (909D-E). This has, we are told, a twofold purpose (771D). Although regular sacrifices are primarily aimed at ensuring the favour of the gods, they also enable citizens to grow familiar (*oikeios*) and well known (*gnōrimos*) to one another through social contact (*homilia*). It is therefore entirely appropriate that Theophrastus' 'Inopportune Man' (*akairos*) should choose to disrupt the proceedings by arriving to ask for the interest on his loan when everybody is busy (and out of pocket) attending to a sacrifice (xx.12).[30]

The social function of sacrifice was something of a preoccupation with Plato. Earlier in the *Laws* (738D-E), the Athenian visitor – usually identified with Plato himself – is made to speak enthusiastically about the value of fixed festivals in allowing people to meet on a regular basis in order to satisfy each other's needs, and also get acquainted with one another's characters. He says: 'There can be no greater benefit for the *polis* than that the citizens should be well known (*gnōrimoi*) to one another' (cf. 640C-D); and, a little later (743C), the underlying aim of the laws is defined as making the citizens as friendly as possible with one another (*malista allēlois philoi*). The speaker has in mind here a small-scale community of a little more than five thousand households (737E). As we have seen (p. 141), it would be fanciful to imagine that in a *polis* the size of Athens even a majority of the citizens could approach the Platonic ideal of intimacy with one another. And yet, there was a formal sense in which all citizens were conceived of as *philoi* with appropriate and mutual obligations. This aspect of civic ideology is brought out by

Aristotle where he describes all *koinōnia* as part of, and subordinate to, the all-embracing *koinōnia* of the *polis* itself (above, pp. 114–15). The *polis* differs from its constituent *koinōniai* in aiming at total as opposed to partial advantage. There exists between all citizens in the *polis* a diluted form of *philia* – *philia politikē* or 'civic friendship' (the phrase is Cooper's, 1976–7: 645–8).[31]

According to Aristotle, the *polis* exists for the sake of the common advantage that its members derive from it (*Eth. Nic.* 1160a11–12); it is therefore essential that the community aim at securing what is needed by its members to support their lives (1160a21–3). *Philia politikē* is based on the experience and expectation that each citizen has of advantage to himself, in common with others, from the membership of the *polis*. *Philia politikē* is therefore friendship for the sake of utility (stated explicitly in *Eth. Eud.* 1242b22–3). To use Cooper's own words (p. 646):

> In a community animated by civic friendship, each citizen assumes that all the others, even those hardly or not at all known to him, are willing supporters of their common institutions and willing contributors to the common social product, from which he, together with all the citizens, benefits. So they will approach one another for business or other purposes in a spirit of mutual goodwill and with willingness to sacrifice their own immediate interests to those of another, as friendship demands.

This is an ideal at which the reader with even a casual acquaintance with the internal affairs of the Greek *poleis* will look askance. Social relations seem to be characterized not so much by consensus and co-operation as by antagonism and tension, regularly spilling over into violence (see the massive compilation by Gehrke 1985: 13–199). But in the case of Athens, ideal and reality may not be too far apart. In the *Nicomachean Ethics* (1159b29), Aristotle explains that the extent of a *koinōnia* is co-terminous with the extent of *philia* between its members. And a few pages further on (1161b9–10) he argues that *philia* exists to the greatest degree in *poleis* which are democratic, 'for there the people are equal (*isoi*) and so have much in common (*koinos*)'. The plausibility of Aristotle's theory is borne out in the broadest way by the almost complete absence of serious *stasis* from democratic Athens (above, pp. 89–90). Arguing along Aristotelian lines, the commitment to democracy in Athens was so widespread as to create a consensus too strong to be challenged. How that consensus was promoted and sustained is a complex question (see above, pp. 76–7). Co-operation within the *demos* played its part, and the practical side of the obligation to help one's fellow-citizens at large is exemplified by the institution of *eranos*-credit, with which this chapter closes.[32]

In his undelivered speech *Against Midias* (xxi), Demosthenes closes a lengthy denunciation of his opponent's behaviour (he punched Demosthenes in the face) with a warning to the jurors against exercising their accustomed *praotēs* or leniency:

> I believe that all men pay contributions (*eranous pherein*) through their whole life; not only those for which they are collectors (*sullegousi*) and contributors (*plērōtai*), but others also. A person who is reasonable, kindly and full of mercy deserves to receive the same from everyone, if he ever suffers want or trouble. But another who is shameless and overbearing, treating others as if they were beggars, the scum of the earth, mere nobodies – he deserves to receive the same payments (*phoras*) that he contributed (*eisenēnoche*) to others. If you will agree to look at things rightly, you will see that, as a contributor (*plērōtēn*), Midias has made the latter contribution (*eranou*) and not the former. (§§184–5; see MacDowell 1990: *ad hoc.*)

As will be seen, the *eranos* metaphor, with its emphasis on reciprocity, is part of the stock-in-trade of Athenian authors. Although no surviving source gives a systematic account of *eranos*-credit, there is no difficulty about the basic mechanism. A typical *eranos*-loan was supplied by a plurality of lenders who gave large or small sums according to their means and the requirements of the borrower. The individual loans were interest-free, with the understanding that they would be paid back as soon as the borrower was in funds. Athenian texts regularly mark off *eranos*-loans from other kinds of lending, and associated with *eranos*-credit was a more or less stable terminology (as reflected in the Midias passage). The word *eranos* could refer to either an individual contribution or the contributors collectively. As individuals, the lenders were called *eranistai* or *plērōtai*, and the regular verbs for making and taking *eranos*-contributions were *eispherein* and *sullagein*.[33]

Occasional *eranos*-loans have cropped up in earlier chapters, but without giving an impression of the frequency with which *eranos*-credit appears in the sources. Even a short text like Theophrastus' *Characters* has five references to *eranos*-operations. The Characters indirectly reveal the ideology underpinning the institution through their refusal to contribute (1.5 and xxii.9), contributing with a thoroughly bad grace (xv.7), boasting about their contributions (xxiii.6), and receiving contributions without any show of gratitude (xvii.9). At least eighteen surviving *horos* inscriptions record credit operations in which the lenders were a group of *eranistai*; there are also some eighteen epigraphical examples of slaves purchasing their freedom with funds supplied by a *koinon* or group of *eranistai*. More generally, the Athenians thought *eranos*-loans sufficiently important to make them subject to the procedure for 'monthly suits' (see Chapter iii, n. 50). The titles have survived of two speeches by Lysias and Dinarchus, which seem to have arisen out of *eranos* operations.[34]

There is further compelling evidence for Athenian familiarity with *eranos*-credit in its regular use as a metaphor, of which the passage by Demosthenes cited above is only a sample. Elsewhere (xxv.22), Demosthenes repeats and extends the image, instructing the jury to assess public behaviour in terms of contributing to an *eranos*. If a man obeys and respects the laws, he deserves commendation for making his own contribution (*phora*) to the well-being of the *polis*. 'For everything done in obedience to the laws', he says, 'is a contribution (*eranos*) to the *polis* and the community (*koinon*).' Needless to say, Demosthenes' opponent is then presented as doing precisely the opposite. The idea that doing one's duty by the *polis* resembles the payment of an *eranos* is a recurring theme right through classical literature. Lycurgus in his *Against Leocrates* (§143) contrasts the cowardice of the defendant with the courage of those citizens who stood fast in the dark days after Chaeronea, making that *eranos* for the safety of the *polis*. The theme even finds its way into Comedy. In *Lysistrata* (ll. 648–55), Aristophanes has the women argue for the superiority of their contribution (*eranos*) to the *polis* over that of the men. While they contribute husbands and sons (*andras eispherein*), the men have squandered the *eranos* of security made over to the *polis* by their forefathers (see Henderson 1987: *ad loc.*, though the *eranos* mechanism is wrongly presented).

The imaging of services to the community as the payment of an *eranos* even appears in what is possibly the most celebrated piece of classical Greek prose. In Thucydides' Funeral Speech (ii.43.1–2), Pericles is made to praise those falling in battle on the grounds that, in giving up their lives, they give to the *polis* their *kalliston eranon* or 'finest contribution'; in return, they receive back 'praise which grows not old'. The phrase *kalliston eranon* recurs in later literature (e.g. [Dem.] LXI.54), and may derive ultimately from a proverbial saying: 'A *kalos eranos* merits an appropriate *charis*', writes Demosthenes in one of his letters (v.6). *Kallistos eranos* is also used to describe the only obligation that a citizen might legitimately put on a level with (or even above) his loyalty towards the *polis*: his duty to his parents. 'Unhappy is that child who does not return with like his parents' services (*charis*), the *kallistos eranos*', says Theseus in Euripides' *Suppliants* (ll. 361–4, with Collard 1975: *ad loc.*), 'for so he gets back from his own children whatever he has given to his parents'.[35]

The highlighting of reciprocity in almost every metaphorical use of *eranos* points to the distinguishing feature of the institution. Hesychius actually glosses *eranion* as *antapodosis* or 'giving back in return'. Confirmation comes from another, concrete meaning of *eranos*, predating its association with cash credit. As far back as Homer, *eranos* has the sense of a communal meal, the burden of which was shared by either having the guests bring individual contributions, or rotating the venue (*Od.* 1.226 and XI.415). Hesiod, in his practical way, advises that these communal feasts are exceptionally good value for money (*Works and Days* 722–3; cf. Vondeling 1961: 4–14). From the mid-fifth century, *eranos* as a communal meal is gradually superseded in our texts by *eranos* as cash loan, but the earlier meaning persists right through the classical period (Xen. *Mem.* III.14.1; other refs. in Vondeling, *ibid.* 15–24). Although the word is not actually used, it is plainly an *eranos*-style feast at which Theophrastus' 'Avaricious Man' (XXX.18) secretes for his private enjoyment a portion of the firewood, lentils, vinegar, salt and oil that his associates have provided (the text is uncertain; see Edmonds and Austen 1904: *ad loc.*).

The development of the idea of a shared loan out of arrangements for a shared meal seems natural enough, even if the stages of the transition evade us. In the analytical section of his monograph, Vondeling argues for an evolution from collective services given and returned, to collective meals, to dining clubs, to formal associations of *eranistai* having a multiplicity of functions, only one of which was the provision of loans (*ibid.* 258–61). Although this scheme is attractive in the prominence given to reciprocity, its culmination in closed groups of eranists seems to diminish the range of mutual support in fourth-century society. Vondeling accordingly interprets the rise, growth and prosperity of these associations as being 'directly related to a decreasing importance of the democratic polis and its citizenship' (p. 264). By dating the beginning of this process to the fourth century, Vondeling subscribes to (and apparently strengthens) the idea of a 'fourth-century decline' (see Chapter II, n. 19). But in his preoccupation with the formal side of *eranos*-credit, Vondeling is in danger of overlooking the detailed evidence for the raising of *eranos*-loans (*ibid.* p. 70, n. 6 – a single sentence). When pieced together, the material makes it clear that mutual assistance between citizens meant far more than predetermined groups of eranists.[36]

The association of *eranos*-loans with *philoi* is routine. In one of the earliest references to *eranos*-credit, the speaker in a speech by Antiphon is made to mention the possibility of raising an *eranos* for his *philoi* in order to pay a fine (II.9). From the other end of the chronological scale, in three of the five occasions on which Theophrastus introduces *eranoi* (XV.7, XVII.9 and XXII.9), *philoi* are also mentioned. The plaintiff in Hyperides *Against Athenogenes* (III.5) describes how he had been a nuisance to his *philoi* as he tried to scrape together an *eranos*-loan. The relationship between *philoi* and *eranos*-credit is manipulated by the speaker in Lysias' *For Polystratus* (XX), who is anxious to distance his father from one Phrynichus, a fellow-demesman. He points out that when Phrynichus became a public debtor, his father 'made no cash contribution (*eispherein*): yet it is in such cases that we see the best proof of a man's *philoi*' (§12). The bond between *philia* and *eranos* is also implicit in Plato's recommendation that, in his near-ideal state (*Laws* 915E), *eranos*-loans would be allowed between *philoi*, but only on the clear understanding that they were not recoverable at law (above, p. 42).

Several of these passages imply that the range of *philoi* from whom an *eranos* might be sought was wider than any established group of *eranistai*. This may also be inferred from texts touching on the technique of raising *eranos*-contributions, suggesting that the process was informal and time-consuming. We have already seen how, when time was of the essence, Nicostratus pleaded with Apollodorus to tide him over with a lump-sum until he had the leisure to raise an *eranos* (p. 56). A similar situation is described in a speech of Isaeus (VII.8). In a mirror-image of the argument from Lysias' *For Polystratus*, noted above, the speaker tries to show how his grandfather was on the best possible terms with one Apollodorus. He points out that when his grandfather was made a prisoner of war, Apollodorus not only contributed (*eispherein*) towards his ransom, but acted as a hostage until the money had been gathered together. There is a hint of the difficulties that might be involved in the search for contributors in Theophrastus' description of the 'Mean Man' (*aneleutheros*). If he sees approaching in the distance a *philos*, whom he knows to be collecting for an *eranos*, he will duck down a sidestreet, and go home by a roundabout way (xxii.9).[37]

The case has already been made for a diluted form of *philia*, generated by the *koinōnia* of the *polis*, and in theory extending across the whole citizen-body. This seems to be the same ideology that underlay the provision of *eranos* credit. Chapter ii opened with an account of Apollodorus' character-attack on Stephanus, harping on his failure to help out his fellow-citizens with *eranos*-contributions. With the opposite intention, the imaginary speaker in one of Antiphon's *Tetralogies* or model speeches (ii.2.12) represents the providing of *eranos*-loans as a civic duty to be associated with liturgy payments. 'I have made', he says, 'many substantial *eisphora* payments, I have performed many trierarchies, I have made *eranos*-contributions to many people, and I have paid out substantial sureties on behalf of many others.' Outside the courts, Theophrastus' 'Boastful Man' (*alazōn*) also links *eranoi* with liturgies as a civic rather than a personal obligation (xxiii.5–6):

In the food shortage (he brags) he gave handouts (*analōmata*) of more than five talents to needy citizens – he doesn't know how to refuse. He then tells the men sitting next to him – who are strangers – to set out some counters; and, reckoning in sums of a thousand drachmas and in round minas, and by plausibly attributing a name to each of them, he makes it ten talents. He says that these are the monies he has contributed in *eranos*-loans; and he adds that it does not include the trierarchies and other liturgies he has undertaken.

The exaggeration is obvious, as is the distortion of the *eranos* ideology (see above, p. 64); but something of the reality behind the boasting can be glimpsed in Demosthenes' catalogue of his father's estate (xxvii.11). He lists as one of the assets, 'about a talent, loaned out (*diakechrēmenon*) in sums of 200 or 300 dr.', and these small loans have been plausibly identified as *eranos*-contributions. Provided that the identification is correct and that Demosthenes is telling the truth (or, at least, lying convincingly), his father's twenty to thirty contributions give an impression of the spread of *eranos*-credit.[38]

It was only to be expected that in a *polis* the size of Athens the reality of mutual support would fall some way short of the ideal. When citizens were looking for contributors in an *eranos*, they would naturally turn towards people with whom they had contacts over and above the bond of citizenship. Plato in his *Apology* (38C) portrays Socrates as being offered spontaneous help in paying a fine by four of his pupils, including Crito – 'my contemporary and fellow-demesman' as Socrates describes him earlier in the speech (33D-E; see above, pp. 76–7). From the other end of the social scale, below the level of citizen, the prostitute Neaera is alleged to have bought her freedom by raising *eranos*-contributions from her former clients ([Dem.] LIX.30–2). Her joint owners, two Corinthians, were about to marry, and expressed their willingness to sell Neaera her own freedom for three thousand drachmas – one thousand drachmas less than her original purchase price. This discount is treated as the equivalent of an *eranos* of 500 dr. from each of them (§). Neaera accordingly summoned to Corinth several of her former customers, including one Phrynion from Athens (§31):

When Phrynion came to her, she told him the proposal which Eucrates and Timanoridas [her Corinthian owners] had made to her, and gave him the money which she had collected from her other lovers as an *eranos* towards the price of her freedom, and added whatever she had gained for herself, and she begged him to advance the balance needed to make up the twenty minas, and to pay it to Eucrates and Timanoridas to secure her freedom. He listened gladly to these words of hers and, taking the money which had been contributed (*eispherein*) to her by her other lovers, added the balance himself and paid the twenty minas as the price of her freedom to Eucrates and Timanoridas on the condition that she should not ply her trade in Corinth.

The procedure described here is complicated by the intervention of Phrynion as Neaera's 'agent', collecting the contributions and completing the transaction on her behalf. Under the circumstances, this made good sense: Neaera was herself allegedly a slave without legal rights or status.[39]

Recruitment of an *eranos*-organizer was not limited to slaves. For citizen-borrowers there were obvious advantages if a well-connected *philos* could be induced to take on responsibility for raising the *eranos*. The third-century philosopher Arcesilaus was apparently eager to assist those making *eranos* collections (Chapter II, n. 23), as were Epaminondas of Thebes (Chapter III, n. 18) and, on occasion, Speusippus (Athen. VII.279f.) and Demosthenes (above, p. 149). A similar rôle was presumably played by the individuals named on a majority of *horoi* recording loans by groups of eranists (30–2, 42, 70, 110 and 31A in Finley 1952: 163A in Millett 1982). The customary formula reads: 'to the eranists, those with' (*tois eranistais, tois meta*), followed by the name of the individual. The background of one of the persons so named on a recently discovered *horos* (*SEG* XXXII 236; see my Appendix I) gives an insight into the kind of person who might be sought to head an *eranos* collection.[40]

The *horos* in question was found in the mining district of Laureion and records (among other things) the offering of surface workings as security to one Simon of Paeanea, and to the eranists headed by Neoptolemus of Melite. Neoptolemus is well known from a range of fourth-century sources (see Osborne 1985a: 86 and 88). He is found elsewhere being honoured in his deme for restoring a shrine (*SEG* XXII 116), and by the *polis* for other religious activities (Ps.-Plutarch, *Mor.* 843F). He was actively involved in politics as an ally of Lycurgus (Dem. XVIII.114), and is described by Demosthenes as a member of a group of men who were 'excessively rich' (XXI.215). He was also one of the persons noted above (p. 150), who in 326/5 made substantial contributions towards the payment of other men's naval debts. Small wonder that, with such extensive connexions, Neoptolemus was able to head a *koinon* of *eranistai* raising anything up to a talent.

CHAPTER VII

Non-professional lending: loans bearing interest

MISER, MONEY-LENDER, BORROWER AND THIEF

An anecdote attributed to Antiphon the Sophist (but also found among Aesop's *Fables*) tells the story of a person in need who[1]

> ...seeing another man earning much money begged him to lend him some at interest (*daneisai epi tokōi*). The other refused; and, being of a mistrustful nature, unwilling to help anyone, he carried it off and hid it somewhere. Another man, observing him, filched it. Later, the man who had hidden it returned and could not find it. He was very upset at the disaster, all the more so as he had not lent to the man who had asked him, because then it would have been safe and would have brought him something extra (*heteron prosepheren*). He went to see the man who had asked for the loan, and bewailed his misfortune, saying that he had done wrong and was sorry not to have granted his request but to have refused it, as his money was completely lost. The other man told him to hide a stone in the same place, and think of his money as his and not lost: 'For even when you had it, you completely failed to use it; so that now too you can think you have lost nothing.'

Consideration of Antiphon's commentary on the story may conveniently be postponed till later. What matters here is the way in which the wealthy miser is criticized for *failing* to lend his money at interest. There is no hint of the antipathy towards interest-bearing credit we have encountered in other texts (25–6 and 99–100). Charging of interest marks the crossing of the boundary between balanced and negative reciprocity (see above, pp. 110–11). But even in the zone of negative reciprocity there are ideological shadings, making the lender's behaviour more or less morally acceptable. The mere making of an interest-bearing loan, at or below the customary rate, was not in itself reprehensible. Athens was a big place, and there were bound to be credit transactions where the bonds of *philia* between the parties were so weak as to make unlikely any reciprocity of service. The place of the return loan could therefore legitimately be taken by the payment of interest.

The factor that distinguished between respectability and relative infamy in the taking of interest seems to have been the occupational status of the lender; or, to use Apollodorus' emotive words about Stephanus (above, p. 25), the frequency with which he regarded the misfortunes and necessities of others as his own good fortune. Casual lenders, such as Antiphon's miser could have become, escaped all ignominy. That was reserved for professional lenders who were thought to derive all or a substantial part of their livelihood from lending at interest. The plaintiff in Demosthenes' speech *Against Pantaenetus* (XXXVII.53) describes them as 'those who make a trade (*technēn*) of the business, with no thought of helping out or of anything else other than gain'. He adds: 'These people are rightly hated by you.' This passage and professional money-lenders in general, are examined in detail in the following chapter. The present chapter is concerned with irregular lenders at interest, who inhabited the grey area between fully reciprocated, interest-free credit (as described in the previous chapter), and professional lending, with interest payments making a decisive contribution towards income.

The terminology here is deliberately vague, as the boundary between casual and professional money-lending cannot be determined with any precision. A case in point is the father of Demosthenes, reported by his son to have had, at the time of his death, close on a talent lent at interest, bringing in an annual income of more than seven minas (XXVII.9). In one sense, that was a substantial sum of money, making a year's wages for a skilled workman. But looked at in another way, the sum on loan made up only one fourteenth of the value of the estate (see below, p. 168), while the annual interest amounted to only one seventh of the profits generated by all the income-earning assets. That was apparently not enough to cause Demosthenes senior to be classed as a professional lender. Much the same could probably be said about most of the isolated loans at interest that appear in our sources (e.g. Lysias XVII.2–3; Isaeus VIII.35 and XI.42–3).

The category of non-professional lending is broad, extending across from unplanned and unforeseen lending at interest to the region in which less-than-casual lending shades off into true professional money-lending. The Antiphon anecdote represents one extreme: asking a man known to be rich for a loan at interest on the off-chance that he might says 'yes'. On this occasion, the answer happened to be 'no'. A degree less casual is the situation in which potential lender and would-be borrower are introduced by a third party known to both of them. This occurred in the Nicostratus case (see above, p. 57), where Apollodorus raised a loan from one Arcesas, who was introduced to him by his friend and neighbour Nicostratus. There is no sign that Arcesas was a professional lender; he was presumably an acquaintance of Nicostratus with some spare cash that he was willing to lend at interest. Absence of any pre-existing bond between Apollodorus and Arcesas justified the charging of interest. Use of a third party in this way to effect introductions between those needing cash and those with some to spare seem to have been a regular feature of lending and borrowing in Athens (e.g. Lysias XIX.22; [Dem.] XX.7; [Dem.] XXXV.6–8 with p. 146, above; Dem. XXXVII.11).[2]

There is also support in the sources for the existence of a group of men who lent out money at interest on a more regular basis, but still without qualifying as professional money-lenders. In his *First Speech Against Onetor* (XXX.11), Demosthenes describes Onetor and Timocrates as men who are 'in the habit of lending out not inconsiderable sums to others' (on the translation, see Pearson 1972: *ad loc.*). And in another speech of Demosthenes (XXXVIII.7), the litigant claims to have heard that: 'Xenopithes and Nausicrates left their entire property in debts (*chrea*), and they possessed only a little tangible property (*phaneran*).' Although we hear about the details of only one of these loans (§11, one hundred staters), the estate was apparently extensive (§20, with *APF* 11263).[3] To this category of citizens with a substantial involvement in lending may be added Moerocles (above, p. 91), and possibly the fifth-century politician, Thucydides son of Melesias. Information, wrongly transposed to the historian Thucydides, tells how after his ostracism he went to Aegina where he lent out most of his fortune at interest, thereby ruining the Aeginetans (Anon. *Life of Thuc.* §7; Marcellinus, *Life of Thuc.* §24). In view of a family connexion with Aegina, Davies is prepared to see an element of truth behind this obvious slander (*APF* 7268 VIII).

These examples of interest-bearing loans by non-professional lenders raise the question whether wealthier citizens 'invested' in loans in order to secure a regular income. The possibility can be extended to include public institutions that occasionally had funds available to be lent at interest. In the following sections I examine the rationale behind these irregular loans at interest, and their bearing on the concept of investment as applied to classical Athens.

LOANS AT INTEREST AND PATTERNS OF PROPERTY-HOLDING

In 345 B.C., as part of his political manoeuverings against Demosthenes, Aeschines prosecuted Timarchus for immorality. Most of the speech *Against Timarchus* is taken up with attacks on his character, including the way in which he is alleged to have squandered his inheritance (§ 105):

> But perhaps some will say that, after selling his father's house, he bought another one somewhere else in the city, and that in place of the farm on the borders and the land at Alopeke and the craftsmen and other things, he set himself up in the mines, like his father before him. But nothing remains to him: not a house, nor a tenement building (*sunoikia*), nor land, nor slaves, nor a loan (*daneisma*), nor anything by which men who are not evil-doers live.

So far as the final sentence is a fair summary of the major sources of income exploited by wealthier citizens, it can be described as a guide to 'investment' in Athens – but investment only in the loose sense of the acquisition of income-producing assets.[4] In the capitalist economic system the concept of investment has a narrower range of reference (see Palgrave, s.v. 'investment'). Apart from investment in the technical sense of expenditure on capital goods (buildings, equipment and stock), the broader concept of acquiring income-producing assets has formal ramifications not always appreciated by ancient historians. Essentially, investment in a capitalist economy is to be regarded as a *rational* activity, planned to generate the maximum financial return, balanced against an acceptable level of risk. In modern discussions of the ancient Greek economy it is often unclear which species of investment the author has in mind. In his otherwise helpful discussion of the sources of wealth in classical Athens (1981: 38–72), Davies seems to use the term in a variety of senses (including 'investments' as a translation of *daneisma* in the Aeschines passage).[5] But there can be no doubt about the stance taken by Thompson in his two papers with the uncompromising titles 'The Athenian investor' (1978) and 'The Athenian entrepreneur' (1982). I take these unashamedly neo-modernist statements as the starting-point for my own analysis.

Thompson states his intentions in a brief introductory paragraph to his earlier paper (1978), couched in the language of modern investment theory (p. 404):

Let us begin with the Athenian who invested his own funds, first the passive investor, then the creative entrepreneur. Afterwards, we can consider the man who tried to turn the resources of others into profit for himself. We shall thus be moving steadily from the safest to the riskiest proposition.

The modernizing tone is sustained almost to the end of the paper, and the ancient evidence is strained beyond breaking point in an attempt to accommodate Athenian practices to contemporary ideas about investment. By way of justification, the reader is referred to the supposed parallel of the Italian merchant of the late Middle Ages (p. 403), 'when commerce and population were roughly on the same scale as in Ancient Athens, and men dealt in the same products, using the same means of transport and communication' – and that is the extent of the methodological debate. But an admittedly brief acquaintance with the literature on the late medieval economy seems to suggest that the *organization* of trade was on an altogether different level of sophistication, complete with letters of credit, bills of exchange, and elaborate manipulation of exchange rates.[6]

According to Thompson (p. 404), Wall Street's 'stock for widows and orphans' has its Athenian equivalent in the use of a 'combination of land and rental property', guaranteed to give a high dividend on a regular basis. 'A similar type of investment', he adds (pp. 404–5), 'is the mortgage, which in Athens usually took the form of a sale with leaseback, with the right of redemption.' Thompson here cites Finley's study (1952: 28–37), but appears to ignore Finley's fundamental point that *prasis epi lusei* is to be considered as a credit and not a sale transaction. The appropriate rates of return are given as eight per cent for 'real estate' and twelve per cent for 'long-term mortgage money' (pp. 406–7) – figures arrived at by disregarding much of the obvious evidence on interest rates (on the figure of eight per cent, see my Appendix IV). Thompson goes on to estimate that money spent on slaves, 'one of the simplest forms of investment, available to everyone', was liable to bring in between fifteen and twenty-five per cent (p. 417). It is enough to note here the different rates of profit estimated by Jones (1956: 5–6): the result of equally speculative calculations. Garlan is surely right to reject attempts to quantify the real or relative profitability of slave labour which, in any case, ignore non-economic considerations of prestige and status (see Garlan 1982: 72–3).

As his case study of an Athenian entrepreneur, Thompson settles on Demosthenes the elder, with the usual unavailing attempts to calculate the profit rates of his 'factories' (pp. 410–12; see above, pp. 95–6). It is argued below that Demosthenes Senior's property holding was probably unique amongst Athenian citizens. Untypical evidence is also brought in to support Thompson's claim that (p. 412) 'there was opportunity for the Athenian investor to place his surplus funds at interest in the various aspects of trade'. But the passages cited (which include the episode of Aeschines the Socratic) are exceptional in character, and are dealt with elsewhere in my analysis.[7] Thompson only adds to the uncertainty by closing his paper with an appeal to a concept of investment that is completely at odds with the formal, neoclassical view implicit in the rest of his study (p. 423):

> Every tree and vine, every dry-wall erected to prevent flooding of the fields, every house, tenement and shop…the abandoned workings of the silver mines…all give mute testimony to the enterprise of the Athenian investor, whether businessman or farmer, and his willingness to save and to reinvest his earnings.

On such a showing there can be few economic activities since the Stone Age that cannot somehow be classed as 'investment', and the term is robbed of precision as a tool of analysis and understanding.

It will be apparent from this selective but not unrepresentative critique of Thompson's study that I am not persuaded by his manipulation of the evidence. This, in turn, stems from a deeper dissatisfaction with Thompson's overall approach, which appears to be at odds with the realities of Athenian economy and society. He assumes throughout his analysis that citizens were preoccupied with the maximization of the rate of return from their assets and made rational investment decisions to achieve that end. As already argued, the Athenians lacked the mentality appropriate to modern conceptions of 'rational economic man'. They did not develop accounting techniques capable of calculating comparative rates of profit. Although it was expected that assets would produce a satisfactory financial return, there were other, equally powerful factors to be taken into account. An obvious consideration is the prestige attached to ownership of land. Something of the flavour of contemporary attitudes comes across in the observations on a range of occupations in the pseudo-Aristotelian *Oeconomica* (1353a25–b5):

> With respect to property (*ktēseōs*), the first care is that it should be according to nature. Agriculture ranks first according to nature; secondly, those activities which extract it from the ground, such as mining and the like. Agriculture is the best because it is just, for it is not at the expense of other men, whether willingly as in trade (*kapēleia*) or wage-earning

(*mistharnikai*) or unwillingly as in war. It is also one of the activities according to nature in other respects, because by nature all creatures receive their nourishment from their mother, and so men receive theirs from the earth. And what is more, agriculture contributes greatly to manly characteristics; unlike manual labour (*hai banausoi*) it does not damage the body, but toughens it, and enables it to face the dangers of war...

Although the statement is cast in a philosophical mould, it reproduces a scale of values found elsewhere in Athenian society. We have already encountered the odium attached to professional money-lending (see n. 4); and there is also the way in which prejudice was raised against the so-called 'Demagogues' whose fortunes depended on the ownership of slave workshops (Finley 1962: 17–18; Connor 1971: 151–8; Davies 1981: 68–72).

The acquisition of income-earning assets paralleled attitudes to profitability by being irrational in any formal economic sense. Finley has described how purchase of property in the Roman world tended to be on a windfall basis (1985b: 117–22). What is known about patterns of property holding in classical Athens implies a similar sort of process: men of substance would typically own several small estates scattered over Attica (Davies 1981: 52–4). There are indications that the acquisition by wealthy citizens of other assets, including interest-bearing loans, was similarly unorganized and unsystematic.

The largest single group of loans falling into this category are sparing of information. A majority of the 150 or so *horos* inscriptions recording *hypothēkē* and *prasis epi lusei* transactions presumably carried interest. The fact that in no case does the name of a creditor appear on more than one stone supports the hypothesis that professional lenders were not involved.[8] This supposition is strengthened by the contexts in which lenders' names reappear. At least eighteen crop up in *Athenian Propertied Families*, suggesting that we are dealing with people from the upper end of Athenian society (Millett 1982: xi). It is not easy to penetrate behind the *horoi* to recover the motives of these irregular lenders at interest. Such evidence as survives concentrates on the intentions of borrowers rather than lenders. There is, however, potentially helpful material in the breakdowns of estates recorded by the Orators. The most fruitful single source is Isaeus, whose inheritance speeches list in usable detail the components of at least six estates, to which may be added the estate of Arizelus, the father of Timarchus (as described by Aeschines). In three cases, loans make up one element in the estates, which are here divided up into real property, movable property, cash and loans.[9]

Isaeus VIII.35	dr.
Farm at Phyle	6,000
House in Athens	1,000
House in Athens	1,300
Slaves producing an income (*andrapoda misthophorounta*)	—
Three female (domestic) slaves	—
Furniture	1,300*
'Considerable sums' (amount not stated) lent at interest	—

*Includes value of slaves.

Isaeus XI.42–3	dr.
Farm at Thria	15,000
House at Melite	3,000
House at Eleusis	500
Furniture, sheep, barley, wine, fruits	4,900
Cash in hand	900
eranos-loans	1,000
Loans bearing interest (reckoned at $1\frac{1}{2}\%$ per month)	4,000

Aeschines 1.97 and 101 (no values stated)

eschatia (hill-land?) at Sphettus*
Farm at Alopeke
Farm at Cephisia
Farm at Amphitropae
Two *ergastēria* (workshops) in the mining area

Furniture

Nine or ten slaves making shoes
Slave-woman working flax
Slave embroiderer

Money owed by various people

*On the meaning of *eschatia*, see Lewis 1973: 210–12.

It is striking that in each case (making due allowance for rhetorical misrepresentation), real property makes up the bulk of the value of each estate. But this was not so with the two other estates known in detail from the Orators: the estate of Diodotus, preserved by Lysias (XXXII.4–15), and the estate of Demosthenes the elder (Dem. XXVII.9–11). In the breakdowns that follow I continue with the categories adopted above, dividing each estate into real and movable property, cash and loans.[10]

Demosthenes XXVII.9–11 *(APF* 3597 XIII–XX)	dr.
House	3,000
Furniture and jewellery	10,000
Ivory, iron, wood	8,000
Dye	7,000
32 or 33 slave sword-makers	19,000
20 slave couch-makers	4,000
Cash in hand	8,000
Deposit at bank of Pasion	2,400
Deposit at bank of Pylades	600
Maritime loan deposited with Xuthus	7,000
Loan to Demomeles (interest-free?)	1,600
Money out on loan at 1% interest per month	6,000
Money loaned out (without interest?) in small sums	6,000

Lysias XXXII.4–15 *(APF* 3885)	dr.
phanera ousia ('real property'?)	—
Furniture and household effects	—
Cash in hand	2,200
Bequest to wife (partly in Cyzicene staters)	2,600
Deposit with Diogiton	30,000
Monies lent out in maritime loans*	46,000
Monies lent out in landside loans	10,000
Money lent out in the Chersonese	2,000

* For 'landside loans' as the meaning of *engeiōi epi tokōi*, see Cohen 1989.

In both cases, real property is conspicuous by its almost total absence, with cash deposits and loans making up a substantial proportion of the estates. Can it be assumed that this pattern was at all typical for wealthy citizens? The answer is emphatically not. Apart from the evidence of the six estates catalogued by Isaeus (n. 9), Davies's exhaustive study puts it beyond reasonable doubt that the estates of Diodotus and Demosthenes Senior were in a class by themselves (*APF* 3597 xiv; Davies 1981: 72).[11]

The small proportion of their wealth that more typical citizens seem to have lent out at interest argues against the practice of systematic investment in loans. That is also the broad implication of the mixed nature of holdings, embracing land, houses, slaves, cash and valuables. Thompson talks in terms of a 'balanced portfolio of investments' (1978: 406); but the diversity of holdings probably reflects the casual acquisition of assets as opportunities arose. The phenomenon can be paralleled in modern, underdeveloped societies. Describing the economy of rural India, Harper (1961: 170) explains how a man who has enough land to yield a cash surplus 'prefers to invest his money in land, but failing this he generally prefers to lend his cash rather than let it lie idle'. The limited opportunities for disposing of surplus cash in village communities are emphasized by Darling (1947: 108 and 205), which may help to account for the prevalence of hoarding throughout the ancient Greek world. 'If people have a very large amount of silver', notes Xenophon in his *Poroi* (iv.6), 'they derive no less pleasure from hiding away the surplus than from putting it to use.' The accuracy of his statement is borne out by a wide range of testimony.[12]

It might be anticipated that Diodotus and Demosthenes the elder would have been more alert than most Athenians to the lost opportunity of having cash lying idle. Yet they both died with substantial sums hoarded in their houses. Moreover, Demosthenes the younger accuses Aphobus of making a false claim before the arbitrator that his father had buried four talents in the ground (xxvii.53–7). We are free to believe or disbelieve this story as we choose, but its apparent plausibility may be reflected in the lengths to which Demosthenes goes to refute it. There are references to sums of money as components of more conventional estates by Isaeus (ix.43 = 900 dr.), in the Demosthenic corpus (xlviii.15 = 1,000 dr. and 7,000 dr.), and particularly in the speeches of Lysias. *On the Property of Aristophanes* (xix.22) mentions a smallish sum of 700 dr., while, at the opposite extreme (§47), the wealth of Nicias was reputed to be not less than one hundred talents and 'most of it in his house' (see *APF* 10808A). Lysias and his brother had extensive holdings of cash and other valuables at home. In his speech *Against Eratosthenes* (XII.11), Lysias claims that a representative of the Thirty Tyrants pillaged the contents of his strongbox (*kibētos*), comprising three talents of silver, four hundred Cyzicene staters, a hundred Persian darics and four silver cups.[13]

In most of these examples, cash and valuables were stored in the house. The possible scale of this hoarding – outdoing even Lysias' strongbox – is hinted at by Plato's passing reference in the *Republic* (548A) to 'storerooms and private strongrooms' (*tamieia kai oikeious thēsaurous*). For those who distrusted or could not afford these precautions, there was always the alternative of burial. The regular discovery of coin hoards bears mute testimony to the relative frequency of concealment in the earth (see Thompson, Mørkholm and Kraay 1973). Apart from incidental references to buried hoards (e.g. Aesop 82 in Chambry 1927; Diog. Laert. IV.16; Athen. XIV.616b), Plato in the *Laws* opens his treatment of movable property with regulations concerning the discovery of buried treasure (913A–14A; cf. 744E–5A), and Davies (1981: 39, n. 3) notes that some seven comedies are known to have had the title *Thesaurus* or 'The Treasure'.

There is an element of truth in the idea that the prevalence of hoarding was a reflection of the high risk involved in lending money (see Michell 1957: 31). Some of the potential difficulties in recovering defaulted loans were outlined in an earlier chapter (pp. 82–4), and Isocrates, romancing about the 'Good Old Days', says that the rich 'felt as confident about what they had given out as about that which they had stored at home' (VII.33, with Millett 1988: 26–8). Even so, I would argue that the most powerful motives behind hoarding were social attitudes which served to restrict the opportunities for semi-systematic lending at interest. In addition to the almost complete absence of productive credit, there was the thriving network of interest-free credit transactions, detailed in previous chapters. It is worth noting that in at least two of the estates examined above (Isaeus XI.42–3 and Dem. XXVII.9–11), lenders combined loans at interest with interest-free *eranos*-loans: yet another illustration of behaviour that would be judged 'irrational' from the point of view of much modern economic theory. The Athenians themselves never show any awareness that extensive hoarding of cash might be economically inefficient. Criticisms of the practice tend to be on the ethical ground of failing to make proper use of one's good fortune (Hyperides fr. D.17 in Burtt 1954, with Gauthier 1976:

125–6; Xen. *Cyr.* III.3.3 and VIII.2.20). Perhaps the best illustration is Antiphon's ponderous moral commentary on the anecdote of the stolen hoard, with which this chapter began:

> For when a person has not used and will not use anything, it makes no difference to him either whether he has it or not. For when the god does not wish to give a man complete good fortune – when he has given him material wealth but made him poor in right thinking – in taking away the one he has deprived him of both.

Or, as Aesop more pithily put it: 'Possession without enjoyment is nothing'.

The picture that emerges from this presentation of non-professional lending at interest is of wealthy Athenians who were far from being investors as the term is commonly understood in the modern, capitalist economy. Although the parallel is by no means exact, they resemble more closely the class of people called *rentiers*, content to draw an income from their assets, with the proviso that these were such as to guarantee (or at least not compromise) social respectability, while maintaining an appropriate lifestyle. This entailed freedom from the trouble of earning one's living through direct economic activity; and, for the typical wealthy citizen, that would have included entrepreneurial activity, manipulating available assets as the basis for further growth.[14]

LENDING BY CORPORATE INSTITUTIONS

'If a deme or members of a phratry or *orgeōnes* of heroes or members of a *genos* or messmates (*sussitoi*) or funerary associates (*homotaphoi*) or *thiasōtai* or those away for plunder or for trade make arrangements in these matters amongst themselves, they shall be valid unless forbidden by the laws.' So runs a law attributed to Solon, preserved in a fragment of the Roman jurist Gaius, in turn quoted in the *Digest* of Justinian (XLVII.22.4).[15] One of the matters about which some of these *koinōniai* did make arrangements was the extension of credit to their members. Of the nine groups mentioned in the law, five are found lending out their funds. The evidence is entirely epigraphic, with references on a handful of *horoi* and a few other inscriptions to lending by demes, phratries, *orgeōnes*, *genē* and *thiasōtai*; to which may be added tribes (not mentioned in the Solonic law). This raises at least the possibility that lending and borrowing on a personal basis were reinforced by credit available from corporate bodies, both subdivisions of the state and private associations.

These institutions are analogous to the private lenders of the previous section in that lending money was not their primary function, but a sideline intended to maintain or boost income. Whether they played anything more than a peripheral part in the overall structure of credit remains to be seen; but immediately apparent is the relative absence of information about this branch of corporate lending. Conspicuous by their non-appearance are the great temples of Athens, which certainly had surplus funds at their disposal and, by analogy with the Delian temple bank, might be expected to have made loans to individuals (Cavaignac 1908: 72). With our unusually detailed epigraphic knowledge of the types of financial operations in which the Athenian temples were involved, it seems safe to conclude that their credit function was restricted to the transfer of resources into empty state coffers (Bogaert 1968: 91–2; cf. Chapter iv, no. 14). Only at deme level does a temple appear as lender, and it is in the demes that the meagre evidence for corporate lending is concentrated. Recent opinion has tended to maximize the part played by deme institutions in the extension of credit to private borrowers. Bogaert sees the temples in those demes away from the city as important leaders, on the grounds that there were probably no bankers in the country demes (1968: 94). As elsewhere, Bogaert under-plays the possibility of *non*-institutional sources of credit acting as a substitute. Andreyev (1974) is even more emphatic about the impact of loans by demes on the overall structure of credit (p. 22): 'The loans which the demes made to citizens were quite regular and existed on a mass scale... This cheap and undoubtedly liberal credit was a comfortable alternative to private loans and must have influenced their nature.' Let us see.

When the scanty evidence for lending by demes is gathered together, it hardly seems to bear the weight of Andreyev's claims. Out of more than 200 *horoi*, only four record loans made by demes (Finley 1952: nos. 5, 67A and 146; Millett 1982: no. 81c ~ Whitehead 1986: Appendix 3, nos. 58 (correcting Finley's deme ascription), 69, 92 and 93). There is a lost speech of Isaeus (fr. 8 in Forster 1927), entitled *Against the Demesmen Concerning a Piece of Land*. In his essay *On Isaeus* (§ 10), Dionysius of Halicarnassus quotes from the introduction to the speech and explains that the speaker had offered the land in question as security to his fellow-demesmen, who had duly seized it. It cannot be determined from the context whether the land was acting as security in a loan or leasing operation. An entry in Harpocration (s.v. 'Sphettus') implies that the demesmen involved were Sphettians. Apart from these specific instances of demes offering credit, there are two inscriptions recording regulations governing the loaning of funds by demes (*IG* I³ 258 ~ Whitehead 1986: 165–6 – Plotheia, *c.* 425–413; *IG* II² 1183 – Myrrhinus, after 340); also, records of the accounts (including loans) of the temple of Nemesis in the deme of Rhamnous for five (consecutive?) years between *c.* 445 and 440 (*IG* I³ 248 ~ *SGHI*² 53 ~ Fornara 90), and a proposal that the deme of Halai Aixonides lend out money generated by the sale of some olive wood (see above, p. 105). This is, on the face of it, an unimpressive catalogue of evidence from a total of approximately 140 demes throughout the whole of the classical period (and beyond).

Although the interpretation of all these texts is problematical, the little that can be deduced generally supports the idea of a low level of lending by deme institutions. Nothing much can be made of the size of loans recorded on three of the four *horoi* (200 dr., 300 or 700 dr., 3,000 dr.). More illuminating are the regulations regarding credit operations by individual demes. In the case of Myrrhinus it is surely significant that the regulations are to be put into effect only (l. 27), 'if there is need of money', implying that deme funds were not automatically lent out on a regular basis. In line with this are the elaborate precautions that accompany any extension of credit, designed to protect the interests of the temple rather than make things easier for would-be borrowers. It was stipulated that the priests were to lend temple funds only on the security of (ll. 28–30), 'land or a house or a tenement house (*sunoikia*) of adequate value, and to set up a *horos* on which is inscribed the god to which the money belongs'. Should the priests fail to comply with these stipulations, they were to bear any loss themselves. Nothing relative to the size of the sums involved should be read into these considered precautions. Some twenty years later (321/0), the deme of Piraeus ruled that anyone leasing deme land and paying an annual rental greater than ten drachmas would be required to supply real security in place of the usual personal surety (*IG* II² 2498, with Finley 1952: 95–6).

Something of the same concern over the security of deme funds can be read in the decree from Plotheia: the subject of a lucid analysis by Whitehead (1986: 166–9). According to his interpretation, an unspecified number of financial officials were to be chosen by lot in order to safeguard the Plotheians' money (ll. 14–15). The portion of deme funds available for lending fell into two categories. Part was to be managed in accordance with existing decrees and was lent out at a rate of interest fixed in advance (ll. 15–18). The other part, lent afresh each year, was to be loaned out to those borrowers offering the highest rate of interest (ll. 18–20). Security for this second group of borrowers took the form of either an *apotimēma* or suretyship (ll. 20–2; see Finley 1952: 95–7). The combined revenue from interest and rents was to be used to pay for sacrifices at various festivals, of which details are given. Above the decree is given a list of eight sums of money apparently designated for specific purposes: 1,000 dr. for the demarch, 1,200 each for the festivals of the Aphrodisia and the Anakia, and so on, giving a total of 22,100 dr. There has been much discussion as to whether these sums represent actual allocations for expenditure, or funds available for loan, only the interest of which was being allocated under each heading. Bibliography and opposing arguments are marshalled by Whitehead (1986: 166–9), who comes down decisively (and surely correctly) on the side of the figures as representing loanable funds. His conclusion offers an inkling of the possible scale of credit available from deme resources: 22,100 dr. represent a considerable sum; enough, in the fifth century, to pay the wages of more than sixty skilled workmen for a year. We have, however, no idea of the sizes of the individual loans. For what it is worth, the two usable figures on deme-*horoi* (above, p. 173) suggest a range somewhere between 110 loans of 200 dr. and seven loans of 3,000 dr. Whereabouts between these two extremes reality lies is impossible to say; but the temple accounts from Rhamnous (discussed below) could imply that small rather than large loans were the norm.

Either way, the figures from Plotheia are impressive, but depend on the assumption – not to be taken as read – that there were takers for all available funds. When the demesmen decreed that funds lent out in the current year should go to those borrowers offering the highest rates of interest, that should not necessarily be interpreted as anticipating for a high demand for deme credit. Although a bare parallel cannot be decisive, the Plotheian arrangements are reminiscent of the situation described by Pliny the Younger during his governorship of Bithynia (*c.* A.D. 220). Pliny wrote to tell the Emperor Trajan how in one of the cities in his province people could not be found who were willing to borrow public funds at nine per cent interest, the going rate for private credit (x.54; see Sherwin-White 1966: *ad loc.*). He accordingly proposed to the emperor that, as a first step, the rate of interest on public funds should be lowered. If funds still remained idle (*otiosae*), then town councillors (*decuriones*) should be forced to borrow the money, furnishing suitable security. Trajan agreed to the first proposal, but not the second (x.55; see Finley 1985b: 118). Willingness to borrow public funds would depend on a combination of personal circumstances, security requirements, and wider social and economic conditions. Pliny makes a point of telling the emperor that opportunities for buying up land were either rare or non-existent. We know nothing about the background to the Plotheia decree, though it may be noted that the broad date favoured by the latest editor (Lewis in *IG* 1³) places it during the Peloponnesian War.

Some of the questions raised by the Plotheian inscription may find partial answers in the accounts from the temple of Nemesis in Rhamnous (always bearing in mind that this material comes from a different date, from a different deme, and is itself elliptical in the extreme). It is not certain that the accounts refer to five consecutive years, and they are anything but systematic in their presentation of the information (see the comments by Meiggs and Lewis, *SGHI*² 53 p. 145). Making due allowance for anomalies, in each of the five years, 37,000 dr. are reported as being 'in the hands of the two-hundred-drachma borrowers'; and, in the fourth and fifth years, first 13,500 dr. and then 14,400 dr. are said to be made up of 300-dr. loans. Matched against these sums of money out on loan are other figures, making it possible to calculate the total liquid resources of the temple, with the implication that the proportion of cash lent out increased over the period covered by the inscription from 75 to 90 per cent (Whitehead 1986: 160). Finley was unable to accept that the entries for two-hundred and three-hundred drachmas referred to loans, 'because it would require 185 debtors and 200 drachmas and 45 or 48 at 300, fantastic numbers...' (1952: 285 n. 3). Pouilloux countered with the suggestion that some of the borrowers might have taken up more than one of the two- and three-hundred units (1954: 148–9). Whitehead accepts this interpretation, which may well be right. An alternative approach would be to link these corporate loans with those made by a private individual some seventy years later. Demosthenes' father had, at the time of his death, one talent lent out in lots of two- and three-hundred drachmas, making a total

of twenty to thirty borrowers (above, pp. 157–8). Their identification as *eranos*-contributions could explain, by association, the
high take-up rate of what were interest-free loans from the Temple
of Nemesis. The large number of borrowers could also reflect the
polis-wide status of the cult, attracting people from outside the deme
of Rhamnous (Whitehead, 1986: 166–9).

The suggestion here is that the credit provided by the Temple of
Nemesis was untypical of other demes in both scale and character.
At the opposite extreme is the inscription from the deme of Halai
Aixonides giving detailed instructions for the leasing of an estate.
The demesmen resolved that unwanted olive wood removed from
the land should be sold to the highest bidder, and the proceeds from
the sale loaned out (ll. 31–41). The sum generated in this way was
hardly likely to be substantial and may be characteristic of the *ad hoc*
way in which demes acquired and exploited loanable funds.
Certainly typical was the charging of interest: the demesmen of
Aixone were specific in their instruction that the rate charged was to
be *epi drachmēi* – 1 per cent per month (l. 37; above, p. 105). This
and similar evidence undermines Andreyev's argument that deme
credit offered a cheap and liberal alternative to private lending. The
position was, if anything, the reverse, with the informal terms
prevailing in personal loans between *philoi* being seen as preferable
to the stringent conditions imposed by deme institutions. With the
possible exception of the *eranos*-type loans from the Temple of
Nemesis, the conditions of deme credit, where they can be
ascertained, qualify as negative reciprocity, with interest charges
and security requirements as appropriate. This is hardly surprising.
The demesmen were understandably keen to keep their temple funds
intact, and Whitehead (1986: 171–5) has charted the increasing
difficulties they faced in 'balancing the budget'. The stringent
conditions the demes imposed on their borrowers are paralleled in
greater detail in the provisions of their leases. Although there was a
bias towards fellow-demesmen as lessees, there is no hint of easy
terms. In the inscription from Aixone already referred to, the
demesmen insist on their right to summary seizure (*enechurasia*) of the
property of the lessee, should he fail to pay his rent (ll. 6–7, with
Whitehead, 1986: 156–8 for a summary of possible safeguards). The
demes leased and lent how and when it suited them best and were
not responsive to changing patterns of demand, even from their own
demesmen.[16]

Much that has been written about lending by deme institutions could be repeated about other corporate (mainly cultic) bodies, for which the evidence is even more meagre. *Genē* appear on *horoi* nos. 41, 146 and 147 (all cited from Finley 1952); a cult body called the *dekadistai* on no. 32; *thiasōtai* and phratries on nos. 41 and 43; and a tribe on no. 146. In addition, one of the *polētai* inscriptions for 367/6 (see above, p. 62) records the sale of confiscated property on which money was owing to (among others) a phratry and a *koinon* of *orgeōnes*.[17]

Although cult bodies do seem to have lent money to their members, the impact on the overall organization of credit was likely to be slight. All the indications are that the sums loaned out were small. Although only nine figures survive, they present a consistent picture, with only one sum higher than 200 dr. (600 dr. on *horos* no. 41), and another sum as low as 24 dr. (*SEG* xii.100). The median figure is only 130 dr., compared with an overall figure from all equivalent *horoi* of 1,000 (Millett 1982: x). Confirming the small scale of credit operations by cult associations is a fragment of a decree of a society of *orgeōnes*, dating from the early third century B.C. (*Hesperia* x 1941: p. 282, no. 55, with Ferguson 1949: 130–1). The decree records, among other things, the decision of the group to take stock of its finances, drawing up a list of borrowers, amounts owed and, it should be noted, interest payments (ll. 5–8). Although the list itself has not survived, the implication of the remainder of the inscription is that the society possibly had insufficient funds to purchase a single ox. Ferguson (1944: 77–9) identifies this group of *orgeōnes* as being comparatively well-to-do, but estimates the annual income of their society at less than 100 dr. Underfunding was apparently a chronic problem for this kind of association (see Finley 1952: 99 and 288 n. 55). A fragmentary third-century inscription (*IG* ii² 1289) records the decision of a group of arbitrators that a society of *orgeōnes* could not offer its land as security, implying that some of its members wanted to do so (Ferguson 1944: 84–6). A similar story may lie behind two identical boundary-*horoi* (*IG* ii² 2631 and 2632) erected on the land of a cultic group meeting on the twentieth of each month to sacrifice to Apollo, and therefore calling themselves the 'Eikadeis'. The inscriptions read: '*Horos* of the land of the *koinon* of the Eikadeis. Let no one make any loan whatsoever on this land.'[18]

The common picture that emerges for both deme and cultic

associations is of a low level of corporate lending. The fragmentary and unsystematic evidence on which this conclusion has to be based is itself a reflection of the discontinuity of the process. Although the institutions described in this section did have a significant rôle to play in the provision of credit for their members, it was not in any formal, collective sense. They offered instead opportunities for the formation or reinforcing of bonds of *philia* between individual members, opening the way for the reciprocal exchange relationships described in the previous chapter. It may be recalled how Plato's enthusiasm for regular sacrifices by the citizen-body was partly based on the scope it gave for enhanced social contact and co-operation (above, p. 151). For something of the mechanics of the process (and the way in which sand could occasionally clog up the works), there is the near-incomprehensible *Accusation Against the Co-associates for Slander*, attributed to Lysias (VIII).[19]

This speech was not delivered before a jury in a law court, but is a diatribe against the iniquitous behaviour of a group of individuals (*sunousiastai*), from whom the speaker formally dissociates himself (§18). The purpose behind the formation of the group was apparently religious; there is an allusion to a trip to Eleusis (§5). But it was also assumed that the members would informally assist one another in various ways. The speaker contrasts his readiness to help his associates to the best of his ability (§3) with the way in which he has been wronged at every turn. The immediate cause of his indignation was a private transaction between himself and one Polycles, a member of the same society. The speaker apparently lent Polycles twelve minas, and received a horse as security (§10). Perceiving that the horse was on its last legs, he wanted to hand it back to Polycles, but a third member of the group (called Diodorus) reassured him that, whatever happened, Polycles would repay the money. When the horse duly died, Polycles kept the loan, receiving the support of Diodorus and many, if not most, of the co-associates: Autocrates, Thrasymachus, Euryptolemus, Menophilus – the names tumble out as the speaker denounces the whole gang as a pack of conspirators. Though on this occasion the association went sour – and the speaker ends by predicting the break-up of the group (§19) – the assumption was plainly that such a *koinōnia* would strengthen friendships and encourage mutual support. That is the expectation behind the speaker's bitter incoherence.

CHAPTER VIII

Professional money-lending

MONEY-LENDING AND MORAL DEGRADATION

One of Theophrastus' more unpleasant Characters is the 'Man Suffering from *aponoia*' (VI). The word is almost untranslatable: 'desperate boldness' (Healey 1616), 'recklessness' (Jebb 1909), and 'moral insanity' (Theophrast 1897) are at best approximations. Theophrastus himself defines and characterizes *aponoia* as (§§ 1–6)

persisting in degrading language and behaviour. The man who suffers from *aponoia* acts something like this. He will swear an oath on the spot and is prepared to hear himself slandered and abused. In character, he is vulgar (*agoraios*), lacking in decency, and without principle... He is notorious for his activities as inn-keeper, brothel-keeper, and tax farmer. He does not reject any trade as beneath his dignity; rather, he acts as herald, cook or gambles. He does not feed his mother, is arrested for theft, and spends more time in prison than in his own house.

So the man smitten with *aponoia* feels no shame about putting himself beyond the pale of decent society through his repeated contraventions of accepted social norms. Given the nature of Athenian society, some unfortunates were bound to end up as inn-keepers, tax-farmers, and even brothel-keepers; but only a person with a severe personality defect would insist on being them all.[1] Such is the background against which this Character's activities as a money-lender are to be read (§9):

He does not think it beneath himself to lord it over the mass of small traders in the *agora*. He lends them money on the spot, and charges interest of $1\frac{1}{2}$ obols on every drachma each day (= 25 per cent per day). He goes the rounds on the hot food stalls, the fresh and salted fishmongers, collecting his interest from their takings, and putting it straight into his mouth.

Aspects of this man's behaviour invite comment which introduces my investigation of professional money-lending.

179

There is, in the first place, the specialist nature of his lending, to traders in the *agora*. Professional money-lenders were defined above (p. 161) as those who generate all or the bulk of their income from lending at interest. But we have already seen in Chapter v how citizens generally had access to a wide range of sources of credit that was free from interest and formal security requirements. And the previous chapter indicated how irregular lending at interest could have further damped down demand for credit from professional lenders. In addition, the overarching ideology of credit relations, taking its tone from the process of reciprocal exchange, meant that those who habitually lent at interest were regarded with hostility. The cumulative effect was to limit the scope for professional money-lending. In the pages that follow, it will be argued that professional lenders occupied specialist and often peripheral positions in the structure of credit.[2]

The second, associated point arises out of the status as a lender of the man who suffers from *aponoia*. There is a tendency in the modern literature to assimilate all professional (and sometimes non-professional) lenders to the status of bankers, which this Character plainly is not.[3] The fundamental distinction drawn by modern economists between bankers and other types of creditors is the source of their loanable funds. Whereas the majority of professional money-lenders hand out their own funds, bankers have the advantage of being able to draw on their customers' deposits. Although this criterion sets down a broad dividing line between bankers and non-bankers in the modern world, in ancient Athens the distinction seems to have been more complex. If bankers are left out of account, the lenders that remain are capable of further subdivision. The most conspicuous sub-category contains usurers, which, as will be seen below, is where the man afflicted with *aponoia* belongs.

USURY AND USURERS

'The taking of a greater interest than it is usual for men to give and take', is how Jeremy Bentham defines usury in his polemical tract *In Defence of Usury* (1787: 8). But that was not always the meaning of the word; in its original sense all lending at interest was 'usury' (see Palgrave, s.v. 'usury'; Cuq in DS s.v. '*usura*'). As such, it was frowned on by early theologians, acting on the biblical prohibitions of interest, reinforced by Aristotle. By extension, any unequal bargain or sharp practice came to be stigmatized as 'usury'

(Tawney 1926: 157–8). But during the later Middle Ages this wholesale condemnation of the taking of interest was effectively challenged, and it was argued that, under certain circumstances, the exaction of a moderate rate was morally justifiable. It was then that the concept of 'usury' came to be limited in scope to lending at an abnormally high rate of interest – its usual meaning today.[4]

There was in Athens no law restricting the rate of interest (quite the reverse; see above, pp. 49–50). Any person lending money could charge a usurious rate if the circumstances warranted it. A case in point is the loan by the banker Sosinomus and his associate Aristogiton to the spendthrift Aeschines, with which this study began. Billeter correctly identifies the interest of 3 per cent per month as usurious (1898: 20), but the banker and his colleague cannot necessarily be identified as professional usurers. In many societies, a distinct group of money-lenders can be made out, who specialize in loans at excessively high rates of interest. These are the true usurers, and they commonly share other characteristics, all or most of which are displayed by the 'Man suffering from *aponoia*'.

At first sight, the money-lending activities of this Character may seem overdrawn; but the plausibility of his behaviour is confirmed by a series of striking parallels, all associating small-scale traders with short-term borrowing at exorbitant rates of interest. 'Many fish and fruit dealers in [nineteenth-century] Glasgow raised a few shillings for the day's trading by pledging their own blankets', says Tebbutt in her survey of working-class credit (1983: 22); and Billeter supplies similar examples from the market of Les Halles in his own day (1898: 45, n. 4). But even more arresting is the material cited by Alfred Marshall in his text-book discussion of capital and interest:

Again, a pawnbroker's business involves next to no risk; but his loans are generally made at the rate of 25 per cent. per annum or more; the greater part of which is really earnings of management of a troublesome business. Or to take a more extreme case, there are men living in London, and Paris, and probably elsewhere, who make a living by lending to costermongers. The money is often lent at the beginning of the day for the purchase of fruit, etc., and returned at the end of the day when sales are over, at a profit of ten per cent.: there is a little risk in the trade, and the money is seldom lost. (1890: 589)[5]

Here is an occasion on which the modern world provides a helpful analogy for ancient society. While there is an enormous gulf between ancient and modern banking institutions, the gap between loans to market traders in the Athenian *agora* and to costermongers in late-Victorian London is narrow.[6] What is striking here is the way the remaining, fragmentary evidence for usury in Athens reinforces the detail of the composite picture provided by Theophrastus and Marshall: the smallness of the sums involved, the short-term nature of the loans, the ruthless exaction of payment, abnormally high rates of interest, and the low social status of the usurers themselves. We will look at each of these features in turn.

Although it is not stated explicitly that Theophrastus' Character lent only small sums to the stall-holders, it is implied by the context (including the limited capacity of his mouth), and confirmed by comparative material. Other passages link usury with loans of only small sums of money – a clear indication of the petty scale of this branch of credit operations. So Aristotle in his *Nicomachean Ethics*, in a passage examining *aneleutheria* or 'meanness', classes alongside brothel-keepers 'usurers (*tokistai*) lending small sums at high interest' (1121b34). He justifies this linking of pimps with usurers in terms that call to mind Theophrastus' description of *aponoia* (1122a1–3): 'For all of these take more than they ought and from wrong sources. What is common to them is evidently love of sordid gain; they all put up with a bad name for the sake of gain, and little gain at that.' The word used in this passage (*tokistēs*) is not the usual term for 'usurer'; nor are *tokogluphos* ('notcher-upper of interest') or *tokopraktōr* ('interest-extorter') – both noted in Bekker's *Anecdota Graeca* (286.31 and 64.30 ~ *FAC* iiia p. 493 fr. 1165). The common term for 'usurer' is *obolostatēs* or 'lender of obols': the word itself is suggestive of the small scale of usurers' transactions.

In a valuable discussion of the etymology of *obolostatēs*, Korver (1934: 113–18) rightly rejects interpretations of the *obolos* element as referring to a rate of interest.[7] An *obolostatēs* is simply a person who lends out sums so small as to be reckoned (almost) in obols, and, for what it is worth, this interpretation receives a dubious confirmation in the lexica. In the *Etymologicum Magnum*, *obolostatēs* is glossed as 'what Attic writers hyperbolically call those lending small amounts'; but also 'a person who lends small sums to his *philoi*', which shows how erratic entries in the lexica can be. On every occasion the word appears in the surviving literature, it has a pejorative sense, far removed from the idea of lending to friends. The *obolostatēs* in a fragment of Antiphanes' comedy *Neottis* ('The Chick') is characterized as a nasty piece of work, 'unsurpassed in villainy' (*CAF* fr. 168 ~ *FAC* II p. 242 fr. 168). Likewise, in Aristophanes' *Clouds* (ll. 1154–6), Strepsiades' song of triumph is an expression of the joy he feels at the prospect of defrauding his arch-enemies, the *obolostatai*. In the pseudo-Platonic dialogue *Axiochus* (367B, discussed in greater detail below), old age is personified as an *obolostatēs* distraining for a debt. Finally, the speaker in a fragment of Lysias (fr. 45 in Gernet and Bizos 1955–9: II) refers to the calculation of interest at rate much lower than that exacted by the *obolostatai*; and in Aristotle's condemnation of the taking of interest (*Politics* 1258b2), the word chosen to do duty for money-lending in general is *obolostatikē*.[8]

The small-scale loans of the *obolostatai* are closely associated with lending at short term. In more recent societies, small loans at high interest are typically lent for short periods – commonly a week (de Vessilitsky and Bulkley 1916–17: 131). According to de Roover (1948: 124), describing credit in medieval Bruges, the Flemish term for 'usurer', *woekeraer*, was popularly understood as deriving from *woeke* meaning 'week'; and Le Roy Ladurie (1966: 215) gives the seventeenth-century nickname for a usurer as 'Monsieur Dimanche'. In the same study (pp. 125–7), Le Roy Ladurie provides a precise parallel for the behaviour of Theophrastus' Character by giving details of a sixteenth-century usurer who (p. 126), 'practised the cruellest form of usury, lending "from day to day at his pleasure"'. Other evidence suggests that daily lending may have been a regular practice with usurers in the Greek world. Diogenes Laertius (VI.99) cites Hermippus as his authority for describing the third-century philosopher Menippus as *hēmerodaneistēs* – 'a lender by the day: Hermippus says that he was a *hēmerodaneistēs*, and so called'. Although the word occurs only in this passage, that need not imply that the nickname was uniquely applied to Menippus; rather, such behaviour was remarkable in a philosopher (see Chapter II, n. 29). The status of Menippus as a usurious lender is discussed below.

Hand-in-hand with short-term lending goes the rigorous exaction of capital and interest. Again, Theophrastus supplies the model, for his usurer takes no chances, grabbing his interest direct from the traders' tills and stuffing it into his mouth (compare Ar. *Birds* 503). A similar idea underlies the passage from the *Axiochus* attributed to Plato, referred to above, (367B). 'If you are not in a hurry to give up your life as if it were a debt (*hōs chreos*)', says the speaker, 'then nature, just like an *obolostatēs*, takes over and distrains (*enechuriazei*) on your sight, on your hearing – often both of them.' The implication here is that loans from usurers – like good health – are of brief duration, with drastic consequences in the event of default on repayment. Although Photius glosses *obolostatēs* as 'one who lends on pledges *(ep' enechurois)*', there is no classical case of a usurer taking any type of security, as opposed to distraining on the possessions of a defaulting debtor.[9] This is what might be expected. Those who were forced to resort to usurers would typically have no property worth mentioning – like the traders in the *agora* – or possess property that was already fully encumbered in more conventional types of credit transaction. This seems to be the situation envisaged in Aristophanes' *Clouds*, where the whole plot hinges on the assumption that Strepsiades is hopelessly burdened with debts and besieged by creditors. His constant fear is that his creditors will distrain on his property (ll. 34–5 and 239–41, with Finley 1952: 222, n. 6). It is in such a desperate plight, having exhausted all other sources of credit, that a person would be forced to turn to usurers – the *obolostatai* over whom he sings his song of approaching victory.[10]

A final piece of evidence completes this picture of the usurer as a merciless distrainer on the property of defaulting debtors. I have argued elsewhere (Millett 1980) that translators have consistently misunderstood the description of Menippus' money-lending activities, as retold by Diogenes Laertius (see above). Briefly, Menippus is usually presented as accumulating his large fortune by making maritime loans 'by the day' and 'taking security' *(exenechuriazein)*. But neither process is appropriate for the mechanism of maritime credit, where lending was for the length of the voyage. Correctly interpreted – and with a minor alteration to the text – Menippus emerges as a usurer who lends by the day at rates *appropriate to* maritime loans, and relentlessly distrains on the property of his debtors – the natural meaning of *exenechuriazein* (Fine 1951: 61, n. 4).

The maritime rates of interest that Menippus allegedly matched in his landside loans are amongst the highest known from the Greek world (Billeter 1898: 40). When Xenophon wished to emphasize the scale of the financial return to those who made the largest initial contributions to his projected fund for increasing the revenues of Athens, he made a direct comparison with the interest on maritime loans *(Poroi* III.9, with Gauthier 1976: *ad loc.*, and Billeter 1898: 36–8). It hardly needs to be added that the inevitable hallmark of the usurer is the charging of an abnormally high rate of interest

(Arist. *Eth. Nic.* 1121b34; Lysias fr. 45: both cited above).[11] Although no weight can be put on what is a hostile gibe against the unethical behaviour of a philosopher, the range of rates associated with maritime credit for each voyage is broadly comparable with the twenty-five per cent charged each day by Theophrastus' usurer. The exaction of compound interest is often linked with usury, and there are a handful of references from the Greek world (Korver 1934: 121–4; Hommel 1964: 616, n. 1). One passage makes an explicit connexion between usury and compound interest: in the *Clouds* (ll. 1155–6, with Dover 1968: *ad loc.*), Strepsiades celebrates his triumph over the *obolostatai*, their principal (*archaia*) and 'interest on interest' (*tokoi tokōn*). Although there was no known law in Athens against compound interest, it was evidently seen as unethical (Plato, *Laws* 842D, with the comments of Caillemer, DS s.v. '*anatokismos*'). This accounts for its inclusion as one of the anti-social activities of Theophrastus' 'Penurious Man' (*mikrologos*), who is merciless in exacting unpaid debts, on which he charges compound interest (x.10). To complete the picture, he comes round to his debtor's house in the middle of the month to collect a half-obol of interest (§2), but he forbids his wife to lend household goods to the neighbours (§13).[12]

From all this hostile material about interest and its exaction it is an easy step to the low social status of usurers. The loathing with which professional usurers are universally regarded turns them, like Theophrastus' Character suffering from *aponoia*, into social outcasts. Sometimes they are outcasts to begin with: the Jew Shylock is only the best known of a string of usurious stage villains. Stonex (1916) lists more than seventy Elizabethan plays in which usurers appear. As a type, they are shown as having stock characteristics (Wright 1934 and 1938); they are old, gouty, miserly, suffer from dropsy, and are prey to suicide. Draper (1935) argues reasonably enough that this repellent portrayal reflects the attitude of contemporary audiences towards professional usurers. More generally, Bentham asks the question whether, 'among all the instances in which a borrower and a lender of money have been brought together on the stage, from the days of Thespis to the present, there was ever one, in which the former was not recommended to favour in some shape or other, either to admiration or to love, or to pity, or to all three; and the other, the man of thrift, consigned to infamy'. Despite Harpocration's gloss on *obolostatēs*, that the word (and presumably the character) appears frequently in Comedy, only hints have survived to bear out Bentham's complaint and complete the Elizabethan parallels. The unfavourable presentation of usurers in Antiphanes' *Neottis* and Aristophanes' *Clouds* has already been mentioned. There were plays by Alexis and Nicostratus, both entitled *Tokistes* ('The Usurer'), of which the former was subtitled *Katapseudomenos* or 'The Liar' (see above, p. 5). Although it may be a coincidence, on the one occasion we are told anything about the origins of a stage usurer, he turns out to be an outsider and a non-Greek. According to Athenaeus (xv.685e ~ *FAC* ii p. 38 fr. 25), Alexis depicted his usurer as an Egyptian. It may be to this play that Plutarch refers in his essay 'How the young should understand poetry', where he quotes a few lines from an anonymous comedy, adding the comment: 'These are bad sentiments, and false too... well suited to an old usurer (*tokogluphos*).' Finally, and from outside Comedy, the speaker in the pseudo-Platonic *Alcibiades* (ii.149E) warns that the gods are not to be won over with gifts, 'like a wicked usurer (*kakon tokistēn*)'.

High rates of interest combined with ruthless exaction of monies owed create the impression that usurers must have been persons of great wealth, if only to compensate for their poor standing in the community. In fact, small-scale lending has seldom been the profitable business it appears, and high rates of interest are more an indication of risks and administrative costs than excessive profits. In a theoretical study concerned with modern rural credit, but applicable to small-scale lending in all societies, Bottomley (1963b) sets out how the small size of loans, lending at short term, and high risk of default all push up costs to the lender. To go back to the past, the *Monts-de-Piété* of medieval Bruges were intended to undercut professional lenders by loaning out small sums to the deserving poor on a non-profit-making basis. But the high costs of administering these small loans made it impossible to reduce the annual rate of interest below 15 per cent (de Roover 1948: 130–1; for similar problems facing modern pawnbrokers, see Tebbutt 1983: 8–9 and 128–30). Returning to the passage from Marshall's *Principles of Economics* which began this examination of Athenian usurers, the paragraph continues:

Now a farthing invested at ten per cent. a day would amount to a billion pounds at the end of a year. But no one can become rich by lending to costermongers; because no one can lend much in this way. The so-called interest on loans really consists almost entirely of earnings of a kind for which few capitalists have a taste.

Although evidence for Athens is almost entirely lacking, Theophrastus' usurer looks less like a billionaire and more like a hustler. It
seems a reasonable assumption that Athenian usurers were like the
rest in having a level of wealth appropriate to their low social
standing.

Despite the scattering of ancient material about usurers, its
concentration does produce a coherent picture which is consistent
with what is known about usurious lending in other times and
places: small sums at short term for non-productive purposes. In
modern macro-economic terms of the volume of credit and its
impact on the economy as a whole, this type of lending is
insignificant; which presumably accounts for its relative neglect by
economists and even historians (Hudson 1982: 13–19). But however
narrow its economic effect, it is now appreciated that the social
significance of petty credit can be disproportionally great – and here
comparative material is particularly suggestive. In recent times,
large numbers of people towards the bottom end of society have
depended on the easy availability of small loans to even out receipts
of income from one week to the next (Bosanquet 1896; de Vessilitsky
and Bulkley 1916–17; Minkes 1953: 15–16). In two recent studies,
Tebbutt (1983) and Johnson (1985: esp. 144–92) have documented
the heavy reliance of working-class families on credit, and the variety
of sources available to them. Apart from the inevitable pawnbrokers,
the cast of characters includes 'dolly-shopmen', 'tally-men', 'scotch
drapers', 'knick-knack men', and 'Johnny Fortnights', collectively
making up their own hierarchy of working-class credit.[13] In
aggregate, all this adds up to a near-astronomical number of loan
transactions. The most closely regulated (and therefore the best
documented branch) of this undergrowth of credit was pawnbroking.
Statistics gathered by Johnson (1985: 168–70) suggest that at their
height, before the First World War, pawnshops took in over the year
a total of 230 million pledges. Such a figure implies that, on average,
every working-class family in Britain made at least one pledge per
fortnight. Other sub-species of working-class credit are by their
nature unquantifiable. But, basing his calculation on the number of
plaints for the recovery of small debts entered in the county courts,
Johnson (1985: 163–5) estimates that on average, in the last decade
of the nineteenth century, one in five working-class families in the
north of England was sued for debt in the course of a year.

Impressive as these figures are, they refer to the working class in
a capitalist society, and are part of a substructure of credit which

cannot be transferred bodily over to ancient Athens. It cannot be coincidental that the rise of pawnbroking in Britain paralleled the growth of urban, industrial communities. Johnson (1985: 170) shows how pawnshops were thickest on the ground in those areas closely associated with the industrial revolution. Pawnbroking and the other types of working-class credit listed above are perhaps best understood as urban alternatives for the informal sources of credit available in rural communities – a substitute, however inadequate, for 'the world they had lost' (Laslett 1983: 79).[14] It was argued in an earlier chapter (p. 35) that classical Athens was remarkable for the extent to which, as a pre-industrial city, it preserved communal networks of credit relations. And yet, no matter how finely spun the safety-net of kinship and community support, there were always individuals who would fall through the net, or miss it altogether. Identification of these people involves speculation, but they presumably included those at the margins of Athenian society: the poorest inhabitants, whose family and friends (if they had any) were as badly-off as they were. In particular, there were the metics, for whom there was no cushion of public pay, and who might miss the range of contact available to most citizens. That perhaps represents the reality behind Theophrastus' usurer lending to traders in the *agora*.

PROFESSIONAL MONEY-LENDERS AND MARITIME LOANS

The thirty-fourth speech in the Demosthenic corpus (*Against Phormion*) is delivered by the joint lenders in a maritime loan, who claim that the borrower has tried to defraud them.[15] The speech ends with an appropriate peroration, urging on the jurors the importance for all concerned of protecting lenders against unscrupulous borrowers (§51):

For you hold that such people not only wrong those who have dealings with them, but also more generally harm your exchange (*emporion*), and that is quite correct. For the resources (*euporiai*) of those involved in trade (*tois ergazomenois*) come not from those who borrow (*tōn daneizomenōn*) but from those who lend (*tōn daneizontōn*); and neither ship nor ship's captain, nor passenger can put to sea if you take away the part contributed by those who lend (*tōn daneizontōn*).

Our immediate concern is not with the accuracy or otherwise of this statement; though it will emerge later that maritime credit was important enough for the jury to pardon the obvious exaggeration.

What matters here is the neutral vocabulary of maritime lending, expressed as part of the verb *daneizein* (see above, p. 28). Usurers and bankers are identified in our sources by their distinctive terminology. But there existed a third group of professional lenders, whose operations were above the petty level of usurers, and who did not offer the services associated with Athenian bankers.[16] Their apparent elusiveness is not merely a matter of terminology. Whereas usurers, thanks to human frailty, find a precarious place in many societies, and bankers provided a range of facilities besides credit, these other professional lenders were pressured and squeezed by aspects of Athenian society already discussed. The prevailing mentality limited the opportunities for lending in productive credit operations where there was no obvious exploitation of the borrower's misfortune. As indicated by the passage quoted above, the exception was the area of maritime credit, which did offer scope for large-scale lending at interest. In this section I will try to demonstrate the overlap between maritime loans and professional money-lending.[17]

The general principles of the maritime loan are straightforward. In order to pay for the cargo being taken on board ship, the merchant (*emporos*) or shipowner (*nauklēros*) borrowed money for the duration of the trading voyage, which could be either one-way (*heteroplous*) or a return trip (*amphoteroplous*). The loan and interest were repaid out of the proceeds of the sale of the cargo, but only on condition that the ship arrived safely at its destination. That is the crucial point about maritime loans, making them different from all other types of loan transaction: if, as the result of shipwreck or piracy, the ship and its cargo were lost, the borrower was freed from all obligation to repay the loan, and the loss was borne by the lender. Because of the risks involved, the rates of interest charged on these voyages were high; anything from $12\frac{1}{2}$ to 30 per cent, per voyage, and perhaps even higher. The sums of money borrowed were substantial, ranging from 1,000 to at least 4,500 dr., with a median value of 3,000 dr. As a partial safeguard against fraud on the part of the borrower, the cargo was offered as security; were the borrower the shipowner, the ship itself could be pledged as security. As a further safeguard against fraud, there was usually a written contract, setting out in some detail the terms and conditions of the agreement.

The evidence on maritime loans is concentrated in four speeches from the Demosthenic corpus, dating from the third quarter of the fourth century (Dem. XXXII, [Dem.] XXXIV, [Dem.] XXXV and [Dem.] LVI). All four cases arose out of the allegedly fraudulent failure of the borrower to repay his loan. What is striking about these speeches is the number of other loans that crop up casually as the speaker presents the facts of the case. Taken together, the four speeches contain allusions to at least twenty separate maritime loans, all having some bearing on the speakers' cases. A few of these loans may be rhetorical inventions designed to bolster up the litigant's case. Even so, the speaker would presumably take care to mirror actual practice in order to avoid raising the suspicions of the jury; the speeches therefore give good indications of the relative frequency of maritime loans.

Apart from this heavy concentrate of maritime credit in traders' speeches, there are scattered references in other speeches that have little or nothing to do with trade. In all, there are at least three references to specific loan transactions (Isoc. xvii.42; [Dem.] xxxiii.4; [Dem.] lii.20), and a further three to individuals lending money in maritime loans (Lysias xxxii.6; Dem. xxvii.11; Hyperides, *Against Demosthenes* fr. iv, col. 17). There are also casual mentions of maritime loans outside the Orators. The 'Boastful Man' in the *Characters* (xxiii.2) brags about the amount of money he has tied up in trading voyages and gives details of his profits and losses. According to Diogenes Laertius (vii.13), it was rumoured that the philosopher Zeno of Citium had more than a thousand talents which he lent out in maritime loans. There are even a couple of references in Comedy to maritime loans (Diphilus *CAF* fr. 43 ~ *FAC* iiia p. 114 fr. 43 ll. 18–22; Scholion to Eupolis, *Marikas*, *P.Oxy.* 2741, with Harvey 1976). Finally Xenophon argues in his *Poroi* (iii.9) that one of his schemes for increasing the revenue of Athens will bring in a return comparable to the profit on maritime loans (*hōsper nautikon*).

That allusion to maritime credit in the *Poroi* is remarkable for its brevity. Xenophon's readers (none of whom would be actively involved in trade) were expected to grasp the significance of a two-word comparison between his own money-making scheme, and the mechanism of maritime loans. The same goes for the other casual references to maritime credit in the literature. Writers and speakers apparently relied on the assumption that the general principles of maritime loans were familiar to all Athenians. Even in the four central speeches, there is no summary of the workings of maritime credit for the benefit of the jury. This may be contrasted with the laboured description of something resembling a letter of credit included in a speech of Isocrates (xvii.35–7). The implication is that whereas the jurors were unfamiliar with the concept of a paper transference of funds (above, p. 8), they knew all about maritime loans.[18]

Although quantification is out of the question, evidence for the familiarity of maritime loans strengthens the impression that they financed a significant proportion of Athens' overseas trade. With interest rates running as high as thirty per cent for a single voyage, the scope was there for people to make a living by lending in maritime credit.[19] Encouraging the participation of professional lenders in maritime loans were three ancillary factors, each involving a different aspect of status.

First comes the status of the loans themselves. If maritime loans were not positively productive in the narrow, neo-classical sense (borrowing from a position of strength), they did at least offer the borrower a return on his money, making the taking of interest appear less reprehensible. Far from the lender exploiting the borrower's misfortune, the peculiar mechanism of maritime loans meant he would share in it.[20] Secondly, there was the dubious status of the borrowers, making it less of a moral issue whether they were forced to pay abnormally high rates of interest. The long-running debate over the distribution between citizen and non-citizen traders is probably insoluble, but it can be sidestepped.[21] Those Athenians who were actively involved in maritime trade were generally of low status; and the few who are known to have been comparatively wealthy were not influential in the sense of being actively involved in politics. In an emotional sense they were something less than full citizens, as their contacts and commitments outside the *polis* were perceived as weakening their ties with Athens (McKechnie 1989: 178–203). To anticipate the provocative boast of Diogenes the Cynic, they were on the way to becoming *kosmopolitai* – 'citizens of the world'. In fact, the world to which they most closely belonged – that of the Piraeus – had its own peculiar character. The rich mixture of non-Athenians resident in the Piraeus from the fourth century onwards has been documented by Garland (1987: 58–68). A more radical theory has been developed by von Reden (1978: esp. 66–72), who sees in the Piraeus a 'world apart' from the *polis*, where untraditional attitudes towards work and wealth were able to flourish. Serving as a symbol for this alternative ideology are the 'men from the Piraeus' to whom Aeschines is supposed to have turned after exhausting all the sources of credit normally available to an Athenian citizen. The implication is that they would consider lending to a person who had put himself outside the community of the *polis* (above, p. 3). As it happened, according to Lysias, the men in the Piraeus refused to lend to Aeschines, reckoning he was a worse risk than financing a voyage into the notoriously stormy Adriatic. This serves to introduce my third aspect of status: that of the lenders, who needed to have the standing of experts in the area of maritime trade. Given the high risk of maritime credit for the lender, they would need to have the knowledge to assess the relative dangers of a voyage, and arrive at an appropriate rate of interest.

Turning to the evidence for lenders appearing in maritime loans, our expectations of professionalism and expertise are largely fulfilled. The only citizen with a casual interest in maritime credit is Demosthenes' father who, at the time of his death, had the substantial sum of 7,000 dr. lent out in maritime loans (Dem. XXVII.11). Demosthenes describes this money as being deposited 'with Xuthus' (*para Xouthōi*). The sum was presumably made up of a plurality of loans, and Bogaert (1965: 141–6) plausibly identifies Xuthus as a middleman with the specialist skill necessary to look after Demosthenes Senior's maritime interests. Other occasional lenders all seem to be actively involved in trade and would therefore know what they were about. In the speech *Against Phormion* ([Dem.] XXXIV.6), there are two casual lenders: Theodorus the Phoenician and Lampis the *nauklēros*, who was probably a slave (§5). Both lent on the outward voyage only, and both travelled with the ship. The circumstantial detail in the speech *Against Lacritus* ([Dem.] XXXV.6–9) suggests that Androcles and Nausicrates were not professional lenders, but Androcles is definitely a trader. The borrowers in *Against Dionysodorus* ([Dem.] LVI.17) are accused by their creditors of appropriating the loan and using it to lend in maritime loans of their own.

The largest group of identifiable maritime creditors are professional lenders, all having some personal experience of the practicalities of maritime trade. The best documented example is the unnamed speaker in the speech *Against Apaturius* ([Dem.] XXXIII.4), who gives a brief account of himself:

I have been involved in maritime trade for a long time now, and up to a certain time risked the sea in my own person. Almost seven years ago, I gave up voyaging, and having made a moderate sum of money, I try to put it to work in maritime loans (*nautikois ergazesthai*).

Chrysippus, in the speech with which this section began ([Dem.] XXXIV.I) claims that he and his partner have frequented the *emporion* or trading area for many years, and have made many maritime loans (*sumbolaia pollois sumballontes*), without ever being involved in a court case. Similarly, Darius opens his speech *Against Dionysodorus* ([Dem.] LVI) by referring to 'those of us who are involved in maritime trade and put our money in the hands of other people'. From an earlier date (*c.* 410), I include in this group Diodotus, whose estate is the subject of Lysias' *Against Diogiton* (XXXII.6). Diodotus made a large fortune in trade, and when he died his estate was worth at least fifteen talents, of which seven talents and forty minas were lent out in maritime loans (above, p. 168). That is by far the largest single component in the estate and easily justifies Diodotus' inclusion as a professional lender.[22]

Although the opportunities for professional lenders lay overwhelmingly with maritime credit, they could extend their operations to landside loans, should the occasion arise. The speech *Against Apaturius* (see above) arose out of a dispute over a non-maritime loan made by the speaker.[23] Although the 'men in the Piraeus' are supposed to have refused to lend to Aeschines the Socratic, it was apparently worthwhile making the approach (or alleging an approach had been made). But by far the best-documented case of a professional money-lender covering both maritime and landside loans occurs in Demosthenes' speech *Against Pantaenetus* (XXXVII). The passage in question is remarkable in that the speaker, Nicobulus, is not accusing his opponent of being a money-lender, but anticipating that attack against himself (§§52–4):

When anyone asks him [Pantaenetus], 'What valid case will you be able to make against Nicobulus?', he says, 'The Athenians hate those who lend money (*tous daneizontas*); Nicobulus is an unpleasant person; he walks fast and carries a cane. All these things (he says) count in my favour.' He is not ashamed to talk in this way, and also imagines that those hearing him do not understand that this is the reasoning not of one who has suffered wrong, but a malicious accuser. For my part, I do not think that a man who lends money (*tōn daneizontōn*) necessarily does wrong, although some of these people are rightly hated by you – those who make a trade (*technēn*) of the business, with no thought of helping or of anything else other than gain. Since I myself have often borrowed money, and not only lent it to my opponent, I know these people well, and I do not like them. But, by Zeus, I certainly do not rob them or bring malicious charges against them. But if a man has traded as I have, making voyages and facing dangers, and having made a small amount of money makes these loans (*edaneise tauta*), wishes not only to oblige people (*charisasthai*), but also to prevent his money being imperceptibly frittered away, why should you set him down as belonging to them? Unless, that is, you mean this, that whoever lends to you ought to be hated by the public.

Read for me the depositions showing what sort of man I am to those who lend money and to those who need help.

Translations of this passage do not always reflect the subtlety of Nicobulus' argument. *Tous daneizontas* of the opening sentence should not be rendered as 'money-lenders', with its overtones of professionalism. The phrase is deliberately neutral – 'those lending money'. In this way, the speaker manipulates the terminology of credit to suggest a flaw in his opponent's argument. The point may be paraphrased as follows. Pantaenetus claims that the Athenians hate money-lenders in general, but this is wide of the mark. As you are all aware, only a distinct group of those lending money are worthy of this condemnation, and I am not one of them.

In his anxiety to distance himself from this type of professional lender, Nicobulus reverts to the idealized view of credit relations. Those who are persuaded to loan money by the prospect of gain, which they raise to the level of a trade (*technē*), ignore the proper motivation, which is showing fellow-feeling (*sungnōmē*). But this is allegedly not the case with Nicobulus, for he claims to make his loans only to 'oblige' people. The key word here is *charisasthai* – a form of the verb from *charis* (above, pp. 123–6). Although the charging of interest can hardly be reconciled with the concept of *charis*, Nicobulus slides over the difficulty by claiming to make a charge (the word *tokos* is tactfully avoided) only by way of preserving intact his hard-won gains. Nicobulus' mention of 'those who make a trade' of lending money is perhaps the most explicit evidence we have for a group of professional lenders in Athens. In spite of his protestations to the contrary, there is a strong presumption that Nicobulus was himself a member of that group. Apart from his protesting too much, there are several inconsistencies in his argument. As we shall see, the account he gives of himself does not square with the description of his activities in the body of the speech.[24]

Pantaenetus purchased an ore-crushing mill (*ergastērion*) and slaves from one Telemachus for an unnamed price. He raised a part of the cash required by 'selling' the plant *epi lusei* ('with right of redemption') to Mnesicles for sixty minas, and the slaves to Phileas and Plistor for forty-five minas. Pantaenetus subsequently paid off this set of creditors by supplanting them with Euergus and Nicobulus. In effect, Pantaenetus was established as tenant of the *ergastērion*, paying rent-interest of 1 per cent per month to two successive sets of owners. The case ultimately arose out of Pantaenetus' failure to keep up the interest payments. The *ergastērion* and slaves are to be seen as the security in a loan that was sought to effect their purchase. In this respect, the transaction is remarkable in resembling a modern mortgage, and therefore approximates to a productive loan (see Chapter III, n. 11). Although it may be potentially misleading to generalize from a single passage, the rich detail of the speech as a whole does respond to a closer analysis.[25]

There is an obvious pointer in the size of the sum loaned, which is some 30 per cent larger than the highest figure on any surviving *horos*. To give some impression of the exceptional scale of the loan for 10,500 dr. secured by Pantaenetus, the median figure for all *prasis epi lusei* transactions inscribed on the *horoi* is only 1,100 dr. A crude calculation from the private orations of Demosthenes gives a median figure for all landside loans anywhere between 1,000 and 1,700 dr.[26] It was possibly the abnormal size of the loan that called for a plurality of creditors at each successive stage of the operation (§§4, 5, 7 and 11–13); at least two of the co-creditors are thought to come from families containing liturgists (Phileas, *APF* 4610; Euergus, *APF* 7094). The reason for the transference of 'ownership' of *ergastērion* and slaves from Mnesicles and his associates to Nicobulus and Euergus is not explicitly stated, though there is a strong hint of a quarrel. Nicobulus claims that he realized the sort of man Pantaenetus was when (§15), 'at the outset, he made charges to us against Mnesicles'. Had Mnesicles and his fellow-creditors exercised their right to withdraw from agreement, Pantaenetus would then have been faced with the urgent problem of raising a replacement loan. A professional money-lender would be an appropriate source to tap under these circumstances – an unusually large sum of money, needed at short notice, for a productive purpose.

Little can be said about the personal relationship between Pantaenetus and his creditors, and between the co-creditors themselves. That is particularly unfortunate in the case of Euergus as he provided the larger slice of the loan; it would be helpful to be able to define his standing as a creditor. The only clue lies in Nicobulus' claim that Pantaenetus and Euergus were once the

closest of friends (§15). There is no way in which the truth behind
this statement can be checked, and the evidence of other speeches
suggests it was a common rhetorical ploy to blacken the character of
an opponent by showing him as abusing the trust of his friends. From
what is said elsewhere, it may be tentatively inferred that the
relationship between Nicobulus and Euergus as co-creditors was
loose and *ad hoc*. Nicobulus certainly appears to be ready to throw his
partner to the wolves in order to save his own skin, arguing at one
point that if Euergus was justly found guilty in an earlier brush with
Pantaenetus, then justice had already been done, and there was no
case to answer (§8). A little later (§10), he says he does not relish the
idea of managing the *ergastērion* with Euergus as his partner. But both
statements could be intended for rhetorical effect.

The impressions that the reader takes away from the Pantaenetus
case are inevitably one-sided and misleading. Even so, Nicobulus
cannot conceal that his deal with Pantaenetus does not correspond
with the apologetic account he gives of his own activities as a lender.
The appropriate conclusion seems to be that Nicobulus is indeed one
of those people who 'make a trade of the business' of lending money.
That is my warrant for including him as a representative of
professional money-lending in Athens.

In the course of his speech, Nicobulus chooses to tell the jury
something about his other business activities. In the passage quoted
above he claims to have made a small amount of money by 'making
voyages and facing dangers'; elsewhere in the speech he gives further
details. As soon as the agreement about the *ergastērion* had been
drawn up between Pantaenetus on the one side, and Nicobulus and
Euergus on the other, Nicobulus sailed for the Pontus. He describes
himself as returning (§10), 'having lost practically everything I had
when I sailed', only to find that, in his absence, his joint agreement
with Pantaenetus had fallen through. Though Nicobulus is not
crystal-clear about his activities as a lender in maritime loans, there
is an obvious parallel with the speaker in the Apaturius case (above,
pp. 192–3), lending out the profits he has made through active
involvement in trade. It may be material that Nicobulus made his
disastrous voyage to the Pontus in the month of Elaphebolion (§6),
before the beginning of the sailing season (de Ste Croix 1974: 43,
n. 8). His loan to Pantaenetus could be evidence for what lenders in
maritime loans tried to do with their money in their winter months,
when the seas were closed to shipping.[27]

BANKERS AND CREDIT

Part of the sixth book of Athenaeus' *Deipnosophistae* (see above, p. 1)
is given over to a denunciation of the iniquitous behaviour of
fishmongers. As evidence against them, one of the diners quotes from
a lost comedy of Antiphanes called *Misoponeros* or 'The Hater of
Rogues' (226d ~ *CAF* fr. 159 ~ *FAC* II p. 238 fr. 159):

A. And are not the Scythians wise indeed? For as soon as their children are
  born, they give them the milk of mares and cows to drink.
B. And, by Zeus, they don't bring in to look after them malignant nurses
  or, later on, pedagogues; there could be no greater pests.
A. Excepting midwives, by Zeus, because they are in a class by themselves.
B. And excepting the begging priests of Cybele; for they are by far the
  foulest breed of all.
A. Unless, by Zeus, you want to call fishmongers the foulest.
B. But only after bankers (*trapezitai*): there is no more pestilential tribe
  than theirs.

This passage is unique in the surviving literature in its hostility
towards bankers as a type; all other accusations involve individuals
(Bogaert 1968: 393–5). In view of the antipathy expressed elsewhere
towards professional money-lenders, this absence of attacks on
bankers seems paradoxical. But the paradox may be resolved by a
closer examination of the functions of Athenian bankers and their
location within the economy and society of the *polis*. That is the task
of the present and following sections of this chapter. I take as my
point of departure the disquiet expressed in the opening chapter (see
above, p. 15) over the established studies of Greek banking by
Bogaert.

Bogaert's analysis of banks and bankers in the ancient world is
dominated by modern banking theory. This is made explicit in a
chapter about the problem of definition with which he prefaces his
earlier study of the origins of deposit banking (1966: 26–31).
Modern authorities on banking apparently agree that the operations
essential to true deposit banking (also called 'credit banking' and
'commercial banking') are acceptance of deposits and extension of
credit (1966: 28–9). There is, however, disagreement as to which of
these operations is of greater significance. It is Bogaert's opinion that
the primary function of a bank is to furnish credit; an opinion
shared, he adds, by the exponents of banking he has personally
consulted. It would not much matter, provided Bogaert were

concerned with settling a definition simply as a piece of convenient shorthand. But, as one reviewer justly remarked (Seager 1967: 378), almost any theory about the chronological and geographical origins of the bank could be supported by the choice of an appropriate definition. And these preoccupations are carried over into Bogaert's broader study of Greek banking (1968), where special emphasis is laid on credit as 'l'opération essentielle' (p. 307). These are the terms of reference for the handful of pages (pp. 367–75) that Bogaert devotes to assessing the significance of banking within Athenian society. To add to the difficulties, his investigation is conducted in pseudo-statistical terms that only serve to illustrate the limitations of a quantitative analysis.

The section on 'Banques et crédit à Athènes' is divided by Bogaert into three subsections: the percentage of their fortunes that Athenians lent at interest; the proportion of wealthy Athenians with bank accounts; and the relationship between the average sums lent out in the various types of credit transactions. Of these, the first issue is quickly dealt with and had, in any case, no direct bearing on banking. Bogaert argues that, as the fourth century wore on, there was a tendency for wealthy Athenians to lend out an increasing proportion of their liquid assets (Bogaert 1968: 368–9). The conclusion is based on a breakdown of the estates of Diodotus, Demosthenes the elder, Nicias, Lysias and Stratocles; but, with the possible exception of Stratocles (Isaeus XI.42–3; see above, p. 167), all these holdings were demonstrably untypical. As we have seen, Diodotus and Demosthenes the elder possessed next to no real property (above, pp. 168–9), the wealth of Nicias derived in large part from the silver mines (Chapter VII, n. 14 with *APF* 10808 A), while Lysias was not even an Athenian citizen (Chapter VIII, no. 13). No more persuasive is Bogaert's broader conclusion that in the course of the fourth century Athenians in general and merchants in particular made increasing use of bank accounts, and turned more frequently to bankers for loans (1968: 370). That merchants were regular customers of Athenian bankers cannot be denied (see below, pp. 207–17). But the handful of references supplied by Bogaert hardly lend themselves to a *dynamic* analysis of change over time.

Deserving more detailed criticism is Bogaert's estimate of the proportion of the Athenian population making use of banks (1968: 370–2). The argument runs as follows. The sources give figures for ten bank loans, averaging 2,250 dr. (p. 370, n. 391); around 370,

Pasion had out on loan a minimum of fifty talents (Dem. XXXVI.5);
the assumption that this sum was made up of loans of average size
gives a total of 133 borrowers as customers of Pasion's bank. There
were at this time at least seven other bankers operating in Athens
(Bogaert 1968: 86); assuming that they did half as much business as
Pasion (p. 371, n. 397), Bogaert suggests a grand total of 750 clients
borrowing from Athenian banks. In order to borrow the average
sum of 2,250 dr., individuals would have to match their debts with
equivalent security. According to the calculations of Cavaignac
(1923: 60–1), in 378/7 as many as 11,500 citizens possessed property
worth 2,500 dr. or more; to this figure, Bogaert adds an estimated
3,000 wealthy metics. From the combined total he concludes that
about 5 per cent of the better-off in Athens ('la population aisée')
borrowed from banks at any one time (1968: 371). In the absence of
usable figures, Bogaert goes on to estimate that a further 5 per cent
would have had deposits with bankers. Accepting a figure of 80,000
for the combined populations of the city of Athens and the Piraeus
(p. 371, n. 398, following Gomme 1933: 46–7), he arrives at a final
figure of one inhabitant in fifty having either an account with, or a
loan from, a banker.

Bogaert rounds off his calculation by citing analogous figures from
medieval Bruges (one in thirty-five to fifty), Venice (one in thirty)
and Barcelona (one in fifteen), taken from studies by de Roover
(1948: 250–4) and Usher (1943: 181). He concludes on the strength
of this comparison: 'Le chiffre que nous avons obtenu par estimation
pour Athènes n'est donc pas exagéré et paraît acceptable, mais nous
devons en souligner le caractère hypothétique' (Bogaert 1968:
371–2). That is something of an understatement. Hardly any of the
figures involved in arriving at the estimate are entirely free from
suspicion and several are no better than educated guesses. Although
the biases are random and to some extent cancel each other out, the
final figure of one client per fifty inhabitants is almost certainly on
the high side.

Several of the sums cited by Bogaert as bankers' loans are of
doubtful status (p. 370, n. 391, where Dem. 52.9 is an error for
53.9). At least three (Isoc. XVII.38, [Dem.] XXXIII.7 and Dem.
XLV.28) do not concern citizens or metics and should therefore be
omitted from Bogaert's calculation. But removal of three figures
from a series of ten lessens the likelihood that the average will have
any meaning. Moreover, Bogaert's choice of the arithmetic mean as

a representative figure raises its own difficulties. Unlike the median, the mean tends to give disproportionate weight to unrepresentative figures at either extreme of the series. Using Bogaert's own figures, the median value for bankers' loans works out at 1,550 dr. – appreciably lower than his average of 2,250 dr. Were there really seven other bankers in Athens 'vers la même époque'? A footnote (p. 371 n. 395) refers the reader to a list of bankers known for the period 394–370, but there is no evidence that all these banks were operating simultaneously. In a separate study (1974), Bogaert has shown how suddenly Athenian bankers could go out of business. The assumption that these other bankers each handled half as many clients as Pasion is, as Bogaert readily concedes, only a guess. On his own reckoning (1986a: 42–7), Pasion was far and away the richest man in Athens at the time. Finally, I do not follow the argument that bankers' customers would have to possess property worth at least 2,250 dr. to cover the average size of the loan. The minimum qualification should presumably correspond to the lowest figure in the series, which is 100 dr. Gomme's estimates of Athenian population are, of course, controversial; even more speculative are Cavaignac's figures for wealthy Athenians.

This catalogue of doubts and queries should make it clear why Bogaert's estimate (however tentative) is to be rejected. If I seem to have dissected his arguments in greater detail than they deserve, it is because this kind of juggling with figures may be thought by some readers to be representative of ancient economic history. Although potentially among the most important, these few pages must be the weakest in Bogaert's book; and yet I am aware of only one reviewer who has expressed even mild misgivings. Pleket (1971: 435) warns that the passage of time tends to turn hypotheses into hard fact. Bogaert's figures have certainly been cited as evidence that Greek banking was more developed than is commonly imagined (Andreau 1977: 1134–5).

The material that Bogaert (1968: 372–3) supplies on the relative size of loans in different types of transaction is less controversial, and his findings may be presented in summary form:

	Secured by land		Maritime loans	Banks	Others
	Orators	*Horoi*			
Average	1,300	1,500	2,600	2,250	1,380

The figures are in drachmas and the average is again the arithmetic mean. There are additional grounds for uncertainty in that Bogaert's choice of figures for inclusion seems sometimes to be arbitrary. It is admittedly difficult to classify material where the circumstantial evidence is limited, but errors can be kept to a minimum by leaving out all sums of dubious status. For example, although Bogaert claims to omit all *eranos*-loans from the category of 'other loans', that is probably the explanation behind the talent loaned out by Demosthenes Senior in parcels of 200 and 300 dr. (see above, p. 157). Leaving these sums out of account raises the mean to 1,830 dr.

In line with Bogaert's questionable methodology are the uneven conclusions with which the section closes (p. 373). Though he is undoubtedly correct to see credit in general as flourishing in Athens, and the rôle of banks as providers of credit coming second to that of private lenders, these conclusions could have been reached without analysis of averages and proportions. But with another of Bogaert's concluding points, disagreement must be fundamental: debtors in general were *not* restricted to 'la classe aisée de la ville', (pp. 373–4). Apart from the in-built bias of the Orators towards the affairs of the wealthy (see Chapter II, n. 16), Bogaert's coverage of different types of credit is patchy. By ignoring *eranos*- and even non-monetary loans, whole areas open to poorer borrowers are left out of account. Nor is it possible to agree with his assumption that the average size of loans is an indicator of the minimum amount of property an individual must possess in order to furnish adequate security. Although this point has already been raised above in connexion with bank loans, it is doubly relevant to loans secured by real property (pp. 372–3). Bogaert assumes that, as security offered had to be twice the value of the loan (possible, but by no means inevitable), this branch of credit would be restricted to citizens possessing property worth more than 2,600 or 3,000 dr. But the *horoi* themselves show that loans of sums below 500 dr. were regularly secured by real property; while the fixing of a median value for all relevant *horoi* at 1,000 dr. (Millett 1982: x) means that approximately half the sums loaned must have been at or below this figure. Loans secured by real property were doubtless difficult for poor citizens, but the property qualification implied by Bogaert is certainly too high.

All these criticisms give a fair indication why, in spite of its many virtues, Bogaert's study is inadequate as a history of Greek banking. As a discriminating collection of source and secondary material, the book could hardly be bettered; but it contains no sustained discussion of the place of banking in Athenian economy and society.

What follows tries to make good that omission, beginning with the background to bankers' credit.

It must be made clear that Bogaert does not let his modern frame of reference push him into modernist conclusions about the mechanisms of ancient banking. Besides the rejection of cheques and giro-payments as anachronistic (pp. 338–45), he comes down firmly on the side of bankers' credit as essentially non-productive (pp. 356–7): a valuable corrective to the view prevailing among his predecessors (Hasebroek 1920: 160; Knorringa 1926: 88; Westermann 1930: 43). It is therefore ironic that so much of the post-Bogaert literature on Athenian banking has been devoted to proving that bank loans were, after all, typically productive. Gluskina (1970) argues that bankers took an active part in financing trade and production within Attica, protesting that (p. 43): 'The prevalence of this sort of lending in fourth-century Attica has not been appreciated.' A later paper (1974: 127) suggests that she reached this conclusion by redefining the concept of productive credit (see Appendix III). A similar technique is adopted by Thompson (1979a: 230–3), who resorts to special pleading to argue that 'commercial loans' were the commonest form of bank credit. Thompson also takes issue (pp. 233–7) with the convincing demonstration by Bogaert (1965) that bankers played no part in providing maritime loans. Again, this involves the strained re-interpretation of what is probably not a maritime loan ([Dem.] XXXIII.4–8; see my note 23 in this chapter). No more persuasive are the inconclusive passages cited by Erxleben (1974: 490–4).[28]

There are difficulties of a different sort about Humphrey's suggestion (1970: 152–3) that Athenian banks acted like their modern counterparts in reconciling discrepancies between lenders' and borrowers' needs, thereby bridging the gap between 'social' and productive credit. She cites the example of a man's deposit with a banker being lent in a maritime loan, with the possibility of the banker making a loan to his client to fund a liturgy payment. For further information, the reader is referred to the study by Bogaert (1968), where it is explicitly stated that there is no known case of a banker lending money in a maritime loan. Finally, there is an equally unsupported argument by Andreau (1977) which by implication favours productive investment by bankers. According to Andreau (pp. 1145–6), Finley has in his *Ancient Economy* (1985b: 141) misapplied Bogaert's study of banking by ignoring as a possible source of potential credit, the direct investment by bankers of their clients' deposits in existing commercial enterprises. In fact, Bogaert (1968: 357) actually argues that such enterprises, if they existed at all, must have been rare: no example survives in the ancient sources.

I have described this secondary material in some detail in order to show the fascination that productive credit continues to exert over writers on Greek banking. At a deeper level, there is room for a reassessment of conventional views of the underlying credit mechanism appropriate to Athenian banks. By Bogaert's definition of deposit banking, the banker's profit derives from the interest differential between deposits received and loans paid out. From the point of view of modern banking practice, the mechanism seems simplicity itself; but the detailed evidence for its existence in the ancient Greek world proves, on closer inspection, to be surprisingly precarious. There is, for example, no conclusive support for the payment of interest on bankers' deposits (see my Appendix VI). This is not necessarily damaging to the deposit-loan mechanism favoured by Bogaert. Considerations of security and convenience have historically proved attractive enough to depositors to overcome the disadvantage of a zero- or even a negative-interest payment.[29] Altogether more serious are reservations relating to the heart of the process, whereby bankers' loans were funded almost exclusively by other people's deposits. Here, I would argue against Bogaert that the relending of deposits made up only a minor part of the business of the typical Athenian banker.

At least one banker is known to have lent out his private wealth in conjunction with customers' deposits. According to the speaker in Demosthenes' *On Behalf of Phormion* (xxxvi.5), less than a quarter of the cash out on loan was made up out of deposits:[30]

For the real property (*engeios ousia*) of Pasion was about twenty talents, but he had in addition to this more than fifty talents of his own (*idion*) lent out. Included in this were eleven talents of bank deposits lent out at interest (*energa*).

Although Bogaert acknowledged this practice (1968: 365–6, with n. 362), he argues that there were other, poorer bankers in Athens who worked entirely with other people's money – in the form of either clients' deposits or borrowed funds. But none of the snippets of evidence gathered by Bogaert is decisive. When Pasion's bank is described (Dem. xxxvi.11) as 'a concern giving a hazardous revenue from other people's money', the allusion is to a banking business that we know to have been dominated by the banker's personal funds. No more conclusive is a paradox of Bion the Borysthenite, an early third-century philosopher, as preserved by Teles (xxvi.2 ~ Kindstrand 1976: fr. 41): 'How is it that some people are short of what they have? – "How do bankers", says Bion, "have money and yet not have it? Because that which they have is not their own."' There need be no reference intended here to working with deposits. Equally plausible is the opposite meaning, that bankers possess money in the form of deposits which they cannot use as belonging to other people. They therefore have to seek funds from other sources.[31]

This introduces a second and more serious difficulty in the wholehearted acceptance of the deposit-loan mechanism. Deposits with Greek bankers are almost invariably referred to as *parakatathēkai* (Korver 1934: 31–9). But if these are to be understood as *parakatathēkai* in the conventional sense of deposits for safe keeping, then for a banker to re-lend these monies to his own advantage would be tantamount to a breach of trust. According to Diogenes Laertius (1.57), a law of Solon inflicted the penalty of death on any person other than the depositor who removed a deposit. That need not be taken too seriously, but the emphasis elsewhere is on the inviolability of deposits. The Peripatetic author of the pseudo-Platonic *Definitions* (415D) characterizes a deposit as 'that which is given in trust (*meta pisteōs*)'; and, in the *Laws* (742C), Plato himself lays down that no one shall deposit money 'with a person he does not trust'. When, in the *Republic* (331E and 332A), attempts are made to define justice, a preliminary effort explores the idea of rendering-up to its rightful owner property deposited for safe keeping. Elsewhere, the handing back of deposits is treated as a benchmark of honest behaviour (Democritus DK 265; Isoc. 1.22), and there are moral tales about the unpleasant fate of those who fail to do so. Notable is the case of Glaucon the Spartan, as told by King Leotychidas in the pages of Herodotus (vi.86). On that occasion, the mere thought of embezzling a deposit was enough to bring about the obliteration of his household (cf. Conon in *FGH* 26 F 1, with Bogaert 1968: 218–9; Aesop in Chambry 1927: no. 298). Perhaps the plainest, practical demonstration of the near-sanctity of deposits is the practice of the so-called 'temple banks'. In his detailed survey (1968: 286–8 and 302), Bogaert can find no case in which their often considerable deposits were lent out to third parties.

This protective attitude towards deposits is, at first sight, difficult to reconcile with the passage quoted above, showing how bankers like Pasion could lend out monies belonging to other people. The answer may be to break away from the straightforward identification of the Greek *parakatathēkē* with the modern concept of a deposit. Harking back to the distinction drawn by the author of the Aristotelian *Problems* (above, pp. 99–100), it might be more fitting to treat those deposits which might be lent out at the banker's discretion as loans to the banker by his creditor-clients. Such an approach helps untangle the problem of interest-payments on deposits, which make better sense if understood as interest on loans, payable only under specified circumstances. These circumstances seem to have surrounded the burning of the Opisthodomos or inner treasury of the Temple of Athena on the Acropolis, some time in the earlier fourth century. The scholiast to a speech of Demosthenes (xxiv.136) recounts how the Treasurers of Athena and the Other Gods either stole temple funds or, alternatively, lent them to various bankers in order to enjoy an illicit gain. When the bankers went bust, the Treasurers tried to cover their tracks by setting fire to the Opisthodomos, but were found out and put on trial. Significant here is the choice of words: the cash is not deposited with the bankers, but lent to them (*tisi daneisai trapezitais*).

Thompson (1979a: 228) is surely right in his conclusion from this episode that in order to receive interest on deposits it was necessary to reach a specific agreement with the banker to lend him the money. The counter-objections offered by Bogaert (1986a: 23–4) fail to carry conviction and reveal the narrowness of his own approach. He bases his argument on the belief that the loans described by the scholiast really represent deposits. This is because loans are for fixed terms, are made openly before witnesses, and call for security or guarantors; deposits, by contrast, can be made in secret, require no security, and are repayable on demand – entirely appropriate for the covert dealings of the Treasurers. He ends with a general statement that people do not lend money to bankers, but deposit money with them; the only exception being loans of *aphormē* or working capital. In fact, the reported failure of the bankers that allegedly led to the firing of the Opisthodomos could be used as an argument that they were in need of funds and willing to pay for the use of them. Bogaert follows modern banking practice in assuming that there were rules governing transactions between bankers and their customers in the ancient world. But, as should emerge below, what distinguished

Athenian bankers was their flexibility and the ways in which they adapted to meet the requirements of different types of clients.[32]

Bogaert's firm ideas as to what constitutes proper banking practice result in his omission of a further way in which Athenian bankers could have met the needs of their customers. The prisoner of modern definitions, he explicitly rejects the possibility that bankers might have functioned as brokers (1966: 30). 'Un dépositaire qui ne placerait les fonds de ses clients que selon les désirs de ceux-ci et aux risques des déposants n'est pas un banquier mais un courtier.' All Bogaert's subsequent discussions of Greek banking are conducted on the assumption that bankers did as they liked with their customers' cash, and never acted as brokers or agents. But the principle of brokerage is well attested for fourth-century Athens in the area of non-professional credit transactions (see above, p. 146); Bogaert himself has put forward compelling arguments in support of the involvement of middlemen in maritime credit (see above, p. 192). Professional brokers are solidly attested in other non-capitalist societies (Humphreys 1970: 151) and, in sixteenth-century England, brokerage was apparently associated with the emergence of modern credit banking (Stonex 1923: 267-9 and 279-81).

This is not intended as a complete solution to the funding of Athenian banking, but rather as an indicator that the question is more open than Bogaert implies. It is a reasonable assumption that Athenian bankers would perform a variety of credit operations, accommodating some borrowers from their personal funds, others from cash they had themselves borrowed, and still others by introducing them to would-be lenders. Misled by modern definitions and analogies, historians have consistently seen lending at interest as the most lucrative, and therefore the characteristic, element in Athenian banking operations.[33] In the following, final section, I try to show how the key to understanding bankers' activities may be found in their peculiar position in Athenian society.

BANKERS, MERCHANTS AND METICS

It has long been recognized that bankers in Athens were almost without exception metics, and often ex-slaves (Bogaert 1968: 386-8; Whitehead 1977: 116). That locates bankers towards the margin of *polis*-society, based as it was on the criterion of citizenship. Much the same can be said of most of their customers. The sources of non-professional credit detailed in earlier chapters – relatives, neighbours, friends and other associates – applied primarily to citizens. An examination of bankers' clientele shows that it consisted overwhelmingly of persons for whom the usual sources of citizen-support were not available. For the most part, that meant non-citizens, though there were exceptions in both directions. Well-established metics might have their own circles of contacts to whom they could appeal for help. To cite an extreme case, it is difficult to imagine Cephalus, the friend and confidant of Pericles, being short of powerful *philoi* (Plato, *Rep.* 328B, with Lysias XII.4). Poorer metics *in extremis* might be able to fall back on the patronage of the obligatory citizen-*prostatēs*. In the passage from Menander's *Hero* cited in an earlier chapter (pp. 63–4), the starving freedman is portrayed as turning for support to his ex-master and *prostatēs*.

Whatever the opportunities open to metics, another sizeable section of the population was without obvious sources of support. These were the *xenoi* – temporary visitors to Athens in the shape of merchants (*emporoi*), shipowners (*nauklēroi*) and sightseers (*theōroi*). Again, there might be exceptions. Occasional merchants could have personal contacts in Athens, passing the time as 'guest-friends' (*xenoi*) with hosts who would supply help if needed. So we are told by the speaker (Apollodorus) in the Demosthenic speech *Against Callippus* (LIII.3) that Lycon from Heraclea on the Black Sea numbered two Athenian citizens among his 'guest-friends'. More generally, it may be that the remarkable upsurge in non-Athenian cultic groups in the Piraeus from the later fifth century, as catalogued by Garland (1987: 101–8), is linked to a desire felt by non-permanent residents for fellowship and mutual support (see above, p. 151). But not all visitors would be fortunate enough to belong to one of these associations, nor could it supply all their needs. Xenophon in his *Poroi* (III.12) advises the building of more lodging-houses around the harbours of Athens for the accommodation of traders with nowhere else to go. If 'friendless' traders like these were faced with an unforeseen shortage of cash, they would be forced to turn to impersonal sources of credit. That was apparently the fate of the merchant Phormion, as described in the Demosthenic speech delivered against him (XXXIV.23). After financing a trading voyage to the Bosporus by raising various maritime loans, his cargo proved unsaleable, so that he was unable to pay off his creditors. The claim was made that he eventually did so by raising a loan in the Bosporus of 120 Cyzicene staters, at an annual rate of interest equivalent to one sixth of the sum borrowed (= $16\frac{2}{3}$ per cent). It is made clear by the speaker that this was a landside and not a maritime loan (*daneisamenos engeiōn tokōn*).

Transferring this sequence of events back to Athens, it comes as no surprise that of the few bankers' loans for which detailed evidence survives, several were sought by traders. Apaturius, a shipowner from Byzantium, arrived in Athens owing forty minas on the security of his ship ([Dem.] xxxiii.5–8). He turned first of all to a fellow-Byzantine who lent him ten minas (§6), and then asked the unnamed speaker for the loan of thirty more. The speaker explains this approach in terms of his own experience as a trader (§5): 'I am on intimate terms (*panu oikeiōs chrōmai*) with these men from Byzantium, through myself having spent much time there.' Having himself no money to hand, he put Apaturius in touch with the banker Heraclides who lent the thirty minas, with the speaker acting as guarantor. It was when the bank failed that his difficulties began (§9).

Connexions between bankers and outsiders are also present in the background to Isocrates' *Trapeziticus* (xvii). The son of Sopaeus (his name is not given) is there described as arriving in Athens from the Bosporus with a sum of money and two shiploads of grain. He was the son of the right-hand man of Satyrus, king of the Bosporus, and travelling 'to see the world' (*kata theōrian*) – an outsider arriving in Athens (§4). Briefly, while in Athens, the son of Sopaeus was introduced to the banker Pasion, with whom he deposited a portion of his funds. At this juncture, political developments back in the Bosporus made it expedient for the son of Sopaeus to conceal his deposit at the bank, and pretend instead that he had borrowed money at interest from Pasion among others (§7). All went well, until Pasion allegedly tried to take advantage of the concealment by embezzling the deposit. In the context of his dispute with Pasion, the son of Sopaeus expresses his fear to the jury that it will be used by his opponent as an argument for his lack of money that he allowed Hippolaidas 'a guest-friend and a companion' (*xenos kai epitēdeios*) to borrow from the banker (§38). So here are examples – both real and imaginary – of outsiders turning to bankers for credit.[34]

The link between banker and trader is even clearer in the case of deposits, a majority of which can be accounted for in these terms. Although the connexion has been made by others, including Bogaert (1968: 355 and 370; 1974: 527), it has not been systematically explored or explained.

The citizen or established resident of Athens would normally have relatives or associates to whom he could, in his absence, entrust affairs, including the safe keeping of valuables. So Apollodorus says of the *stratēgos* Timotheus ([Dem.] XLIX.37) that, 'Many important citizens were close to (*oikeioi*) the defendant, and looked after his affairs while he was in the service of the king [of Persia].' Apollodorus claimed to have a similar arrangement of his own with his neighbour Nicostratus (above, pp. 53–9). Details about deposits made under these circumstances usually find their way into the sources after the cash or valuables have been embezzled, as is allegedly the case in Isocrates' speech *Against Euthynus* (XXI.1–10). Nicias was a wealthy Athenian who feared that his property would be confiscated by the Thirty Tyrants. He therefore conveyed his slaves out of Attica, removed his furnishings to the house of a friend (who delivers the speech on his behalf), took out a loan on the security of his house, and deposited three talents of silver with his cousin Euthynus. He then left the city and went to live in the country (§2). Shortly after, he decided to quit Attica altogether, but when he asked for the return of his deposit, cousin Euthynus would hand back only two talents. The terms in which the speaker attempts to justify Nicias' trust of his relatives are revealing. 'In my opinion', he says (§9), 'knowing as I do their intimacy (*oikeiotēta*), Euthynus would not have ever acted unjustly towards Nicias if he could have defrauded someone else of so large a sum.' The implication is that even a villain would rob his relatives only as a last resort.[35]

Traders in a strange town would have no relations, however untrustworthy, to whom they could entrust valuables or turn for support. In search of an alternative, they would naturally look towards a banker, with whom they might have good personal contacts, as affording the best protection available under the circumstances. That this protection could be less than complete is shown by the case of Timosthenes, a resident of Athens, who arrived back from a trading voyage to find that two silver bowls left at Pasion's bank along with other valuables for safe keeping had accidentally been lent out ([Dem.] XLIX.31–3). According to Apollodorus, his father took responsibility for the loss and paid over to Timosthenes the value of the bowls: an interesting contrast to the difficulties apparently experienced by Nicias in the case detailed above.

The value of an honest banker protecting the interests of his non-

Athenian client is illustrated by Callippus' attempt to confiscate a deposit made with Pasion's bank by the Heraclean merchant Lycon. The details are supplied by Apollodorus in the Demosthenic speech *Against Callipus* (LII), delivered after Pasion's death. Before leaving on a voyage to Libya, Lycon reckoned up his account with Pasion in the presence of witnesses, ordering that the sum of 1,640 dr. be paid over to a trading partner, Cephisiades of Scyros. While making his voyage, Lycon was killed by pirates, with the result that Callippus, in his capacity as Heraclean *proxenos* in Athens, tried to appropriate the deposit meant for Cephisiades (§§ 3–7). Apollodorus claims to repeat to the court Callipus' words to Pasion (§9):

It happens that I am *proxenos* of the Heracleotes, and you would be glad, I should think, to have me get the money rather than a metic-type (*metoikion anthrōpon*) who resides in Scyros, and is a man of no account.

Right through the speech (§§25 and 29), the contrast is emphasized between the high-status citizen *proxenos* and the metic trader from Scyros (Whitehead 1977: 49–50).[36] But in this case, if Apollodorus can be believed, the banker kept faith with his client's wishes and the cash was handed over to Cephisiades.

From detail towards the beginning of the speech (§3), it is clear that Lycon did not deposit his money in the bank immediately before his departure from Athens, but already had an account. Apollodorus describes him as 'using my father's bank, like the other merchants', which is not an empty generalization. Even a trader who, like Lycon, had personal contacts in Athens might be unwilling to leave large sums of money in a private house, let alone public lodgings. As bankers presumably had the facilities for looking after valuables, merchants might hand over their cash for safe keeping. This seems to have been the case with the son of Sopaeus: after selling his grain (§4) 'Pythodorus the Phoenician introduced Pasion to me, and I made use of his bank'. So the introduction was made by a non-Athenian who was almost certainly a trader and a customer of Pasion's bank. There is a possible parallel in the Demosthenic speech *Against Apaturius*, where the unnamed defendant – himself a retired trader – acts as guarantor for a loan made to the Byzantine merchant by the banker Heraclides 'with whom I have dealings' (§7). The sensible suggestion is made by Bogaert (1968: 355, n. 293) that Heraclides would more willingly accept the speaker as guarantor for a thirty-mina loan if he were himself in credit with the bank.

Other snippets of information strengthen the link between traders and bankers. Theophrastus' 'Boastful Man' (XXIII.2) stands in the trading quarter of the Piraeus (Garland 1987: 154) and impresses *xenoi* with tales of non-existent maritime loans, sending off a slave to see how his account stands at the bank. Also deserving a mention is an epigram attributed to Theocritus which has the form of a banker's advertising slogan (*Epigr.* XIV ~ *Anth.Pal.* IX.435). Although the precise interpretation (and even the authorship) of the poem is disputed, it is clear that the banker boasts how his customers – both citizens and non-citizens (*astoi kai xenoi*) – can withdraw deposits at any hour of the day or night. This has led to speculation that the banker's customers may have been merchants, anxious to catch a fair wind (see Bogaert 1968: 275). Finally, there is the evidence of the physical location of the banks themselves (Bogaert 1968: 375). Apart from a cluster of banks in the *agora* (Plato, *Apology* 17C and *Hippias Minor* 368B), there was a concentration in the Piraeus ([Dem.] XLIX.6, LII.8 and 14, and XXXIII.6–7). According to a story in Polyaenus (VI.2.1–2), when Alexander of Pherae raided the Piraeus in 362, his men seized money belonging to the bankers.[37]

Traders' deposits with bankers account for the majority of bank deposits known from the surviving sources.[38] Implicit in this material is the notion that a banker's services towards his mercantile clients were not limited to emergency loans and the safeguarding of deposits. For a friendless merchant in an unfamiliar city, a banker could function as a general agent and personal confidant. Although the son of Sopaeus was obviously anxious to present himself as the innocent dupe of Pasion, there is presumably some plausibility in his claims (Isoc. XVII.6; cf. Herman 1987: 95):

When I found myself in such embarrassing difficulties, men of the jury, I related my troubles to Pasion. For I was on such intimate terms with him (*oikeiōs*) that I had the greatest confidence in him: not only in matters of money, but in everything else as well.

Bankers could also perform less irregular services for non-citizens. When the son of Sopaeus was let down by his father's guest-friend in Athens, it was Pasion who found for him a citizen guarantor (§43). The banker himself might act as guarantor for his clients: Pasion stood as surety in a financial transaction, again on behalf of the son of Sopaeus (§37). There are two known cases of contracts recording maritime loans being deposited with bankers ([Dem.] XXXIV.6 and LVI.15); and in each case the parties involved were non-citizens. It

may be noted in contrast that of the sixteen written agreements
mentioned on the *horoi*, recording transactions between citizens, only
one is thought to have been deposited with a banker (Finley 1952:
no. 39, with 174, n. 2).

Although I have presented the rôle of the banker as a non-citizen
substitute for the services usually performed by citizens and friends,
over time a bond of *philia* might develop between banker and client.
The son of Sopaeus warned it was difficult to bring successful
prosecutions against bankers, because 'they have many *philoi*' (§2).
There is support for his claim in the behaviour of Apollodorus in the
Demosthenic speech *Against Polycles* (L; see above, pp. 68–70). While
on the island of Tenedos, serving as trierarch, Apollodorus found
himself short of cash (§56):

I therefore borrowed from Cleanax and Eperatus, *xenoi* of my father in
Tenedos, and gave the sailors their provision money. On account of my
being Pasion's son, and the fact that he was connected by ties of *xenia* with
many, and was trusted throughout the world, I had no trouble in
borrowing money wherever I needed it.

Apollodorus also made use of his late father's associates at Lampsacus
(§18), again referred to as *xenoi* (see Herman 1987: 93).

Traders are the obvious, but not the only, group outside the circle
of citizen-support. A small proportion of bankers' clients consisted of
citizens to whom, for one reason or another, the regular sources of
credit were closed. Such a situation could arise if an individual
consistently broke the ethical code governing reciprocal lending and
borrowing between *philoi*. That was the position of Aeschines the
Socratic. The background to the speaker's version of events may be
reconstructed as follows. Aeschines fraudulently acquired possession
of a perfumery, but needed cash to run it. His reputation as a man
who did not repay his debts is exploited to the full by his opponent's
humorous sallies in the later sections of the fragment. Since this anti-
social behaviour closed off the usual sources of personal credit,
Aeschines was forced to fall back on impersonal, interest-bearing
credit, securing a loan from a banker and his associate.[39] As his
reputation had preceded him, he could find accommodation only at
the punitively high rate of 3 per cent per month: a rate of repayment
which it proved impossible to keep up. Aeschines was therefore
fortunate to convert the first loan to another at $1\frac{1}{2}$ per cent, though
even that proved intolerable in the end. So the banker in the story

has the rôle of a 'lender of last resort', offering credit to debt-ridden citizens.[40]

There is support for this interpretation in the Demosthenic speech *Against Timotheus* (XLIX), delivered by Apollodorus some time after his father's death (see above, pp. 71 and 84–5). He recounts in detail the circumstances surrounding the various loans made by Pasion to the Athenian commander Timotheus during the period *c.* 374–372.

We are told by Apollodorus that the first loan was made during April of 383, immediately before Timotheus set out to relieve Corcyra (§§ 6–8). Although Timotheus was already short of cash – witness his financial expedients while campaigning in 376–5 ([Arist.] *Oec.* 1350a23–b15) – the speech as a whole gives the impression that it was as a result of the voyage to Corcyra that his financial position became desperate (§§ 11–15). This first loan is best thought of as a response to a sudden and unforeseen demand for cash (§6):

[Timotheus] was about to sail on his second expedition, and was already in the Piraeus on the point of putting out to sea when, being short of money, he came to my father in the port and urged him to lend him (*chrēsai*) 1,351 drachmas 2 obols, declaring that he needed the additional sum...

The odd sum involved supports the idea of a loan to meet some specific, unexpected payment. As the journey was needed urgently, none of the usual types of credit would be suitable; an *eranos*-loan was certainly out of the question. Under these circumstances, Pasion's bank in the Piraeus would be an appropriate source to tap. This banker's loan did nothing to settle Timotheus' long-term money problems. While stationed at Calauria, an island off the Peloponnese, in order to retain the loyalty of certain Boeotian trierarchs serving with him, he was forced to borrow 1,000 dr. from Philippus the shipowner (*nauklēros*) and his treasurer (*tamias*) Antiphanes (§§ 14–15). On Timotheus' return to Athens this pair immediately put him in an awkward position by demanding repayment. In order to compensate the trierarchs for expenses imposed on them during the expedition, he had already pledged a part of his estate as security, the other part being encumbered in a *misthōsis oikou* operation. Apollodorus paints a vivid if exaggerated picture of Timotheus' distress (§§ 11–13):

...he was in desperate need of money. All his property was pledged as security (*hupochreōs*), *horoi* had been set up on it, and other people were in control. His farm on the plain had been taken over as security by the son of Eumelidas; the rest of his property was encumbered for seven minas each to the sixty trierarchs who set out on this voyage with him, which money he as commander had forced them to distribute amongst the crew for maintenance...he gave them his property as security. Yet now he is robbing them by digging up the *horoi*. He was hard-pressed on every side, his life was in extreme danger because of the seriousness of the misfortunes which had befallen the *polis*...

Under such delicate circumstances, Timotheus was naturally unwilling that the disclosure of financial irregularities while on campaign should add to his difficulties. He was therefore anxious to settle the matter with Philippus as quickly as possible in order to stop the truth coming out. Speed and secrecy were essential, which again ruled out the possibility of an *eranos*, and there was no real property left to hypothecate. Circumstances once more forced Timotheus to turn to Pasion, who would lend without security, and presumably keep quiet about it. 'He came to my father and begged him to settle with Philippus, and to lend him the thousand drachmas to pay Philippus' (§18). So says Apollodorus, who goes on to explain that Pasion felt pity for the plight of Timotheus and lent him the money.

Late in 373, Timotheus was caught unprepared by the arrival of Alcetas, king of the Molossi in Epirus, and Jason the tyrant of Pherae, who had come to Athens to support him at his trial. He was without the money and articles appropriate for entertaining two such distinguished guests and, as it was late in the evening, there was little time left in which to act (§§22–3):

Being at a loss how to entertain them, he sent his personal slave Aeschrion to my father and told him to ask for the loan of some bedding and cloaks and two silver bowls, and to borrow a mina of silver. My father, hearing from Aeschrion the personal slave of the defendant, that they had both arrived and the urgent need for which the request was made, both supplied the items for which he had come, and lent the mina he asked to borrow.

Once again, when other sources of credit were not available, the banker was able to perform a useful supplementary service. Pasion's final loan to Timotheus took place after his acquittal, and after his departure from Athens to take mercenary service with the king of Persia. Before he left, he took Pasion to one side and asked him to pay the freighting cost of a load of timber he was expecting from Macedonia. This Pasion agreed to do, and the cost of 1,750 dr. was added to Timotheus' account (§§25–30). By this time, Timotheus had apparently exhausted all the sources of credit available to him as a well-connected Athenian citizen. Not only was all his property encumbered, he had also borrowed from other citizens without security, 'having no equivalent security to give' – Apollodorus produces a deposition to this effect (§61). Here, if anywhere, Pasion was acting as 'lender of last resort'. Although there were apparently many important citizens looking after Timotheus' affairs in his absence (§37), none of them was prepared to lend him any money.[41]

Non-resident traders and citizens deep in debt make up the majority of the known clientele of Athenian bankers. And the handful of other customers we hear about can be explained along similar lines: they are citizens who turn to bankers because more conventional sources of support are somehow inappropriate. One of the few examples of potentially productive credit from classical Athens concerns a loan by two citizens from the banker Blepaeus for the purchase of mining concessions ([Dem.] XL.52). Although there is no other evidence to speak of, it would be consistent with prevailing attitudes if people wanting a loan for productive purposes were forced to look outside the usual network of credit relationships. *Eranos*-loans and the like were meant to help people out of their difficulties, not help them make a profit.

Similar considerations apply to the few citizens found with bank accounts. In the probable absence of interest on deposits (see Appendix VI), it is hard to imagine what incentive ordinary citizens might have to give their money to bankers. Security need not have been much of a motive, with the ground regarded as the safest of safe deposits (above, pp. 169–70).[42] The Attic Orators have, in fact, only four examples of citizens depositing cash with bankers (Demosthenes Senior: Dem. XXVII.11; unnamed speaker: [Dem.] XLVII.51, 57, 64; Comon: [Dem.] XLVIII.12; ?Epicrates: Hyperides, *Athenogenes* 5). At least two of these citizens were untypical in the degree of their involvement in manufacturing. Comon had slaves weaving cloth and grinding colours; Demosthenes had slaves making swords and building couches. It seems a fair assumption that their bank deposits were tied up with their trading interests. The other two citizens had deposits that were different in character from those of Demosthenes and Comon. These were not regular accounts, but temporary deposits for a specific purpose. The unnamed speaker in the Demosthenic *Against Euergus* (XLVII) deposited with a banker a sum of money owed as damages arising out of a court action. He arranged that his opponent should meet him at the bank, where the obligation was to be discharged. The position in the speech by Hyperides is much the same. The citizen-speaker wished to purchase the freedom of two slaves owned by a metic perfume-seller. After collecting *eranos*-contributions from his friends, he deposited the purchase price of forty minas in a bank.

It is probable that in both these transactions the banker had a supervisory rôle; not merely as a disinterested witness (see Chapter v, n. 27), but in his technical capacity as an expert assessor of the quality of coins. Literary and epigraphical testimony confirm this as an ever-present consideration when receiving payments in the Greek world (Bogaert 1976). In Theophrastus' *Characters* there are allusions to handing over worn as opposed to new coins (IV.11 and XXI.5); and a fragment of Menander has the motif of taking a dowry to the bank to have the tester (*dokimastēs*) see if the coin is good (*CAF* fr. 532 ~ Allinson 1921: p. 478, fr. 532). In the Demosthenic speech *Against Lacritus* (XXXV.24) it is stipulated in advance that a debt is to be discharged in 'good coin' (*argurion dokimon*). Finally, there is the well-known inscription of 375/4, making provision for public testers of coins in both *agora* and Piraeus (Stroud 1974 ~ Epigraphica III 21 ~ Harding no. 45).

The skill of bankers in identifying false or underweight coins derived from their activities as money-changers. The monetary chaos of the Greek world, with each state having its own coinage (Bogaert 1968: 308–15), forced travellers to rely on the expertise of professional changers. Right through the fourth century and beyond, changing would have played an important part in the range of services offered by bankers. It is now generally agreed that banking institutions as known in the classical period had their origins in money-changing, with the term *trapezitēs* referring to the changer's table (Bogaert 1966: 135–44). It is, however, impossible to be precise about the point at which the word ceased to mean merely 'money-changer'.[43]

Here is another area in which preoccupation with the principles of modern banking has diverted attention away from a crucial aspect of Athenian banks. Given the available evidence, it is possible to argue that the bulk of a banker's profits would not have come from lending at interest, but from changing money. In contrast to a loan with all its associated risks, possibly extending over several months (above, pp. 81–4), a money-changing operation need have taken only a few moments, and the banker got an instantaneous payment, with no danger of default. Evidence from all over the Greek world (but not Athens) suggests a minimum of 5–6 per cent profit on each transaction (Bogaert 1968: 323–31), which compares favourably with the prevailing rate of interest on loans of 1 per cent per month.

Bogaert is not the only historian of Greek banking who would disagree with this promotion of changing over lending as the most profitable service offered by fourth-century bankers. In a passage which is in danger of denying that Athenian bankers had any profitable activities, Hasebroek envisages a gradual decline in the significance of money-changing (1928: 85, n. 3): 'As banks grew, it became less and less important, and the most developed of them – e.g. that of Pasion – seem to have abandoned it altogether.' The conclusion is apparently based on a statement in Isocrates' *Trapeziticus* (XVII.40), where the son of Sopaeus claims to have 'purchased' staters from several different people. From this it is inferred by Hasebroek (1920: 142–3) that Pasion no longer acted as a money-changer. But it seems more likely that even he did not hold sufficient reserves to cover a demand for more than a thousand staters. If references in the Orators to bankers changing money are few, that is because money-changing – unlike the lending of money – was unlikely to end in litigation.

The account of Athenian bankers contained in these final pages goes some way to resolving the paradox with which my study of banking began (p. 197). The toleration of bankers, in spite of their status as professional lenders, can be explained by two considerations. As I have tried to show, whatever modern theory might seem to suggest, Greek bankers were not primarily money-lenders. The extension of credit was only one of a range of services which included safe keeping of deposits (including valuables and documents), acting as witnesses and guarantors, and changing money. Also, bankers – usually non-citizens themselves – would typically lend to those who were either outside the community of citizens by reason of birth, or had forfeited its protection by failing to respect social norms. As a result, bankers in Athens were not seen as a threat to the citizen solidarity that was considered essential for the well-being of the *polis*.

CHAPTER IX

Conclusion

> Neither a borrower, nor a lender be;
> For loan oft loses both itself and friend,
> And borrowing dulls the edge of husbandry.

Polonius' advice to his son survives as a proverbial reminder of conventional wisdom about personal borrowing. The mood is unfailingly negative. 'He who goes a-borrowing goes a-sorrowing.' 'He that borrows must pay again with shame and loss.' 'Better to go to bed supperless than to rise in debt.' 'Out of debt, out of danger.' Debt is popularly conceived as disruptive of relationships, morally reprehensible and economically damaging. From the mass of corroborative literature from Shakespeare's time onwards, one might single out Samuel Johnson's repeated and Polonius-like warnings to Boswell about the danger of borrowing: 'Let it be your first care not to be in any man's debt' (1791: IV, 154).[1] From the nineteenth century, a recurring theme in art and literature is the awful spectre of insolvency: what Carlyle writing in *Past and Present* (almost) called 'the Hell of the English' (Weiss 1986: 13). The combination of folk wisdom with Victorian melodrama may sound like voices from the past; but there are those who would interpret the unacceptable face of the credit explosion in the late 1980s as the penalty for neglecting Victorian values.[2]

What has emerged from this study of credit in Athens is the existence of another, more positive side to the lender–debtor relationship. The Athenians were keenly aware of the unpleasant possibilities of debt (see above, p. 5), but they would have looked askance at Polonius' denunciation of lending and borrowing as dangerous to friendship and best avoided. Citizens viewed loan transactions as one of the many ties that could create and sustain *philia*. Although traces of this more constructive attitude survive in our own industrial society, only in non-capitalist economies does it emerge as the dominant ideology. Some modern misconceptions about debt as it occurs in the Third World are exposed by Hill in her critique of what she identifies as the false assumptions behind development economics (1986). In a chapter called 'The need to be indebted' (pp. 83–94), her aim, as she puts it (p. 84), is to 'decolonialize the attitude to debt' by introducing the idea that lending and borrowing within the local community are inevitable and need not involve moral censure. 'Throughout the colonial empire', she writes, 'rural indebtedness was ignorantly and priggishly regarded as a moral problem, a sign that "natives" lacked the virtues of thrift, self-reliance and so forth. Village credit-granting was never seen as the converse of stultification – the sign of a lively economy.' Much the same (though with a different emphasis) could be said about modern attitudes to credit relations in classical Athens. Hill goes on to identify semantic barriers to understanding already familiar from this study (pp. 21 and 191–4): how harping on the idea of 'debt' as opposed to 'borrowing' gives a misleading impression of 'indebtedness'; how indiscriminate use of the term 'money-lender' implies that rural lenders are professionals, whereas most are villagers and fellow-farmers (pp. 84–5). Most revealing of all is Hill's emphasis on the structural rôle of credit within village economy and society (pp. 86–94): how lending and borrowing are on a largely informal basis, with creditors often simultaneously debtors, and debt seen as something natural.

On this general level, the analogy with ancient Athens seems promising: credit is in both cases firmly embedded in the fabric of everyday society. In Athens that is clear from the pervasiveness of credit operations, and also from the intrusion of concepts drawn from credit into ways of thinking. This cuts deeper than the metaphorical use of the terminology of lending and borrowing familiar from our own experience. Where credit appears in Athenian literature it is sometimes impossible (and inappropriate) to distinguish metaphor from reality. This is a consequence of the close identity of personal credit with gift-giving and reciprocity. In addition to the familiar function of relocating resources, credit operations in Athens were a way of defining and regulating relationships. Absence of interest, security, witnesses and written agreement made an unambiguous statement about the bond between lender and borrower. The effect was reinforced by the availability of an alternative set of credit relations that assumed or imposed an impersonal and potentially exploitative relationship, signalled by the charging of interest. It is onto this non-reciprocal (and more familiar) branch of credit that modern historians have directed most of their attention. I have tried to show how these impersonal credit operations were concentrated in the sphere of trade and typically involved non-citizens. Although essential to the survival of the Athenian state, trade and traders were seen as external to the *polis* in its sense of a *koinōnia* or community of citizens. My systematic survey of lending and borrowing seems to show that the reciprocal, integrative side of credit was easily the more important in the lives of ordinary citizens. Fears expressed by conservative thinkers like Plato and Aristotle about the corrosive effect of impersonal credit were misplaced. The two systems were complementary and where they interlocked, as in the law courts, it was the ideology of reciprocity that generally prevailed. In a Western, capitalist economy, that would be unthinkable.[3]

What distinguishes the Athenian model of credit and makes a sharp break with the framework of Hill's study (and much of my other comparative material) is the scale of the process and its relationship to the formal political structure. Hill is explicit about her concern with rural communities, and she draws a firm line between countryside and city (p. xii). In the case of Athens, the practice of reciprocal lending was understandably concentrated in small-scale groupings of relatives, neighbours and other associates. But the ideal of co-operative credit, expressed in the support that fellow-citizens owed to one another, extended over the whole *polis*. This promotion of mutual assistance to the status of civic ideology may be read as an expression of the democratic *ethos* – stronger in Athens than in any other *polis*. In view of our relative ignorance about social relations in *poleis* other than Athens this has to remain a hypothesis. But, moving away from classical Greece, a case can be made for a contrast between mechanisms of support in Athens and those that occur elsewhere. Assistance in Athens was along broadly horizontal lines, between people of notionally equal status as citizens; in the non-democratic remainder of the ancient world, vertical relations predominate, designed to reinforce hierarchy and control. The 'euergetism' of the Hellenistic East was not primarily concerned with philanthropy or even honour, but with more material rewards (Veyne 1976: 185–374; Garnsey 1988: 82–6). Aristotle in his *Politics* (1321a31–42) highlights the connexion between spending by wealthy individuals and the preservation of oligarchy. From the Roman world, the patron–client relationship involves an obvious element of social control (Wallace-Hadrill 1989a; Garnsey and Woolf 1989).[4]

'In the end, therefore, a genuine "synthesis" of the history of ancient slavery can only be a history of Graeco-Roman society.' So wrote Moses Finley as the conclusion to an essay on the interplay between ancient slavery and modern ideology. The same can be said, if in a more modest way, of the history of lending and borrowing in ancient Athens. If nothing else, my study at least bears out Polanyi's dictum that in the ancient world the economy was embedded in society. And perhaps it goes further to make a point which bears repetition. Non-capitalist societies should not necessarily be seen as backward or primitive. As the case of credit in ancient Athens suggests, they are capable of their own kind of sophistication.

Appendices

I: RECENT WORK ON THE *HOROI*

Since the appearance of my reassessment of the *horoi* in 1982 (summarized in *SEG* xxxiv 158–68), at least three further inscriptions have come to light, of which only one has so far been published.

A limestone plaque from Laureotike in Attica, found in excavations of the Asklepiakon mine at Soureza in 1976–8 (Conophagus 1980: 389 no. 2 ~ *SEG* xxxii 236):

[ὅρο]ς ἐργαστηρίου καὶ ἀνδρα-
πόδων πεπραμένων ἐ-
πὶ λύσει [rasura]
[rasura] καὶ ἐρανισταῖς
τοῖς μετὰ Ἐπιτέλους ἐκ
Κεραμέων Χ Η Δ
   vacat
καὶ ἀπέργαστρα καμί-
νωι τῆι Σίμου Παιανιέω
ΔΡΙΡΙ καὶ τοῖς ἐρα-
νισταῖς τοῖς με-
τὰ Νεοπτολέμου
Μελιτέως Τ

This *horos* (dated to *c.* 350) is briefly discussed in the text (p. 159, above). The two unpublished *horoi* are also from the mining area of Attica, from the excavation of a silver-mine site at Agrileza. In his preliminary report, Ellis-Jones records (1984–5: 122) 'two... boundary stones recording mortgage leases, both using the common *oros... pepramenou epi lusei* formula; one, with six lines of neat *stoichedon* lettering of fourth-century B.C. date, came from the washery's SW sedimentation basin, and the other with five lines of less regular letters from alongside the washery.' The three inscriptions will make a useful addition to the analysis of *horoi* from the mining area by Lauffer (1979: 89–97).

Several recent publications have a bearing on specific *horoi*. Whitehead (1986: Appendix 3, no. 58) questions Finley's ascription of a *horos* pledging property to the Halaieis (1952: no. 5) to Halai Aixonides rather than Halai Araphenides. The *horos* published as *SEG* xxx 122 has already appeared in print as *SEG* xxi 656 (see Chapter vii, n. 8). An inscription identified by Fine as a *horos* marking property pledged as security to the Thymaitian phratry (1951: no. 11 ~ Finley 1952: no. 101c) has been convincingly reread by Hedrick (1988) as the boundary-marker of a sanctuary. My querying (1982: xxviii–xxix) of Vanderpool's rereading of an inscription as a security *horos* (1971, with Aleshire 1988) receives independent support from Oikonomides, who identifies the text as a lease (see *SEG* xxix 158).

Other studies have a broader impact on our appreciation of the *horoi*. The conclusions reached by Osborne (1985: 59–60), which relate to patterns of property-holding in Attica, are briefly noted in the text (pp. 146–7). Germain (1982–4) has made a special study of the small group of *apotimēma* inscriptions which do not refer to pupillary or dotal security (Finley 1952: 45–6). Combining the testimony of five relevant *horoi* (Finley 1952: nos. 32, 160, 162 and 163; Millett 1982: no. 163A) with other epigraphic evidence concerning terms of leases (*IG* ii² 1172 ll. 20–2; 2494 l. 7; 2498 ll. 3–6), Germain argues that there is in this category no certain case of property encumbered in favour of an individual. Where detail is preserved, the creditor or lessor is either a deme, a temple, or a group of *eranistai*. (He interprets the Dionysus of *horos* no. 163 as referring to a temple to the god rather than to an individual of that name.) Germain's suggestion that *apotimēma*-type security was considered appropriate for privileged creditors or lessors seems reasonable enough. But the evidence is altogether inadequate to support his theory (based on a strained interpretation of Isaeus fr. 34; see above, p. 70) that *apotimēma* should somehow be connected with *antichrēsis*.

In an important study of the relationship between oral tradition and written records in Athens, Thomas (1989: 55–60) singles out security-*horoi* as exemplifying the combination of written and non-written elements characteristic of the use of documents in the ancient world. In the case of the *horoi*, existence of the obligation was marked by placing, in the presence of witnesses, a physical object, supplemented by a brief bit of writing. In this way, the transaction was protected by a blending of oral, symbolic and written methods. Thomas also makes the tentative suggestion that, in view of the residual function of the written element, some *horoi* marking loans may have carried the single word *horos*. If so, it would help to explain the apparent absence of security-*horoi* from before the beginning of the fourth century.

The relationship between the *horoi* and literacy also appears in a paper by Harris (1988a: 379–80), who offers the use of these inscriptions as evidence for widespread (if rudimentary) literacy in Attica. The apparent logic of the argument is, however, called into question by Thomas's considered examination of the rôle of documentary evidence; and it may be thought that my own researches cast similar doubts on Harris's other concluding remarks about the evolution of credit in Athens (pp. 380–1). But these are not major concerns of Harris's study, which provides a penetrating analysis of the security aspect of the *horoi*. In the body of his paper (pp. 361–77), he explores the notorious discrepancy between the terminology of security operations as found on the *horoi* and in the Orators (see Millett 1982: xii–xiv). After an exhaustive scrutiny of relevant operations involving real security in literary and epigraphical sources, Harris concludes that differences in terminology (between *hypothēkē* and *prasis epi lusei*) are just that, and do not conceal separate types of security. He also argues that, seen from the perspective of the creditor, pledging property as security amounted to temporary transference of ownership. What is attractive about Harris's approach is the emphasis he places on the perceptions of the parties involved in the transactions, and his suggestions may well be right.*

II: METIC MONEY-LENDERS AND CITIZEN AGENTS

A recurring theme in M.I. Finley's writings on Athenian economy and society has been the existence of a wall or barrier between the land owned by citizen borrowers and the liquid resources of metic

---

* I am grateful to Professor Harris for the trouble he has taken in elaborating his views in correspondence with me.

lenders. Metics were barred by law from owning land and so could not foreclose on the real security that was a regular feature of loan transactions between citizens. The idea did not originate with Finley (see, for example, Böckh 1817: 140; Zimmern 1911: 312; Glotz 1920: 242; Weber 1909: 192 and 1921: 218); but he has been its most forceful proponent. In *Land and Credit in Ancient Athens* (1952: 77–8), Finley suggested that the economic history of Athens might well be written with this 'basic economic cleavage' as the point of departure. Thirty years later, in his *Ancient Economy* (1985b: 48), he gave as an illustration the anomalous position of the wealthy metic, Cephalus of Syracuse:

Cephalus could own neither farmland nor a vineyard nor the house he lived in; he could not even lend money on land as security since he had no right of foreclosure. In turn, Athenian citizens who required cash could not easily borrow from non-citizens, the main money-lenders. This wall between the land and liquid capital was an impediment in the economy, but, the product of a juridically defined and enforced social hierarchy, it was too firmly based to be torn down.

In a society where land was both the basis of wealth and the obvious symbol of status, use of movable property as security could only be a partial substitute (see Andreau 1977: 1147–8, with pp. 74–8, above).

Finley's formulation of the gulf between land and money as an economic hindrance has generally been accepted by Greek historians. But there are hints that the gap could be bridged if the need arose, and was not so detrimental to the smooth functioning of the economy as Finley seems to suggest.

An obvious way around the difficulty was for a would-be metic creditor to make use of a citizen agent or middleman. The device is well attested elsewhere: Roman money-lenders apparently evaded the legal restrictions on interest charges to fellow-Romans by using Latins as intermediaries (Livy xxxv.7); and medieval Jews might lend at interest to fellow-Jews by using a Christian as a 'straw man' (Rabinowitz 1944). For Athens, there is only one indisputable example of a metic money-lender operating through a citizen agent. In the Demosthenic speech *On Behalf of Phormion* (xxxxvi.6), the speaker explains how it came about that Pasion was set down as owing eleven talents to the bank which he had leased to Phormion, his former slave:

So, when the defendant leased the business of the bank and took charge of
the deposits, he realized that as he had not yet received the right of
citizenship from you, he would be unable to recover such monies as Pasion
had lent on the security of land and tenement houses. He therefore chose
to have Pasion himself as debtor for these sums, rather than the other
creditors to whom he had lent the money.

Although Finley acknowledges this case as a breach in the
land–money wall (1952: 77), he gives three reasons why it should be
regarded as exceptional. No parallel example is known from the
sources; the relationship between Pasion and Phormion was
unusually close, as evidenced by the marriage of Phormion to the
widow of his former owner; and Pasion's retention of the land-
secured debts in his name was not primarily in his own interests – it
was so that Pasion could preserve his estate intact for his heirs. Each
argument can be qualified in some way, and I take them in reverse
order.

Although Pasion's action was in his heirs' (and his own) interests
as much as Phormion's, that is not necessarily evidence for the
uniqueness of the mechanism. The same could presumably be said
about some middlemen in other times and places. Was the
relationship between Pasion and Phormion exceptionally close?
Further into the speech (§§ 28–9), the speaker names three other
bankers who made provision for their widows to marry their former
slaves. Even if the 'many other instances' to which the speaker
loosely alludes are the product of his rhetorical imagination, the four
named examples look like more than a coincidence. The apparent
absence of parallels to the Pasion–Phormion mechanism is a more
serious objection, which needs a more detailed examination.
Although there are no obvious parallels, a hard look at the sources
does suggest at least the possibility that analogous arrangements
were available to other bankers (see Michell 1953).

Nothing is known of the status and circumstances of the three
bankers who anticipated Pasion's matrimonial plans for his former
slave. The speaker implies by what may be a rhetorical trick that all
were in precisely the same situation as Pasion and Phormion, but it
is possible that none of the three possessed the right to own land.
Other examples are more promising: one of Pasion's former owners
could have acted as his agent in the way he was later to act for
Phormion. We know that at least one of the original owners of the
bank (Archestratus) not only possessed Athenian citizenship (Isoc.

XVII.43), but retired from banking in favour of Pasion, as Pasion was himself to do in the case of Phormion. Speculation about whether the bankers Archestratus and Antisthenes formed a citizen–metic partnership is pointless, but there are other possible examples of bankers with citizen-associates. The plaintiff in Isocrates' *Trapeziticus* (XVII.33–4) describes in less than flattering terms the behaviour of a citizen called Pythodorus, 'who does and says everything on behalf of (*huper*) Pasion'. According to Apollodorus in his *First Speech Against Stephanus* (Dem. XLV), his opponent acted as agent or associate for more than one banker. He paints a hostile picture of the way in which Stephanus courted Aristolochus the banker so long as he enjoyed prosperity (§§64–5); and how he then transferred his attentions to Phormion, acting as his representative (*presbeutēs*).

Other possible pairs of bankers and citizens include the association of Sosinomus with Aristogiton in a loan at 3 per cent per month to Aeschines the Socratic (see above, pp. 1–2, with VIII, n. 39). Literally all we know about Aristogiton is his name, which does at least confirm that he can never have been a slave in Athens (Gellius, *Attic Nights* IX.2). A metic (ex-slave) banker is indubitably linked with a citizen in a fragment from Isaeus' speech *For Eumathes* (Forster 1927: fr. 18). The speaker (unnamed, but presumably the Xenocles mentioned in the following fragment) was so impressed with Eumathes' honest dealing over a deposit left in his hands that he 'became even more intimate with him and, when he set up his bank, supplied him with money' (see Chapter VIII, n. 31). Admittedly, the two do not appear as joint creditors, but the trusting relationship between them at least admits the possibility that Xenocles might play the part of Pasion to Eumathes' Phormion.

The discussion so far has been conducted in terms of metic bankers lending through citizen agents, but the range may be widened to include metics in general. A hint is provided here by the mysterious *enguētai* who put in a fleeting appearance in the Demosthenic speech *Against Apaturius* (XXXIII.10). These 'guarantors' appear only after Heraclides' bank has gone bust and the banker himself has gone into hiding. The unnamed speaker reports to them that Apaturius owes the bank thirty minas, a loan for which he is guarantor, and hands over into their keeping the appropriate security. There has been much speculation about the nature of these *enguētai*, most of it revolving around the idea that they somehow guaranteed repayment of the bank's deposits (see Bogaert 1968: 398–9). I would prefer to identify them with the sureties apparently required of non-citizens in public and private transactions. In his presentation of the citizen–metic divide, Finley (1952: 76–7) stresses the dependence of non-citizens on personal guarantee. It was, for example, only with the co-operation of a citizen-surety that metics were able to rent the houses in which they lived (Thür 1989). Acting as middleman for metic lenders was an additional possibility. That could conceivably have been the rôle of the otherwise unexplained co-guarantors (*sunenguētai*) appearing on a *horos* (Finley 1952: no. 18). The creditor, Hagno-demus, has no demotic and therefore *might* have been a metic (but see Finley 1952: 77). As often, the problem is one of identifying the metic.

An existing procedure could have supplied metics with suitable citizen guarantors. The law of Athens stipulated that every metic had to have a citizen *prostatēs* or patron (Harrison 1968–71: 1, 189, n. 4). The rôle of these *prostatai* has been much debated, with discussion focussing on the need for citizen representation in the courts (Arist. *Pol.* 1257a7; see Whitehead 1977: 89–33). Although there are certainly cases of non-citizen defendants appearing before the polemarch and providing citizen sureties (Dem. XXXII.29; [Dem.] LIX.40; Isoc. XVII.12), a *prostatēs* could also (and did more regularly) stand in as his metic's *enguētēs* whenever a citizen was needed as surety. An entry in one of the lexica (*Anec. Bekk.* 201 s.v. '*aprostasiou*') actually glosses *prostatēs* as 'one who takes care of public and private matters on a metic's behalf, being a kind of *enguētēs*'. The law required that freedmen take their former owner as *prostatēs*, and it is a reasonable assumption that an ex-slave who needed a citizen representative would turn to his former master. That is, in fact, the arrangement behind Phormion's lease of his former owner's banking business: Pasion, who acts as Phormion's citizen agent, must also have been his *prostatēs*.

Although the material gathered here cannot be conclusive, it shows the relative ease with which the *prostatēs–enguētēs* link could be deployed to breach the wall between land and money. The rarity with which breaches seem to have occurred says more for the wider organization of credit than the solidity of the wall. As I have tried to show in my study of lending and borrowing, citizens who needed to borrow had access to a range of possible sources of credit, before being forced to fall back on impersonal loans from metic money-lenders or bankers. It cannot be a coincidence that evidence for the use of citizen agents is concentrated around non-citizen bankers. The smooth working of the middleman-mechanism depended on fore-closure remaining the exception. In a period of crisis, where default might become the rule, the strain on the citizen–metic relationship would be great. Something like this seems to have happened at Byzantium, as recorded in an undated anecdote from the Aristo-telian *Oeconomica*:

Certain metics had lent money on the security of property. As they did not possess the right to own real property, the people voted that anyone who wanted to pay one third of the loan into the treasury would have a legal right to the property. (1347a1–4; see Bogaert 1968: 119).

The solution adopted by the *polis* amounted to a blanket offer to non-citizen lenders of an opportunity to purchase *enktēsis gēs kai oikias* (ownership of land and house). In Athens, by contrast, extension to non-citizens of the right to own real property remained a privilege granted to only a few (see Pečírka 1966).

III: PRODUCTIVE AND NON-PRODUCTIVE CREDIT

The most determined attack on the position I have sought to defend in the text (above, pp. 59–71) has been made in a series of papers by Thompson (1978, 1979a and 1982; for a recent summary: 1988). Attention is here confined to those parts of Thompson's writings which promote the idea of productive credit as a feature of Athenian economy and society. For the sake of completeness, I merge with his arguments the points raised by other supporters of productive credit in Athens. Combined support for the concept seems to fall into three categories, which are here examined in turn.

(i) The definition of productive/non-productive credit

It needs to be emphasized at the outset that loans are always judged to be productive or otherwise from the point of view of the borrower and not the lender. Confusion over this seems to have resulted in an unfortunate misapprehension in the review of the first edition of Finley's *Ancient Economy* by Frederiksen (1975). When Frederiksen writes that Finley 'infers from two letters of Cicero and Pliny that loans were mainly political and non-productive. The Roman lawyers, however, show a different world, wherein money is...regularly presumed to be interest-bearing and have a living value', he confuses a productive loan with an interest-bearing loan. Productive credit may be defined more closely as referring to loans taken out with the expectation that the resulting return will be greater than the interest charge. There is therefore no idea of economic compulsion on the part of the borrower. This is admittedly a narrow definition, but it (or something close to it) must be adhered to if the concept of credit is to be used as a gauge in assessing economic attitudes.

In his review of Bogaert's *Banques et banquiers...* (1968), Pleket (1971: 434) offers the hypothetical case of a peasant borrowing money to replace broken or worn-out tools. He admits that this would not result in any increase in agricultural yield, but suggests that 'the ancients may well have had a production mentality, provided one gives the word "productive" a less modern and anachronistic twist'. True enough; but what Pleket has done is to change the terms of reference away from the capitalist conception of productive credit. A similar line is taken by Thompson (1979a: 230–2) in a paper which has critical things to say about Bogaert's views on bankers' loans. In order to minimize the extent of non-productive credit, Thompson invents a sub-group which he calls 'political loans', consisting of four loans made to the *stratēgos* Timotheus by the banker Pasion (see above, pp. 213–15). He also suggests that two 'imaginary' loans attributed to bankers can be classed as commercial loans ([Dem.] XLIX.26–42; Isoc. XVII.12). Thompson's reasoning is effectively called into question by Bogaert (1986a: 24–5).

Before leaving the problem of definition, it may help to anticipate attempts to re-establish a productive element in Athenian credit relations by moving away from the idea of a purely monetary return. As is clear from my text (above, pp. 64–71), the Athenian élite did borrow heavily in order to fund public services which brought them a non-material, but still potent, return of *charis* (see the passage by Davies above, pp. 64–5). It is, however, precisely this willingness to borrow and spend in the hope of symbolic rewards that differentiates sharply between classical Athenians and the entrepreneurs of classical economic theory.

(ii) Concentration on untypical loan transactions

This is not a difficulty in Thompson's analysis as he is keenly aware
of the dangers involved in generalizing from inadequate data. On
the contrary, this is a failing of which he accuses the 'minimalists'
(see below). Concentration on the uncharacteristic is, however, a
weakness in the analysis of Athenian credit relations by Gluskina
(1970). In the English summary to her paper (p. 43), she writes:
'Trapezitae took an active part in financing trade and production
enterprises within the confines of Attica. The prevalence of this sort
of lending in fourth-century Athens has not been fully appreciated.'
But she bases this conclusion on just two examples ((i) and (ii) in the
list given in Chapter III, n. 11).

Outside Attica, Vial (1984) has made a detailed study of the civic
institutions of Delos during its period of independence (314–167
B.C.). From the evidence of inscriptions, he has compiled a dossier of
almost 150 citizens borrowing from the temple treasury (pp. 369–
72). Although Vial acknowledged that Finley's conclusions on the
exceptional nature of productive borrowing might be appropriate
for Attica, he argues that the easier conditions of Delian credit (long
or unlimited term; no danger of foreclosure) encouraged the use of
loans for profit-making purposes. But his evidence, which depends
on inferring the motives of borrowers from the size and sequence of
the sums borrowed, is at best inconclusive. Four loans of five 500 dr.,
borrowed on the same day by four Delians and repaid (again, on the
same day) five months later, are interpreted as funds for some short-
term commercial venture (pp. 375–7). It is also argued that a Delian
who regularly borrows large amounts (in one case as much as
13,400 dr.) cannot be borrowing for prestige purposes, but in order
to finance some productive enterprise (pp. 377–8). The fragility of
the arguments will be apparent, and other hypothetical explanations
are easily found. The four Delians could be borrowing (say) to
ransom a friend out of slavery; and the repeated borrowing of large
sums might be compared with the loans Timotheus raised from
Pasion. What is striking about the mass of information gathered by
Vial is the way in which it seems to support Finley's association of
non-productive borrowing with the lifestyle of the Athenian élite. As
Vial himself points out (p. 372), there is a massive overlap between
his lists of borrowers and of those involved in political or liturgical
activities.

(iii) Assuming the existence of 'missing persons'

This refers to persons (and institutions) whose non-appearance is explained away by references to the bias and imperfections of our sources. So Thompson writes: 'In an Athenian court one brags about how much money one has spent on public services, not how much one has acquired by investing. That is why we hear more about borrowing to meet one's social responsibilities, such as ransoming a friend, than to expand one's business' (1982: 57). The missing-persons argument is Thompson's major defence against the people he calls 'minimalists'. He is, in fact, reviving an argument made many years ago by Harrison (1954) in his review of Finley's *Land and Credit* (1952): 'There would surely be a greater tendency for loans for non-productive purposes to come into court, contracted as they often would be under stress.' There is an element of truth in the suggestion, but both Harrison and Thompson neglect the many incidental references to loan transactions which occur in the Attic Orators. Nor are the Orators, in spite of their overwhelming importance, the only source of information about credit relations. As shown in my opening chapter, there are casual references to credit in almost every branch of literature. It is a weakness of Thompson's analysis that he relies on other people's collections of data; see 1982: 80, n. 153, where his 'review [of] the evidence we have for borrowing' is based on lists of loans compiled by Bogaert and Gluskina.

Finally, I must acknowledge a response by Andreau to my earlier statement (1983: 43), which was in turn a reaction to his comments on productive credit in the Greek world (1977: 1144–8). In his later paper (1984: 113, n. 45), Andreau states that I have misunderstood his position, and announces his intention of devoting an article to an examination of my conception of productive credit. If Andreau's arguments have been misunderstood, that is to be regretted; but further comment must be postponed until the appearance of the promised paper.[1]

IV: THE RATE OF CAPITALIZATION OF LAND IN ATTICA

The rate of capitalization of an asset refers to the ratio between its market value and the annual income it produces, usually expressed as a percentage. In the ancient world, the foremost income-earning asset was land. The rate of capitalization for land in Attica has regularly attracted the attention of historians, who have made the percentage size of rental payments the basis for generalizations about the Athenian economy.

The most detailed discussion is by Billeter (1898: 15–18), who envisages a shifting relationship between rate of interest, rent and the price of land. For an outline of the mechanism, we may turn to Adam Smith's account of how the price of land depends on the rate of interest (1776: II, 45–6). A person who wishes to draw a regular income from his capital is assumed to have the choice of buying land to lease or lending at interest. Says Smith: 'The superior security of land, together with some other advantages which almost everywhere attend on this species of property, will generally dispose him to content himself with a smaller revenue from land, than what he might have had by lending out his money at interest.' But he adds that if the difference between rent and interest becomes too great, ownership of land will look less attractive and its price will fall.

Billeter argues that his findings bear out the general rule that the rate of capitalization for land should be significantly lower than the ordinary rate of interest. The key to his conclusion is a clause in the terms of a lease agreed by the demesmen of Halai Aixonides (ll. 31–47; see above p. 105). It was proposed that the proceeds resulting from the sale of olive wood cleared off the land should be loaned out at 1 per cent per month, and the resulting revenue shared equally between deme funds and leaseholders. Billeter seems to assume that the ratio between the value of a part of the property (the olive wood) and the annual income from that part of the property taken up by the demesmen (half of 1 per cent per month), must somehow be identical to the ratio between the value of the entire property and the whole annual rent. This means that the rate of capitalization for farmland in fourth-century Attica was approximately $\frac{1}{2}$ per cent per month – 6 per cent per annum, or half the ordinary rate of interest. It hardly needs to be added that the chain of Billeter's reasoning is hopelessly weak. It makes better sense to see the division of the interest-revenue into two equal parts as just that. The only recent writer to take Billeter's figure seriously is Behrend (1970: 118–19), in a study of Attic lease agreements. In a sequence of suggestions, the logic of which frankly escapes me, Behrend claims to find other evidence to support Billeter's rate of 6 per cent. If I understand Behrend correctly, he sees some significance in the possibility that real security in loan transactions might be twice the

value of the loan; also, that certain leases contain a clause halving
the rent payable in the case of destruction resulting from enemy
action. He tentatively suggests that this had something to do with
the two-field system, which meant that only half the available land
was productive at any one time. A serious study of leasing land and
property is now available by Osborne (1988).

Billeter's final estimate for the rate of capitalization for land is
between 6 and 8 per cent, with the higher figure coming from a
speech of Isaeus (XI.42). The litigant lists as components of an estate
a farm worth $2\frac{1}{2}$ talents, bringing an annual rent of twelve minae (=
8 per cent), and two houses which had been bought for 3,000 and
500 dr. respectively, bringing a combined rent of three minas (=
$8\frac{4}{7}$ per cent). Billeter rejects as evidence the figure calculated for
houses on the grounds of complications through building costs and
amortization, but both are accepted by a majority of historians.
Encouragement apparently comes from a third figure, derived from
an inscription of the later fourth century (*IG* II² 2496 11.9–28 ~
IJG I p. 240 no. XIII *ter*), recording for a workshop and adjoining
house an annual rent of fifty-four drachmas. We are also told that
the property was assessed for taxation purposes at seven minas,
giving a ratio of $7\frac{5}{7}$ per cent. These three figures are commonly
merged to arrive at 8 per cent as the 'standard rate' for rents in
Attica (see, for example, Jones 1957: 139, n. 72). Tod expresses
surprise that the figure should be so far below the current rate of
interest (*CAH*¹ v 20).

In fact, a fourth figure, again taken from an inscription, is less
accommodating (*IG* II² 1241). By the terms of a lease, dating from
300/299, a phratry rent out a piece of land for ten years at an annual
rate of 600 dr. At any point during the term of the lease, the tenant
is given the option of purchasing the property for 5,000 dr., giving a
ratio of 12 per cent. Billeter (1898: 17, n. 3) explains the figure as
reflecting the possibility of sale to a sitting tenant at a price below the
land's market value, thereby suggesting an artificially high rate of
capitalization. Thompson, on the other hand (1978: 406), sees the
tenant as paying over the odds in return for the option to purchase
the property. Here, I exceptionally find myself in agreement with
Behrend (1970: 92, n. 201), who raises the possibility that the lease
conceals a loan agreement. If so, the transaction is analogous to the
situation described in Demosthenes' *Against Pantaenetus* (see above,
pp. 193–7). The 'lessee' borrowed 5,000 dr. from the phratry,

handing over land as security. He continued to live on the land as quasi-tenant, handing over rent-interest at the customary rate of 1 per cent per month. At any time, he was free to cancel the agreement by repaying the 'purchase price' of 5,000 dr. If, by the end of the ten-year period, no repayment had been made, the land could become the full property of the phratry. Historians who accept 12 per cent as a realistic rent either see the rate of capitalization extending from 8 to 12 per cent (Jardé 1925: 156; Andreyev 1974: 39), or assume an increase over time (Glotz 1920: 239).

Whichever way they are expressed, the figures we have are hardly conclusive; only one, it should be noted, is exactly 8 per cent. This would not matter much, had the ratios not been used for comparisons and calculations. Casson concludes that, from the point of view of the Athenian investor, one of the drawbacks of real estate was that (1976: 35) 'it yielded a return of only about 8 per cent, far less than other easily available investments...' (cf. Thompson 1978: 404-7). The rent-ratio has also been used as a multiplier to calculate the likely capital value of rented plots. Andreyev (1974: 39) assumes in this connexion that public land will have been leased out on a 'non-entrepreneurial basis', and sets his rate at 5-6 per cent. This results in land values that are suspiciously high – mostly more than one talent, and some as high as ten talents. 'Although there is insufficient evidence to claim that 8 per cent was the "standard" classical Athenian rent, it is clear that rents were often of that order.' So says Osborne (1985: 57), who uses the figure in his re-interpretation of the so-called 'hekatostai inscriptions' as property leases (pp. 56-9). The idea is economical and appealing; but doubts remain over the status of 8 per cent as even an approximation to the rate for Athenian rents.

V: FOUNDATIONS AND LENDING AT INTEREST

Absent from classical Athens were the foundations or endowment funds that are such a feature of civic life in the Hellenistic and Roman worlds (Larsen 1938: 361-8 – still the best short account). These foundations were usually established by gift or bequest with the intention of providing funds in perpetuity for the celebration of festivals, upkeep of shrines and temples, commemoration of the dead and the well-being of the community in general (supplies of grain, oil and the like). The assets by which the funds were generated were typically either land to be leased or money to be lent at interest (Larsen 1938: 363–5; *IJG* II 77–145 for selections of both sorts). The standard collection of testimonia by Laum (1914: II – now out of date) lists well over 200 individual foundations from the Greek world.

What is striking about all this material is its chronological distribution, firmly labelling foundations as a Hellenistic phenomenon. Taking the dates supplied by Laum, the breakdown by centuries B.C. is approximately as follows: fifth – 1, fourth – 2, third – 26, second – 22 (and see the statistical summary by Laum I, 8–11). This upswing in the creation of foundations is not easily explained. Many of the earlier examples are concerned with commemoration of the dead, which Kamps (1937) interprets as a preoccupation dating from the late fourth century: a response to structural changes in the relative strengths of 'clan' and family solidarity. But that accounts for only a part of the picture. Foundations existed for a variety of purposes, and occasional examples are found as early as the second half of the fifth century. The Plotheian decree (above, pp. 173–4; not included in Laum's catalogue) is a clear case of the 'foundation mentality', with the income from specified funds being earmarked for the fixed purpose of celebrating religious festivals. And yet, despite this early (possibly the earliest) appearance of a loanable-fund foundation in Athens, that particular institution never flourished there, as elsewhere in the Greek world. For the whole of Attica, from the fifth century B.C. to the second century A.D., Laum lists only ten examples of foundations (nos. 14–20), of which perhaps three were made up of monies lent at interest (19b, 20 and 20a). By contrast, Ziebarth (1917) identified on Delos a minimum of twenty-four loan-fund foundations.

Part of the explanation may rest with the practical requirements for a successful foundation; in particular, those made up of money lent at interest. Apart from the Plotheia inscription, the earliest known foundations drew their income from land (Mannzmann 1962: 127–8). Plutarch tells how Nicias purchased an estate for 10,000 dr., the revenue of which was to provide for sacrifices on Delos and supply the Delians with a feast, at which they were to pray for blessings for Nicias from the gods (*Nicias* III.5; Laum II, no. 53). Perhaps forty years later (*c.* 385), Xenophon set aside a portion of the produce from his estate at Scillus for the performance of sacrifices to Artemis and the maintenance of her temple (*Anabasis* V.3; Laum

II, no. 12). A foundation was essentially a gift with strings attached, and there was always the danger that at some future date all or some of those strings would be snapped. We are told how both Nicias and Xenophon tried to bind posterity by setting up inscriptions recording the terms of their endowments. If there was a threat that a foundation based on land might somehow fail, the danger was magnified many times over with cash out on loan. Those responsible for managing foundation funds faced the dilemma of wanting a respectable return of interest to generate funds and, at the same time, requiring cast-iron security. In very general terms, those people in a position to offer the best security would be able to borrow elsewhere on less binding terms.

Something of the paradox can be seen in the arrangements for a number of foundations, of which only a sample are examined here. The queen of foundation inscriptions is a decree from Corcyra, probably dating from the third century B.C. (*IG* IX 1 694 ~ *IJG* II 117–29 and 137–44 ~ Laum II, no. 1 ~ Mannzmann 1962: 39–77, where it forms the centrepiece of an examination of the legal side of foundations in the Greek world; note the searching review by Hommel 1964). This long inscription gives (and then repeats) detailed instructions for a joint donation of 120 minas to the *polis* of Corcyra to pay for the annual hiring of performers in honour of Dionysus (ll. 1–7). The cash is to be lent out at the equivalent of 16 per cent per annum, 'neither more nor less' (ll. 53–5; on the calculation of interest, see *IJG* II 139–41; Hommel 1964: 615–17). Responsible for placing and recovering the loans each year are the three wealthiest men in the *polis* (ll. 9–10; cf. 42–9), who publicize the availability of credit by having it 'cried' for at least five days (ll. 42–3). The authors of the inscription envisage some difficulties. If it is, in the estimation of the council and assembly, possible to place the funds and yet the three men fail to do so, they are to be heavily fined (ll. 66–72). It is to be presumed that, as the wealthiest citizens, they would be in a position to put pressure on others to take up the loans or, as a last resort, take up any surplus cash themselves.

Turning to a second foundation from the city of Aegiale on Amorgos in the second century B.C. (*IG* XII 7 515 ~ Laum II, no. 50; partly trans. by Hands 1968: 177 D.5), it is clear that the loans were destined for the wealthy. A gift of 2,000 dr. for the support of festivals and games was to be placed at 10 per cent interest per annum. Individual loans were not to exceed 200 dr., and in return the borrower had to offer security of land worth at least ten times that amount. The loans, once taken out, were perpetual and could not be repaid, so that borrowers had effectively 'sold' property worth 2,000 dr. for only 200 dr. and, in order to have the use of it, had to pay an annual 'rent' of 20 dr. Taking up a loan from the Aegiale foundation looks like the performance of a civic duty (for Roman parallels, see Hands 1968: 109–10). This helps to explain the reluctance (and eventual refusal) of the Achaean League to accept from Eumenes an offer of 720,000 dr., the income from which was to be used to pay a salary to the Achaean council (Polybius XXII.7.3; 185 B.C.). The men of wealth who controlled the League presumably realized that they would end up having to borrow the money themselves (against the over-elaborate explanation of Larsen 1938: 366–7, involving the opposition of business and banking interests).

How this and the other Hellenistic material on foundations relates to Athens must remain problematical; but, in combination with the interpretation of the Plotheian inscription offered in the text, it goes some way towards explaining the relative rarity of loanable-fund foundations in fourth-century Athens. Alternative sources of credit were available, and the wealthy had plenty of other calls on their cash in the performance of liturgies. Possible changes after the abolition of the democracy, and the liturgies that went with it (Ferguson 1911: 55–8 and 99–100), are at present a subject for speculation.

VI: BANK DEPOSITS, INTEREST AND THE PATRIMONY OF DEMOSTHENES

Payment of interest on bank deposits has been the source of a long-running debate; the earlier literature is surveyed by Bogaert (1968: 345–51, with nn. 236–9). Bogaert himself comes down on the side of interest payments on timed deposits (*dépôts de placement*) but not on demand deposits (*dépôts de paiement*). But this is a modern distinction which may not be appropriate for the ancient Greek world. The detailed evidence offered by Bogaert in support of limited interest payments (1968: 345–51) seems to be successfully challenged by Thompson (1979a: 225–30), whose objections are not overturned by Bogaert's counter-arguments (1986a: 19–24). The arguments on both sides are, to say the least, attenuated; I see no need to rehearse them here. But one point calls for further discussion: Bogaert's choice of 10 per cent as the likely annual rate paid out on timed deposits (1968: 347).

Interest at 10 per cent per annum was not a common rate in fourth-century Athens (see above, p. 104). Although that need not be a serious objection to Bogaert's hypothesis, there are other explanations of his evidence, which consists of a discrepancy between two figures in different speeches of Demosthenes. In the *First Speech Against Stephanus* (XLV.34), Apollodorus argued that Phormion had embezzled eleven talents of his father's banking funds; but, in the speech *For Phormion* (XXXVI.3), the speaker reveals that the repayment actually claimed was twenty talents. This discrepancy of nine talents has generated a literature out of all proportion to the importance of the problem, with contributions by Wolff (1966: 54, n. 1), Beyer (1968: 65), Talamanca (1971), Erxleben (1973), and Thompson (1981). The bibliography is judiciously surveyed by Bogaert (1986a: 23–35), who opts for the solution offered by Sandys (Paley and Sandys 1910: II, xxiv, n. 4). Briefly, Sandys suggests that the additional nine talents are to be understood as interest on the eleven originally embezzled. Taking the period of the lease as eight years (Dem. XXXVI.37) gives an annual interest charge of (almost) 10 per cent, which Bogaert interprets as the probable equivalent of the rate paid on timed deposits.

The difficulty here is the rate of interest needed to generate nine out of eleven talents in eight years. The precise figure is 10·22 per cent – '10% en chiffres arrondis', says Bogaert. But that is an odd way of arriving at an approximation, as it was surely the final sum of money and not the rate of interest that would be rounded up or down? A possible way forward might be to see the eight-year span of the lease as an exaggeration, rounded up from seven years and an unspecified number of months (see the chronological summary of Pasion's bank in Isager and Hansen 1975: 225–6). When Demosthenes made his claim against his guardians, the interest charge he levied on his defrauded property was 1 per cent per month (Dem. XXVII.17, 23, 35; XXVIII.13); as argued in the text (above, pp. 105–6), that was the prevailing rate of interest in fourth-century Athens. Seven years of interest on eleven talents at 1 per cent per month yields slightly less than $9\frac{1}{4}$ talents, which might be rounded down to nine talents. I offer these figures *exempli gratia*, as the problem seems insoluble in narrow terms of interest charge and duration of the alleged fraud.

The question of Demosthenes' patrimony prompts discussion of another part of Bogaert's analysis (1986: 34, n. 76). He points out that the estate as bequeathed to Demosthenes was estimated to be worth fifteen talents, with the guardianship lasting for ten years. As the guardians were collectively ordered by the court to repay a grand total of thirty talents, that implies an annual interest charge of 10 per cent per annum. Demosthenes himself describes this as (XXIX.60), 'the lowest rate (*elachistos*), and not that at which estates are usually let'. Bogaert sees this intended as a contrast to the 1 per cent per month claimed by Demosthenes (see above), and as support for his hypothesis that bankers paid 10 per cent on timed deposits.

Once again, there are difficulties about this interpretation. In the first place, it implies an odd procedure in assessing the damages, with Demosthenes suggesting an appropriate rate of interest which was then reduced by the jurors. It seems more likely that Demosthenes proposed a final figure for damages which the jurors would adjust as they saw fit. Thirty talents may be seen as a straightforward doubling of the original fifteen. But was the estate valued at fifteen talents? Demosthenes himself gives a value of 'almost fourteen talents' (XXVII.4), and that is borne out by the piecemeal listing of items, totalling thirteen talents, forty-six minas (*APF* 3597 XIII). The higher valuation of fifteen minas is ascribed to the guardians by Demosthenes in a series of what Davies rightly calls 'obscure passages' (*APF* 3597 XVI). This is a piece of rhetorical posturing on Demosthenes' part, and it seems certain that in assessing damages he would work from his own itemized valuation. In fact, thirteen talents, forty-six minas at 1 per cent per month over ten years yields sixteen talents, thirty-one minas and 200 dr., making a total award for damages of 30 talents, seventeen minas and 200 dr. – a natural candidate for downward rounding to thirty talents. In any case, the duration of the guardianship may have been less than the ten years claimed by Demosthenes, anxious to present the guardians in the worst possible light (*APF* 3597 X); compare the possible exaggeration of Phormion's lease of Pasion's bank.

If the damages were calculated, as I have suggested, on the basis of 1 per cent per month, how can this be reconciled with Demosthenes' claim that the jurors allowed him compensation 'at the lowest rate'? The answer may again be the striking of a rhetorical posture. When Demosthenes was claiming his compensation, he repeatedly described it as 'only' (*monon*) 1 per cent per month (see Chapter IV, n. 14); and when that rate was actually awarded, he continued to harp on its being (if anything) on the low side. An alternative (and more attractive) solution is to regard the anomalous reference to an award 'at the lowest rate' and the figure of thirty talents as additional evidence for the forging of the *Third Speech Against Aphobus*. In which case, my own reinterpretation of Demosthenes' damages joins Bogaert's original presentation as vain juggling with figures.

Notes

I. APPROACHES TO LENDING AND BORROWING

1 Fr. 38 in Gernet and Bizos 1955–9: II, omitting the section of the speech summarized by Myrtilus; the fullest commentaries on the fragments are by Blass 1887–98: I, 630–3 and Messina 1948. The translation in the text is adapted from the Loeb edition of Gulick 1927–41: IV, excluding for the sake of brevity less important sections of the fragment and all irrelevant comments by Myrtilus. The text of the two sections marked off by obelisks may be corrupt, but without affecting the general sense of the passage. See Millett (forthcoming), arguing that the speaker told the jury not about the seizure of a branded slave, but about a house offered as security; on the second, longer section, see Messina 1948: 245–50.

2 To add to the uncertainty, Lysias' authorship of the speech has been disputed, though on no very good grounds. The elaborate arguments against authenticity put forward by Welcker (1834) are more than adequately refuted by Baiter and Sauppe 1839–43: II, 170–1, Blass 1887–98: I, 630–1 and Messina 1949.

   Provided that the speeches in question are genuine examples of fifth- or fourth-century forensic oratory, disputes over the authenticity of *authorship* normally have no bearing on the value of the Orators as evidence for Athenian economy and society. On the tendency of works by lesser writers to be attributed to better-known authors, see Dover 1968b: 23–7 and 1974: 8–10. Concerning so-called 'private' speeches, in only a very few cases does the problem of authenticity go beyond attribution to involve the whole speech. Where a speech is suspected of being a forgery – typically, a late rhetorical exercise – it has no independent value as evidence for Athenian social institutions. For this verdict on Dem. XXIX, see Finley 1952: 24, n. 10 (reinforced by Jackson and Row 1969: 49–50), against Calhoun 1934 and Burke 1974–5 arguing in favour of authenticity.

3 For general comments on the use of the Orators to write the history of society: Finley 1952: 16–17, Dover 1968b: 71–2 and 148–74, and 1974: 1–45 (esp. pp. 13–14), Ober 1989: 43–9; in greater detail: Todd 1990a. The technique of inference as described in the text is not entirely unproblematic, depending in part on the social composition of the jury

and the speaker's perceptions of what they might expect to hear; see
Todd 1990b. Some of the possible pitfalls are revealed by Wevers's
reading of Isaeus (1969). In spite of sensible introductory remarks (pp.
94–120), he tries to demonstrate how the anti-social behaviour described
in these speeches about disputed inheritances proves that (p. 121):
'Athens in the fourth century was living in a fading tradition.' But,
apart from the problem of deducing the dynamic concept of a decline
from a single source, it is only natural that family quarrels, accusations,
illegitimacy and the like should have a high profile in inheritance suits.

With rare exceptions (notably Kamps 1938), attempts to determine
the relative strength or weakness of a speaker's case are unconvincing
and only marginally relevant to the understanding of Athenian society.
The studies of the Demosthenic *paragraphē* speeches by Isager and
Hansen (1975) and Thompson (1980), and the series of papers by Miles
(1951a, 1951b, 1952 and 1955), display great ingenuity, but only serve
to show up the impenetrability of the Orators' arguments. Even on the
rare occasions that speeches representing both sides of a case survive
(e.g. Isaeus XI and [Dem.] XLIII; on which see Thompson 1976),
certainty is still impossible. The rhetorical sleights of hand detected by
Wyse in *every* speech of Isaeus strongly suggest that twisting of the facts
was in order even when the client had right on his side.

4 See the confused misinterpretation of the Lysias fragment in the
textbook by Glotz (1920) – still cited and read as an introduction to the
ancient Greek economy. I cite three conflicting quotations taken from
the same chapter and all apparently referring to Aeschines. 'Aeschines
the philosopher kept his perfume-works going by means of borrowing'
(p. 241); 'The highest rates [of interest] were imposed on industry. A
perfume manufacturer borrowed from friends at nine obols in order to
repay bankers who were taking twice as much from him' (p. 243); 'The
36 per cent required by bankers from a suspicious client... is almost
without interest except in the history of manners' (p. 244).

5 The use of Comedy to write the history of society is complicated by the
constraints of performance. Whereas a litigant has to persuade the jury
of the truth of his argument and necessarily presents a plausible picture,
the comic playwright has to make his audience laugh, and everything
else may be subordinated to that end. This is more apparent with the
Old Comedy of Aristophanes where fantasy has a large part to play in
the creation of comic effect. See the common-sense observations by
Dover 1951–2 (a review of Ehrenberg 1951); on the apparently
intractable relationship between the plays of Aristophanes and
contemporary politics, see Heath 1987. With New Comedy the emphasis
seems to be different. Since antiquity it has been assumed that
Menander's plays somehow reflect 'real life', and it can be argued that
their humour arises, not out of fantasy, but from closeness to reality.
There remains, nevertheless, plenty of scope for argument, with modern
opinion about the historicity of the plays ranging from total scepticism

to almost complete acceptance; earlier bibliography is cited and summarized by Préaux (1957) and Perlman (1965), to which the more recent discussion by Turner (1984) adds little.

Broad interpretations of Menander as history try to place the plays at some appropriate point along a 'spectrum' of historicity. A more promising technique might be to abandon the monolithic approach and try to distinguish the different elements in the plays that are either more or less liable to distortion for comic effect or dramatic convenience. Menander does, in fact, share with Aristophanes elements of comic fantasy. Tarn was surely right to object (Tarn and Griffith 1952: 273) that life in later fourth-century Athens was 'not entirely composed of seductions and unwanted children, coincidences and recognitions of long-lost daughters, irate fathers and impertinent slaves'. But on a lower dramatic level, both Aristophanes and Menander adopt the same technique (familiar from the Orators) of piling up circumstantial detail as a plausible launching-pad for the more fantastic parts of their plots (Handley 1985: 8–9). In this connexion, Robin Osborne has pointed out to me the wealth of accurate local detail in Menander's *Dyscolus* and the way in which it is made integral to the play. That is the kind of material which, once identified, can be used to illuminate Athenian society.

6 Compare *Lysistrata* 1050–7 (with Henderson 1987: *ad loc.*), where the chorus of women are moved to offer their audience loans that need never be repaid – the catch being that no one will be given any money in the first place.

7 For a selection of references to credit in the *Characters* see the index to the excellent Leipzig edition (Theophrast 1897) s.v. 'Leihen'. The *Characters* have in the past been dismissed as a Byzantine compilation, but recent editors agree on the traditional attribution to Theophrastus (though with occasional interpolations), and a date for composition/ publication around 320 (Ussher 1960: 12–14). Although the text of the *Characters* is in a poor state, the underlying sense is usually clear. Quotations in this study generally follow the text established by Steinmetz (1960–2), with translations adapted from the version by Vellacott (1973).

The potential of the *Characters* for writing the social history of Athens has been neglected; the paper by Giglioni (1980) is helpful within limits, but preoccupied with *histoire événementielle*. The most illuminating study of the *Characters* for the historian of society is probably Smeed's examination of the Theophrastan 'Character' as a literary genre (1985). He correctly identifies the 'inner man' of each Character as emerging from 'externals' which can be manipulated to recreate a range of aspects of contemporary Athenian society (pp. 1–5). More particularly, the *Characters* differ from Comedy in the absence of any danger that reality might be subordinated to plot. The description of each individual has the sole purpose of creating the character-trait he is supposed to possess. By observing how negative behaviour transgresses norms it is theoretically possible to infer the norms themselves. Such is the technique used to make historical sense of the *Characters* in this study. There are, of course, complications: whose norms do the *Characters* transgress and how far were they appropriate to the Athenian *polis* as a whole? I hope to enquire further into these and other questions in a forthcoming paper on the *Characters* and Athenian society.

8 Although the *Demodocus* is almost certainly not by Plato, it is thought to date from the later fourth century (Souilhé 1930: 37–42; Isnardi 1954). As in the case of the Orators (above, n. 2), attribution is of secondary importance. The attitudes of Plato and Aristotle to credit in general are discussed in greater detail in the following chapter.

9 Other common images drawn from credit are introduced elsewhere in the text: obligation of children to look after aged parents expressed as repayment of a debt (pp. 133–5); imagery based on the payment of interest (p. 46); metaphors derived from *eranos*-credit (pp. 153–5).

10 Compare the vivid image in the pseudo-Platonic *Axiochus* (367B): if you delay in giving back your life as if it were a debt (*hōs chreos*), then nature (*phusis*) steps in like a usurer (*hōs obolostatis*) and distrains on your sight and hearing (see further pp. 183–4, below).

11 The association of paying the penalty for impiety with repayment of a debt is not restricted to Aeschylus (see, for example, Soph. *OC* 235; Eur. *El.* 858). For references (ancient and modern) to the concept of justice as retaliation, see Blundell 1989: 26–31.

12 The importance of *pistis* in making and returning deposits is underlined in Herodotus' story of the Spartan, renowned for his probity, who nevertheless planned to embezzle a quantity of silver left with him for safe keeping (IV.86; see Bogaert 1966: 35–6, with pp. 204–5, below).

The usual Athenian equivalent of 'debt' (*chreos*) has a range of meanings easily as wide as *pistis* ('obligation, affair, matter, purpose, duty, task', according to LSJ⁹). On the broadness of the concept of debt in early Greece and other 'primitive' societies, see Lintott 1982: 17; Gluckman 1965: 209–13.

13 On credit instruments in general, see Hawtrey, *ESS* s.v. 'credit'; Spufford 1986: xxxvii–1; on their place in maintaining the growth of economic activity in modern capitalist society: Anderson 1970. Some of the implications of the eventual development of paper credit are sketched in by Braudel 1979: 470–8. His claim that notes and cheques between market traders and bankers were known in Greece (p. 472) need not be taken too seriously. Nadler (*ESS* s.v. 'financial organisation') argues that credit instruments 'could only become widely used if they attained unquestioned legal standing and if the rights of drawers, drawees and holders were properly safeguarded by legal provisions'. None of these precautions applied in the classical Greek world.

14 Familiarity with the practice may be inferred from a fragment of a lost

speech by Antiphon (Maidment 1941: fr. c 1). The speaker lists among legitimate reasons for travelling overseas 'the collection of a private debt (*chreos idion*)'.

15 On the perceived rôle of banks in the creation of the modern, industrial economy, see Mathias 1983: 130–59; and in greater detail: Cameron, Crisp, Patrick and Tilly 1967 (with Lévy–Leboyer 1968).

　　In so far as neo-classical economics is descriptive of any system, it is to be associated with the modern, capitalist economy. The 'school' of neo-classical economists is very approximately as old as this century. The prime statement of neo-classical theory in English is Alfred Marshall's remarkable book *The Principles of Economics*, first published in 1890 and reprinted many times. The title of Marshall's book is significant in that classical economists (notably Smith, Ricardo and Mill) wrote studies of *political* economy. The dropping of the political element marks an attempt to disembed economic theory from its surrounding society, in favour of a more objective, pseudo-scientific approach. Theories of price, markets, marginal utility and economic equilibrium are predominantly neo-classical creations (see Millett 1990: 167–9). Although neo-classical theory is at present the prevailing orthodoxy, there are doubts concerning its ability to make sense of even capitalist economies. The fallacies of the neo-classical school are exposed in Robinson and Eatwell 1974: 1–51.

16 There is an uncomplicated narrative account of the 'House of Pasion' by Glover 1917: 302–36; for full analytical detail, see Bogaert 1968: 63–79. Pasion's bank is untypical by virtue of its size: one explanation for the unusual and misleading richness of our information. Pasion himself was arguably one of the wealthiest of classical Athenians with a fortune of approximately seventy talents (*APF* 11672, with Bogaert 1986a: 42–7).

17 Most conveniently in Austin and Vidal-Naquet 1977: 1–8, with additional material in Gernet 1933, Pearson 1957, Humphreys 1970 and Nippel 1982. The fullest account of the debate (though dated) remains Will 1954.

18 The standard juristic studies are by Caillemer 1870, Beauchet 1897: IV, 226–34, and Lipsius 1905–15: 716–38. Much of the earlier literature on guaranty is discussed by Finley 1952, on real security by Harrison 1968–71: I, 96–121.

19 The standard edition of Böckh's *Staatshaushaltung* for reference purposes is the third edition of 1886 edited by Fränkel; for the sake of convenience, references in the text are to the English translation by Lewis (1842).

20 Also known as the '*oikos* debate' (Pearson 1957) and the 'Bücher–Meyer controversy' (Finley 1979). Bücher's *Entstehung* went through many editions – a sixteenth appeared in 1922. References in the text are to the fifth edition of 1906, as reprinted by Finley (1979), along with other major contributions to the debate by Meyer and Beloch. An English

translation of the third edition of *Entstehung* (*Industrial Evolution*, by S. M. Wickett, London and New York, 1901) was not available to me. The antecedents of Bücher's staged theory of development are set out briefly by Gras 1930 and at greater length by von Below 1901 (who summarizes on p. 8 the substance of Bücher's paper of 1876).

21 In the first edition of his massively influential textbook of Greek history Beloch described Pasion as 'der Rothschild dieser Zeit' (1893–1904: II, 350–2) – a comparison rightly ridiculed by Bücher (10, n. 1), and actually omitted from the second edition of Beloch's history (1912–27: III.1, 333–4). The Rothschild parallel is accepted with reservations by Gomme (1937a: 55–6), who is forced to admit that the evidence for the sophistication of Greek bankers is not impressive, but adds: 'I expect they did more than we know of' – a classic case of the so-called 'missing persons' argument (see my Appendix III).

22 References in the text are to the English translation by Frank, *The Agrarian Sociology of Ancient Civilizations* (1976): unfortunately marred by a weak supplementary bibliography (pp. 30–3) and occasional lapses of accuracy. The most glaring example is p. 43, n. 1: 'The remarkable thing about these ancient "factories" is that they could be "confiscated" (*aphobos*) or lost through dissipation (*timerokos*)...' What is presumably a misprint in the German original (Timerokos for Timarchus) has resulted in the transformation of the titles of forensic speeches (Demosthenes XXVII; Aeschines I) into non-existent technical terms!

23 Hasebroek seems to have reached these uncharacteristic conclusions under the influence of work on the Egyptian papyri by Preisigke 1910. His second thoughts were the result of criticisms by Laum 1922 (and see Hasebroek 1923). The supposed evidence in support of giro and associated operations has been carefully examined by Bogaert (1968: 30 and 336–45), who scrupulously ignores the papyri.

24 References in the text are to the useful but sometimes erratic English translation by Jonkers, *Economic Life in Greece's Golden Age* (1958). According to Jonkers' preface (p. vii), the influence of Weber on Bolkestein came second to that of Zimmern's *The Greek Commonwealth* (1911). Zimmern's work stoutly refuses classification as primitivist, modernist, Weberian, or anything else. The extensive bibliographical index to the fifth and final edition of 1931 omits the names of Bücher, Weber and Hasebroek. But throughout the book, Zimmern emphasizes distinctions between the ancient and modern worlds, and his chapter on 'Money' (pp. 301–13) has a number of penetrating suggestions about lending and borrowing in Athens.

25 About other general studies of Greek economic and social history little need be said. They are numerous and almost invariably include chapters on banking and money-lending, but display either ignorance of, or indifference to, the contributions of Weber and Hasebroek. They therefore tend to represent only a marginal advance on the antiquarian

researches of Büchsenschütz. For the sake of completeness I list the most influential of these general works with a minimum of comment. Glotz (1920) discusses credit under two headings, both indicative of his approach: 'Investment and interest' (pp. 238–44) and 'Commercial companies and banks' (pp. 301–7). The relevant sections of Cavaignac (1951: 17–18, 30–1 and 91–2) are concerned mainly with rates of interest. Probably the most widely read survey of the Greek economy in English is still Michell (1957), which is thoroughly modernist in tone, talking in terms of 'loans for highly productive purposes...of vital importance for both industry and commerce' (p. 30; cf. pp. 311–51). Concerning French (1964), see the sharply critical review by Finley (1965b). The chapter on 'Finance and banking' in Hopper (1979: 118–25) is a hotch-potch of material, full of errors of fact and interpretation. For details of relevant entries in encyclopaedias, see Heichelheim 1938: II, 193.

26 The more general material in *Land and Credit* is summarized in Finley 1953a; those aspects of Finley's study relating specifically to the *horoi* are updated in the light of recent discoveries of *horos* inscriptions by Millett 1982) subsequently reprinted with minor additions as the preface to a corrected reprint of *Land and Credit*. Relevant material that has come to light only very recently is included in Appendix 1 to this study.

27 Bogaert reaches similar conclusions about the terminology of banking (1968: 59–60), and Chantraine about Greek words for 'sale' (1940). Compare my brief comments on the range of meanings of *pistis* and *chreos* (above, p. 7, with n. 12).

28 Korver's study began as a doctoral thesis, supervised by Bolkestein. Other monographs by pupils of Bolkestein having some bearing on Athenian credit relations include Bongenaar 1933, a detailed commentary on Isocrates' *Trapeziticus* (XVIII), and Endenburg 1937 on the concept of *koinōnia* (see the brief review by Rose 1938).

29 Note also Bogaert's article in *RAC* s.v. 'Geld': an interesting mixture of material on credit drawn from the ancient world as a whole.

　　Recent literature on Greek banking either swallows Bogaert's findings more or less whole or is restricted to the modification of relatively minor points. Into the first category fall Isager and Hansen 1975: 88–98, Andreau 1977 and Hopper 1979; into the second: Talamanca 1971, Erxleben 1973, Andreyev 1979, Thompson 1979a and 1981. The substance of all these papers (and Bogaert's own researches) is conveniently summarized by Bogaert 1986a and 1986b.

30 The need for economic growth as stimulated by the inevitability of unlimited wants is challenged by Sahlins 1968. Analogous is the evolutionary approach to law and legal theory, associated in the English-speaking world with Henry Maine in his *Ancient Law* (1861; see Kuper 1988: 17–41; Cocks 1988: 52–78). The problems involved in applying the evolutionary paradigm to Athenian law and society are briefly examined by Millett 1990: 180–2). The origins and development

of the evolutionary vision of society are described by Robertson 1989: 7–8 and Burrow 1966.

31 This is not the place to examine in detail why Lowry's eloquent plea fails to persuade; but one may wonder whether 'in the field of economics even classicists by 1970 were led to accept the tenet that economic science sprang full-blown from Zeus's head in 1776 with Adam Smith's *Wealth of Nations*' (p. xiv). See the review-article by Meikle 1989: not averse himself to identifying an ancient thinker with a nineteenth-century economist (1979).

32 If I seem to labour the point it is in response to an earlier misapprehension of my position. In an otherwise perceptive paper, Harris (1988a: 37, n. 81) interprets my statement about the extent of credit in Athens (Millett 1983: 42) as the grudging concession of a primitivist.

33 What is probably the best-selling textbook on economics of all time by Samuelson (1970) has less than one page out of 850 given over to consumption loans. In marked contrast are the many valuable entries in the *Encyclopaedia of the Social Sciences* (*ESS*), notably s.v. 'loans, personal', 'small loans', 'pawnbroking' and 'usury'. The *International Encyclopaedia of the Social Sciences* (*IESS*) represents a complete rewriting of *ESS*, omitting much of the helpful historical material.

34 Coverage of comparative material on lending and borrowing is bound to be unsystematic, but one omission from my study calls for comment. In the absence of any comprehensive study of Roman credit relations, I have made only occasional use of the Roman material. The themes which recur in modern work on Roman credit parallel Athenian preoccupations: debt in politics (Frederiksen 1966; Royer 1967), interest rates (Barlow 1978) and banking (Andreau 1984). In Andreau's massive and painstaking study of *La Vie financière dans le monde romain* (1987) the debt to Bogaert's work on Greek banking is explicit (p. vii). Although expressing doubts and qualifications, Andreau takes as his starting-point a definition of 'bank' almost identical with that adopted by Bogaert (pp. 1–17). In the event, Andreau's coverage is wider, embracing 'les métiers de manieurs d'argent'; but his analysis largely ignores the informal credit relations that make up the bulk of my own study (Chapters II–VII), and presumably had some significance in the overall structure of credit at Rome.

For similar reasons I have decided against the use of the plays of Plautus and Terence as testimony for Athenian credit practices. In a long and illuminating study of banks and bankers in Roman comedy, Andreau (1968) tentatively concludes that much of the institutional detail is Greek in origin. He accordingly draws up guidelines for the use of Greek and Roman 'colour' and lists passages which appear to reflect either Greek or Roman influence (pp. 523–5). But without a comprehensive statement of Roman credit relations for the Middle Republic – for which the materials probably do not exist – it seems impossible to be precise about Greek and non-Greek elements in the plays. My own conclusion is that the Roman versions may broadly reflect the wealth of allusions to credit and debt present in the Greek originals. The references to banking operations collected by Andreau represent only the tip of a large credit-iceberg in Roman Comedy (see his footnote on *danista/fanerator*, p. 475, n. 4).

35 The majority of references to credit in the two historians are metaphorical in character (e.g. Hdt. 1.41–2 and v.99; Thuc. 111.63 and iv.19.3). Herodotus does, however, single out (presumably in contrast to the Greek practice) the aversion of the Persians to borrowing (1.138). This is on the grounds that the borrower is somehow compelled to tell a lie (either about need for the loan or ability to repay?). His account of an episode in Egyptian history in which people borrowed on the security of their fathers' mummies is apparently included as a curiosity (11.136).

36 Although speeches no doubt continued to be delivered in the courts, with some of them being preserved for a time, they ultimately proved unable to compete with the so-called 'Canon' of the ten Attic Orators which had become established as models. The Canon, as enshrined in the 'Lives of the Ten Orators' attributed to Plutarch (*Moralia* 832B–850E), is possibly Alexandrian in origin (see Kennedy 1963: 125). The inclusion in the Canon of Isaeus – the only one of the ten not known to have involved himself in politics – may be a consequence of the tradition that he taught Demosthenes (*Moralia* 839F).

37 On the continuity between Aristophanes and Menander, see Treu 1984: briefly, but effectively, undercutting the arguments of those who present New Comedy as reflecting the 'transformation' of fourth-century society (see above, n. 5). The bearing that credit has on the conventional picture of the fourth century as a period of crisis and decline will emerge as one of the broad conclusions of my study. Central to the debate is the issue of periodization by both century and age. The relevance of the label 'Hellenistic' to post-classical economic institutions is examined critically by Kreissig (1982) and more briefly by Finley (1985b: 183). Finley argues for two sectors to the Hellenistic economy: the Eastern regions, where economic and social systems were essentially non-Greek, and the old Greek world, where the economy underwent no fundamental changes. As regards security practices in post-classical Athens, the survival of dated *horos* inscriptions implies at least an element of continuity down to the early second century B.C.(Finley 1952: xl–xli; Millett 1982: ix–x). A brilliant but impressionistic study of continuity and change in *polis* institutions through the Hellenistic period is given by Davies (*CAH*[2] vii pt. I 257–320, esp. 290–6 and 304–15). Davies adopts a consciously empirical approach, rejecting a crude division between East and West, and stressing the complex amalgam that was 'Hellenistic Society' (p. 290): 'A convenient but misleading label for a set of developing and *ad hoc* solutions to the

various immediate or longer-term needs and problems which had to be solved (or lived with) within certain boundary conditions by governments and individuals'. As a major force for change within the period, Davies singles out the pressure of debt (pp. 293–4). He draws a contrast between classical Athens – free from troubles generated by debt – and the later fourth century and Hellenistic age, when tensions deriving from debt were common. The analysis is suggestive, particularly with reference to the debt problems of northern and central Greece in the early second century B.C. But, for reasons given in the text, I prefer to see the contrast in ideological rather than chronological terms, between *democratic* Athens and the rest of the Greek world.

38 The citation goes on to attribute, on the authority of Aristotle, a similar practice to the Ithacans. The fullest discussion of the passage is by Kelly (1985: 154–5), who gives slightly the wrong emphasis by translating *tous daneizontas* as 'money-lenders' rather than 'those lending money' (see below, p. 194). These tallies are conceivably to be identified with the *klaria* (tokens) supposed to have been symbolically burnt in the cancellation of debts under Agis (MacDowell 1986b: 106–7).

39 Christien (1974) claims to detect a Spartan debt crisis behind the so-called 'Rhetra of Epitadeus' (Plut. *Agis* V), which she dates to the early fourth century. Apart from doubts over the historicity of the Rhetra itself (Cartledge 1979: 165–8, opposed by MacDowell 1986a: 99–110), the sources make not the merest mention of debt to substantiate her theory.

40 For the sake of convenience, I reproduce Asheri's catalogue of laws relating to debt in tabular form and with additional items.

(1)	594/3	Athens	?Arist. *Ath. Pol.* VI
(2)	after 570	Megara	Plut. *Greek Quest.* XVIII = *Moralia* 295C–D
(3)	after 510	Croton	Iamb. *Life of Pythag.* 262 (trans. Clark 1989)
(4)	504	Cumae	Dion. of Halic. VII.8.1–2
(5)	408	Selymbria	*SIG*³ 122
(6)	403	Athens	Andoc. 1.87–8; Dem. XXIV.56–7
(7)	400–350	Arcesine	*IG* XII 7.3
(8)	*c.* 390–60	Delphi	*Bull. de Corresp. Hell* 50 (1926): 14–106
(9)	367/6	Syracuse	Justin XXI.1.5
(10)	*c.* 365/4	Herclea Pontica	Justin XVI.4
(11)	after 362/1	Byzantium	ps.-Arist. *Oecon.* 1347b1
(12)	before 360	Abydos	ps.-Arist. *Oecon.* 1349a3
(13)	*c.* 353/2	Athens	Dem. XXIV.39
(14)	mid-fourth century	Chios	ps.-Arist. *Oecon.* 1347b35
(15)	346/5	Heraclea Pontica	Memnon *FGH* 434 F 3
(16)	331	Olbia	Macrob. *Sat.* 1.2.33

(17) after 329/8	Priene	*Inschr. v. Priene* no. 8
(18) 324/3	Tegea	*SIG*³ 306 37–48
(19) 316/5	Syracuse	Diod. XIX.9.5
(20) *c.* 303	Teos–Lebedos	Welles no. 3 §§6–7
(21) *c.* 300/299	Ephesus	*SIG*³ 364 69–85
(22) *c.* 297/6	Ephesus	*SIG*³ 364
(23) *c.* 280	Carthaia	*IG* XII 5.1065
(24) *c.* 280	Naxos	*OGIS* no. 43
(25) *c.* 280	Samos	*SEG* I 363
(26) *c.* 250–40	Syros	*IG* XI 4.1052
(27) 243/2	Sparta	Plut. *Agis* VIII.1, XI.1 and XIII.2–3
(28a) *c.* 230	Olbia	*SIG*³ 495B 161–70
(28b) *c.* 230	Olbia	*SIG*³ 495B 179–88
(29) 227	Sparta	Plut. *Cleom.* x.6
(30) *c.* 206/5	Aetolia	Polyb. XIII fr. 1–1a
(31) 197	Argos	Livy XXXII.38.9
(32) 197	Arycanda	Agatharcides *FGH* 86 F 16
(33) after 188	Orchomenos	*IG* VII.21
(34) 179/8	Macedonia	Polyb. XXV.3.1–3
(35) before 174/3	Aetolia	Diod. XXIX.33
(36) 174/3	Thessaly	Livy XLII.5.7–10, 13.9; Diod. XXIX.33
(37) 174/3(?)	Phalanna	*IG* IX 2.1230
(38) 147/6	Achaea	Polyb. XXXVIII.2.10; Diod. XXXII.26.3
(39) end of second century	Malla	*IC* I xix.3(A)
(40) 86/5	Ephesus	*SIG*³ 742

To the list may be added a decree from 306, in honour of Antigonus I, cancelling all non-sacred debts on the island of Ios (*IG* XII 5.168). From an earlier period, there are repeated references to lending and borrowing in the Gortyn Code (see Willetts 1977: via the index, s.v. 'creditor', 'debt' and 'pledge'). Possibly fictitious are laws involving credit attributed to early lawgivers: Zaleucus, legislating for early seventh-century Locri, is said to have forbidden the use of written agreements in loan transactions (see above, p. 42); and a law attributed to Oxylus of Elis forbad the securing of loans on a certain proportion of a man's property (Arist. *Polit.* 1319a12). Asheri's account of a similar restriction on plots of land possessed by Athenian settlers in sixth-century Salamis and Lemnos (1963: 3) depends ultimately on Luria's unsupported restoration of *hupothenai* in *IG* II² 30 (*SEG* III 73).

41 The examples given in the text are by no means exhaustive. In the early third century, all the citizens of Itanos on Crete swore an oath not to cancel debts (*SIG*³ 526.21–4). An undated anecdote preserved by Aelian (*Varia Historia* XIV.24) describes murderous attacks by debtors

on their creditors in Corinth and Mytilene (the consensus is for a fourth-century date – Fuks 1979–80: 56–8). The idea of a comic dance descriptive of 'debt-cancelling' (*chreōn apokopē*) is appealing, but 'meat stealing' (*kreōn apoklopē*) seems more likely (the correction suggested by Cobet and Bapp for the text of Athenaeus xiv.629f.; see Asheri 1969: 104).

42 For possible dates of the incidents described in the anecdotes, see the commentaries by van Groningen 1933, and van Groningen and Wartelle 1968 (with Finley 1970). The translation in the Loeb series by Armstrong (1935) is not always accurate.

43 Hennig (1987) sees credit operations as the likely explanation behind the so-called 'deeds of sale' of real property from fourth- and third-century Olynthus, Torone and Amphipolis. Publicity may also lie behind the series of eight inscribed lead plaques from Corcyra, the subject of some speculation (SEG xxx 519–26). According to Calligas (1971), the plaques date from *c.* 500 and record maritime loans: an interpretation accepted by Bravo (1977: 2–8) and tentatively built on by Salmon (1984: 149). But the only positive indication that maritime credit might be involved is the findspot of the plaques near the harbour. Other arguments put forward by Calligas have no force. He cites Finley (1952: 22) to the effect that 'it was in the commercial field, more narrowly in the speculative field of maritime loans, that the written contract became more or less universal'. Finley gives as the reason behind this development the complexity of maritime loans. But the contents of the plaques could hardly be more basic: lender, borrower, loan sum and witnesses; nothing about interest or the terms and conditions of the voyage (contrast the written agreement in [Dem.] xxxv.10–13). Calligas suggests (p. 86) that 'these factors could be uniform and commonly known, and so have no need to be written down'. But it was precisely in order to fix these details that a written contract was desirable. The further references that Calligas gives to Finley's book relate to landside loans and have nothing to do with maritime credit. In their brevity, the plaques are reminiscent of the Attic *horoi*, but the comparison is not to be pressed. The theory of Vélissaropoulos (1980), attempting to equate the plaques with a symbolic counter-gift in a transaction resembling a reciprocal gift-exchange, is ingenious but gratuitous.

44 I have tried to ensure that none of the conclusions reached in the body of my study depend on evidence from outside Athens. Above all, I have avoided the deceptively rich testimony of the papyri, which are at best an uncertain guide to the institutions of mainland Greece (see Todd and Millett 1990: 7–11). Concerning credit, there is sufficient warning against using the papyri to illuminate Athenian practices in the debate over Jewish influence on loan transactions in the *Adler Papyri* (*Ad.Pap.* 5–6, with Wilcken 1939: 218–23, and Tscherikower and Heichelheim 1942). There is a general survey of credit in the papyri by Rupprecht

1967, with specialized studies by Husselman 1961, Pestman 1971, Bagnall and Bogaert 1975, Herrmann 1975, Foraboschi and Gara 1982, and Bogaert 1984, 1987 and 1988.

II. THE IDEOLOGY OF LENDING AND BORROWING

1 For an impressionistic account of Apollodorus' litigious progress through the Athenian courts, see Bonner 1927: 113–34; aspects of his family relationships and financial affairs are set out in *APF* 11672 §§x–xii; his career as a political figure is covered by Schäfer 1858: 130ff. A detailed study of Apollodorus is being prepared by Jeremy Trevet.

2 The detailed documentation for the dates and events given in the text is supplied (with minor discrepancies) by Bogaert 1968: 71 and 75–8, and *APF* 11672 §§ii–iv and ix. It cannot be stressed too strongly that in their progress from rags to riches (and Athenian citizenship) the careers of Pasion and Phormion were utterly untypical.

3 As for all the private speeches in the Demosthenic corpus, Gernet provides an acute introduction and brief notes (1954–60: 1, 199–223). The older commentary by Paley and Sandys (1910: ii, 1–57) is still occasionally helpful.

4 If the ancient attributions are to be believed, we have here a case of Demosthenes writing speeches for both sides in the same dispute. It is significant (though not decisive) that Aeschines thought it worth while to accuse Demosthenes of divulging the contents of his speech *On Behalf of Phormion* to Apollodorus (ii.165; cf. iii.173). No fewer than seven speeches in the Demosthenic corpus were written for delivery by Apollodorus (xlv, [xlvi], [xlix], [l], [lii], [liii] and [lix]); but, with the exception of the *First Speech Against Stephanus*, none are regarded as genuinely Demosthenic. On the possible relationship between the Apollodoran speeches and the rest of the work of Demosthenes, see Pearson 1966 and 1969.

5 The translation in the text is based on the Loeb version by Murray (1936–9: v), adopting in the antepenultimate sentence the alternative translation proposed by Fine (1951: 85–7).

6 In the absence of any extended discussion of the moral and ethical aspects of liturgies, see the brief but complementary accounts by Hands (1968: 26–48), Davies (in *APF*, xvii–xxi), Adkins (1972: 119–26), Finley (1985b: 150–4), Veyne (1976: 185–200) and Lauffer (1974).

7 The Orators as a source of evidence about conventional morality are discussed by Dover (1974: 1–14; note the searching criticisms by Adkins 1978). The crucial questions of the likely composition and outlook of the jury are examined by Todd 1990b.

8 The themes of Mauss's essay are significantly refined and extended by Lévi-Strauss 1949: 161–70, Sahlins 1965, Gregory 1982 and Macherel 1983. As Mauss himself noted (1925: 121, n. 43), early Greece was not one of the societies on which he drew in his reconstruction of gift-giving. In an earlier paper on gift-exchange amongst the ancient Thracians

(1921), he remarked how classical scholars had sometimes been misled by their ignorance of primitive institutions. Application of gift-exchange to the dark-age society of Homer by Finley (1977) has been extended into the archaic period by Morris (1986). In this important paper, Morris argues for a wider application of gift-giving as a primary mechanism of exchange, outside the kinship-based, non-state societies to which it has been restricted by Mauss and some of his followers. For the persistence of a strong element of reciprocity in the classical period, see Millett 1990.

9 Mention might also be made of the Latin terminology of credit: *mutuum* – the regular word for 'loan' – originally involved the idea of mutuality. The attempt by Kelly (1970) to assimilate *mutuum* to barter seems to ignore Mauss's theory about the origins of sale and credit in gift-giving.

10 Hence the failure of attempts by Caillemer (1870: 1; DS s.v. *foenus* – an otherwise helpful article) to equate *chrēsis* and *daneismos* with the categories of *commodatum* and *mutuum* familiar from Roman law. For subsequent attempts to differentiate between the two terms, see Beauchet 1897: IV, 230–3, Cvetler 1935a and 1935b (with the criticisms by Pringsheim 1950: 513–14), and Simon 1965: 40–7. The only passage in the classical literature in which *chrēsis* and *daneismos* appear as alternatives is from Aristotle's *Nicomachean Ethics* (1131a2–4), where – along with sale, purchase, surety, depositing and leasing – they are classed as 'voluntary transactions' (*sunallagmata hekousia*).

11 See briefly Gernet 1948–9: 151. Detailed bibliography on the legal and ethical implications of the concept of *sumbolaia* is cited by Cataldi 1982.

12 With the exception of a bizarre and ambiguous passage in Aristotle's *Nicomachean Ethics* (1148b23): Black Sea tribes 'lending' (*daneizein*) children to be eaten.

13 The late appearance of *tokizein* may well be a quirk of the distribution of the surviving sources – the result of the fourth-century concentration of the Orators' private speeches. But use of the word is not confined to law-court speeches; for an early epigraphic example, see a fourth-century inscription from Delphi, regulating the rate of interest (Epigraphica III 41 6–7; trans. Asheri 1969: 105–8). Compare also the non-oratorical use of the cognate term *tokismos* ('loaning at interest') by Xenophon (*Poroi* IV.6) and Aristotle (*Politics* 1258b21). Although an argument from silence cannot be decisive, it is surprising that *tokizein/tokismos* do not appear in the plays of Aristophanes (e.g. *Clouds*) where their presence would be utterly appropriate.

14 Millett 1984a: the text follows 100–3, with minor modifications. I take this opportunity to correct an unfortunate misprint in my earlier paper: on p. 93, l. 23, for 'Hesiod was himself a poet', read 'Hesiod was himself a peasant'. Several of the ideas offered in that paper are developed by Bovill 1985. See also Bravo 1984, 1985 and Zanker 1986; and, from the earlier bibliography, Glover 1942a and Green 1959.

15 This paradoxical interplay of self-sufficiency and co-operation finds an analogy in the dark-age *oikoi*, described in the Homeric poems. The

keen sense of competitive rivalry between the aristocratic heads of the
Homeric *oikoi* is tempered by the need for gift-exchange. See the classic
statement by Finley (1977: 61–6 and 118–19), with additions and
modifications by Donlan (1982 and 1989) and Hooker (1989).

16 Our ignorance of the class of small farmers, probably the largest single
occupational group in fourth-century Attica, is partly through selective
survival of the sources. Peasants, impoverished or otherwise, were
amongst the last people liable to appear in a published law-court
speech. Only the better-off citizens would be able to afford the services
of a Lysias or a Demosthenes (see Casson 1976: 52, nn. 54–5). Of course,
the problem goes beyond source-survival in that peasants were so
ubiquitous as rarely to attract the interest of the literary élite. The plays
of Aristophanes are, for obvious reasons, a partial exception (see
Ehrenberg 1951: 73–94). Such material as does survive is pieced
together (to reach varying conclusions) by Jameson 1977–8, Osborne
1987 and Wood 1988.

17 For the ideal of the peasant citizen, see Austin and Vidal-Naquet 1977:
151. I am, however, not persuaded by their argument (based, ironically
enough, on Theophrastus' 'Rustic'!) that in the fourth century the
ideal corresponded less and less to reality (pp. 372–5). As they
themselves note (p. 151), the rustic is opposed to the city-dweller
(*asteios*) as a figure of fun at least as early as 423 and the *Clouds* of
Aristophanes. On the implications of the distinction between *agroikos*
and *asteios*, see Osborne 1985a: 185.

18 Nothing certain can be deduced from the vague statement by Diodorus
(1.79.5) that a majority of Greek lawgivers, 'forbade that weapons,
ploughs and other indispensable things be taken as pledges (*enechura*) for
loans'. Although Aeneas Tacticus advises that weapons should not be
accepted as pledges in cities under siege (x.7), the only actual example
of such a law comes from the Gortyn code (see Willetts 1955: 221). The
list of unpledgeable items (if such it be) includes looms, wool, iron tools,
ox-yokes, hand-mill stones, equipment from the men's quarters and the
marriage bed – apart from the ploughs and weapons mentioned by
Diodorus and Aeneas. Prohibitions like this are common in non-
capitalist societies: 'No man shall take the upper or nether millstone to
pledge, for he taketh a man's life to pledge' (Deuteronomy xxiv.6); cf.
de Roover 1948: 134 (medieval Bruges) and Thorburn 1886: 114
(nineteenth-century India).

19 In marked contrast to the upheaval of the Solonic crisis (see the final
section of this chapter). The mystique that has grown up around the
fourth century as a period of crisis and decline deserves a study to itself.
For a selection of 'crisis theories' see Pečírka 1976. The brief discussion
that follows is limited to the part supposedly played by debt in fourth-
century developments.

Finley's elimination of the *horoi* as evidence for widespread peasant
indebtedness in Attica destroyed one of the foundations of the crisis
theory (1953a: 63–7). More recently, a valuable study by Hanson

(1983) has undermined the view of extensive and irreversible damage to smallholdings by the Peloponnesian invasions of Attica and occupation of Decelea. All the indications are that, after overcoming initial difficulties brought about by the war, peasant smallholders were able to re-establish themselves on the land in substantial numbers (Andreyev 1974). And yet the crisis mentality, which found its classic expression in an early study by Mossé (1962), continues to flourish (e.g. David 1984). Although Mossé has modified her position (e.g. 1972), the conviction remains that the peasants of fourth-century Attica underwent a decline in status (Mossé 1973, with Millett 1982: xi–xii).

On a point of detail, Mossé detects a hint of difficulties arising out of debt in the oath of the Athenian jurors, quoted in a speech by Demosthenes (XXIV.149): 'I will not allow private debts (*chreōn idiōn*) to be cancelled, nor lands nor houses of Athenian citizens to be redistributed.' Mossé rightly notes (1973: 183) that the attribution of the law to Solon is almost certainly false; but I am not persuaded by her admittedly cautious attempt to link its sentiments with events in later fourth-century Athens, which (she claims) betray 'une certaine inquiétude face à des revendications agraires'. She points out that the wider terms of the oath, with their promise not to vote for a tyranny or oligarchy, are reminiscent of the so-called 'Decree of Eucrates against Tyranny', dated to 337/6 (Merritt 1952 ~ Harding no. 101), about which Mossé has her own, unorthodox ideas (Mossé 1970). She reminds the reader of the association of tyranny with the redistribution of land and cancellation of debts, and wonders whether, in the aftermath of Chaeronea, it was felt necessary to revive measures introduced in the wake of the oligarchic revolution of 404–3, as preserved by Andocides (1.87–8). After quoting a law to the effect that all verdicts given in private suits under the democracy were to be valid, Andocides provides his own gloss, telling the jury that this was done 'in order to avoid the cancellation of debts (*chreōn apokopai*) and the re-opening of such suits, and to ensure the enforcement of private agreements'. The fragility of the line of argument advanced by Mossé, albeit tentatively, will be apparent. The purpose of the decree of Eucrates is disputed (see Ostwald 1955), and it seems more economical to associate the formulation of the jurors' oath with the restoration of the democracy in 403; that is the interpretation of Asheri (1969: no. VI, with pp. 98–101). It is to be hoped that the jurors' oath will follow in the way of the *horoi* as evidence for agrarian discontent in fourth-century Attica.

20 The antithesis is between *epidōsō* and *epimetrēsō*, which Korver (1934: 73) interprets as between giving and lending; 'What you give', he says, 'you don't need to measure.' But elsewhere in the *Works and Days* (and often in other literature), *didōmi* does refer to lending objects.

21 Regarding social relations in local communities in seventeenth-century England, Wrightson specifically remarks 'Of this kind of daily co-operation, comparatively little trace is left to the historian...Yet it must have been of major significance in the ability of many families to make

their living (1982: 52). He cites the failure of poorer peasants to possess ploughs, with the presumption that they made arrangements to borrow from their neighbours. Such was the position of the imaginary neighbour to Theophrastus' 'Rustic'.

22 The translation in the text is from the Loeb edition by Arnott (1979). Incredibly, Wiles (1984) takes the motif of pestering neighbours in the *Dyscolus* as somehow related to the sumptuary legislation of Demetrius of Phaleron (p. 173): 'The extra utensils that the slaves attempt to borrow are not really needed (520). In the final scene, Getas and the cook taunt Knemon with symbols of consumption: tables, cauldrons, foreign fabrics, wine (914, 916, 923, 946).' But this is to burden a comic device with weightier interpretation than it will bear. The verses in question are explicable entirely in terms of making people laugh.

Some glimpses of the etiquette to be observed in borrowing from neighbours in late nineteenth-century England are given in the idyllic, autobiographical picture of village life by Flora Thompson (1939: 107–8).

23 Aristophanes: kneading-trough (*Frogs* 1158–9), razor and dress (*Thesm.* 219 and 250), pestle (metaphorically for Brasidas: *Peace* 283–4); Plato the Comic Poet: cloak (*CAF* fr. 205 ~ *FAC* I p. 555 fr. 205; cf. Diog. Laert. VI.62); Plato the Philosopher: sword (*Rep.* 331C); Machon: stones for house repairs (Ath. VI.254d), shield (Ath. XIII.579c); Herodas: dildo (VI.27); Menander: wig, cloak and stick (*Aspis* 377–8; cf. *P.Hib.* 17). A fragment of papyrus published by Handley (1975) contains a piece of dialogue between a slave and another person. One of the matters discussed is an inventory of possessions (col. A 14–15): 'in detail / all that's inside, and all we've loaned (*kechrēkamen*) to people'. The antithesis seems to lie between two categories of household objects: those still in the house, and those lent out to other people. Handley has suggested that the fragment might belong to Menander's *Aspis*, but certainty is impossible (see Arnott 1979: 7–10).

Non-monetary loans from the world of the Orators are naturally more substantial: horses (Lys. XXIV.11; Dem. XXI.174); bronze pitcher – specifically said to be 'worth a lot' ([Dem.] XLVII.52); bowl and gold jewellery (Dem. XLI.8); gold basins and censers (Andoc. IV.29); best bronze plate (Lys. XIX.27); bedding, cloaks and two silver bowls ([Dem.] XLIX.22). Humphreys (1970: 151) takes this final reference, along with Thucydides' account of the tricking of the Athenian envoys at Egesta (VI.46), as traces of competitive gift-giving. But they resemble more closely the non-monetary loans between friends and neighbours described above and in the text. The connexion is strengthened by a further example of lending plate in an anecdote attributed to the early third-century philosopher, Arcesilaus, preserved by Diogenes Laertius (IV.38). In a passage stressing the generosity (*eleutheria*) of Arcesilaus, there is a description of how he helped people in general ways, and especially by collecting *eranos*-contributions (*sunēranizein*) on their behalf. The passage continues:

Someone once borrowed his silver plate in order to entertain friends and never brought it back, but Arcesilaus did not ask him for it and pretended it had not been borrowed. Another version of the story is that he lent it on purpose, and, when it was returned, made the borrower a present of it because he was poor.

24 The relatively rare word *protelein* is also used to describe credit operations by Xenophon (*Anabasis* VII.7.25; *Poroi* III.9). On the dating of Democritus to the later fifth century, see Kirk, Raven and Schofield 1983: 404.

25 The presentation in the text is necessarily schematic. As will emerge from later chapters, the transition from interest-free to interest-bearing credit was not always as clear-cut as this provisional picture seems to suggest. The model as a whole owes its inspiration to Sahlins's conception of 'primitive exchange' (1965). He visualizes reciprocity as encompassing a whole range of types of exchange, forming a continuum. At one end of this spectrum stands the 'pure gift' with no open stipulation of a return; at the other extreme, there is appropriation by trickery or force, calling for an act of retaliation. 'The extremes', explains Sahlins (p. 191), 'are notably positive and negative in a moral sense. The intervals between them are not merely so many gradations of material balance in exchange, they are intervals of sociability. The distance between poles of reciprocity is, among other things, social distance...' The concept is developed in a subsection entitled 'Reciprocity and kinship distance' (pp. 196–204), and concrete examples are gathered in an appendix (pp. 231–46). The scope of Sahlins's analysis is narrowed by his concentration on ties of kinship to the exclusion of other bonds that could be equally effective in the more open society of classical Athens.

26 The ramifications of *philos* and *philia* are examined in Chapter v. Here and elsewhere in the text, translations of the *Nicomachean Ethics* are by Irwin (1985). In the earlier version by Ross (1925), the terms *ethikē*, *nomikē* and *epi rhētois* are rendered respectively as 'moral', 'legal' and 'on fixed terms'.

27 For what it is worth, the lexica record the term *cheirodoton*, glossed by Pollux (II.152) as 'loan without agreement' (*daneisma to aneu sumbolou*); cf. Bekker, *Anecdota Graeca* 89.23.

The relationship between writing, literacy and exchange is a complex problem which deserves further study. What matters here is the impersonal rôle of written records and agreements. Goody (1986: 77–82) singles out the tendency of writing to formalize exchange relationships (p. 82): 'The calculus of precise reciprocities has replaced, in part at least, that of the closeness of the relationship.' A similar idea is among those developed in a necessarily speculative paper on the use of writing and early trade by Lombardo (1988: esp. 181–5).

Lombardo plays down traders' use of letters and documents, particularly those written on lead, before the fourth century, pointing to their relative rarity (175–6). But his figure of six lead letters, cited from Bravo (1974: 111–16), is already out of date:

(i) letter of Mnesiergus from Attica, *c.* 400 (Wilhelm 1904 ~ *SIG*³ 1259); (ii) letter of Artikon from Berezan'(?), fourth century (Wilhelm 1909 ~ *SIG*³ 1260); (iii) fragmentary letter from Agathe in southern France, fourth century (*Bull. épigr.* 1944, no. 90); (iv) fragmentary letter(?) from the Pnyx in Athens, late fifth or earlier fourth century (*Hesperia* Suppl. VII, 10, no. 17; cf. *Bull. épigr.* 1944, no. 90); (v) fragmentary letter (?) from Emporion in southern Spain, late fourth or earlier third century (*Bull. épigr.* 1955, no. 282); (vi) letter of Achillodorus from Berezan', *c.* 500 (Bravo 1974).

To which may now be added:

(vii) letter of Apaturius from Olbia, *c.* 500 (apparently unpublished, but summarized by Vinogradoff 1981: 18–20); (viii) letter from Emporion in southern Spain, *c.* 500 (Sanmarti and Santiago 1987 and 1988); (ix) letter(?) from Pech-Maho in southern France (Lejeune and Pouilloux 1988; Chadwick 1990). It seems probable that letters will continue to come to light, and not only through excavation; item (i) was originally published as a curse-tablet, and (ix) was for thirty years thought to be a weight from a fishing-net. (For a possible tenth letter on lead from Attica, see below, Chapter III, n. 9.) The content of the three most recent discoveries, directly concerned with traders' business, goes against Lombardo's further observation, that none of the letters already known were true 'lettres d'affaires'. His final point, that 'business letters' are not alluded to before the fourth century, can be explained as a consequence of selective source-survival. There is a similar difficulty behind Pringsheim's attempt to trace the transition from witnessed to written transactions to the middle of the fourth century (1955; cf. Finley 1952: 21–7; Thomas 1989: 41–2). Frequency of reference depends in part on the distribution through time of appropriate law-court speeches (see Ober 1989: 349). Also problematic is Pringsheim's conception of the fourth century as the period which saw (p. 289) 'the transformation of Athens from a more or less rural community to a commercial town. This change inevitably destroyed, together with the aristocracy, the close village relationship and the spirit and economy of the peasant.' One of the major themes of the present study is that this was not, in fact, the case.

28 The translation is adapted from Storey 1930–5. The passage contains an untranslatable pun on the double-meaning of *tokos* as 'offspring' and 'interest'. Compare *Rep.* 507A (with Storey's note *ad loc.*), and see n. 29 below.

29 Plato's opposition to interest, placed in the mouth of Socrates, gives point to the anecdote, preserved by Plutarch (*Aristides* 1), that Socrates possessed a sum of seventy minas which he lent at interest to Crito. Plutarch gives as his authority a book by Demetrius of Phalerum, but the original source of the story may have been Aristoxenus, the fourth-century philosopher, musical theorist, and author of a hostile biography of Socrates. According to Diogenes Laertius (II.20), Aristoxenus accused Socrates of having made money by systematically lending at interest.

Although no trust can be placed in the truth of the accusation, it does show how a fourth-century figure could go about undermining a person's reputation – by accusing him of habitually taking interest.

Diogenes tells other anecdotes about money-lending philosophers. Arcesilaus (IV.35) is said to have rebuked a money-lending student (*daneistikon kai philologon*), who could not answer a philosophical question, with a quotation from Sophocles' *Oenomaus* (fr. 477 in Pearson 1917): 'For the hen is not aware of the passage of the winds, save when breeding time (*tokos*) is at hand.' The point seems to be that people pay little attention to things that are important until their own 'interests' are concerned (for the play on words, see above, n. 28). The reprimand would be all the more appropriate coming from Arcesilaus, given his reputation for interest-free lending and giving (above, n. 23). Diogenes' account of the money-lending Menippus (VI.99) is discussed in Chapter VIII.

30 In spite of this weakness, Grote's digression remains the most helpful discussion of philosophical attitudes towards lending and borrowing (cf. Gordon 1982: 415–18). His misapprehension regarding the prevalence of commercial credit in fourth-century Athens is shared by more recent writers on Plato and Aristotle; see Klingenberg 1982, with Millett 1990: n. 42.

31 The argument traditionally attributed to Aristotle, derived from the *Politics* (1258a39–58b9), that the sterility of money renders the taking of interest 'most contrary to nature' has been tremendously influential (see Langholm 1984: 54–69). Whether that was Aristotle's intended meaning is another matter; for the view that it was probably *not*: Cannan *et al.* 1921–2. The emphasis in the passage seems to lie on interest being contrary to nature because 'it involves men in taking things from one another', but without equivalent return.

32 For an analogous process, compare the attempts of the Latin grammarians to explain *fenus* (interest) as a derivation of *fetus* (progeny or parturition): Varro, cited by Gellius XVI.2.7.

33 In his discussion of Hesiod's advice about returning more than the original loan, Korver (1934: 63) suggests that the practice continued right through the classical period. In the absence of any clear evidence, he points to the frequent stipulation 'without interest' (*atokos*) in the papyri (but see Pestman 1971). Given the bias of fifth- and fourth-century sources away from peasant-type society, Korver's suggestion seems entirely reasonable. The degree of bias may be reflected in the near-uniqueness of the terminology of the Hesiod passage (l. 349): *eu men metreisthai para geitonos*. Although *metreisthai* has the literal sense of 'measure out', one of its recognized meanings was apparently 'lend'. Hesychius glosses *metreisthai* with *daneizesthai*; and when in Aristophanes' *Acharnians* (l. 1021) the ruined farmer begs Dicaeopolis '*metrēson* a bit of peace to me', the scholiast explains that the word stands in place of *daneion*. As an alleged parallel he cites a line from Theopompus' comedy *Kapelides* (*CAF* fr. 22): 'Either share it, or lend it (*metrēson*) or

accept its value.' As the passages from Hesiod and Aristophanes suggest, *metreisthai* is appropriate to the *Naturalwirtschaft* of peasant society; by contrast, I am aware of only one passage from the whole *corpus* of the Orators where a natural commodity seems to take the place of coined money (Lysias XXXII. 6 and 15).

34 For the metaphor of the poem as discharging a debt, but without the interest-element, see *Ol.* III.12, *Pyth.* VIII.45. Other, later metaphorical examples of the use of interest include: Menander, *Thesaurus* (*CAF* fr. 235 ~ Allinson 1921: 359), those who fall in love in old age have to pay a heavy burden of interest to Eros; Demosthenes 1.15, the Athenians behave recklessly in their extra-*polis* relations, like men borrowing at high interest (cf. Dem. XIX.99); Plato, *Politicus* 267A, an exceptionally full argument is compared with a repayment plus interest (cf. *Rep.* 612C).

35 This is, of course, against the usual interpretation of Hesiodic society as being in a state of crisis (Millett 1984a: 104–6).

36 For a compendium of survival strategies: Garnsey 1988: 43–68. The date of Alciphron is obscure, though *c.* 200 has been suggested; see the discussion by Benner and Fobes (1949: 6–18), from whom the translation in the text is taken. The idea of peasants writing letters to one another is as fanciful as the names of the correspondents ('Lamb to Love-Calf'), but some of the circumstantial detail seems accurate enough. The allusion to imported grain rings true for Athens in the fourth century – apparently the imagined setting for many of the letters (another mentions the banker Pasion: 1.13.4).

37 Recent literature on the Solonic problem is listed and discussed by Will (1965: 59–94), Cassola (1964), Manfredini and Piccirilli (1977), Rhodes (1981: 90–130) and *AO* 37. Scholars continue to imagine that a close reading of the *testimonia* will reveal fresh insights into the Solonic crisis and reforms: see the convincing critique of Cataudella (1966) by Will (1969). Even the wider-ranging analysis by Sakellariou (1979) depends on the unsafe assumption that *every* detail in the ancient sources must be somehow significant. His credibility is further weakened by the unwarranted introduction of merchants competing for loan capital, encouraging wealthy landowners to impose higher interest payments on struggling *thetes* (108–9). Similarly speculative are the Solonic debts described by Miller (1968: 70–3) as 'arising from advances of credit, e.g. for investments in industry as Athenian pottery (and other exports) expanded'. There is no evidence for any of this. For more promising attempts to locate the Solonic crisis in appropriate agricultural and archaeological contexts, see the studies by Gallant (1982) and Morris (1987: 205–8).

38 The remark is directed at Starr (1977: 183), who wonders 'how debt could become so mighty a machine'. After rightly rejecting coinage as a factor in the crisis, Starr plumps for entry into the market economy as the probable explanation of long-term indebtedness in Solon's Attica. Certainly, intrusion of the market into a subsistence economy can cause

an expansion in the volume of peasant debt; see the perceptive comments of Darling (1947: 202–47) on prosperity and debt in British India. But peasant access to commodity markets is a relatively recent phenomenon (see below, n. 45), and there is nothing remarkable about a high incidence of rural debt. Robinson and Eatwell in the introduction to their book on modern economics (1974: 71) are able to construct a plausible model of peasant indebtedness without introducing markets.

39 The claim of Androtion, recorded by Plutarch (*Solon* xv) that 'Solon relieved the poor, not by wiping out their debts, but by reducing the interest on them' is almost certainly a fourth-century invention; see Billeter 1898: 5–9 and Rhodes 1981: 127. The same can be said about the fictitious loans attributed to Solon and his friends (*Solon* xv; cf. the Aristotelian *Constitution of Athens* (*Ath. Pol.*) vi.2). The attempted rationalization by Woodhouse (1938: 182–90) is imaginative, but superfluous.

40 A precise date for the Megarian affair (which may never have happened as described by Plutarch) is an impossibility. Legon (1981: 115) favours a date shortly before 600, Asheri (1969: 14–16) favours the years after 570 and Figueira (1985: 146–9) the 540s. The probable source and background to the Plutarch passage are discussed by Halliday (1928: 99–102), who concludes the most likely source to be Aristotle's lost *Constitution of the Megarians*. The reconstruction of events proposed by Oost (1973) is utterly unreliable, based on the demonstrably false assumption that peasants have nothing to do with interest and loans.

41 The fragmentary evidence for the period is assessed in detail by Rhodes 1981: 179–88, and by Andrewes in *CAH*² iii part 3 392–8. Herodotus is explicit (if condescending) about support for Pisistratus from people in the countryside. It would be nice if the backing described in the Aristotelian *Constitution of Athens* (*Ath. Pol.* xiii.5) as coming from 'men deprived of debts due to them, discontented because of the hardships resulting from this' could be made to mean 'those who had been freed from debt' (as by Hopper, 1961: 195, n. 73). But Rhodes (1981: *ad loc.*) is probably correct in judging the former to be the natural meaning of *hoi te aphēirēmenoi ta chrea*.

42 For detail on these two themes, see Lewis in *CAH*² iv 287–302, Frost 1985 and Ober 1989: 65–8.

43 The word *prodaneizein* is examined from different angles by Wyse (1892), Korver (1934: 136–43) and Migeotte (1980a). The collective opinion seems to be that *prodaneizein* is normally used in connexion with public finance, in transactions involving an intermediary which are interest-free. All these characteristics apply to the passage cited in the text. Chambers (1984) appreciates the importance of the passage in explaining the basis of Pisistratus' support, but argues that the *chrēmata* were given rather than lent, and not only to peasants.

44 Assuming that *chōrion ateles* refers to a category of land, and not to a

specific plot. For alternative versions of the hill-farmer anecdote, see Rhodes 1981: 216. According to the *Constitution of Athens* (*Ath. Pol.* XIV.4), the levy on produce was fixed at 10 per cent (*dekatē*), but Thucydides (VI.54.5) gives a figure of 5 per cent (*eikostē*). Day and Chambers (1962: 95) see Thucydides as right and the *Constitution of Athens* as wrong; others (most recently Pleket 1969: 46, n. 95) suppose that the rate was reduced to 5 per cent by Pisistratus' sons; Dover (1965: 63) points out that *dekatē* ('tithe') may be used generically, and so subsumes the tax of one-twentieth. As a fourth, faint possibility, it could be argued that Pisistratus' levy was progressive, linked to the Solonic property groups: 10 per cent for the *pentakosiomedimnoi* and *hippeis*, 5 per cent for the *zeugitai*, and nothing for the *thetes* (in line with the interpretation of *chōrion ateles* offered above). But there is probably nothing in it.

Little can be said in favour of a proposal by Holladay (1977: 50) – tentatively accepted by Rhodes (1981: 214–15) – that Pisistratus' loans had the limited purpose of tiding over the peasantry during their supposed transition from grain-growing to the production of olive oil: 'By switching from subsistence farming to the more profitable cash crop (and by buying imported corn) the small farmers could stand on their own feet.' But there is no contemporary evidence that the peasants of Attica *ever* shifted from subsistence to cash crops. Pericles was no peasant, yet Plutarch singles out as remarkable his eccentric behaviour, selling his crops in the market, and buying what was needed on a day-to-day basis (*Pericles* XVI). In any case, at least one other tyrant is associated with a programme of 'soft loans'. According to a fragment of Memnon (*FGH* 434 F.3), Timotheus, the fourth-century tyrant of Heraclea Pontica (*c.* 345), not only cancelled outstanding debts, but also 'lent money without interest to those who were in need, for trading or other means of subsistence' (details in Asheri 1969: 35–6).

45 For the sake of completeness, I note here the proposal of Themistocles (483/2), as recorded by the *Constitution of Athens* (*Ath. Pol.* XXII.7), that the hundred-talent surplus from the silver mines at Maroneia should be 'lent' (*daneisai*) to the hundred richest citizens to use as they thought fit. The passage continues: 'If they (the *dēmos*) were satisfied with the way in which the money was spent, it should be put down to the city's account; but if not, the money should be reclaimed from those to whom it had been lent.' In the event, each of the hundred individuals used the cash to build a trireme. Rhodes (1981: *ad loc.*) is surely right to see in this story some liturgical-type arrangement (possibly an anachronistic retrojection of the *proeisphora* system), whereby wealthy citizens assumed responsibility for overseeing state expenditure.

One further text calls for comment. In a lengthy passage in his mid-fourth century speech *Areopagiticus* (VII.32–5), Isocrates harks back to the 'Good Old Days', when everything in the Garden was lovely. He waxes lyrical about the way in which the poor showed respect to the rich, who in return responded by helping out the poor with loans at low interest so that they might engage in trade or other occupations. In spite of determined attempts to make this passage yield up clues about the organization of Athenian trade (e.g. Erxleben 1974: 471–3; Bravo 1974: 151–3 and 1977: 4–5), its historical interest lies, as I have argued elsewhere (Millett 1989a: 25–8), in supplying an insight into contemporary crypto-oligarchic ideology.

46 For the Peloponnesian War as a period of 'shattering social change and consequently of changes in attitudes of which Thucydides gave a remarkable analysis', see Humphreys 1970: 143. There are certainly examples of formerly prosperous people being reduced to poverty by the war: Atrometus, father of Aeschines (II.147), Isocrates (V.161), Aristarchus (Xen. *Mem.* II.7) and Eutherus (Xen. *Mem.* II.8). In both the *Memorabilia* passages, the possibility of borrowing money is at least canvassed (II.7.2 and II.8.1).

III. BORROWING AND REPAYMENT

1 *Against Nicostratus: A Denunciation Concerning the Slaves of Arethusius.* Authenticity and date of delivery are discussed by Paley and Sandys 1910: li–lix; helpful introduction with brief commentary in the Budé edition by Gernet 1954–60: III, 82–101; translations in the text are adapted from the Loeb edition by Murray 1936–9: VI. For the probable identification of Nicostratus and his brothers in inscriptions, see *APF* 12413, n. 1.

2 In the text as printed (§2), Apollodorus talks about his entitlement to three-quarters (*ta men tria merē*) of the value of the slaves. For the near certain correction of *tria* to *trita* (one-third), see Lewis 1966: 191, n. 67, with Osborne 1985b: 44–5.

3 On the transformation of loans into gifts, compare the behaviour of the philosopher Arcesilaus as related by Diogenes Laertius (IV.38, cited above, Chapter II, n. 23). Also preserved by Diogenes Laertius is an illustration of the characteristically outrageous behaviour of Diogenes the Cynic (VI.62): 'When someone asked that he might have back his cloak, "If it was a gift," he replied, "I possess it. If it was a loan, I am using it."'

4 There is negative support for a less than formal relationship in Apollodorus' silence about the payment of interest. Had interest been charged by Theocles, as in a typical 'impersonal' loan transaction, it might be expected that Apollodorus would harp on this as further evidence of his generosity towards the treacherous Nicostratus (compare the detail on interest in §13). Theocles is not known outside this passage.

5 Herman incorporates this transaction into his account of *xenia* or 'ritualized friendship' (1987: 93). But it takes special pleading to identify these money-lending *xenoi* as a species of *philoi*: the clause in the agreement stipulating payment within thirty days was, says Herman,

'merely intended as a safeguard for lenders either short of cash or having a low opinion of Nikostratos' credit'. All the signs here indicate an impersonal relationship between strangers, an interpretation which actually simplifies and strengthens Herman's larger analysis.

6 There is a complication here. Towards the end of the speech (§28) it is implied that the three brothers held their property separately. This seems to suggest that Nicostratus had borrowed money from Arethusius, offering his land as security. For a broadly similar dispute between brothers, see Isaeus II.28, with Wyse 1904: *ad loc.* The legal implications of both passages are discussed by Harrison 1968–71:I, 267–8 and 291–2.

7 His precise words, following on from the passage in the text, are: 'When I heard these things from him, having no idea that he was lying, I answered as was natural for a young man who was an intimate friend (*oikeiōs chrōmenos*), and who was far from thinking that he would be defrauded...' About what is Nicostratus accused of lying? Presumably (and plausibly) Apollodorus refers to his opponent's expressed intention of raising an *eranos*-loan. And yet an alternative interpretation might see the lie as referring, not to Nicostratus' intention to repay Apollodorus, but to his citation of laws relating to the rights of a ransomer over the person ransomed. 'If an Athenian paid the ransom for a fellow-citizen who had been captured in war and the latter did not repay him the ransomed man became the slave of his ransomer'; so says Harrison (1968–71:I, 165; cf. MacDowell 1978: 79–80 and Garlan 1987: 15). But the sole authority for this remarkable law turns out to be the passage from the Nicostratus speech, which is immediately followed by Apollodorus' accusation that the speaker was telling lies. As it stands, the law is, to say the least, anomalous, providing the only set of circumstances under which an individual Athenian was empowered to enslave a fellow-citizen. Stranger still, it seems to imply that *non*-citizens were able to enslave citizens. The point is picked up by Gernet (1954–60: III, 85), who envisages Nicostratus as referring to 'droit commun hellénique', and he cites a possible parallel from the Gortyn Code (VI.49); but in ideological terms aristocratic Gortyn was a long way from democratic Athens. Taking into account all the improbabilities involved, I am inclined to see Nicostratus' claim (if he ever made it) as intended to put pressure on Apollodorus and not as an accurate statement of Athenian law.

8 All attempts to explain the unusually high rate fail to convince. In spite of analogous cases where a lower rate is charged, Billeter (1898: 25–6) interprets $1\frac{1}{3}$ per cent per month as appropriate to *Konsumptivkredit.* Thompson (1978: 407, n. 17) talks in terms of long- and short-term lending, with interest rates adjusted accordingly. But this depends on an anachronistic reading of the evidence, and I am unable to understand Thompson's argument: 'In Dem. 53 the borrower apparently had to pay slightly less than his lender could get by lending short-term on inferior security.' Of course, if the interest charge was ultimately to be borne by Nicostratus, its size would not have concerned Apollodorus;

and if Nicostratus had no intention of repaying the loan, it would not
have bothered him either. But this is speculation, reading too much into
the text.

9 For the sake of completeness, I note a possible, though as yet
unconfirmed control on the reliability of Apollodorus' narrative. Mr
David Jordan has kindly provided me with an advance copy of his text
and commentary on an unpublished lead letter, the author of which he
identifies as Pasion, father of Apollodorus. The text of the letter (so far
as it survives) calls on one Satyrion to take action against (among
others) Nicostratus, brother of Deinon and Arethusius, on the grounds
that he is plotting to evade some payment. As Jordan points out in his
provisional commentary, Pasion's earlier encounter with the three
brothers gives the lie to Apollodorus' protestations of his naive,
unthinking trust in Nicostratus being monstrously abused. Apollodorus
makes it clear that he became particularly friendly with Nicostratus
after his father's death in *c.* 370. The letter therefore serves to strengthen
the sceptical reader's suspicion that Apollodorus' underlining of his
youth and inexperience is so much rhetorical posturing to gain the
sympathy of the jury.

Further comment on the letter and its contents must await
publication of text and commentary by Jordan. One's immediate
reaction is that the whole thing is almost too good to be true. The
provenance of the letter is unfortunately unknown; it is at present held
in a private collection in Athens.

10 (i) *xenoi* loan 26 minas to Nicostratus (§10); (ii) Apollodorus loans/gives
300 dr. to Deinon (§7); (iii) Theocles lends 1,000 dr. to Apollodorus
(§9); (iv) Apollodorus lends/gives 1,000 dr. to Nicostratus (§9); (v)
Arcesas lends 16 minas to Apollodorus (§13); (vi) Apollodorus lends 16
minas to Nicostratus (§13); (vii) possibility of *eranos*-loans of 16 minas
to Nicostratus (§11); (viii) Nicostratus' debt(?) to Arethusius (§10);
(ix) Arethusius' loan at interest to Archepolis of Piraeus (§20). Had the
eranos-loans of (vii) actually taken place, the number of separate credit
operations would have been substantially increased.

11 The eight possible examples are:
(i) Lysias fr. 38 (see pp. 1–3, above); (ii) [Dem.] XL.52 (loan from
banker to purchase a mining concession); (iii) Xen. *Mem.* II.7 (loan to
set up a destitute family as cloth-makers: see pp. 71–4, below); (iv)
Dem. XXXVII *passim* (series of loans to purchase mill for processing silver
ore); (v) Isaeus, Forster 1927: fr. 18 (loan or gift to freedman wishing
to become a banker); (vi) Lycurgus, *Leocrates* 23 and 58 (loan to
purchase metalworkers); (vii) *horos* no. 3 in Finley 1952, and (viii) *horos*
no. 12A in Millett 1982 (both recording loans to purchase real
property).

Maritime loans are excluded from the list. In my earlier statement
(1983: 188, n. 15), five examples are listed as possible exceptions; the
additional items are (v), (vi) and (viii).

12 The ratio in the text is intended only as an order of magnitude. Both

slave-prices and the price of ransom were variable within wide ranges; see Garlan 1982: 54–5, with Dem. XIX.169 (suggesting three and five minas as reasonable ransoms for prisoners of war).

13 Were there people at Aegina (and other slave markets) who specialized in buying likely-looking slaves from pirates and ransoming them? This could explain the rôle of the mysterious *xenoi* in the case of Nicostratus. Although the risks of non-repayment would be high, so were the potential profits – the difference between the price of a person as a slave and his or her value when ransomed. That would also explain the absence of any mention of an interest payment by Nicostratus to the *xenoi* (see Herman 1988: 93). It is entirely characteristic of Diogenes the Cynic (or our perceptions of him) that he is supposed to have refused an offer of his friends to ransom him out of slavery (Diog. Laert. VI.75). This was on the grounds that as a slave he resembled a lion, inspiring fear in those whose job it was to keep him fed.

14 Text and translation of the Eryximachus fragments in *P. Ryl.* III no. 489, reading Körte's *tōn allōn triērarchōn* (1941: 134–6) for *tōn emōn* of the papyrus.

15 It is possible that in his description of events in Macedon Demosthenes deliberately manipulates the terminology of credit so as to present his own actions in a particularly favourable light. When the prisoners ask to 'borrow' the money for their ransoms (§169), they are made to use the verb *daneizein*, which usually has overtones of lending at interest. But Demosthenes depicts his actual lending of the money with the term *kichranai* (§170), which typically has the sense of an interest-free loan (see above, p. 29). He then explains how, in the event, he gave the money as a straight gift: *edōka dōreian* he twice says (§§170 and 171), which is the exact phrase used by Apollodorus to describe his gift of 1,000 dr. towards the ransom of Nicostratus (above, p. 55). Aeschines in his opposing speech *On the Embassy* (II.100) predictably gives a different assessment of Demosthenes' intentions and capabilities as a would-be ransomer.

16 Missing from the list is help in paying-off fines, where scope for assistance would naturally be limited to family and friends. Antiphon II.2.9 and v.63 both refer to friends (*philoi*) providing cash to pay a penalty or fine; and Plato in the *Laws* (855B) seems to envisage friends contributing to pay a person's fine (cf. *Apol.* 38B; see above, p. 158).

17 The background to the purchase on credit of some funerary equipment, as recorded in a speech of Isaeus (VIII.23), remains obscure. This seems the appropriate place to record a true 'emergency loan' from Aristophanes' *Peace* (ll. 374–5). Threatened with imminent death by Hermes, Trygaeus asks the god for a loan of three drachmas to purchase a piglet. Its sacrifice will (he implies) raise him to the ranks of the Eleusinian initiates, who enjoy a happy afterlife.

18 For what it is worth, Nepos' *Life of Epaminondas* seems to provide fourth-century Theban evidence for friends lending money to pay for dowries (xv.5–6):

When one of his fellow-citizens was taken prisoner by the enemy, or the daughter of a friend was of marriageable age, but because of poverty could not be given in marriage, he held a meeting of his friends, and determined how much each should give, according to his resources.

The passage is interesting as seeming to describe, for the benefit of Roman readers, the institution of the *eranos*-loan, complete with Epaminondas as *eranarchēs* or sponsor. As proof that the combination of dowry and *eranos* existed outside Athens, there is the so-called 'dowry register' from Myconos (*SIG*³ 1215 ∼ *IJG* I vi 48–62). The inscription is of uncertain date and may be post-classical. The first entry (§ 1) gives details of a dowry of 1,300 dr., of which only 300 dr. were paid outright by the bride's father. The remaining 1,000 dr. were raised by *eranos*-contributions, for which an *eranarchēs* is named. At least two other fathers seem to have had difficulty in raising the agreed sums (§§ 4 and 6). In the former case, the father guaranteed the shortfall by offering his house as a pledge of eventual repayment.

It has been argued by Pomeroy (1982: 123–33) that the Athenians made formal state provision for the dowering of daughters of poor citizens. Her evidence is highly circumstantial, and in all comparable areas – ransom, burial, food-shortage – the obligation to help seems to have rested on the citizen-body as a collection of private individuals.

19 See Garnsey 1988: 163, with references to private donations of grain during the crisis-years of the later fourth century (pp. 150–62).

20 Compare the supporting statements made elsewhere by Davies (1981: 26 and 92). It is impossible to give precise English equivalents for the three Greek terms in the quotation. *Philotimia* (lit. 'love of honour') might be rendered as 'ambition': for a detailed discussion, see Whitehead 1983. *Lamprotēs* (lit. 'brilliance') is roughly equivalent to 'distinction'. *Charis* can be translated as 'gratitude', though the term has clear overtones of the return of a reciprocal obligation (see above, p. 58).

21 I take over this quotation (in the excellent translation by Crawley) from Davies in *APF* xvii (cf. 1981: 97–8).

22 There are other, oblique indications of Alcibiades' financial difficulties. They may be reflected in the tradition that Alcibiades, having taken possession of the enormous dowry of ten talents, extorted a further ten on the birth of his first child. This could also be the explanation behind his refusal to divorce his wife, which would have cost him control over her dowry ([Andoc.] iv.13–15, with *APF* 600 viii).

Also suggestive of financial embarrassment through conspicuous expenditure is the background to Alcibiades' quarrel with Tisias, of which four versions have survived ([Andoc.] iv.26–7; Isoc. xvi *passim*; Diod. xiii 74.3–4; Plut. *Alcib.* xii.3). Briefly, Tisias was a wealthy Athenian citizen who wanted to win an Olympic victory and heard of an outstanding racing team at Argos. He persuaded Alcibiades, who had excellent connexions in Argos, to buy the team on his behalf. Alcibiades duly completed the purchase, but kept the team for himself and ran it under his own name at the Olympics of 416. (The story goes that it was with this very team that he won his victory.) The presumption is that Alcibiades purchased the team using Tisias' cash – the sum is fixed at either five or eight talents – and refused to hand over either cash or horses. Whatever the rights and wrongs of the dispute, it was still running twenty years later (*APF* 13479); *c.* 396, Tisias brought an action for damages against Alcibiades' son, with Isocrates writing the speech for the defence (XVI).

There is one final, faint link-up between Alcibiades, extravagant living and debt. A thread running through contemporary and near-contemporary accounts of Alcibiades is the accusation that he aimed at tyranny; Thucydides links this fear with his dissipated life style (VI.15.4). In the *Republic* (573D–E), Plato examines the character of the 'tyrannical man', whom he portrays as given over to a depraved, luxurious way of life: 'And so any income there might be is quickly expended...And after this there are borrowings (*daneismoi*) and fritterings away of the estate.'

23 Extravagance need not be the preserve of the élite – or even of humans. Aesop (Chambry 1927: no. 162) tells of the jackdaw who 'borrows' the finer plumage of other birds in an unsuccessful attempt to win a beauty contest. The moral is aimed at those who finance a sumptuous life style through debt. Xenophon (*Mem.* II.6.2) has Socrates talk in general terms about the spendthrift (*dapanēros*) who never has enough, but is always borrowing from his neighbours. Aeneas Tacticus (V.2) describes how Leucon, tyrant of Bosporus (393–353), would discharge any of his guards who were in debt through gambling or other excesses. Compare (or contrast) an epigram by Callimachus (XLVIII – *Anth.Pal.* VI.301), recording the dedication by one Eudemus of his salt-cellar, 'with which, by eating frugal salt for relish, he escaped the mighty storms of debt' (trans. Mair and Mair 1955).

24 I have an impression (nothing more) that a substantial number of trierarchs were inscribed as 'public debtors' – presumably because they failed to return state property borrowed in connexion with their duties (e.g. [Dem.] XLVII.21–3). I know of no systematic study of public indebtedness (see the article by Schulthess in *RE* s.v. '*opheilontes tōi dēmosiōi*'), but state debtors regularly appear among the propertied élite in the pages of *APF*.

25 The argument in the text goes against de Ste Croix's attempt (in a valuable study) to minimize the impact of *eisphora*-payments on wealthy individuals (1953: 49 and 69–70). But his calculation that the burden of the *eisphora* over time was equivalent to an annual income tax of between $2\frac{1}{2}$ per cent and 5 per cent depends on an unrealistically high ratio between assets and income of 5–10 per cent (see his warning note, p. 49, n. 80).

26 (i) Unspecified amount, using real property (*ousia*) as security: cash raised in order to hire rowers (§7); (ii) 30 minas, land (*chōrion*) as

security, borrowed from Archeneus and Thrasylochus (possibly the trierarch encountered later in the speech (§52) – *APF* 9719, but see Ballin 1977: *ad loc.*): money used to pay crew (§13, cf. 28 and 61); (iii) loan of 15 minas from Archidemus of Anaphlystus, contracted away from Athens: used to hire rowers (§17); (iv) loan of 800 dr. from Nicippus the shipowner (conditions obscure: see below), contracted away from Athens: used to hire new rowers and pay old ones (§17); (v) loan of unstated size from Cleanax and Eperatus in Tenedos, apparently without security: used to provide ration-money (*sitēresion*) for crew (§56). To this list may be added Apollodorus' abortive attempt to borrow from Polycles on the security of the ship's equipment (§55–6).

Not everything is clear about all these loans. Only two (iii and iv) are explicitly said to carry interest. In the case of (ii), Apollodorus tells the jury, as part of his catalogue of woes: 'Those who lent the money came to collect their interest when the year came to an end, unless someone paid up(?), according to the agreement' (§61). It is uncertain what had to be paid up or handed over, according to the agreement. If it was the principal (so Murray 1936–9: VI, *ad loc.*), then this could be a case of a loan that was interest-free, provided repayment took place within the year: see Harrison 1969–71: I, 226, n. 3. Even more obscure are the terms of loan (iv). The extreme anacolouthon of the relevant sentence makes translation difficult, but a possible version might be: 'I secured from Nicippus the shipowner, who happened to be in Sestus, 800 dr. – a maritime loan (*nautikon*) at $12\frac{1}{2}$ per cent – on condition that I should pay him the money with interest when his boat (*ploion*) arrived safely at Athens.' The problem lies in reconciling Apollodorus' contracting of a maritime loan (*nautikon*) with the safe arrival, not of his warship, but of the cargo boat (*ploion*) of Nicippus. Possible interpretations are put forward by Ballin (1977: *ad loc.*) and Bogaert (1986a: 48), both of whom join Gernet (1954–60: III, 42, n. 5) in seeing Apollodorus as taking a share in a conventional maritime loan contracted by Nicippus. An alternative approach might be to play down the idea of a formal maritime loan, and take *nautikon* as referring loosely to the terms of the interest payment – calculated and expressed along lines familiar from maritime credit. In purely practical terms, the loan would indeed be repaid to Nicippus 'when his boat arrived safely at Athens'.

27 Apollodorus says as much in the *First Speech Against Stephanus* ([Dem.] XLV.78):

Whatever concerns the *polis*, however, and whatever concerns you, I do as brilliantly (*lamprotata*) as I am able, as you are all aware. For I fully realize that for you who are citizens by birth, it is sufficient to perform liturgies as the laws require; but we who have been made into citizens ought to make it clear that we perform our liturgies as if repaying a debt of gratitude (*hōs apodidontas charin*).

To the modern reader, Apollodorus seems to be suffering from an acute sense of his own inferiority; and no wonder if a reported gibe was at all true or typical. Apollodorus tells how Polycles, having heard about Apollodorus' financial difficulties, replied (§26): 'The mouse has just tasted pitch (i.e. bitten off more than he can chew), for he wanted to be an Athenian.' Elsewhere, Apollodorus explains how he adapts his behaviour to suit his unusual status. In the speech *Against Nicostratus* ([Dem.] LIII.18), he claims that in his earlier suit against Arethusius (see above, p. 53), he begged the jury not to pass a sentence of death, as they had a mind to, but to let off his opponent with a fine. 'I did this', he says, 'not because I wished to save Arethusius from the death penalty...but so that I, Pasion's son, made a citizen by a decree of the people, might not be said to have caused the death of any Athenian.'

28 For the fragility of Athenian finances in the fourth century, see the passages collected by de Ste Croix 1981: 607, n. 37 (cf. Davies 1981: 128–9).

29 (i) From Aristophanes: 5 talents (§§22 and 43); (ii) from Aristophanes' friends: amount not stated (§22); (iii) from Aristophanes' brother: 40 minas; (iv) projected loan from Aristophanes of 16 minas with gold cup as 'security' (*sumbolon*) and earning 4 minas interest (§§25–6; see Vickers 1984).

After the Battle of Mantinea (362), Agesilaus apparently compensated for an empty Spartan treasury by raising loans and levies from his friends (Plut. *Ages.* xxxv). On the eve of his Asian campaign, Alexander is reported to have been in debt to the tune of 200 talents (Plut. *Alex.* xv; see Hamilton (1969: *ad loc.*), who regards the tradition as credible). For a similar funding operation, but non-Greek and from an earlier epoch, see Nicolaus of Damascus (*FGH* II A 360–1), with the lengthy discussion by Bogaert (1966: 133–4).

The problems of finding cash to pay mercenaries are almost a commonplace in the literature (e.g. Xen. *Anab.* 1.2.11; *Hell.Ox.* XIX.2 (cf. Isoc. IV.142), with McKechnie and Kern *ad loc.*). Xenophon both advises and reports borrowing as a possible solution (*Anab.* VII.5.5 and *Hell.* V.3.17; cf. Dem. VIII.26).

30 There is an impressive demonstration of the unproductive character of non-capitalist credit in the many biblical references to lending and borrowing. Although the conspectus of passages collected by Gamoran is nowhere near complete (1971: 131, n. 32), he is correct in his belief that there is no case of a 'commercial' loan in the Old Testament (see the following chapter, n. 10).

31 Phormion, not yet a citizen, was unable to take ownership of any real property offered as security for loans from the bank; Pasion therefore acted as intermediary (see my Appendix II).

It may be significant that the comparatively rare word *philergia* (only twice in the Demosthenic *corpus*) is applied to two other Athenians whose behaviour is untypical. In Xenophon's *Oeconomicus* (XX.22–8), Ischomachus describes the behaviour of his father, who specializes in buying up run-down farms, which he improves and then sells at a profit. This he does, says Ischomachus, through *philergia* (§26). Everything that is said about Ischomachus' father (including Socrates' amazed reaction) implies that his behaviour is exceptional, if not unique. This undermines Mossé's interpretation of the passage as evidence for an agrarian crisis in Attica, following on the devastations of the Peloponnesian War (in Will, Mossé and Goukowsky 1985: II, 107, against Finley 1952: 270, n. 46). As Robin Osborne points out to me, the bought-up land is unworked through neglect or incapacity (*ameleia, adunamia*: §22), which has nothing to do with the Peloponnesian War. Also unique, so far as the surviving sources are concerned, is the only citizen known to have laboured himself in the silver mines ([Dem.] XLII.20). At the end of his speech he appropriately calls on the jurors to take note of his *philergia*. For an attempt to invest this character with qualities typical of Athenian entrepreneurs, see Thompson 1982: 60.

32 An analogous anecdote strengthens the novelty effect. Aristotle is the earliest author to recount how Thales turned the tables on those who mocked him for his poverty (*Politics* 1259a9–19). Using his meteorological skills he predicted an unusually heavy crop of olives. He therefore 'raised a little money while it was still summer and paid deposits (*arrhabōnas diadounai*) on all the olive presses in Miletus and Chios, hiring them cheaply because no one bid against him. When the appropriate time came, there was a sudden rush of requests for the presses; he hired them out on his own terms and so made a large profit, thus demonstrating that it is easy for philosophers to be rich, if they wish, but that it is not in this way that they are interested.' Again, the emphasis is on the uniqueness of the sage's behaviour.

33 Conveniently available in the Loeb edition by Fowler (1936), from which quotations in the text are taken. The structure and coherence of the essay are examined by Russell (1973), who rightly sees no need to relate the work to any particular debt crisis. Compare the briefer sayings on expenditure and debt attributed to Simonides (*P.Hib.* 17; trans. Edmonds II, 253–5).

34 My comments on the debt crisis of the late Republic are heavily dependent on the paper by Frederiksen (1966). Professor Michael Crawford reminds me that the Republican credit crisis differed from Athenian experience by having its origins in a shortage of liquidity. I have accordingly tried to limit my comparison to the impact of debt on politics and society.

35 Is all this agitation about debt, paralleled in other non-capitalist societies, a natural outcome of unproductive borrowing in agrarian societies? Compare the existence in various early societies of formal mechanisms for the periodic cancellation of debts, the most familiar being the Jewish Sabbatical and Jubilee release (Leviticus xxv; Deuteronomy xv.1–4; see Finley 1965a: 162–3). For Babylonian laws on debt remission, see Bottéro 1961. From the Greek world, the Spartan

cancellation of public debts on the death of a king (Hdt. vi.59) finds a close parallel in medieval India (Sharma 1965–6: 74). Although there is no mention of debt as a mechanism of property transfer, reference might also be made to the decision of the Lipari islanders in the late archaic period to redivide their land every twenty years (Diod. v.5; see Figueira 1984).

36 Robin Osborne would like to hear a whisper in Androtion's fourth-century rewriting of Solon's cancellation of debts as a reduction in the rate of interest (Plut. *Sol.* xv.3). 'It was important', he suggests (in a personal communication), 'to deprive those who might agitate for debt cancellation of a historical precedent.' That is ingenious, but Androtion's revisionism could also be seen as part of a broader attempt to deradicalize Solon, without having any detailed bearing on conditions in fourth-century Attica.

37 On the distinction see Hemelrijk 1928 (summarized by Finley 1985b: 41) with Markle 1985: 267–71.

38 For the legal background to pledges as security, see Harrison 1968–71: I, 260–2. It cannot be a coincidence that the pledging of commonplace items appears in Comedy as opposed to Oratory (cf. Chapter ii, n. 23).

39 To the references supplied by de Ste Croix (1981: 163; Lysias xii.98, Isoc. xiv.48, Ar. *Plutus* 147–8) may be added a late fifth-century inscription from Halicarnassus, suggesting that those defaulting on sums owed to the local temple underwent a form of debt-bondage (*SIG*³ 46, with Bogaert 1968: 271–2; cf. Glotz 1904: 365–7).

40 For evidence of 'voluntary servitude' in the Roman world, see Frederiksen (1966: 129, n. 13). Worthy of special mention is the biblical example of Jacob's fourteen-year service to Laban in order to earn the right to marry the daughter of his choice (Genesis xxix.15–28).

   In very general terms, the corn dole at Rome had a function analogous to public pay in Athens, preventing the urban *plebs* falling *en masse* into dependence on the rich. But Pericles was no Clodius, nor even a Gaius Gracchus, and the analogy should not be pressed (see Chapter ix, n. 4).

41 Apart from the obvious factor of the prestige value of real property, sight should never be lost of the extent to which the Athenian élite depended on land as a generator of income. Sale of land would permanently reduce income, whereas land offered as security remained in the possession of the borrower, who retained the right to dispose of whatever crops it might produce (Finley 1952: 10–13). The corollary of this is that a man taking out a loan might conceivably lease additional land in order to service the debt. I would tentatively identify this as the motive behind Timotheus' involvement in a *misthōsis oikou* or 'renting of an estate' ([Dem.] xlix.11). In a *misthōsis oikou* operation, an individual leased the property of an orphan on agreed terms, offering a portion of his own land as security against eventual repayment (Finley 1952: 38–44). Such a transaction could have benefited Timotheus, who had

heavy debts to discharge (above, pp. 70–1). The incidence and implications of leasing in the Greek world are examined in an important paper by Osborne (1988).

A further factor inhibiting sale was the possibility that a property offered for sale would fail to fetch a reasonable price. According to Francis Bacon in his essay of 1625 *Of Usury* (p. 289): '...were it not for this easy borrowing upon interest, men's necessities would draw upon them a most sudden undoing, in that they would be forced to sell their means (be it land or goods) far under foot, and so, whereas usury does but gnaw them, bad markets would swallow them quite up.' The existence of 'bad markets' in Attica is attested by Aeschines (1.96), who accuses his opponent Timarchus of selling his property for what it would fetch, far less than what it was worth. It may be noted that the state, when selling confiscated property, allowed purchasers up to five years to find the full price of houses, and ten for land (?Arist. *Ath. Pol.* XLVII.3). For a dishonest attempt to inflate the price of a sow being sold to discharge a debt, see Aesop's account of the 'Athenian debtor' (Chambry 1927: 10).

42 Examples of public loans from the Greek world are collected with translation, commentary and valuable concluding chapters by Migeotte. Although his catalogue of 118 items is compiled with meticulous care, there is bound to be disagreement over what constitutes 'public credit' (for a possible omission, see below).

43 Apart from the raising of cash at Byzantium (1346b30), Clazomenae (1348b17) and Selymbria (1348b33) in time of food shortage, at Antissa (1347a25) to fund a particularly lavish festival, and at Caria (1348a4) to pay tribute, all other devices are linked with finding money for warfare. Compare in this connexion the Corinthian proposal, on the eve of the Peloponnesian War, that loans be raised from the funds held at Delphi and Olympia in order to hire mercenaries (Thuc. 1.121.3, 143.1 ~ Migeotte no. 22). From the other end of the Peloponnesian War, both sides in the Athenian civil war of 404–403 borrowed funds to carry on the fight (?Arist. *Ath. Pol.* XXXIX.6 ~ Migeotte no. 1F). In the fourth century, the Thebans borrowed from the Eleans the sum of thirty talents to help finance their invasion of Laconia in 370 (Xen. *Hell* VI.5.19 – not included in Migeotte). Against this background of war-related credit (further examples in Migeotte 361), it is a reasonable assumption that the 'bribe' of one talent that Demosthenes is alleged by Aeschines to have taken from the city of Oreus was in reality the repayment of a loan (III.103–4). According to Aeschines, Oreus was 'exhausted by war and completely without means', and therefore paid Demosthenes interest on his promised bribe at the rate of 1 per cent per month (again, not included in Migeotte's catalogue). For examples of public loans made by individuals in other states, see the sequence of loans secured by the city of Arcesine on Amorgos during the late fourth and early third centuries B.C. (Migeotte nos. 49–53).

44 Given the volume of evidence for public borrowing to meet unforeseen expenditure, often arising out of an emergency, and the relative frequency of default (below, n. 51), it is difficult to agree with the theory of Tarn and Griffith (1952: 116–18) that '... most of the city borrowing met with was mere machinery; it had no more to do with poverty than does municipal borrowing today... There was sometimes deliberate procrastination over repayment, but this had nothing to do with poverty.' I find it hard to accept that the cities of Cyme and Lampsacus which, by default on public loans, respectively lost control over their public stoa (Strabo XIII.3.6 ~ Migeotte no. 81) and acropolis (Ath. XI.508f. ~ Migeotte no. 75), were not suffering from poverty. In support of the historicity of these anecdotes, see Migeotte 1980b.

45 The process of staged repayment may lie behind two *horos* inscriptions, on which loan-sums have been partially erased (Finley 1952: nos. 28 and 154). At the other extreme was the reported good fortune of 9,000 guests at a banquet given by Alexander the Great. According to Plutarch (*Alex.* LXX.3), Alexander paid off all their outstanding debts at a total cost to himself of 9,870 talents.

46 The practice of embarrassing people by demanding payment in public may lie behind the law noted by Demosthenes (XXI.10–11) that on festival days it should not be lawful to seize or distrain on the property of a defaulting debtor (for other plausible explanations, see MacDowell 1990: *ad loc.*). In Boeotia the practice of publicly humiliating debtors was apparently an established institution. According to Nicolaos of Damascus (*Ethon Synagoge* XXXI), those who did not discharge their debts were made to sit in the *agora* with a basket on their heads. Recalcitrant debtors may make up some of the persons appearing on curse tablets (see Jordan 1985). The Ifugao tribe of the Philippines invoke up to forty deities who (according to Barton, 1922: 425–6) 'torment the debtor with reproaches of conscience or pride until his nights are sleepless, until he imagines his fellow-men look on him with scorn as one who borrows but does not pay'. The same tribe also makes extensive use of professional debt-collectors.

47 On the legal process of debt-recovery, see Cohen (1983: 18–22), who shows how litigants could try in their speeches to assimilate embezzlement of a loan (*aposterein*) to the more serious crime of theft (*kleptein*). The possibility that *atimia* (loss of civic rights) might have been a possible sanction for non-payment of certain types of private debt is raised by Hansen (1982). Creditors in court had to pitch their demands at realistic levels, according to the circumstances. If the speaker in Lysias' *On the Property of Eraton* (XVII) can be believed, he now feels able to claim back only fifteen minas (§7) or one-eighth of a two-talent loan made by his grandfather (§2).

48 The ancient lexicographers (Harporation, *Souda* s.v. *dēmarchos*) and the scholion to Aristophanes' *Clouds* (l. 37) state that the demarch assisted in distraining on the goods of defaulting debtors (see Harrison 1968–71:

II, 189, n. 2). But as pointed out by Bonner & Smith (1930–8): I, 322), there is no clear case of a demarch helping in the recovery of private debts. Strepsiades' complaint that he is being 'bitten by a demarch' (*Clouds* 37) is vague enough to refer to monies owed to the deme, as collected by the demarch described in [Dem.] LVII.63. Whitehead (1986: 125–7) is prepared to go a little further, advancing the tentative hypothesis that a demarch was authorised to intervene in disputes over debts within his own deme. It may be that the demarch could be used to bring informal pressure to bear on debtors.

49 The trials and tribulations of lending money at interest entirely escape Thompson, who baldly states that a capital sum of forty-five minas lent out at the 'going rate of interest (12 per cent)', would provide the lender with an annual income of 540 dr. 'without lending a finger' (1982: 60). He also ignores the odium incurred by professional money-lenders (see Chapter VIII).

50 Speeches arising out of a defaulted debt: Dem. XXXII (maritime loan), [XXXIII], [XXXIV] (maritime loan), [XXXV] (maritime loan), XXXVII, XXXVIII, XLI, [XLIX], [LIII] and [LVI] (maritime loan); Isaeus fr. 16 in Forster (1927); Lysias VIII and XVII. Of Lysias' speeches involving 'agreements' (*sumbolaia*), several of which apparently arose out of unrepaid loans, only fragments survive (cited from Gernet and Bizos 1955–9: II): fr. 36 *Against Alcibus*, fr. 37 *Against Archebiades*, fr. 38 *Against Aeschines the Socratic* and fr. 39 *Against Theomnestus*.

The importance of court cases arising out of debt may be gauged by their designation as 'monthly suits' (*dikai emmēnoi*). These were a privileged category of suit which, according to the traditional view, had to be settled within the space of one month (but see Cohen 1973: 3–95, with Rhodes 1981: 583). Out of the ten types of *dikai emmēnoi* listed in the Aristotelian *Constitution of Athens* (*Ath. Pol.* LII.2), four are directly concerned with credit. Privileged treatment was accorded to cases arising out of money borrowed at 1 per cent per month, out of borrowing *aphormē* (stock?) to trade in the *agora*, out of *eranos*-loans (contrast the attitude of Plato in his *Laws*; above, p. 156), and banking transactions (*trapezitikai*).

51 The difficulties inherent in securing repayment or judgement and executions were magnified many times if the debtor lived in another *polis* (e.g. Dem. XXXVIII.11–12). Not for nothing does Theophrastus portray his 'Avaricious Man' (*aischrokerdēs* – lit. 'shameful-gaining') as borrowing from a visitor (*xenos*) who is staying overnight with him (XXX.3). The question of private settlements between citizens of different states is covered by Bravo (1980), with a lengthy critique by Gauthier (1982).

This is perhaps the place for a brief comment on non-repayment of public loans; the detailed analysis by Migeotte (pp. 392–400) makes a full presentation unnecessary. On the face of it, cities seem to have offered solid guarantees against default. A popular method was the granting of a lien on future public revenues. Alternatively, creditors might be offered security in the form of the property of all the citizens. Repayment was occasionally made the responsibility of designated wealthy citizens. For all these mechanisms (on which see Migeotte pp. 389–92), there exist medieval parallels (de Roover 1948: 126). And yet, in spite of apparently cast-iron guarantees, default seems to have been a regular problem. Indicative of the precariousness of repayment is the way in which the Athenians under the restored democracy repeatedly pat themselves on the back for having repaid a loan from the Spartans, raised by the oligarchs (refs. in Migeotte no. 1). At the opposite extreme was the decision (*c.* 300) by a board of arbitrators from Cnidos that the city of Calymna need not repay an apparently substantial public loan. The disappointed claimants were the great-grandchildren of the original claimants, two citizens of Cos (Epigraphica iii: 42).

52 The possibility that Athenians reaped substantial personal rewards from their administration of the Second Confederacy is raised by de Ste Croix (1981: 604, n. 27) as part of an attack on Finley (1978). The examples offered by de Ste Croix are not particularly persuasive. He assumes that Timarchus could have been willing to bribe his way into the office of archon on Andros – raising a loan of thirty minas at interest in the process (Aeschines 1.107 – in order to make 'a substantial profit'. No doubt; but the possibility should not be neglected that Timarchus (if guilty of the bribery charge) wanted prestige rather than financial profit. It might be expected that Aeschines would at least hint at possible extortion on the part of Timarchus; he refers instead to his sexual irregularities. De Ste Croix also cites the case of Androtion, who was rewarded for his loan to the city of Arcesine (used to pay for a garrison and meet other shortfalls in public revenues) by being made hereditary Athenian *proxenos* (*GHI* ii 152 ~ Migeotte no. 48 ~ Harding 68). That was a post, observes de Ste Croix, 'which *might be* both financially lucrative and politically advantageous...Other Athenian governors and phrourarchs, in the fifth century as well as the fourth, *may well have taken the opportunity* to lend money to the cities they governed at a handsome rate of interest' (my italics). This is, unfortunately, pure speculation. I am aware of no Athenian official lending money in this way, and de Ste Croix's supporting reference to a paper by Perlman (1958) provides nothing in the way of evidence. Androtion's loan to Arcesine, it is to be noted, was interest-free.

53 The only case known to me of a would-be *stratēgos* being held back by poverty involves Phormion in the fifth century. According to an anecdote preserved by Pausanias (1.23.10), he was deeply in debt and withdrew to his deme until the Athenians elected him to command a naval expedition. At first he refused to take up the appointment on the grounds that he was too distracted by debts to think about the men under his command, but the story has a happy ending (for Phormion). So determined were the Athenians to have him as one of their *stratēgoi* that they paid off all his debts.

54 A persuasive case for viewing not the fifth but the fourth century as the 'Golden Age' of Athenian democracy (against, e.g. Mossé 1962: 262–332), is made by Ober (1989). His examination of shifting attitudes to wealth in fifth- and fourth-century Athens (pp. 205–12) complements my comments in the text. For a summary and preliminary assessment of Ober's arguments, see Millett 1989b.

IV. THE ROLE OF INTEREST

1 For a conspectus of references to Moerocles, and an attempt to explain his connexions with the worlds of politics and finance, see Ampolo 1981 (but note the reservations of Osborne 1985a: 236, n. 44). Inconclusive attempts to identify the occasion of Moerocles' comment are cited by Billeter 1898: 13–14.

2 Figures for the bank rate for the 1930s from Mitchell and Deane (1962: 456–9). It is often ignored that the effective or 'real' rate of interest has to take into account changes in the price level. As it happens, the examples in the text are from periods of moderate deflation and rapid inflation. The appropriate adjustment (real rate = money rate − rate of inflation) suggests that the real rate of the 1930s was as high as, if not higher than, the 'record' rates of the 1980s – sufficient warning against accepting interest rates at their face value. The section on ancient Greece in Homer's summary listing of interest rates across the centuries has no value for the ancient historian (1977: 32–43).

3 For a taste of the complexity of modern interest theory, try Ingersoll in Palgrave, s.v. 'interest rates'. The standard critique of interest theories down to the later nineteenth century is by Böhm-Bawerk (1884): the contents page gives an impression of the range of possibilities. Böhm-Bawerk's own theory of interest is analysed, along with later developments, by Conard (1963). For a lucid account of interest theory in a short compass, see Knight, *ESS* s.v. 'interest'.

A part of the difficulty in getting to grips with interest theory is the intrusion of ideology – often in the crude sense of political prejudice. It may be noted in this connexion that the most recent English translation of Böhm-Bawerk's standard work on interest is published by the 'Libertarian Press'. Its biographical sketch of the author opens with praise of his 'stout resistance against the rising flood of interventionism and socialism. He was one of the first to see the imminent destruction of our civilization through Marxism and all its related schemes of socialism' (p. v). So much for positive economics.

4 Of course, other things rarely are equal, and the immediate impact of an increase in the money supply will depend on who gets the extra cash and what they do with it. Hume does envisage circumstances in which a sudden influx of precious metals from foreign conquests (like those of Alexander) might result in a short-term fall in interest rates, lasting until price rises have worked through (1752: 57–8). But if this is the mechanism imagined by Glotz, Bury and Meiggs, and the rest, they do

not say so. It is ironic that although few, if any, of Hume's contemporaries held the quantity theory of interest in its crudest form (Blaug 1968: 23–4), the same cannot be said of his successors.

5 Commentaries on Demosthenes' inheritance speeches by Gernet (1954–60: I, 24–109) and Pearson (1972: 103–203). On the component parts of the estate, see *APF* 3597 XIII–XX. The most recent presentation of the evidence by Hopper (1979: 120–1) is marred by a remarkable sequence of errors which seem to have escaped the notice of reviewers: (c) for 7·2 per cent, read 7·2 minae; (d) for 80 minae value, read 150 minae value; (e) for valued at 100 minae, read valued at 130 minae; (h) for 6 with Demomeles, read 16 with Demomeles. Not surprisingly, Hopper draws from this combination of errors a false total for the estate of 656 minas, which he compares with the rounded total of 14 talents (840 minas) claimed by Demosthenes. Hopper concludes from this wide discrepancy (p. 219, n. 36): 'There is probably here a manuscript corruption of figures, a warning against basing too close calculations on such.' In fact, substitution of the correct figures gives a grand total of 826 minas – just 14 minas short of the rounded figure.

The bibliography on Demosthenes' inheritance is extensive: see *APF* 3597 XIII. The most uncompromising attempt to rework the material in the speeches along rational economic lines is by Schwahn (1929), with a devastating review by Calhoun (1930). Concerning the studies by Oertel (1930) and Korver (1942), see the brief comments by Finley (1952: 67–8, 116; 1985b: 116); on Costouros (1976), see Macve (1985: 262–4). The body of Macve's paper consists of a valuable reworking of the conclusions reached by de Ste Croix (1956), which, with some qualifications and changes of emphasis, are found to hold good.

6 See, for example, Böhm-Bawerk (1884: 10), Marshall (1890: 584) and Robinson (1951), who prefaces her classic study of the rate of interest by clarifying the scope of her analysis (p. 92):

> The most important influences upon interest rates – which account for, say, the difference between 30% in a Chinese village and 3% in London – are social, legal and institutional... and in the broad sweep of history these considerations are more significant. But we are here concerned with an economy in which the most up-to-date credit facilities must be taken for granted and a capitalist system is fully developed.

> Perhaps the earliest appreciation of the disjunction between non-productive credit and the rate of profit was made by Marx: 'The form of interest is older than profit. The level of interest in India for communal agriculturists in no way indicates the level of profit' (1857–8: 851–2, and cf. 862; 1867–94: III, 215).

7 Application of the loanable fund theory to Athens may be doubly anachronistic. The supposed rôle of the rate of interest as a regulator, restoring equilibrium between demand for and supply of loans, is disputed by some economists, and seems to mark a decisive break between neo-classical and Keynesian models: see Keynes (1937).

8 For what it is worth, Hesychius (s.v. *tokopherein*) glosses *tokos* as 'a kind of greed' (*eidos pleonexias*); and the scholiast on Demosthenes (at XXIV.213) talks vaguely about 'private rules' (*idiōtikoi nomoi*) against the exaction of too much interest (see Beauchet 1897: IV, 248).

9 I ignore disputed details of text and interpretation (see Stein 1952; Neufeld 1955), and reproduce the translation of the New English Bible (1970).

10 Perhaps a majority of biblical scholars take the Old Testament laws on interest as referring to 'commercial credit': notably Neufeld (1955: 371–2; citing earlier writers on p. 361). He is followed by Meislin and Cohen (1963–4), who re-interpret the later laws as a response to the development of commercial loans. But the style of argument (see, for example, Neufeld 1955: 377–8), and the evidence of actual credit operations in the Old Testament, suggest that this is a case of misconceived modernism (see Chapter III, n. 30, with Gordon 1982).

11 On the principle of the exaction of interest from heretics, see Noonan 1957: 101–2; for a precise Indian parallel, Sharma 1965–6: 57–8. In this connexion may be noted a telling misinterpretation of an Athenian law, cited by Nelson (1969: 22, n. 49). The sixteenth-century theologian, Petrus Gregorinus of Toulouse, argued that to extend interest-free loans to enemies and foreigners was to offer them illicit aid. This point, he claimed, was appreciated by the Athenians, who inflicted on offenders the gravest penalties. This can only be explained as a misunderstanding (or misremembering) of the laws restricting lending in maritime loans (e.g. [Dem.] XXXV.51).

12 The same principle, though without a time element, is used to calculate the *epōbelia*, or fine of one obol for every drachma claimed as damages, imposed on a plaintiff who failed to win more than one-fifth of the jurors' votes (e.g. Dem. XXVII.67). The *epōbelia*, with a time dimension, is introduced as a fine in Plato's *Laws* (921C) for failing to pay for goods received on credit. A parallel principle was involved in calculating the *aparchai* or fractions of allied tribute that the Athenians dedicated to Athena: one-sixtieth, or a mina in the talent. Likewise, the *epiphorai* or fines for late payment of tribute amounted to three minas in the talent (= 5 per cent) for each month in arrears (see Meiggs 1972: 236 and 432–3).

13 Left out of the list is the doubtful appearance of 7 per cent on a *horos* (Finley 1952: no. 27, with 273, n. 66). Beyond the scope of my study are the interest-bearing loans made by the Temple of Athene to the Athenian treasury in the later fifth century (see, for example, *SGHI*^{2} 72 ~ Fornara 134). The *rationale* behind these loans remains obscure (Pritchett 1977; Thompson 1979b), as does the charging of interest (from 7 to 1.2 per cent per annum: Wade-Gery 1930).

14 On each occasion Demosthenes mentions this 'interest' charge, he adds the qualification that it is 'only' (*monon*) 1 per cent per month; but this is rightly dismissed by Billeter as a rhetorical trick (1989: 11).

15 The 1 per cent figure from the Aixonides inscription is used by Billeter

(1898: 15–18) as the basis of a precarious calculation of the rate of capitalization in fourth-century Attica. Needless to say, the concept is a development of classical economic theory and has little or no meaning for the non-capitalist economy of classical Athens (see my Appendix IV).

16 Böckh (1842: 130) suggests that 1½ per cent per month could have been the usual rate of interest when the law was framed, but more recent opinion favours a deliberately high rate (Harrison 1968–71: I, 57–8; MacDowell 1978: 89). Full references for application of the 1½ per cent rate in divorce cases by Billeter (1898: 46–56).

17 The list of rates compiled by Heichelheim (1930: 126–7) adds nothing to the argument; supposed evidence for rates of interest in Hellenistic Athens is rightly dismissed by Day (1942: 250, n. 241).

18 Bogaert (1968: 290) contrasts the stability of the Delian rate with apparent changes in interest levels throughout the rest of the Greek world and concludes that the figure of 10 per cent has some sacred significance, akin to a tithe (*dekatē*). It is, however, my belief that the consistency of the Delian rate was not abnormal but typical, and had a comparable range of material survived from Attica, it would show much the same stability. I have argued elsewhere for the importance of custom and tradition in the formation of prices in Athens (Millett 1990).

V. *PHILIA* AND FRIENDSHIP

1 Compare 1162a29–33. The part of the *Nicomachean Ethics* concerned with friendship is available in an expanded translation by Percival (1940), which occasionally clarifies obscurities resulting from Aristotle's highly elliptical style (see Chapter II, n. 26).

2 See, for example, Earp 1929: 32–3. In fact, the expression of relationships as a series of concentric circles is found in Stoic writings (Sandbach 1975: 34–5). Implicit in Plato's *Laws* is the idea of a hierarchy of relationships, starting with parents and children, and moving downwards through relatives, friends and citizens to *xenoi* (718A; cf. 729B–730A).

3 Elsewhere in greater detail (1160a1–19):

> What is just is also (like *philia*) different, since it is not the same for parents towards children as for one brother towards another, and not the same for comrades as for fellow-citizens, and similarly with other types of *philia*. Similarly, what is unjust towards each of these is also differentiated, and becomes more unjust as it is practised on closer friends. It is more shocking, for example, to rob a comrade of money than to rob a fellow-citizen, to fail to help a brother than a stranger (*othneiōi*), and to strike one's father than any one else.

For the context, see above, pp. 114–15.

4 Some of the common maxims concerning friendship are strung together by Isocrates in his advice *To Demonicus* (1.24–6). For collected references to the blessings of friendship, see Blundell 1989: 31–2.

5 The works in question being the *Nicomachean Ethics* (*Eth. Nic.*), the *Eudemian Ethics* (*Eth. Eud.*) and the *Magna Moralia* (*Mag. Mor.*); corresponding sections of the three texts relating to friendship are usefully tabulated and summarized by Hamburger 1951: 112–16. Fashions regarding the priority and even the authenticity of these works change periodically. The present orthodoxy seems to be to regard *Eth. Nic.* as the definitive statement of Aristotle's ethical theory, with *Eth. Eud.* as an earlier, interim effort, and *Mag. Mor.* as a post-Aristotelian compilation (Hardie 1980: 1–10; in detail, Rowe 1971: esp. 52–60). It should, nonetheless, be noted that Kenny (1978) has recently made out a powerful case for the philosophical primacy of *Eth. Eud.* over *Eth. Nic.* Almost all the references to Aristotle in my text are taken from *Eth. Nic.* So long as the Aristotelian credentials of *Eth. Nic.* are not compromised, the debate is of passing interest.

6 The basic bibliography on Greek friendship is listed (with critical comments) by Gauthier and Jolif (1970: II, 654–8); to these may be added: Landfester 1966, Fraisse 1974, Huxley 1979: 7–20, Taillardat 1982 and Price 1989. The attempt by Hutter (1978) to approach Greek politics and friendship from a sociological perspective deserves to be better known.

7 Ramsøy's article is a useful introduction to the sociology of friendship. Also helpful are the programmatic essays by Paine, Du Bois and Schwimmer in the collection edited by Leyton (1974). Friendship has not been a central subject of sociological enquiry (see Mullett 1988: 4), but the items by Eisenstadt (1956), Wolfe (1966), Allen (1979) and Eisenstadt and Roniger (1984) shed some light on the ancient Greek experience.

8 The contrast with Plato's Socrates is striking. Whereas Plato tries to justify Socrates' exasperating behaviour in terms of his contribution to philosophy, Xenophon's defence depends on presenting a Socrates who was utterly respectable (Lacey 1971: esp. 31–40). Marchant (1923: xiii) is probably correct in seeing as much Xenophon as Socrates in Book II of the *Memorabilia*. Although the division into books is post-Xenophontic, the deliberate structuring of the *Memorabilia* is one of the main themes in the painstaking studies by Gigon (1953 and 1956).

9 The classic statement is by Ross (1949: 230) – 'any mutual attraction between two human beings'. But it is fairly objected by Cooper (1980: 302) that attraction *alone* is not enough to count as *philia*. In order to arrive at his own definition ('mutual well-wishing and well-doing out of concern for one another'), Cooper turns to the treatment of *philia* in Aristotle's *Rhetoric* (1380b35–81b36), and seems to be in danger of over-stressing the altruistic element in *Eth. Nic.* Of no immediate help are the various conflicting theories about the etymology of *philos*; see Benveniste 1969: 273–8, Hamp 1982, and Schwartz (in Figueira and Nagy 1985: 27, §5, n. 3).

10 The missing section (1160a1–9) is quoted in full in n. 3, above. The

Oxford Text of Bywater (1890) brackets as spurious the penultimate
sentence ('Some *koinōniai … sunousias*'); but more recent editors accept it
as Aristotelian (see Gauthier and Jolif 1970: II.2 *ad loc.*). The proverb
that *philoi* have everything in common also appears in Plato's *Laws*
(739c).

11 The concept of *koinōnia* is examined in detail by Endenburg, 1937 (in
Dutch, with German summary; brief review in English by Rose, 1938).

12 The argument is compressed and needs expansion. Aristotle seems to be
saying that because things differ in degree (more or less *philia*), that
need not exclude the possibility of differences in type (various kinds of
philia).

13 For *boētheia* as the appropriate term for help needed by and offered to
philoi, see Herman (1986: 121–2), with special reference to *xenia* (further
discussed in n. 18, below).

14 The wine he sells to a friend is watered (§5); he borrows a cloak from
an acquaintance and keeps it for so long that the lender is forced to ask
for it back (§10); if a friend is selling something cheap, he beats the price
down still further, and then resells at a profit (§12); when he's travelling
with some acquaintances, he uses their slaves and hires out his own
(§17); if a friend or friend's daughter is getting married, he goes away
to avoid having to send a present (§19); he borrows from his
acquaintances the sorts of things they would never dream of asking to
be returned (§20). Other Characters also show their unpleasant sides in
their dealings with *philoi* (see Edmonds and Austen 1904: index s.v.
'friendship'); the work could almost be read as a guide to friendship in
reverse.

15 See Bolkestein 1939: 156–60; Hands 1968: 11–16. There is, of course,
a sense in which even 'Christian Charity' is giving for a return (Rubin
1987: 1–2). Tredennick (1970) is evidently embarrassed by Socrates'
calculating approach to the acquisition of friends, excusing it on the
grounds that (p. 115) 'Xenophon's Socrates, like Plato's, often speaks
with his tongue in his cheek, or at least with a twinkle in his eye.'
Nothing, I suspect, could be further from the truth.

16 Xenophon does not tell the whole story: the relationship between
Agesilaus and his *philoi* was complicated by the king's almost uniquely
high status. A proverbial expression – quoted with approval by both
Plato (*Laws* 757A) and Aristotle (*Eth. Nic.* 1157b35) – identifies *philia*
with equality (*isotēs*). Aristotle does envisage the possibility of friendship
between unequals (1158b11–59b25), but only provided that the gap in
virtue, vice, wealth or whatever is not too wide (1158b29–59a5). The
case he cites by way of illustration is that of a king and his 'far inferiors'.
Although Aristotle does not say so, the relationship here resembles
patronage, and the people to whom Agesilaus dispensed favours
without requiring a specific return may plausibly be identified as
clients. The theme of Agesilaus' exploitation of the patron–client
mechanism for political ends is developed by Cartledge (1987: 139–59).

The relationship between kings and inferiors is presented from a different perspective by Isocrates in his letter to Nicocles, the young king of Salamis on Cyprus. He opens and closes his letter (II.1 and 54) with the suggestion that those who present rulers with valuable objects are not really making a gift (*dosis*), but are engaging in trade (*emporia*) – and highly profitable trade at that.

17 For enmity (*echthra*) as the mirror-image of *philia*, with identical rules of reciprocity (including paying back more than the original hurt), see Goldhill 1986: 83–9; Blundell 1989: 30–1. The part played by enmity as an element in the Roman political process is set out (with some exaggeration) by Epstein 1987.

18 In what is probably the best brief account of non-philosophical *philia*, Herman (1987: 29–30) cites Apollodorus' version of the growth of his relationship with Nicostratus (§4) as typical of the way in which friendships were formed within the *polis*.

> Confidence was generated through a lengthy process of interaction, and the resulting relationship was sustained – or disrupted – through permanent interaction…Ritualised friendship (*xenia*), by contrast, was concluded between persons who originated from different, and at times, drastically dissimilar social systems, and who had no previous record of social intercourse. Intimacy was established not through a lengthy interaction, but abruptly, as in marriage, through a ritual act.

As in illustration of initiation between *xenoi*, Herman summarizes the anecdote from Herodotus (III.139–40), describing a chance meeting between Darius and Syloson and its consequences (Darius got a brightly coloured cloak, and Syloson got – some years later – the island of Samos). While agreeing with Herman's overall formulation of *xenia* as opposed to *philia*, it should not be presumed that people *never* became *philoi* through chance encounters – especially in a *polis* the size of Athens. Stripped of its picturesque detail, the story of Darius and Syloson shows the main characteristics of *philia*: an initial gesture, creating an obligation to reciprocate. If Herman's study has a fault, it is treating *philia* as a sub-species of *xenia*, when the reverse is surely the case.

19 In the last two verses, Menander plays on the semi-technical distinction – common in the Orators – between property which is 'visible' and 'invisible' (see Chapter VII, n. 11). For parallels, and for the sentiment of the speech as a whole, see the commentary by Handley (1965: *ad loc.*). There is no need for Finley's dismissal of this passage as representing a 'minority ethical note' (1985a: 248, n. 43); its classical credentials are entirely orthodox.

20 The theory of continuity of outlook between Homeric and classical Greece appears in earlier work by Adkins (1960: 226–32); note, however, the objections to his interpretation of Homeric *philos* by Hooker (1987). Adkins necessarily limits his discussion of friendship in Homer and Aristotle to the upper reaches of Greek society; but the

account of *philia* given in the text can be applied to all levels of citizen society. Although the most striking examples of helping out friends involve members of the élite (e.g. Crito: Diog. Laert. II.121; Plato: Diog. Laert. III.24; Arcesilaus: Diog. Laert. IV.37), three jokes in Aristophanes' *Plutus* seem to imply that obligations between *philoi* were generally appreciated (ll. 237–41, 335–42 and 380–1).

21 Although the general sense of the passage is clear, I omit several words which are so ambiguous as to defy translation. On the wider significance of Thucydides' words, see Hooker (1974).

22 The complex (and surprising) evolution of the Charites is traced by Zielinski (1924); on their cult in Athens and elsewhere, see Rocchi (1979 and 1980). The Charites are associated with democracy by Oliver (1960: 91–117).

23 There is no recent, comprehensive study of *charis*. Hewitt (1927), Franzmann (1972) and Scott (1983) all break off before the fourth century. The older study by Loew (1908) was not available to me (but see Hewitt 1927: 142).

24 Aristotle in his *Rhetoric* (1385a16–b10) includes *charis* as one of the qualities with which the would-be orator needs to be familiar. There are instructions on how to manipulate the circumstances of an individual act of *charis* so as to maximize or minimize its apparent significance.

25 The Orators' use of *charis* with the sense of reciprocity is not limited to the public-service theme. The following selection is chosen to illustrate the range of the concept. In a speech of Antiphon (v.57), the speaker finds it necessary to ridicule the suggestion put forward by his opponent that he killed a man 'as a favour' (*chariti*): 'But who has ever done this for another person as an act of *charis*?' In Lysias' *On the Scrutiny of Evandros* (XXVI.15), the accuser reassures the jury that he is not making his attack on the would-be archon in order to show *charis* to his friend, who had already been rejected on a scrutiny (on the transitivity of *philia* and *echthra* see Blundell 1989: 47–8). In a fragment of Lysias (*For Pherenicus*, Gernet and Bizos 1955–9: II, fr. 34.2–3), the Athenian speaker explains how he owed (*opheilein*) *charis* to a Theban who offered him hospitality while in exile (see Herman 1987: 28). Elsewhere, there are references to freed slaves showing *charis* to the person giving them their freedom (Hyp. *Athenog*. 6), a man expecting to receive *charis* from a prostitute on whom he spends money ([Dem.] LIX.21), and a sailor showing *charis* to Apollodorus in return for financial assistance when in need ([Dem.] L.47).

26 For *aposterein* as the appropriate term for failure to repay a loan (used ten times in the speech *Against Timotheus*), see Cohen 1983: 18–22.

27 Opinion is divided over whether Timotheus paid interest on his loans from Pasion (Bogaert 1968: 356, n. 300). Apollodorus' lavish references to *charis* and the *philia*-type relationship between Timotheus and the banker imply that the loans were interest-free; this is apparently supported by the claim that Pasion required neither witness nor security

(§2). That the absence of witnesses was characteristic of personal loans between friends may be inferred from Lysias' *Against Theomnestus* (Gernet and Bizos 1955–9: II, fr. 39.6.iv), and from an anecdote of Plutarch involving the third-century philosopher Persaeus ('On Being Put to Shame' 533B). Persaeus apparently caused a stir by insisting that a friend receive a loan from him with a banker as witness. All this is not quite decisive for the Timotheus episode. As noted by Gernet (1954–60: III, 7–8), Apollodorus is guilty of sophistry in implying that it was unusual for bankers to lend without witnesses: it was, in fact, the rule. It also seems strange that Apollodorus does not exploit a possible advantage by stating explicitly that the loans were interest-free. The problem could be resolved by assuming that although interest *was* charged, Apollodorus wanted to mislead the jury into thinking that the loans were interest-free. But it is probably impossible to penetrate Apollodorus' rhetorical posturing, and the question of an interest charge must remain open.

VI. NON-PROFESSIONAL LENDING: LOANS WITHOUT INTEREST

1 The norm may be inferred from Thucydides' description of the dangers of extreme *stasis* or political conflict (III.82.6). In order to emphasize the abnormality of personal relationships under these conditions, he argues that links between *hetairoi* were counted stronger than family ties (*to sungenes*). For other, near-identical hierarchies of *philia*, see Chapter V, n. 2 (with Plato, *Alcib.* I 126c).

2 Only after extreme provocation would a father formally disown his son or daughter (see below p. 133). Brothers might choose to ignore or even to fight one another but they remained brothers. See Cooper (1980: 334, n. 2), who cites Euripides, *Phoenician Women* (l. 1446): Polynices, mortally wounded by his brother Eteocles, whom he has just killed, tells his mother that although Eteocles was *philos* and became *echthros*, yet he was still *philos*.

3 The classic definition by Rivers identifies kinship as 'the social recognition of biological ties' (quoted by Mair 1972: 69–82; but see Needham 1971c: 3–5). For the full range of descent groups in Athens (tribe, phratry, *genos*, *oikos*), see Littman 1971: 5–14, Humphreys 1978: 194–202; fundamental on *oikos* and *oikia* is Lacey 1968. The terminology of Greek kinship is discussed by Miller 1953.

4 The extent and complexity of the literature is potentially baffling. A good starting-point is the article on Kinship in *IESS* by Eggan, Goody and Pitt-Rivers. There are brief introductions by Mair (1972: 69–82) and Lewis (1985: 234–80); at greater length by Fox (1967) and Goody (1974). The origin and development of kinship studies as a component of social anthropology is traced by Fortes (1969).

5 The tone of Needham's introductory essay is instructive (and note the

dissenting voice in the dedication of the volume to Edmund Leach on p. v). For a summary of his own views on the value of kinship in anthropology, see Leach 1982: 176–211.

6 For the familiar picture of the *genos* as a late and fictitious creation, see the detailed studies by Bourriot (1976) and Roussel (1976), conveniently summarized by Smith (1985). Other aspects of the kinship structure are re-examined in a series of papers by Humphreys (1978, 1980, 1983b and 1986).

7 The translation in the text is adapted from the version by Maidment (1941). The peculiar circumstances of the case are the warrant for MacDowell's judicious discussion of Andocides' innocence and guilt (1962: 167–76).

8 There is an extended version of the 'unnatural behaviour' theme in a speech by Antiphon (1), where the speaker claims to have been orphaned as the result of a family poisoning. Playing on the duty of a murdered man's relations to seek vengeance (MacDowell 1963: 8–32), he opens the speech by confessing to the jurors his terrible dilemma (§1): 'On the one hand, how can I disregard my father's solemn injunction to bring his murderers to justice? On the other hand, if I obey it, I shall inevitably find myself ranged against the last persons with whom I should quarrel – my half-brothers and their mother.' The rôle of his relatives as defendants is presented as a paradox (§2): 'One would have expected them to seek vengeance for the dead and support the prosecution; but as it is the opposite is the case: they are themselves my opponents and the murderers, as both I and the indictment state.' This makes possible an emotional appeal to the jury (§3): '...avenge the dead man, and in doing so give me, a lonely orphan, your aid. For you are my kin (*anagkaioi*); those who should have avenged the dead and supported me are his murderers and my opponents.' The speaker may here be playing on the idea of the citizen-body (through the myth of autochthony) as a single kinship group (cf. Andoc. 1.148–9); see Ober 1989: 261–3. It may be noted that the legal limit of 'kin' (*anchisteia*) for the purpose of avenging death (and inheriting property) was children of first cousins (see Lacey 1968: 28–9; opposed by Littman 1979: 6, n. 2, who favours *second* cousins).

9 Although Tragedy has plenty of sharp confrontations between close relatives, the plays are rightly ignored by Lacey as direct evidence for his reconstruction of the classical Greek family (1968: 10). The evidence of the Orators suggests that disputes reaching as far as the courts were generally between more distant relatives.

10 As often, manipulation of the accepted norm adds to our understanding. The anonymous author of the *Dissoi Logoi* or 'Contrasting Arguments' (*c.* 400) is out to shock. Having proved to his own satisfaction that all good things are also bad (and *vice versa*), he holds an imaginary conversation with a person who claims to have done good to his parents, advising him (since what is good is also bad) to do bad instead (1.12,

with Robinson 1979: *ad loc.*). Also illuminating is the dramatic background to Plato's *Euthyphro*. Socrates falls into conversation with Euthyphro, whom he discovers to be prosecuting his own father for murder, much to the disgust of his own relatives (4D). Socrates can hardly believe his ears, and immediately assumes that the victim must also have been a relative (4A–B). Euthyphro sets him straight with his opinion that what matters is the justice or otherwise of the act, and not one's relationship to the victim (in this case, his *pelatēs* or 'client'; see Millett 1989: 30, n.1). This is evidently meant as a minority view; Burnett (1924: *ad loc.*) thinks it almost certain that Euthyphro would have had his suit disallowed by the competent magistrate.

11 The following list of passages is not meant to be complete. The debt owed by children to their parents is commonly expressed as an *eranos*-contribution. 'My son', says a father in a fragment of Alexis (*CAF* fr. 280 ~ *FAC* II p. 510 fr. 280), 'the greatest *eranos* I can give you is to bring you up properly (*kata tropon*). That is what I received from my father, and I must pay it back (*apodounai*) to you' (see also: Thales, in Stobaeus III 119H; Antiphanes *CAF* fr. 260 ~ *FAC* II p. 296 fr. 260; Eurip. *Supp.* 361–4; Arist. *Pol.* 1332b35–41; [Dem.] x.40). The minority of passages without the *eranos* element includes a fragment from the prologue of Menander's *Xenologos* or 'Hirer of Mercenaries' (Kock fr. 354 ~ Allinson 1921: p. 416 fr. 354; cf. *Samia* 4–18): 'The son of a poor man, who had been brought up beyond his father's means, saw that his father had only a little and was ashamed. Being well trained, he paid back at once the fair fruit (*karpon*) of gratitude (*charitos*).' *Karpos* may here have the additional, figurative sense of 'interest' or 'profit'. In Euripides' *Alcestis* (ll. 681–4) the debt motif is stood on its head by a father who angrily denies he is under any obligation to die on behalf of his own son. The idea of debts owing to parents is explored by Cameron (1964) in the course of making sense of an otherwise obscure passage in Aeschylus' *Seven Against Thebes*.

12 This is not the place to get drawn into the massive debate (and literature) about attitudes towards women in classical Athens, but three brief points can be made about the status of wives with respect to *philia* within the family. First, there is the relative ease with which *philia* between husband and wife could be cancelled by divorce; contrast the enduring bond between other members of the *oikos* (above, n. 2). Secondly, the *philia* between husband and wife and (say) father and son was asymmetrical. Whereas the woman would always be in a position of relative inferiority, there was the expectation that the son would, in due course, become a father in his own right (Arist. *Pol.* 1332b35–41). Finally, the scope for women's contributions to the *oikos* via exchange operations was limited (at least in theory; see Xen. *Oec.* VII.1–X.13). Aristarchus accepts his obligation to provide for his female relatives (Xen. *Mem.* II.7), but they are not allowed to contribute to the upkeep of the *oikos*; at least, not until Socrates has brought to bear all his powers

of persuasion. They are then able to accuse Aristarchus of failing to pull his weight (above, pp. 71-4).

13 For the background to this arrangement and some of its legal and financial implications, see Finley 1952: 48-50.

14 The loan of property to Spudias to act as security in a further loan transaction is reminiscent of the arrangement between Apollodorus and Nicostratus (above, pp. 56-7). Other loans are mentioned in the speech. The speaker contrasts his own virtuous behaviour with that of his opponent, telling the jury that he paid the price (and interest) on everything he received from Polyeuctus and his wife; also that he has restored to the estate everything that he previously owed (§9). More specific is his claim that his wife 'advanced' (*proanaliskein*) one mina to pay for her father's funeral expenses (§11). This and other passages from the speech noted in my text are revealing as suggesting that women could participate in credit operations involving valuable objects and substantial amounts of cash. Other scraps of evidence for female creditors in Athens are collected by Schaps (1979: 63-7).

15 A little later in the speech (§24), Lycurgus gives details of how Philomelus and Menelaus (both Athenian citizens) received from the hand of Amyntas some forty minas owed them by Leocrates. (For what is known about Philomelus, see *APF* 14671, where Davies seems to assume that the borrower was not Leocrates but Amyntas.) For the significance of the *eranos*-contributions owed by Leocrates, see the final section of this chapter.

16 Editors have consistently had difficulty with this passage on the grounds that a payment of one mina in interest, calculated on a monthly basis, works out at $2\frac{6}{7}$ per cent per month ($= 34\frac{2}{7}$ per cent per annum). As this excessively high rate is not paralleled in any Athenian loan transaction – let alone between relatives – there have been at least three attempts to emend away the anomaly (see Petrie 1922: *ad loc.*). In fact, the difficulty probably arises out of a misunderstanding about what the mina of interest represents. It was possibly no more than a conveniently round sum to cover the whole period of the credit sale, the duration of which is not known. An alternative, unsatisfactory explanation is offered by Thompson (1982: 72), who accepts the figure of one mina interest, which he grosses up to an annual figure of 34 per cent. This he explains, without apparent support from the text, as the equivalent of rent in a leasing operation. He also seems to envisage the possibility (again, without obvious justification) that Timochares leased the 'shop' to a third party.

The Lysicles with whom the agreement was deposited may reappear in a similar rôle in Hyperides' *Against Athenogenes* (§9); but there is no need to follow Burtt (1954: *ad loc.*) in identifying him as a banker.

17 Introduction and commentary in Paley and Sandys (1910: lxviii–lxxix and 245-75). Legal aspects of the case are considered by Wolff (1943); discussion of the topography of the two properties by Gomme (1945).

In a close reading of the speech, Osborne (1985a: 17–18) suggests that the two litigants, though members of the same community, probably owned adjacent properties on which they were not normally resident; note, however, the objections raised by Roy (1988).

18 *Geitōn* – sharing the same *gē* (land); *homoros* – having the same *horos* (boundary); *paroikos, prosoikos* – living beside; *perichōros* – around the locality; *pelas, plēsion, pelatēs* – nearby (cf. the English 'neighbour' as 'one who has his bower nigh'). The bibliography specifically on neighbours in Greek society is unsatisfactory (on demesmen, see the following note). Radermacher (1918) is helpful so far as it goes; the relevant sections of Bolkestein (1939: 88–9 and 122–8) and den Boer (1979: 62–92) make only a few general comments before broadening out into discussions of the Greek view of mankind ('who is my neighbour?').

19 For a detailed account of the demes, see the complementary studies by Osborne (1985a) and Whitehead (1986). As will be seen from the text, my own presentation of neighbourly relations draws heavily on their researches. In particular, my view of the neighbourhood as intermediate in terms of exchange relations between *oikos* and *polis* echoes Osborne's theory that the deme mediated political power between local community and central authority (1985a: 88–92).

To avoid possible confusion, it should be appreciated that the 'demotic' or deme ascription borne by all Athenian citizens is not an infallible guide to the place of residence. The demotics formally acquired by citizens at the time of the Clisthenic reform were passed on from father to son, irrespective of changes of domicile within Attica. The current view seems to be that, as late as the end of the fourth century, a majority of citizens continued to live in their ancestral demes (Osborne 1985a: 58 and 184; Whitehead 1986: 352–8).

20 The figure of 35,000 adult male citizens should be taken as a maximum (Hansen 1985: 65–9 and 1988: 7–13). Approaching the question from a different direction (the size of bouleutic quotas), Osborne arrives at maximum and minimum sizes for deme communities of 1,500 and 130 free persons (1985a: 42–5).

21 This is an over-simplification (Allan's study refers to urban rather than rural communities). Neighbourly expectations can be very different from those living in (say) a terraced house in working-class Leicester, and in a detached (or even semi-detached) house in middle-class Cambridge.

22 But they are not to be pressed too far. Wrightson repeatedly underlines the provisional status of his conclusions, which may be subject to regional variations not yet researched. (Though it may be noted that other historians have questioned the conventional emphasis on kinship in other periods and places; e.g. Bulloch (1969) on early medieval Europe.) Accounting for possible divergences in kinship relations, Wrightson (1982: 50) places at the top of his list differing patterns of

population mobility. This is an aspect of Athenian society about which
we are almost wholly ignorant. The assumption that ancestral estates
consisted of a single piece of land, redivided in each generation so as to
create an ever-increasing number of neighbours linked by kinship ties,
is no longer credible (Burford-Cooper 1977-8: 163-8). Equally
untenable is the once-popular theory of a 'flight from the land' in the
classical period (Whitehead 1986: 353-5, with n. 19, above). For the
little that can be deduced from the sources, see Osborne 1985a: 47-63.
It may be inferred that networks of local support would tend to
discourage mobility. Describing the poor of Victorian London, Stedman
Jones (1984: 87-8) remarks on the economic importance of 'being
known' in a district. 'From the viewpoint of the labourer, it provided
a further incentive against mobility. Credit arrangements which had
been built up in one neighbourhood over a period of time could not
immediately be transferred to another.' The arrangements referred to
here were with local tradesmen. For the possibility of *philia*-type
relationships (including credit) between Athenian shopkeepers and
their regular customers, see Millett 1990: 189-91.

23 On the informal support expected from neighbours in emergencies, see
Lintott (1982: 20-2). There were certain states where obligations
between neighbours were on a formal footing. A fragment of Heraclides
Ponticus (XI.4) tells how at Cyme neighbours had to contribute in the
event of loss by theft. In his *Laws*, Theophrastus preserves details of
regulations relating to the sale of real property at Thurii and Aenos,
where neighbours were required to guarantee the transaction (fr.
21.2-3 in Szegedy-Maszak 1981). Glotz (1904: 195-203) treats these
laws as archaic survivals which he uses in support of an idiosyncratic
reinterpretation of passages in the *Works and Days*.

24 The mutual assistance of neighbours assumes an element of equality;
what Wrightson (1982: 57) calls 'reciprocity of comparable services
between effective equals'. When Euripides' Electra is asked by
Clytemnestra why she delivered herself of a child alone, without the
help even of neighbours, she replies that no one wishes to have *philoi*
who are poor (ll. 1130-1). Help which did come from those who were
superior in wealth and status could take on the characteristics of
patronage, which include exploitation. I have argued elsewhere (Millett
1989) that the political patronage so effectively wielded by Cimon with
the deme as his power-base (Whitehead 1986: 305-15 for details), was
largely suppressed by a combination of democratic ideology, public pay
and mechanisms of mutual support between near equals. Largesse by
wealthy demesmen did not completely die out. Two of Lysias' speeches
(XVI.14 and XXXI.15-19) refer to individuals supporting poorer fellow-
demesmen with cash handouts and weapons in time of war. An
inscription from the late fourth century (*IG* II^2 1187; trans. Hands 1968:
125-6) honours the *stratēgos* Dercylus in recognition of his support for
the education of boys within the deme of Eleusis, where he apparently
owned land (*APF* 3248; Mitchel 1964). Also from the later fourth

century, one Leukios of Sounion presented an *agora* to his fellow-demesmen (*APF* 9057). All this seems to be indicative of deme solidarity rather than political ambition.

25 The wills of Theophrastus and of five other philosophers, also preserved by Diogenes Laertius (Plato: III.41–3; Aristotle: v.11–16; Strato: v.61–4; Lyco: v.69–74; Epicurus: x.16–21), are discussed in detail by Bruns (1880). The influence of Roman testamentary law on Bruns's interpretation is criticized by Dareste (1882b). The authenticity of the wills (periodically questioned) is convincingly reasserted by Gottschalk (1972). Translations from the wills in the text are adapted from the Loeb edition by Hicks (1925).

26 Hipparchus seems to have acted as Theophrastus' treasurer and financial agent (Bruns 1880: 28–9). A clause in the will (§56) stipulates that any agreements (*sumbolaia*) made in Chalcis by Hipparchus in the name of Theophrastus are to become the property of Hipparchus. The nature of these *sumbolaia* is not known, but some form of loan agreements seem likely. Matters of credit and debt crop up in other philosophical wills. Plato (III.43) records that Euclides the stone-cutter owes him three minas, whereas he himself owes nothing to anybody (§44). Strato cancels an agreement involving an unspecified obligation (v.63), as does Lyco (v.73), who also makes general arrangements to discharge any debts he may have incurred at the time of his death (§§69 and 71). It is unfortunate that Gottschalk (1972: 319) should make a point of dismissing these sections of the wills as containing 'little of importance to the historian'. Although the evidence is slender, they give an impression of the way in which debts were recorded in non-philosophical wills.

27 Relationships between fellow-travellers could have repercussions for the future. See Humphreys (1985: 333–5) for the use of travelling companions as witnesses in court.

28 On all aspects of the *hetaireiai*, Calhoun (1913) remains indispensable. The persistent fault in his analysis is a tendency to assume that 'clubs' were widespread at all levels in Athenian society (pp. 1–2). His supporting evidence is meagre (Plato, *Apol.* 36B), and is rightly rejected by Connor (1971: 28, n. 45). I do not follow Calhoun (pp. 44–5) in his identification of a 'club of sycophants' grouped around Melas, the Egyptian metic, who figures in Isaeus' *On the Property of Dicaeogenes* (v.7–9). According to the speaker, Melas and his *philoi* had encouraged his opponent to lay claim to the estate at issue, even lending him money in the expectation of a favourable outcome – money which he now refuses to pay (§40). Calhoun is himself forced to admit that there is no positive evidence for a permanent grouping around Melas and that 'passing alliances' were no doubt frequent (p. 95, n. 3). The vague accusation that Melas and his *philoi* were so bold as to 'bear false witness on each other's behalf' (§8) is mere law-court rhetoric.

29 A similar process may lie behind other examples in *APF* of individuals having their public debts discharged by people other than their heirs

(6366 with 14627; 1461). In at least two other cases, either debtor or benefactor were active in politics: Leptines (9046) and Hyperides (14160). There is a literary parallel (though possibly without a political element) in an episode described in Antiphon's *On the Murder of Herodes* (v.63). When the Athenian Lycinus was imprisoned for a public debt of seven minas, it was his *philoi* who contributed to his release. Nothing much can be said about the *philos* of Pericles from whom his son borrowed money under false pretences (above, pp. 66–7). Equally anonymous is the *philos* from whom the unfortunate Phocion was forced to 'borrow' 12 dr. – the price of the dose of hemlock with which he ended his life (Plut. *Phoc.* XXXVI.4).

For the existence of political *philoi* as distinct from *hetairoi*, see Connor (1971: 30–2, with refinements by Strauss 1986: 20–7). The distinction (though possibly without political undertones) appears in a fragment from the fourth-century comic playwright Philemon (*CAF* fr. 213 ~ *FAC* IIIa p. 89 fr. 213). A character called Cleon (not the fifth-century politician) is interrogated about his wealth. When it is pointed out to him that cash and even real property tend to disappear, he falls back on the possibility of raising an *eranos*-loan by going the rounds of his *hetairoi*, *philoi* and *sunētheis* (intimates). The response – that people will not help out a person who has had bad luck – need not be taken seriously.

30 Other Characters reveal their unpleasant sides through anti-social behaviour at sacrifices (IX.2, XIX.4, XXI.7 and 11, and XXII.4). The *Characters* as a whole are testimony to the pervasiveness of religion in Athens; see Edmonds and Austen 1904: via the index, s.v. 'religion'.

31 The summary of civic friendship that follows in the text draws heavily on the helpful account by Cooper (1976–7; compare the analysis by Price 1989: 193–205). Civic friendship is one of the few areas of *philia* to receive a fuller treatment in the *Eudemian* (1242a1–19) rather than the *Nicomachean Ethics*.

32 Contrast the position in oligarchic Sparta, where sharing of property was encouraged as a means of strengthening Spartiate solidarity against the helot threat. Aristotle (*Politics* 1263a21–37) specifically mentions the sharing of slaves (helots?), horses, dogs, and food stored in the fields (cf. Xen. *Const. Lak.* VI.3).

33 The terminology of *eranos*-operations is fully catalogued in the predominantly philological study by Vondeling (1961). Whatever its limitations (above, pp. 14–15), this painstaking collection of material is the natural starting-point for a more searching analysis. Vondeling's monograph has, however, been almost completely ignored outside Holland (see the solitary review by Pleket 1962), and is apparently unknown to Longo (1983), the most recent writer on *eranos*. Of the earlier literature, surveyed and supplemented by Finley (1952: 100–6), the brief article by Reinach (DS s.v. '*eranos*') is still valuable. The summary by Gluskina (1974: 127–9) of a longer paper in Russian on the social aspect of *eranos*-credit would seem to add nothing significant

to the discussion. The dissertations by Maier (1971) and Benvenuti (1980) were not available to me.

34 *Eranistai* on *horos* inscriptions: 8, 30–2, 40, 42, 44, 70–1, 110, 112–14, 31A and 114A in Finley 1952; 163A in Millett 1982; 236 in *SEG* XXXII 1982. Slaves purchasing freedom through groups of *eranistai*: Vondeling 1961: 118–19; Lewis 1968: no. 49 (the so-called 'Freedmen's Bowls' inscriptions; see n. 39). Speeches linked to *eranos*-operations: Lysias, *Against Aristocrates, Concerning the Surety for an eranos* (fr. XVI in Thalheim ~ Harpocration, s.v. '*eranizontes*'); Dinarchus, *Against the Children of Patrocles, Concerning an eranos* (Dion. Hal. *Dinarch.* 12).

35 The debt that children owe to their parents is often expressed in terms of an *eranos*-loan (see n. 11). On the debt owed by citizens to their *polis* as 'fatherland' see the references collected by Blundell (1989: 44).

The range of *eranos* imagery is impressive; only a selection is given in the text. Other striking examples include Isocrates' description of Theseus as owing an *eranos* to Pirithous for his help in abducting Helen, and discharging the obligation by accompanying him down to the underworld (X.20). In Plato's *Symposium* (177C), one of the speakers jocularly talks in language appropriate to an *eranos*-contribution about making an offering to the neglected god of love. Finally, the plaintiff in the Demosthenic speech *Against Neaera* (LIX.8) ominously informs the jury that he and his brother-in-law intend to use the court-case to give their opponent an appropriate *eranos* in return for the harm he has done them. The full range of metaphorical references is gathered by Vondeling (1961: 169–206).

36 Although Vondeling repeatedly stresses the reciprocity at the heart of every *eranos*-operation, which he locates within the wider context of gift-giving in other primitive societies (citing Bücher, Mauss and other anthropological studies), he fails to relate his conclusions to the broader structuring of Greek society. He concentrates instead on etymological investigation (pp. 232–57), relying on the possible derivation of *eranos* to recreate the Greek society of the second millenium BC (p. 266), 'a society of a strongly military and hierarchic structure, bearing a pronounced feudal stamp'. As positive evidence for his conception of a decline in mutuality between citizens in the fourth century (followed by Gluskina 1974: 128–9), Vondeling cites two passages. The one (from Theophrastus, XV.7) shows unwillingness to contribute to an *eranos*, the other ([Dem.] LIII.13) shows unwillingness to repay. But, in both cases, as we have seen (p. 57 and p. 154), the point at issue is the unacceptability of unco-operative behaviour.

37 There is a vivid – though not necessarily Greek – description of an attempt to raise an *eranos*-loan in Plautus' *Asinaria* (I.3, ll. 90–5):

> If I don't get hold of that twenty minas I've had it; really, unless I make away with that money, I'm done for. So now I'll go to the forum and try out all my resources, all my endeavour. I'll beg and I'll earnestly entreat every friend I see – both good and bad. I'm determined to ask and try them

out. And if I can't borrow interest-free (*mutuas*), I'll take it up at interest (*faenore*).

38 For possible parallels for these small-scale contributions, see Bogaert (1986a: 22–3). It is true that other figures for *eranos*-loans suggest much larger contributions (Isaeus XI.43, 1,000 dr.; Lysias fr. 11.43 in Gernet and Bizos 1955–9: II, 2,000 dr.; [Dem.] LIII.8–9, 1,000 dr.); but this may reflect the bias of what gets discussed in the law courts. The relatively petty scale of a typical *eranos*-contribution may perhaps be inferred from Aeschines' disparaging contrast between those who are awarded crowns by assembly and council, and those who merely *eranizōn* crowns from demes and tribes (III.45).

39 A similar procedure may lie behind certain entries in the inscriptions listing the 'Freedmen's Bowls' (see n. 34, above). The dedication of these bowls was connected in a way not now fully understood with the process whereby slaves in Athens gained their freedom. On those occasions where the entry mentions an *eranos* it seems likely that the organizer of the loan was the owner himself; in a minority of cases, a third party appears to have been involved, as in the Neaera affair. For detailed discussion of the problems arising out of these inscriptions, see Finley (1952: 104–5), Lewis (1959 and 1968), and Kränzlein (1975).

40 In later literature, the person taking responsibility for overseeing the *eranos* is referred to as *eranarchēs* or '*eranos*-leader' (see Harpocration, s.v. '*plērotēs*'). It was to such an *eranarchēs* that Diogenes the Cynic is said to have refused a contribution (Diog. Laert. VI.63), quoting by way of rebuff a line of Homer not known in our texts: 'Exact your due (*eranizein*) from the rest, but from Hector keep your hands.'

VIII. NON-PROFESSIONAL LENDING: LOANS BEARING INTEREST

1 DK 87 fr. 54. In the version by Aesop (Chambray 1927: 344) no request is made to borrow the money. On the difficulty of identifying Antiphon the Sophist (thought to have been a contemporary of Socrates), see Guthrie 1962–81: III, 285–6 and 292–4, with Pendrick 1987 for the latest bibliography. The translation of Antiphon here and elsewhere in the text is adapted from the version by Freeman (1947).

2 In two of the cases listed in the text ([Dem.] LII.13; Dem. XXXVII.11), the borrowers describe their introduction to potential lenders by using a part of the verb *proxeneō*. Michell (1957: 231) argues that so far as the *proxenos* was concerned: 'One definite duty that he performed was that he could introduce traders to the local bankers and payments made or received by them were made in his presence.' Michell supplies no references, but is presumably building on an episode in the pseudo-Demosthenic *Against Callipus* (LII.5–11), in which a *proxenos* expresses a corrupt interest in a bank deposit made by a dead Heraclean trader (see p. 210). In fact, the only case in which *proxenos* has anything like the

sense suggested by Michell is in a letter of Alciphron (II.5 in Benner and Fobes 1949); but even here it seems unlikely that the word is meant in any technical sense. On the institution of *proxenia*, see Herman 1987: 130–42.

3 The status of these persons is not clear. Murray (1936–9: I, 418) describes Nausicrates as a 'rich banker and merchant'. Mention of the hundred-stater debt as being contracted in the Bosporus supports his identification as a trader, but there is nothing to suggest that he also acted as a banker.

4 For an alternative listing of income-earning assets, see Xenophon, *Memorabilia* III.11.4, with Finley 1952: 245, n. 1. The importance of income from renting property is brought out by Osborne 1988. Aeschines' neutral *daneisma* may be contrasted with Aristotle's slanted inclusion of lending at interest in his discussion of ways of getting a living (*Politics* 1258a39–58b27). The legitimate acquisition of wealth through domestic production (*oikonomikos*) is matched against the 'discredited' branch involving exchange (*metablētikos*). This is further subdivided into trading (*emporia*), money-lending (*tokismos*) and wage-earning (*mistharnia*). *Tokismos* has overtones of exploitative lending at interest not present in *daneisma* (see Chapter VIII).

5 See p. 72 (other references to investment on pp. 59, 60, 63, 64, 64 n. 50, 66 and 72). Compare the greater confusion in the discussions by Glotz (1920: 238–44) and French (1964: via the index, s.v. 'investment'). In the Loeb edition of Hyperides' *Against Athenogenes*, Burtt (1954) describes what seem to be *eranos*-loans to a perfumer as 'sums which customers have invested in the perfumery' (§6). Thompson (1982: 80) tentatively identifies these sums of money with mechanisms found in Renaissance Florence and pre-revolutionary France whereby people contributed capital to merchants in return for a fixed income. But a glance at the evidence cited (de Roover 1948: 40–1; Taylor 1964: 485) suggests a scale and complexity of operations of an altogether different order from that of Athenogenes' stall on the market.

6 See, for example, de Roover 1944, 1954, 1957 and 1965; Spufford 1986: xxx–xxxvi. Thompson's implied equation of the classical Athenian economy with that of fifteenth-century Italy is reminiscent of Meyer's notorious identification of the seventh, sixth and fifth centuries B.C. with the fourteenth, fifteenth and sixteenth in the modern world (Meyer 1895: 118–19; cited by Austin and Vidal-Naquet 1977: 4–5).

7 [Dem.] XL.52; Dem. XXXVII; Lysias fr. 38; [Dem.] XLIX.35: see Chapter III, n. 11. Thompson adds a section on 'gearing' (417–19) – the practice of borrowing money at low interest to invest at a higher rate of return. But, in the absence of a system of productive credit, the mechanism has little meaning. Much of the remainder of Thompson's paper is concerned with maritime trade, which is discussed in the following chapter.

8 Although published as different inscriptions (and so interpreted by

Osborne 1985a: 247, n. 43), two *horoi* naming Hieron of Rhamnous as joint creditor are in reality the same stone (*SEG* xxi 656 ~ Millett 1982: no. 95A; *SEG* xxx 122 ~ *Arch.Eph.* 1979: 42).

9 For a brief (and not always accurate) summary of the contents of these estates, see Jones 1957: 151, n. 161. The full references are:

  Aeschines, *Against Timarchus* (1.97-101)
  Isaeus, *On the Estate of Dicaeogenes* (v.22) *APF* 3773
  Isaeus, *On the Estate of Philoctemon* (vi.33) *APF* 15164
  Isaeus, *On the Estate of Ciron* (viii.35) *APF* 8443
  Isaeus, *On the Estate of Hagnias*, *APF* 2921   – Theophon (xi.41)
                                                       – Stratocles (xi.42-3)
                                                       – Theopompus (xi.44)

In two of these estates, not detailed in the text (Isaeus v.22 and vi.33), money was actually owed by the deceased. It hardly needs to be added that all these estates belonged to wealthier members of Athenian society. The sizes of the estates mentioned by Isaeus are summarized by Wevers (1969: 96-7).

10 This means disregarding Demosthenes' own division of his father's property into the categories of 'active' (*energa*) and 'inactive' (*arga*). The distinction is not without apparent contradictions (money lent in maritime loans is classed as 'inactive'). For successive attempts to disentangle what Finley (1985b: 116) rightly calls 'a remarkable conception of "capital"', see Schwahn 1929: 6-7, Oertel 1930: 243-6, and Korver 1942 (and compare *aphanēs/phanera* in the note below).

11 On the date, authenticity and detailed interpretation of the speech *Against Diogiton* see the commentary by Carey (1989). Davies infers that the unspecified *phanera ousia* of Diodotus' estate cannot have been substantial. The terms *phanera* and *aphanēs ousia* echo *energa* and *arga* (see the note above) as indicating the non-economic categories into which the Athenians habitually classified their property (Gernet 1956). See the valuable study by Gabrielsen (1986), who concludes that the terms represent flexible attitudes towards property on the part of owners.

  A further item in Diodotus' estate calls for comment. The interest of the loan of 2,000 dr. in the Chersonese (§6) was apparently paid annually in grain (§15; see Chapter II, n. 33). There is, however, no reason to follow Mossé's explanation that the payments were rent owing to Diodotus in his capacity as absentee landlord of a cleruchy (1962: 61). Given the difficulties in recovering debts from abroad, Athenian citizens would lend outside the *polis* only under exceptional circumstances.

  (i) If the parties were *xenoi* in a formal sense, bound by ritual ties of reciprocity (Herman 1987: 92-4). (ii) If the lender was a merchant or otherwise involved in trade, giving extensive overseas contacts ([Dem.] xxxiv.23). That is presumably the explanation behind the loans made by Diodotus, Nausicrates (above, n. 3) and Pasion (Dem. xlv.28).

Included in Pasion's will was 'a talent from Peparethus' (the creditor here was not Phormion as reported by Davies, 1981: 63). (iii) If Athens as a *polis* wielded power overseas that could be mobilized by individual citizens to override local obstacles in the way of recovering monies owed, or foreclosing on securities. That this had been the practice during the fifth-century empire may be inferred from the decree of Aristoteles (378/7), recording the terms of the so-called 'Second Athenian Confederacy' (*IG* II^2 43 $\sim$ *GHI* II 123; most recent text and translation in Cargill 1981: 14–47). A clause of the decree specifically prohibits the Athenians from acquiring house or land in allied territory by either purchase or foreclosure. The implications of this clause are examined in detail by Gauthier (1973: 174–6). Some thirteen years after the end of the Peloponnesian War, the Athenians were still hoping to reclaim monies lent in subject states. In his speech *On the Peace with Sparta* (III.15) of 391, Andocides listed among Athenian war aims, 'the recovery of the Chersonese, our colonies, our property overseas, and our debts (*chrea*)'.

12 In his later paper (1982: 75; see my Appendix III), Thompson returns to the theme that a random spread of assets should not be read as evidence for the absence of 'entrepreneurial spirit' (against Humphreys 1970: 153). Thompson's technique is to reject the usual picture of the 'textbook capitalist of 1880 or 1980 solely intent on "maximizing profits"', and to examine instead 'the typology of the entrepreneur'. A study by Redlich (1971: 17) is cited to the effect that the first entrepreneurs 'were after business whenever and in whatever form it presented itself. Exponents of this type could run a mercantile house, a bank, and a textile mill simultaneously or successively with equal skill. The business aspect of enterprises of all kinds was still essentially the same, so that they could be handled by any capable businessman.' Thompson equates all this with Demosthenes' father, 'with his two factories, his safe loans at 12 per cent and his risky naval loans'. The same technique is used elsewhere in the paper, arguing that the modern economy is not really as modern as people think (p. 82): 'The "minimalists" are correct in arguing that the Athenian businessman operated on a small scale, but this in itself is no reflection on his spirit of enterprise. And in some areas even the size of Athenian business will bear comparison with that of a later age.' There follows a comparison between 'the large workshops at Athens, such as the hundred or so slaves that Lysias had working for him, and the thirty-odd cutlers and twenty couchmakers who belonged to Demosthenes' father', and numbers of employees in English mills, according to a government survey of 1833 (modal figure: 25–49 employees).

This kind of argument can be criticized on two different levels. Apart from detailed criticisms (we know nothing about the safety or otherwise of Demosthenes Senior's loans at 12 per cent; the 'risky' maritime loans were apparently managed by a middleman – see above, p. 192;

outside the silver mines, the slave holdings of Lysias and Demosthenes' father are the largest known from the classical Greek world), there is the problem of what Thompson hopes to prove. However welcome this revisionism might be, its redefinition of entrepreneurship and the factory system threatens the modernist conception of economic development, and not the reality of the ancient economy (compare the attempts to redefine productive credit, Appendix III). No amount of redefinition can alter the fact that Demosthenes' father acquired one of his batches of slave craftsmen as security on a defaulted loan – surely the antithesis of planned investment. To call that a manifestation of the 'entrepreneurial spirit' is to rob the term of all precision as an analytical concept.

13 As metics, Lysias and his brother were, of course, legally debarred from ownership of real property, which may account for their untypically large holdings of movable property and slaves (see n. 12, above). Gabrielsen (1986: 109) suggests that the tendency, for whatever reason, for citizens to conceal their wealth, may have resulted in the under-representation of liquid funds as components of estates.

14 On the original and subsequent meanings of *rentier*, see the entry in Palgrave. The application of the *rentier*-ideal to the citizens of the Greek *poleis* is traced by Gauthier (1976: 245–52) from its origins with Weber, via Hasebroek and Bolkestein, to Finley and Humphreys. Although Gauthier rightly modifies the extent to which Xenophon's *Poroi* can be used in support of the *rentier*-mentality, he quotes with approval Humphreys' formulation that (1970: 153), 'the majority of Athenians were quite ready to give up the effort to make money as soon as they could afford a comfortable *rentier* existence'. The concept of the *rentier*-mentality is attacked by Thompson (1982: 67–74), who concentrates his efforts on showing that the owners of slaves were directly involved in their management, and not content to draw a fixed income. He sees as the substantive issue whether the owners 'sub-contracted' the organization of the workshop to a third party (typically, a freedman *epitropos* or overseer) in such a way as to insulate himself from fluctuating profit and loss. A good case is made out (against Francotte 1900: I, 12) for the slaves belonging to Demosthenes' father as being operated on the owner's own account. On the other hand, Thompson says nothing about the case of the father of Timarchus (Aeschines 1.97), who owned nine or ten slave-shoemakers, each paying a fixed *apophora* of two obols per day, and the *hēgemōn* (foreman) of the *ergastērion* paying three obols. Or, again, there is the well-known case of Nicias, who sub-contracted his thousand mine-slaves to Sosias the Thracian, 'on condition that Sosias paid him an obol per day per man clear profit, and this number he always supplied undiminished' (Xen. *Por.* IV.14). Xenophon goes on to name other Athenians who had smaller numbers of slaves let out under similar terms. Given the incompleteness of our evidence, it is impossible to reach a verdict about the preferred method

of managing slaves by counting up examples. Nor does Thompson's analogy of John D. Rockefeller and Henry Ford having foremen but running the business themselves advance the argument in any way. They are, after all, classic representatives of the 'textbook capitalists' rejected by Thompson elsewhere in his analysis (above, n. 12). A single passage cannot be decisive, but Aristotle in his *Politics* is clear about the desirability of having a slave or freedman to manage other slaves (1255b31–6). 'This knowledge (of employing slaves) is of no particular importance or dignity: the master must know how to direct the tasks which the slave must know how to execute. Therefore all people rich enough to be able to avoid personal trouble have an overseer (*epitropos*) who takes office, while they themselves engage in politics or philosophy.' On the rôle of the *epitropos* in agriculture, see Audring 1973; on the wealthy Athenian's conception of a leisured existence, see Stocks 1936: 180–2.

15 The law is generally allowed to be authentic and, even if not genuinely Solonic, to contain archaic elements; for text and translation, see Ferguson 1944: 62–6, Finley 1952: 88–9, and Whitehead 1986: 13–14. All the associations mentioned here and immediately below in the text have brief descriptive entries in the *OCD*², s.v. '*dēmoi*', '*genos*', '*thiasos*', '*phratriai*', '*orgeōnes*' and '*phylai*'.

16 The local temples of modern India have credit provisions that parallel lending by demes in terms of discontinuity and emphasis on security and interest charges. According to the brief account by Harper (1961: 171): 'It is not uncommon for a village temple to have a fund of several thousand rupees. Extreme care is taken to ensure that only better-than-average credit risks borrow this money as it is feared a loss would incur the wrath of [the goddess] Mariamma. When loans are made from this fund a promissory note is always required and an interest charge of 12·5 per cent per annum is charged.'

Patterns of deme lending may help to explain the absence from classical Athens of the endowment funds or foundations that are such a feature of civic life in the Hellenistic and Roman worlds (see my Appendix V).

17 The *dekadistai* were a cultic group, meeting to perform sacrifices on the tenth day of each month. For the sake of completeness should be added the appearance of *orgeōnes* on three *horoi* from Lemnos (Finley 1952: nos. 107–9), and a damaged *horos* from the Athenian *agora* (Millett 1982: no. 85D) recording some unidentifiable group as creditor. An inscription identified by Fine as a *horos* mentioning a phratry (1951: no. 11 ~ Finley 1952: no. 101C) has been reread by Hedrick (1988) as a boundary marker.

18 Owing to the ambiguity of the key-word *sumballein*, editors have generally interpreted these inscriptions as prohibiting the dumping of rubbish; for the interpretation offered in the text, see Finley 1952: 286, n. 47.

19 Although the speech is probably not by Lysias it is usually accepted as
an authentic document as opposed to a rhetorical exercise. The
unintelligibility of the piece is a powerful argument in favour of
authenticity. Bibliography is cited by Finley (1952: 288, n. 56), to
which add Dover (1968b, via the index). The otherwise helpful
reconstruction of the speech by Gernet (Gernet and Bizos 1955–9:
121–3) is compromised by his assumption that the co-associates had
some semi-formal rôle in the contracting of the loan.

VIII. PROFESSIONAL MONEY-LENDING

1 On reading the *Characters* as history, see Chapter I, n. 7. The meaning
of *aponoia* (moral degradation?) is discussed in detail in the standard
commentaries by Edmonds and Austen 1904, Jebb 1909, Ussher 1960
and Steinmetz 1960–2.
2 The point has not been adequately appreciated in the standard
textbooks of Athenian economic life: Böckh 1817: 127–8, Glotz 1920:
240–1, Ehrenberg 1951: 220 and 232–3, Michell 1957: 336–7 and
Hopper 1979: 118–25.
3 On the false identification of lenders as bankers, see Bogaert 1986a: 86,
n. 156, and 452; to which add Vanderpool 1966: 279 (on *horos* no. 163A
in Millett 1982).
4 The shifting attitude towards usury is analysed in detail by Nelson 1968.
It needs to be noted that some modern writers continue to apply 'usury'
to all loans at interest; see, for example, Heichelheim, *OCD*[2] s.v.
'usury'.
5 On the place of Marshall's book in the evolution of economic theory, see
Chapter I, n. 15. Zimmern (ch. I, n. 24) was an admirer of Marshall
and, in his far-sighted if erratic essay 'Suggestions towards a political
economy of the Greek city-state' (1928a), argued that the only fruitful
way of approaching the economic history of Greece was with Marshall
in one hand and a text of Thucydides in the other. But that is going a
bit far.
6 The hand-to-mouth existence of costermongers is confirmed by remarks
in Booth's famous study of life and labour in late-Victorian London
(1902–3: final volume, p. 83).
7 The only evidence in support of the interest-rate interpretation are
entries in the lexica and a garbled reference by the Scholiast to
Aeschines. Hesychius and the *Souda* gloss *obolos* as 'interest' (*tokos*); the
Etymologicum Magnum and Bekker's *Anecdota Graeca* (286.31) explain
obolostasēsai as 'to exact interest' (*labein tokous*). More precise is the note
to a passage from Aeschines (1.39: Dindorf 1852: *ad loc.*), where a
mention in the text of the Thirty Tyrants moves the scholiast to list
other 'thirties', amongst them being 'thirty *obolostatai* chosen from the
wealthy; this meant to lend money at the rate of one obol on the mina'.
As calculated by Korver (1934: 115–16), an obol on the mina, taken as

a monthly rate, works out at only 2 per cent per annum – easily the lowest rate of interest known from the classical period!

8 Korver (1934: 117) interprets this passage as implying that Aristotle disapproved of only petty usury, and cites in support the attack in the *Nicomachean Ethics* (1121b34) on those who lend small sums at high interest. But it seems clear from the context that Aristotle disapproves of all lending where interest is involved, no matter what the rate. The word *obolostatikē* has presumably been chosen as a strong hint that all such transactions deserve the distaste usually reserved for usury.

9 Alciphron's letter (II.5 in Benner and Fobes 1949), describing the imaginary visit of a farmer to a city usurer (*tokogluphos*) who demands real security, has no independent status as historical evidence (but see Chapter II, n. 36). We can only agree with the farmer when he writes at the beginning of his letter: 'I don't know what came over me; I ought to have gone to you or some other of my country neighbours since I had run short of money.' It is unfortunate that Michell (1957: 337), who quotes this letter *verbatim* as part of his brief discussion of professional money-lending, should neglect to mention its character as an artificial literary composition, of late date.

10 The *obolostatai* never actually appear in the play. In the introduction to his commentary (1968a: xxix–xxxiii), Dover argued persuasively that neither of the creditors who do put in an appearance were professional money-lenders. There is no need for the second thoughts he has subsequently had about the First Creditor (Dover 1974: 21, n. 5). The First Creditor is a fellow-demesman of Strepsiades (ll. 1214–58) and reluctant to press for payment. The Second Creditor (ll. 1259–1302) is presumably an associate of Strepsiades' son, sharing his passion for chariot-racing; it is to Phidippides that he has lent the money (ll. 1267–9). Although the loan is not interest-free, that may be in order to introduce an elaborate joke about interest (ll. 1289–97). Neither of the creditors are professional money-lenders: it would not suit Aristophanes' dramatic purpose if they were. Had Strepsiades rebuffed a pair of *obolostatai*, the audience would have applauded his action rather than seen him as the cheat and rogue which the rest of the play shows him to be. The creditors may be ridiculous, but they are not villains.

11 High interest rates are also mentioned in a metaphorical passage from the *First Olynthiac* of Demosthenes (1.15). The orator criticizes the Athenian people for their failure to take active measures against Philip:

> I am afraid, men of Athens, that just as men who borrow money recklessly at high interest (*megalois tokois*) enjoy a temporary accommodation only to forfeit their estates (*archaiōn*), so we may find that we have paid a heavy price for our indolence...and we may finally endanger our possessions here in Attica itself. (Trans. by Vince 1926–35: 1)

Does *ta archaia* mean 'estates'? In the context of lending and borrowing, the obvious (but not inevitable) meaning should be 'principal' as opposed to 'interest' (see Korver 1934: 101–3). Beauchet accordingly suggests that in this passage *hoi daneizomenoi* signifies not 'borrowers' but 'lenders'. He supports his interpretation with a gloss in Bekker's *Anecdota Graeca* (239.2), giving as alternative equivalents of *daneizomenoi*, *hoi hupochreoi* (debtors) and *hoi daneistai* (lenders). *Ta archaia* can then keep its natural meaning, and the creditors are presented as raking in a handsome profit from high interest rates, but losing everything when the debtors default on repayment of the principal. This otherwise attractive idea unfortunately makes nonsense of Demosthenes' image, for the Athenian people surely need to be seen as foolish, improvident borrowers and not greedy money-lenders. Paul Cartledge suggests that the emphasis in the passage may be on *archaia* in the sense of *ancestral* estates (paralleled with the loss of parts of Attica itself to Philip; cf. Dem. xix.99).

For the sake of completeness, I include under this heading of usurious interest rates a passage from Plautus' *Epidicus*. The play is presumably based on a Greek original from the first half of the third century; the dramatic date may be inferred from references to an Athenian expedition against Thebes, *c.* 290. While absent on military duty in Thebes, a young Athenian purchased a slave girl, and his slave gives details of the transaction (1.i.ll. 52–5). It turns out that the girl cost forty minas and the money was borrowed at interest from a money-lender (*danista*) at Thebes (l. 54), *in dies minasque argenti singulas nummis*. Use of *danista* suggests that the Greek play contained the word *daneistēs*, and that Plautus has not invented this part of the plot (for the reverse of this argument, see Bogaert 1968: 394, n. 530). Much ingenuity has been devoted to determining the scale of the interest payments. Estimates vary from 1 per cent and 2 per cent to 10 per cent per day, depending on the Greek coin chosen to stand in place of Plautus' *nummus* (Billeter 1898: 71). The point is not of pressing interest. Daily payment (or reckoning) of interest marks this down as a usurious transaction – the conclusion reached by Billeter.

12 Reading with Jebb (and against Diels) *elthōn* (§2), *chrēsai* (§13). The 'Penurious Man' also (§9) 'inspects his *horoi* every day to see if they remain the same'. In view of his association with the seamier side of lending, there is a temptation to interpret this as a reference to hypothecation-*horoi* (see Edmonds and Austen 1904: *ad loc.*; Giglioni 1980: 87–8). The temptation should be resisted, as the allusion is to the familiar motif of removing a neighbour's landmark (Plato, *Laws* 843c, with Finley 1952: 213, n. 49).

13 Even after the growth of pawnbroking in the later eighteenth and earlier nineteenth centuries, there remained (and still remain) groups of lenders providing loans at exorbitant rates for the near destitute. 'Dolly shops' were unlicensed pawnshops, catering for those with goods to offer too low in value to interest legitimate pawnbrokers (Johnson 1985: 186). As the rate of interest was at least twice the legal maximum for a

licensed pawnbroker, neither records were kept nor tickets given. De Vesselitsky and Bulkley (1916–17: 129), assessing attitudes towards borrowing among the London poor, describe how 'the atmosphere of secrecy and gloom which envelops the subject of loans, and the people's disinclination to give any information concerning them, is in striking contrast to the readiness – one might almost say pride – with which pawntickets are displayed'. Their observation is borne out by the personal reminiscences of Robert Roberts about borrowing by the poor in Salford before the First World War (1974: 13). 'Only those in dire straits, with the certainty of cash cover to come, patronised the local blood sucker... To be known to be in his clutches was to lose caste altogether. Women would pawn to the limit, leaving the house utterly comfortless, rather than fall to that level.' And no wonder, if the street money-lender charged one penny in the shilling per day (Johnson 1985: 191) – an annual rate of more than 3,000 per cent, and over twice the going rate for a dolly shop. That was the fate of those who, like Mayhew's orphaned flower-girl, had nothing to pledge and therefore had no choice but to apply to a usurer (Tebbutt 1983: 13).

14 Although this is not the place to go into detail, the terminology of the alternative credit organizations created by the working class for their own benefit hints at a different conception of lending and borrowing, with 'friendly societies', 'co-operative societies', and 'mutuality clubs' (Johnson 1985: 126–43). In earlier days, these societies combined 'feasting and festivities' with their proper business of taking in and giving out money.

15 The Phormion attacked in the speech is no relation to the banker of the same name. Introductions to and commentaries on the speech by Paley and Sandys 1910: 1, 1–48 and Gernet 1956–60: 1, 151–68. For both lenders taking a share in delivering the speech, see Lofberg 1932. Several legal and economic aspects of the speech are discussed by Bogaert 1971; on the attempt by Thompson (1980) to reconstruct the background to the speech, see Chapter 1, n. 3.

16 Although Heichelheim (1938) recognizes the existence of this third group of lenders, he oversimplifies the problem by seeing money-lenders as classified (II, 82) 'in accordance with the size of their business, either as *daneistai*, if they had capital above a certain amount at their disposal, or as *obolostatai*, if they conducted small-scale business obscurely in corners'. In fact, *daneistēs* hardly ever appears in surviving classical sources; see Korver 1934: 111–13 (to which add Plut. *Phocion* IX.1).

17 What follows in the text is a selective restatement of parts of my earlier treatment of maritime credit (1983), which is in turn dependent on the fundamental study by de Ste Croix (1974).

18 Cohen (1973: 93–5) argues that in *dikai emporikai* the jurors were specially chosen from among those commercially active in the Piraeus. In support of his hypothesis he appeals to modern American practice in maritime law; but all the ancient evidence he marshals can be

explained in terms of rhetorical posing by the litigants, intended to flatter the jury.

19 For what it is worth (and it is not very much), Garland (1987: 85) builds on an estimate by Isager and Hansen (1975: 62) to arrive at a very approximate figure of twelve ships per day unloading at the Piraeus during the sailing season. If only a tenth of these voyages were funded by maritime loans from Athens, it would add up to a substantial volume of maritime credit – hundreds of thousands of drachmas. But Garnsey's reassessment of Attica's potential for grain production throws all these estimates back into the melting pot (Garnsey 1985; 1988: 89–106).

20 On the question of the motive behind borrowing in maritime loans, Thompson (1982) concludes that when traders topped up loans towards the purchases of cargoes with an equivalent contribution from their own funds, they were (p. 65) 'not borrowing out of poverty, but to achieve that advantage which we call "economies of scale"'. He continues: 'By doubling his cargo with borrowed money he stood a chance to be compensated twice for his time and physical danger.' For maritime loans as evidence of underfunding, with traders being forced to borrow in order to augment their own, inadequate resources, see Millett 1983: 42–7.

21 On the problems involved in identifying traders, and lenders and borrowers in maritime loans as citizens or non-citizens, see Millett (1983: 37–8), citing the contradictory head-counts of Hansen and Erxleben. Not all writers on maritime trade seem to appreciate the way in which these two sets of figures undermine each other. Each set is referred to in different articles by Thompson (1982: 66; 1978: 417, where the identification of Erxleben's figure of '41' as a misprint for '14' is wishful thinking). Strauss (1986), in a rather muddled section on 'Commerce, culture, real-estate and finance' (all in less than three pages, 48–51), cites in a single footnote (p. 65, n. 33) pages from Isager and Hansen, and Erxleben containing opposite conclusions about the personnel involved in financing trade. Erxleben's identifications of citizens and non-citizens are subjected to a searching criticism by Hansen (1984; and rightly so; cf. Bogaert 1986a: 47–9). But her own careful attempts to arrive at maximum and minimum figures only underline the precariousness of basing any conclusion on these statistics. The study by Montgomery (1986) adds nothing to the discussion.

22 Other, dubious examples of professional lenders of maritime loans include Zeno of Citium (above, p. 190) and Demon, speaker in Demosthenes' *Against Zenothemis* (XXXII). It is difficult to know what to make of the allegation in Hyperides' *Against Demosthenes* (fr. IV, col. 17) that Demosthenes himself had lent out in maritime loans the state funds he was supposed to have embezzled. As an accusation it would be difficult to confirm or refute, which is perhaps why it was made. Theophrastus' 'Boastful Man' (above, p. 190) is to be understood as

exaggerating or inventing entirely the large amounts of money he has tied up in maritime credit. But it may be significant that Theophrastus places him in the Piraeus, standing on the Diazeugma or Pier, where he tells his stretchers to the *xenoi* gathered round him (Garland 1987: 154). There may be one or two references to professional maritime credit in Xenophon's *Poroi*. In the first passage (IV.6), Xenophon explains how, when crops are abundant and food is cheap, farmers turn to trading, retailing and lending at interest (*ep' emporias kai kapēleias kai tokismous*). Certainty is impossible, but the context suggests that lending in maritime loans may be intended. Similarly, when the benefits of peace as encouraging trade and immigration are under discussion (V.3), Xenophon mentions in the same breath as 'shipowners and merchants', 'those who are able to make themselves rich by their wits and their money (*gnomēi kai argurioi*)'. Again, the context and description fit those who make a living through maritime credit. For alternative interpretations of these passages, see Gauthier 1976: *ad loc.*

23 The status of the debt as a non-maritime loan is asserted and reasserted by Harrison (1968–71: I, 272–4) and de Ste Croix (1974: 52).

24 The complexity of the speech adds to the difficulty of reconstructing the details of the transactions that lie behind it. The interpretation offered in the text broadly follows the version by Finley (1952: 32–5), and is in general agreement with the lucid commentary on the speech by Carey and Reid (1985). Note, however, the reservations of Harris (1988a: 370–7) in his careful reassessment of the relationships between the different sets of creditors (see my Appendix I). Some juristic questions raised by the speech are discussed at length by Cataldi (1982).

25 In view of continuing confusion (Miles 1951: 52; Germain 1973: 432), it needs to be stressed that the dispute centres on the purchase price of the *ergastērion* and slaves, and not Pantaenetus' lease of a mining concession from the state, costing him ninety minas (§22). The distinction between *ergastērion* and *metallon* was drawn almost a century ago by Ardaillon (1897: 102 and 109; see Finley 1952: 259, n. 110; Fine 1951: 146, n. 8).

Fine (1951: 147) sees an unnecessary difficulty in the discrepancy between the 105 minas borrowed to buy the property from Telemachus (§31) and its eventual sale for approximately twice that amount (§50). On the grounds that Telemachus would have driven a harder bargain had he been the true vendor, Fine prefers to see Pantaenetus as the original owner, having acquired the property in some way not stated in the text. In the process of working the mill he needed ready cash, which he borrowed from Telemachus, with *ergastērion* and slaves acting as security. But it is nowhere stated that 105 minas was the full purchase price of the property when it passed into Pantaenetus' hands. A part of the price was possibly paid out of his own resources (after the fashion of a maritime loan; see Harrison 1968–71: I, 274–9, esp. 275).

26 Difficulty in discriminating between loans and other transfers of cash

makes a precise figure impossible. Disregarding Timotheus' loan of 420 minas from his trierarchs ([Dem.] XLIX.11; see Gernet 1954–60: III, *ad loc.*), the largest figure in the Demosthenic corpus is for one talent, shared between two creditors ([XLII]. 28).

27 Describing his involvement in maritime trade (§54), Nicobulus uses a part of the verb *ergazomai*, which may be applied either to voyaging (*kata thalattan*), or to lending money in maritime loans (*nautikois*). The speaker in the Apaturius case ([Dem.] XXXIII.4) uses the word in both senses within a few lines. It is possible that Nicobulus travelled to Pontus in his capacity as a lender, choosing to travel with the ship as supercargo. For possible inferences and speculation about Nicobulus' status, see Erxleben 1974: 474–5 (with Hansen 1984: 90, n. 16).

28 For the record, the 'commercial loans' identified by Thompson are (i) Lysias fr. 38 (see in the text, pp. 1–3 and 212–13); (ii) [Dem.] XL.52 (see p. 215, below); (iii) [Dem.] XLIX.25–30 and 36; (iv) Isoc. XVII.7–12 and 38.
The claims of (iii) and (iv) to be read as productive loans are convincingly refuted by Bogaert (1986a: 24–5), who also dismisses attempts by Thompson and Erxleben to show bankers making maritime loans (pp. 27–9). It is unfortunate that Salmon, in his discussion of the mechanisms of Corinthian trade (1984: 149), identifies bankers as 'the pivot of the system' of maritime credit in Athens.

29 Bogaert (1968: 336, n. 180) offers as evidence for bank charges on deposits a passage in [Dem.] LII.26, where Apollodorus, 's'insurge contre l'idée que son père aurait touché une commission pour l'exécution du mandat qu'il avait reçu de Lycon'. But Apollodorus is here defending his father against the possible charge of having appropriated a part of Lycon's deposit for his own use (cf. Isoc. XXI.17). For the payment of interest by depositors in Mesopotamia, see Bogaert 1966: 84, n. 235, and 98.

30 Editors have had difficulty with this passage, seeing it as impossible that eleven talents could be deposits belonging to the bank's clients, and still be counted in with Pasion's property. Many modern editors and commentators therefore follow Blass in omitting *idion* ('of his own'); see Paley and Sandys 1910: II, *ad loc.*, with Davies (in *APF* 11672 VIIID), and Pearson 1972: *ad loc.* It is, however, entirely typical of non-capitalist enterprises to draw no clear distinction between personal and business funds (see Weber 1904–5: 21–2); as Thompson rightly says: 'The word (*idion*) makes excellent sense rhetorically' (1981: 92, n. 18). Other interpretations of the passage are summarized and assessed by Bogaert (1986a: 35–42).

31 For a possible case, see the fragment of Isaeus' speech *For Eumathes* (fr. 18 in Forster 1927 ~ Dion. Hal. *On Isaeus* §5). The speaker, a citizen called Xenocles, defends the status of Eumathes as a freedman against an attempt to re-enslave him. He explains how, having deposited some cash with Eumathes, he went off to serve as a trierach and was reported

killed in a sea battle. Eumathes thereupon behaved with exemplary honesty, calling together the relatives and friends of Xenocles in order to hand the money over to them. When Xenocles returned safe and sound, so impressed was he with this conduct that: 'I became even more intimate (*echrōmēn*) with him and, when he set up his bank, I supplied him with money (*proseiseuporēsa arguriou*).' It is not clear why Xenocles should have deposited money with Eumathes *before* he became a banker. There are other possible examples of bankers associating with persons who may have been non-active partners, supplying them with funds: Aristolochus and Antidorus (*APF* 1024 and 1946), Sosinomus and Aristogiton (see n. 39).

32 The distinction I have drawn between deposits (for safe keeping) and loans (to be used at the borrower's discretion) should not be pressed too far. In the passage describing Pasion's wealth quoted in the text, the eleven talents lent out are said to be 'from the deposits (*apo ton parakatathēkōn*) of the bank'. And in the Demosthenic speech *Against Lacritus* (XXXV.38), the speaker is filled with righteous indignation because the men to whom he and his associate made a maritime loan had 'made use of our money as if it had been their very own (*idiois*)'. In the case of Pasion, it may be that the speaker did not want to give the jury the impression that the banker was in financial straits by talking in terms of borrowed funds rather than deposits. Concerning the maritime loan, it was a condition of the agreement (stipulated by written contract) that the cash be used for the specific purpose of purchasing a cargo, and not be relent.

33 So say Hasebroek (1928: 114) and Calhoun (1926: 102). There are exceptions. According to Bolkestein (1923: 127–8), 'lending against interest was of such a modest nature that it excluded banking of any importance'. On the strength of the trading and manufacturing interests of Pasion and Phormion (on which see Hasebroek 1920: 164–5; Mickwitz 1939: 9–10; *APF* 11672), it is argued by Laum (1922: col. 429) that *trapezitai* were three-quarters traders and only one-quarter bankers. Bogaert (1968: 358, n. 313) objects that Pasion and Phormion must have made their money in banking before investing it in other fields. But, in line with views expressed elsewhere (p. 169, above), I interpret this move across into non-banking activities as a response to the limited opportunities for deployment of funds in private banks. The banker Blepaeus, it may be noted, is also found acting as a *misthōtēs* or contractor (*PA* 2876).

34 The relationship between Pasion and the son of Sopaeus is discussed by Bogaert (1968: 64–7) and, at greater length, in the commentary by Bongenaar (1933). Legal aspects of the speech are examined by Bogaert (1962) and Thür (1975).

35 In a close parallel to the Euthynus case, Aeschines (II.166) accuses Demosthenes of having embezzled a deposit of three talents entrusted to him by his friend Aristarchus, who was going into exile on a charge of

murder. Themistocles in exile is reported by Thucydides (II.137.3) to have received funds which he had deposited with *philoi* in Athens.

36 Or is Cephisiades resident in Sciros in Attica? (The interpretation favoured by most editors – see Gernet: 1954–60: III, *ad loc.*, with Diller 1937: 161, n. 2).

37 According to Garland (1987: 68): 'Another Piraeus banker was Charion, whose gravestone depicts the deceased holding what is possibly an oblong or cylindrical book-roll.' But in the photographs and description by Clairmont (1970: 58 with plates 26–7) I can find no hint (beyond the book-roll) that Charion is to be identified as a banker.

38 A non-trading visitor to Athens making use of a bank deposit was Crates, the philosopher from Thebes. Diogenes Laertius (VI.88) preserves an anecdote that, while staying in Athens, he deposited a sum of money with a banker to be placed in trust for his sons. If they chose not to follow their father in the philosophic life, the money was to be theirs. If they embraced philosophy, they would have no need of money, which the banker was to give to the people (see Bogaert 1968: 84).

39 The banker Sosinomus is found elsewhere (Dem. XXXVI.50). Why he should here appear in association with Aristogiton is not clear from the context. Bogaert sees Aeschines as being forced to tap two sources in order to scrape together the funds he needed (1968: 370, n. 390). My own preference (see n. 31) is to see in Aristogiton some kind of partner to the banker. The relationship may possibly go deeper, with Aristogiton acting as a citizen-agent on the banker's behalf. The hypothesis (it can be no more than that) is developed in detail in Appendix II.

40 There is, as it happens, independent testimony for Aeschines as a spendthrift in a story told by Diogenes Laertius (II.62): 'It is said that when he was suffering hardship through poverty, Socrates jokingly advised him to make a loan to himself (*par' heautou daneizesthai*) by cutting down on the size of his meals' (cf. Simonides *P.Hib.*17). This is further evidence against those who read the Lysias fragment as evidence for 'productive investment' in 'factories' (Thompson 1978: 412; Davies 1981: 42). The likely scale of a perfumer's business is indicated by the background detail in Hyperides' speech *Against Athenogenes*: stocks of raw materials, a stall on the market, and a couple of slaves.

41 For the political and military background to Timotheus' borrowing, see the bibliography at the head of *APF* 13700; the date of the speech is discussed by Harris 1988b.

42 Burying cash in the ground was also the safest way of making it invisible for the purpose of liturgy-dodging. A citizen could only deposit money in a bank with this intention if he had a close and trusting relationship with his banker (Dem. XLV.66). If a banker were dishonest enough to connive at defrauding the state, there was always the danger that he would turn round and cheat his client (see Gabrielsen 1986: 103).

43 The first Athenian *trapezitēs* known to have been a banker in the conventional sense as opposed to a money-changer is Pasion, dating

from the early fourth century (Isocrates' *Trapeziticus* is probably to be dated to the late 390s; see Mathieu and Bremond 1924–62:1, 68). There is an attempt by Bogaert (1974: 521–2) to push the documentation for credit-banking back into the fifth century by arguing that Archestratus, the original owner of Pasion, must have been more than a simple changer. It is known that, at a later date, Archestratus possessed Athenian citizenship. Assuming that (like most bankers) he was not a citizen by birth, Bogaert suggests he was probably granted this status by the people as a reward for services to the state. Such services, he argues, could only have been performed by a banker with extensive resources, and Archestratus therefore cannot have been a money-changer. The argument is ingenious, but no confidence can be placed in a conclusion reached via such a string of assumptions. More promising (but still inconclusive) is the case of 'Antimachus the banker'. The scholiast on Aristophanes' *Clouds* (l. 1022) gives Antimachus as the name of 'the *trapezitēs* Eupolis mentions in the *Demes*'. Eupolis was active from *c.* 430 to 410, and the *Demes* was one of his last plays. As Archestratus the owner of Pasion is known to have had a son called Antimachus (Dem. xxxvi.45–6), it is cautiously suggested by Bourriot (1987) that the Antimachus of the *Demes* was the father of Archestratus, who named his own son after the grandfather. Bourriot also tentatively suggests that Antisthenes, partner of Archestratus, may have been his brother, making up a whole family of bankers from late fifth- and early fourth-century Athens. Whatever the reality behind this reconstruction, there is nothing to show that Antimachus Senior was a fully fledged banker as opposed to a simple money-changer. The earliest attested changers appear in Corinth, possibly in the last quarter of the sixth century (ps.-Aristotle, *Oecon.* 1346b24–6, with Bogaert 1968: 120).

IX. CONCLUSION

1 From earlier in the same year (1791: IV, 152): 'I say nothing of the personal wretchedness of a debtor, which, however, has passed into a proverb' ('Let him who sleeps too much, borrow the pillow of a debtor', according to the editor). Johnson refers elsewhere to the power that a creditor has over his debtor (1791: V, 113).
2 'Unacceptable face' refers to the present high rate of default among private borrowers in the UK. In 1986, more than two million individuals were sued for debt in the county courts, and it was estimated that in excess of 10 per cent of households had taken on obligations that were not being met. The source for these figures is Ford's study of Britain as 'The indebted society' (1988: ix), the whole of which makes salutary reading. Contemporary attitudes to credit and debt are, of course, more complex than my summary in the text suggests. There is, for example, something paradoxical about a mentality which preaches the virtues of thrift while simultaneously offering financial incentives to

take on massive mortgages in pursuit of home ownership (see Ford 1988: 12–40).

3 For the view as imagined from the other side, there is Shylock's verdict on Antonio (1.iii.43):

> I hate him, for he is a Christian;
> But more for that in low simplicity
> He lends out money gratis, and brings down
> The rate of usance here with us in Venice.

The wider implications of this passage are brought out by Nelson (1969: 142–51) and Wills (1990). The clash of the two types of credit is brilliantly brought out in Breen's study (1988) of the tobacco-planters of Virginia in the late eighteenth century. Between themselves, the planters operated a system of mutual trust and support with interest-free loans; but the English merchants with whom they traded had very different ideas about sound business practices.

4 These concluding remarks necessarily simplify the situation. An additional factor in the case of Athens was the availability of public pay, which may be seen as supplementing the network of reciprocal exchange (above, p. 76). In a valuable essay on patronage as a tool of comparative analysis, the sociologists Johnson and Dandeker question my choice of democracy as part of the explanation for the absence of patronage networks in Athens (1989: 233–4). They stress instead the rôle of public support: 'That is to say, in Athens the potentiality for the development of private and personalised ties of patronage was inhibited by the existence of both an "ethic" of "euergetism" (public benefaction) and the institutions of public allocation.' They go on to draw a parallel with the introduction of the corn dole in Rome and the emergence of embryonic 'universal patrons' like the Gracchi. Of course there were overlaps between the Athenian, Hellenistic and Roman worlds, but the argument offered by Johnson and Dandeker comes close to saying that everything was like everything else. The character of public pay has political implications that are at odds with the euergetism of wealthy individuals; and the embryonic universal patrons who appear in fifth-century Athens (for example, Cimon and Pericles) disappear in the fourth. In both cases the different path taken by the Athenians can be explained in terms of their democratic *politeia*.

APPENDIX III

1 While this book was in press there appeared a further statement of the modernist case by E. E. Cohen: 'Commercial lending by Athenian banks: cliometric fallacies and forensic methodology' (*Classical Philology* 85 (1990) 177–90). La lutte continue.

Bibliography

References are given to reprints, translations and volumes of collected papers where they are known to exist. Where alternative versions of a book or article are available, citations in the text are usually taken from the more accessible source, as indicated in the bibliography.

Adkins, A. W. H. (1960): *Merit and Responsibility. A Study in Greek Values.* Oxford.

   (1963): '"Friendship" and "self-sufficiency" in Homer and Aristotle', *Classical Quarterly* 13: 30–45.

   (1972): *Moral Values and Political Behaviour in Ancient Greece.* London.

   (1978): 'Problems in Greek popular morality' (review-article of Dover 1974), *Classical Philology* 73: 143–58.

Ad. Pap. = *The Adler Papyri*, E. N. Adler, J. G. Tait, F. M. Heichelheim and F. L. Griffith (eds.). London 1939.

Aleshire, S. B. (1988): 'The Athenian archon Hoplon', *Hesperia* 57: 253–5.

Allan, G. A. (1979): *A Sociology of Friendship and Kinship.* London.

Allinson, F. G., trans. (1921): *Menander, the Principal Fragments* (Loeb edition). London and Cambridge, Mass.

Ampolo, C. (1981): 'Tra finanza e politica: carriera e affari del signor Moirokles', *Rivista di filologia* 109: 187–204.

Anderson, B. L. (1970): 'Money and the structure of credit in the eighteenth century', *Business History* 12: 85–101.

Andreau, J. (1968): 'Banque grecque et romaine dans le théâtre de Plaute et de Térence', *Mélanges d'archéologie et d'histoire* (Ecole française de Rome) 80: 461–526.

   (1977): 'M. I. Finley, la banque antique et l'économie moderne', *Annali della scuola normale superiore di Pisa* 7: 1130–52.

   (1984): 'Histoire des métiers bancaires et évolution économique', *Opus* 3: 99–114.

   (1987): *La Vie financière dans le monde romain. Les métiers de manieurs d'argent.* Rome.

Andrewes, A. (1977): 'Kleisthenes' reform bill', *Classical Quarterly* 27: 241–8.

Andreyev, V. N. (1974): 'Some aspects of agrarian conditions in Attica in the fifth to third centuries B.C.', *Eirene* 12: 5–46.

(1979): 'Demosthenes on Pasion's bank. An interpretation', *Vestnik Drevnej Istorii* 134–9 (Russian with English summary).

Annas, J. (1977): 'Plato and Aristotle on friendship and altruism', *Mind* 86: 532–55.

AO = Athenian Officials 684–321 B.C., R. Develin (ed.). Cambridge 1989.

APF = Athenian Propertied Families 600–300 B.C., J. K. Davies (ed.). Oxford 1971.

Appleton, C. (1919): 'Contribution à l'histoire du prêt à intérêt à Rome. Le taux du *fenus unciarium*', *Nouvelle revue historique de droit français et étranger* 43: 467–543.

Ardaillon, E. (1897): *Les Mines du Laurion dans l'Antiquité*. Paris.

Armstrong, G. C., trans. (1979): *Aristotle, Metaphysics X–XIV, Oeconomica and Magna Moralia*. (Loeb edition). London and Cambridge, Mass.

Arnott, W. G., trans. (1979): *Menander* vol. I, (Loeb edition). London and Cambridge, Mass.

Asheri, D. (1963): 'Laws of inheritance, distribution of land and political constitutions in ancient Greece', *Historia* 12: 1–21.

(1969): 'Leggi greche sul problema dei debiti', *Studi classici e orientali* 18: 5–122.

Audring, G. (1973): 'Über den Gutsverwalter (*epitropos*) in der attischen Landwirtschaft des 5. und des 4. Jh. v.u.Z.', *Klio* 55: 109–16.

Austin, M. M. and P. Vidal-Naquet (1977): *Economic and Social History of Ancient Greece. An Introduction*. London (revised translation by M. M. Austin of *Economies et sociétés en Grèce ancienne*. Paris 1972).

Bacon, F. (1625): *The Essays or Counsels, Civil and Moral*. London (cited from the edition by S. H. Reynolds. Oxford 1890).

Badian, E., ed. (1966): *Ancient Society and Institutions. Studies Presented to Victor Ehrenberg*. Oxford.

Bagnall, R. S. and R. Bogaert (1975): 'Orders for payment from a banker's archive', *Ancient Society* 6: 79–108.

Baiter, J. G. and H. Sauppe, eds. (1839–43): *Oratores Attici* 2 vols. Zurich.

Ballin, T. N., ed. (1977): '*A commentary on [Demosthenes] L, Against Polykles*' (unpublished Ph.D. thesis). Chapel Hill, N.C.

Baltensperger, E. (1989): 'Credit' in Eatwell, Milgate and Newman 1989: 97–102.

Banton, M., ed. (1966): *The Social Anthropology of Complex Societies*. London.

Barlow, C. T. (1978): 'Bankers, moneylenders and interest rates in the Roman Republic' (unpublished Ph.D. thesis). Chapel Hill, N.C.

Barnes, J., M. Schofield and R. Sorabji, eds. (1975–9), *Articles on Aristotle*, 4 vols. London.

Barton, R. F. (1919): 'Ifugao law', *University of California Publications in American Archaeology and Ethnology* 15: 1–127.

(1922): 'Ifugao economics' *University of California Publications in American Archaeology and Ethnology* 15: 385–431.

(1949): *The Kalingas. Their Institutions and Custom Law*. Chicago, Ill.

Beard, W. M. and M. H. Crawford (1985): *Rome in the late Republic*. London.

Beauchet, L. (1897): *Histoire du droit privé de la république athénienne*, 4 vols., Paris (reprinted Amsterdam, 1969).

Behrend, D. (1970): *Attische Pachturkunden*. Munich.

Beloch, J. (1893–1904): *Griechische Geschichte*, 4 vols., Strasburg; (second edition: 1912–27, 4 vols. in 8).

(1902): 'Zur griechischen Wirtschaftsgeschichte', *Zeitschrift für Sozialwissenschaft* 5 (reprinted in Finley 1979; printed in modified form in Beloch 1912–27: III.2, 419–49).

Benner, A. G. and F. H. Fobes trans. (1949): *The Letters of Alciphron, Aelian and Philostratus* (Loeb edition). London and Cambridge, Mass.

Bentham, J. (1787): *Defence of Usury*. London.

Benveniste, E. (1969): *Le Vocabulaire des institutions indo-européennes*, 2 vols., Paris, (translated as, and cited from, *Indo-European Language and Society*, London 1977).

Benvenuti, P. (1980): 'ERANOS' (unpublished dissertation). Padua.

Beye, C. R. (1972): 'The rhythm of Hesiod's *Works and Days*', *Harvard Studies in Classical Philogy* 76: 23–43.

Beyer, H. V. (1968): *Über den Sachverhalt der demosthenischen Rede für Phormion*. Berlin.

Bickerman, E. J. (1980): *Chronology of the Ancient World*. London.

Billeter, G. (1898): *Geschichte des Zinsfusses im griechisch-römischen Altertum bis auf Justinian*, Leipzig, (reprinted Wiesbaden 1970).

Biscardi, A. (1982–4): *Studi in onore di Arnaldo Biscardi*, 5 vols. Milan.

Blass, F. (1887–98): *Die attische Beredsamkeit*, 2nd edn, 3 vols., Leipzig, (reprinted Hildesheim 1962).

Blaug, M. (1968): *Economic Theory in Retrospect*, 2nd edn. London.

Blundell, M. W. (1989): *Helping Friends and Harming Enemies. A Study in Sophocles and Greek Ethics*. Cambridge.

Böckh, A. (1817): *Die Staatshaushaltung der Athener*. Berlin, (translated as, and cited from, *The Public Economy of Athens*, 2nd edn, by G. C. Lewis, London 1842; reprinted New York 1976).

Böhm-Bawerk, E. von (1884): *Geschichte und Kritik der Kapitalzinstheorien*, Stuttgart (translated as, and cited from *History and Critique of Interest Theories* by G. D. Huncke and H. F. Sennholz. South Holland, Ill. 1959).

Bogaert, R. (1962): 'A propos de la *phasis* (Isocrate, Trapézitique §42). Contribution à l'histoire du droit athénien)', *Revue internationale des droits de l'antiquité* 9: 158–67.

(1965): 'Banquiers, courtiers et prêts maritimes à Athènes et à Alexandrie', *Chronique d'Egypte* 40: 140–56.

(1966): *Les Origines antiques de la banque de dépôt*. Leiden.

(1968): *Banques et banquiers dans les cités grecques*. Leiden.

(1971): 'Notes critiques, juridiques et économiques sur le discours contre Phormion' in Volterra 1971: III, 123–34.

(1974): 'Die Krise der Banken im 4.Jahrhundert v.u.Z.' in Welskopf 1974: I, 521–30.

316 *Bibliography*

(1976): 'L'Essai des monnaies dans l'antiquité', *Revue belge de numismatique* 122: 5–34.

(1984): 'Les Banques affermées ptolémaïques', *Historia* 33: 181–98.

(1986a): 'La Banque à Athènes au IVe siècle avant J.-C. Etat de la question', *Museum Helveticum* 43: 19–49.

(1986b): *Grundzüge des Bankwesens im alten Griechenland.* Constance.

(1987): 'Banques et banquiers dans l'Arsinoïte à l'époque Ptolémaïque', *Zeitschrift für Papyrologie und Epigraphik* 68: 35–75.

(1988): 'Les Opérations en nature des banques en Egypte gréco-romaine', *Ancient Society* 19: 213–24.

Bolkestein, H. (1923): *Het economisch leven in Griekenlands bloeitijd*, Harlem, (translated as, and cited from, *Economic Life in Greece's Golden Age* by E. J. Jonkers, Leiden 1958).

(1939): *Wohltätigkeit und Armenpflege im vorchristlichen Altertum*, Utrecht, (reprinted New York 1969).

Bongenaar, J. C. A. M. (1933): *Isocrates' Trapeziticus, vertaald en toegelicht.* Utrecht.

Bonner, R. J. (1927): *Lawyers and Litigants in Ancient Athens*, Chicago, (reprinted New York 1969).

Bonner, R. J. and Smith, R. (1930–8): *The Administration of Justice from Homer to Aristotle*, 2 vols., Chicago, (reprinted New York 1970).

Booth, C. (1902–3): *Life and Labour of the People in London*, 17 vols. London.

Bosanquet, H. (1896): 'The burden of small debts', *Economic Journal* 6: 212–25.

Boswell, J. (1791): *Life of Samuel Johnson*, London, (cited from the edition by G. Birkbeck Hill, 6 vols. Oxford 1934).

Bottéro, J. (1961): 'Désordre économique et annulation des dettes en Mésopotamie à l'époque paléo-babylonienne', *Journal of the Economic and Social History of the Orient* 6: 113–64.

Bottomley, A. (1963a): 'The return for risk as a determinant of interest rates in underdeveloped rural areas', *Quarterly Journal of Economics* 77: 637–47.

(1963b): 'The cost of administrating private loans in underdeveloped rural areas', *Oxford Economic Papers* 15: 154–62.

(1964): 'Monopoly profits as a determinant of interest rates in underdeveloped rural areas', *Oxford Economic Papers* 16: 431–7.

Bourriot, F. (1976): 'Recherches sur la nature du génos: étude d'histoire sociale athénienne – periodes archaïque et classique'. Lille and Paris.

(1987): 'Une famille de banquiers athéniens, celle d'Antimachos ve–ive s.', *Zeitschrift für Papyrologie und Epigraphik* 70: 229–34.

Bovill, S. (1985): 'Hesiod's *Works and Days*: The social and economic structure of an archaic peasant society' (unpublished dissertation). Leicester.

Braudel, F. (1979): *Les Structures du quotidien: le possible et l'impossible*, Paris, (translated as, and cited from, *The Structures of Everyday Life* by S. Reynolds. London 1981).

Bravo, B. (1974): 'Une lettre sur plomb de Berezan': colonisation et modes de contact dans le Pont', *Dialogues d'histoire ancienne* 1: 111–87.

(1977): 'Remarques sur les assises sociales, les formes d'organisation et la terminologie du commerce maritime grec à l'époque archaïque', *Dialogues d'histoire ancienne* 3: 1–59.

(1980): 'Sulan: représailles et justice privée entre les étrangers dans les cités grecques', *Annali della scuola normale superiore di Pisa* 10: 675–987.

(1984): 'Commerce et noblesse en Grèce archaïque', *Dialogues d'histoire ancienne* 10: 99–160.

(1985): '*Les Travaux et les jours et la cité*', *Annali della scuola normale superiore di Pisa* 15: 707–65.

Breen, T. H. (1988): *Tobacco Culture. The Mentality of the Great Tidewater Planters on the Eve of the Revolution*. Princeton, N.J.

Bruns, G. (1880): 'Die Testamente der griechischen Philosophen', *Zeitschrift der Savigny-Stiftung für Rechtsgeschichte* (Roman. Abt.) 1: 1–52.

Bücher, K. (1893): *Die Entstehung der Volkswirtschaft*, Tübingen, (reprinted in Finley 1979).

Büchsenschütz, A. B. (1869a): *Besitz und Erwerb im griechischen Altertum*, Halle, (reprinted Aalen 1962).

(1869b): *Die Hauptstätten des Gewerbefleisses im klassischen Altertum*. Halle.

Bull. épigr. = *Bulletin épigraphique* (published annually in *Revue des études grecques*).

Bulloch, D. A. (1969): 'Early medieval social groupings: the terminology of kinship', *Past and Present* 45: 3–18.

Burford-Cooper, A. (1977–8): 'The family farm in Greece', *Classical Journal* 73: 162–75.

Burke, E. M. (1974–5): 'A further argument on the authenticity of Demosthenes 29'. *Classical Journal* 70: 2: 53–6.

Burnett, J., ed. (1924): *Plato's 'Euthyphro', 'Apology of Socrates' and 'Crito'*. Oxford.

Burrow, J. (1966): *Evolution and Society. A Study in Victorian Social Theory*. Cambridge.

Burtt, J. O., trans. (1954): *Minor Attic Orators*, vol. II (Loeb edition). London and Cambridge, Mass.

Bury, J. B. and R. Meiggs (1975): *A History of Greece*, 4th edn. London.

Bywater, I., ed. (1890): *Aristotelis Ethica Nicomachea* Oxford.

CAF = *Comicorum Atticorum Fragmenta*, T. Kock (ed.), 3 vols. Leipzig 1880–1.

CAH[1] = *Cambridge Ancient History*, 12 vols. Cambridge 1924–39.

CAH[2] = *Cambridge Ancient History* (new edition). Cambridge 1970–.

Caillemer, E. (1870): 'Le Contrat de prêt à Athènes' in his *Etudes sur les antiquités juridiques d'Athènes*, 1–38, Paris 1865–72, (reprinted New York 1979).

Calhoun, G. M. (1913): *Athenian Clubs in Politics and Litigation*, Austin, Tex., (reprinted Rome 1964).

(1926): *The Business Life of Ancient Athens*, Chicago, Ill., (reprinted New York 1968).

(1930): Review of Schwahn 1929, *Classical Philology* 25: 86–9.

(1934): 'A problem of authenticity (Demosthenes 29)', *Transactions and Proceedings of the American Philological Association* 65: 80–102.

Calligas, P. (1971): 'An inscribed lead plaque from Korkyra', *Annual of the British School at Athens* 66: 79–93.

Cameron, H. D. (1964): 'The debt to the earth in the *Seven Against Thebes*', *Transactions and Proceedings of the American Philological Association* 95: 1–8.

Cameron, R., O. Crisp, H. T. Patrick and R. Tilly (1967): *Banking in the Early Stages of Industrialization. A Study in Comparative Economic History.* Oxford.

Cannan, E., W. D. Ross, J. Bonar and P. H. Wickstead (1921–2): 'Who said "Barren metal"?', *Economica* 1–2: 105–10.

Carey, C. ed. (1989) *Lysias, Selected Speeches.* Cambridge.

Carey, C. and R. A. Reid, eds. (1985): *Demosthenes, Selected Private Speeches.* Cambridge.

Cargill, J. (1981): *The Second Athenian League. Empire or Free Alliance?* Berkeley, Calif.

Cartledge, P. A. (1979): *Sparta and Lakonia. A Regional History 1300–362 B.C.* London.

(1983): '"Trade and Politics" revisited: Archaic Greece' in Garnsey, Hopkins and Whittaker 1983: 1–15.

(1987): *Agesilaos and the Crisis of Sparta.* London.

Cartledge, P. A. and F. D. Harvey, eds. (1985): *CRUX. Essays Presented to G.E.M. de Ste Croix on his Seventy-fifth Birthday*, Exeter (= *History of Political Thought* VI, 1/2).

Cartledge, P. A., P. C. Millett and S. C. Todd, eds. (1990): *Nomos: Essays in Athenian Law, Politics and Society.* Cambridge.

Cassola, F. (1964): 'Solone, le terre e gli etemoroi', *Parola del Passato* 19: 26–88.

Casson, L. (1976): 'The Athenian upper class and new comedy', *Transactions and Proceedings of the American Philological Association* 106: 29–55, (reprinted in Casson 1984: 35–69).

(1984): *Ancient Trade and Society.* Detroit, Mich.

Cataldi, S. (1982): 'La struttura del rapporto creditizio e il diritto reale del creditore nell'orazione demostenica "contro Panteneto"' in Biscardi 1982–4: III, 423–44.

Catanach, I. J. (1970): *Rural Credit in Western India 1875–1930.* Berkeley, Calif.

Cataudella, M. R. (1966): *Atene fra il VI secolo.* Catania.

Cavaignac, E. (1923): *Population et capital dans le monde méditerranéen antique.* Strasburg.

(1951): *L'Économie grecque.* Paris.

Chadwick, J. (1990): 'The Pech-Maho lead', *Zeitschrift für Papyrologie und Epigraphik* 82: 161–6.

Chambers, M. H. (1984): 'The formation of the tyranny of Pisistratus' in Harmatta 1984: 1, 69–72.

Chambry, E., ed. (1927): *Esope*, '*Fables*' (Budé edition). Paris.

Chantraine, P. (1940): 'Conjugaison et histoire des verbes signifiant *vendre*', *Revue de philologie* 14: 11–24.

    ed. (1968–80): *Dictionnaire étymologique de la langue grecque: histoire des mots*, 4 vols. Paris.

Chase, A. H. (1933): 'The influence of Athenian institutions upon the *Laws* of Plato', *Harvard Studies in Classical Philology* 44: 131–92.

Christien, J. (1974): 'La Loi d'Epitadeus: un aspect de l'histoire économique et sociale à Sparte', *Revue historique de droit français et étranger* 52: 197–221.

Clairmont, C. W. (1970): *Gravestone and Epigram*. Mainz am Rhein.

Clark, G., trans. (1989): *Iamblichus, 'On the Pythagorean Life'*. Liverpool.

Cocks, R. J. C. (1988): *Sir Henry Maine. A Study in Victorian Jurisprudence*. Cambridge.

Cohen, D. (1983): *Theft in Athenian Law*. Munich.

Cohen, E. E. (1973): *Ancient Athenian Maritime Courts*. Princetown, N.J.

    (1989): 'Athenian finance: maritime and landed yields', *Classical Antiquity* 8: 207–23.

Collard, C., ed. (1975): *Euripides, 'Supplices'*, 2 vols. Groningen.

Conard, J. W. (1963): *An Introduction to the Theory of Interest*. Berkeley and Los Angeles, Calif.

Connor, W. R. (1971): *The New Politicians of Fifth-Century Athens*. Princeton, N.J.

Conophagos, C. (1980): *Le Laurium antique*. Athens.

Cooper, J. M. (1976–7): 'Aristotle on the forms of friendship', *Review of Metaphysics* 30: 619–48.

    (1980): 'Aristotle on friendship' in Rorty 1980: 301–40.

Coser, L. A. and B. Rosenberg (1976): *Sociological Theory. A Book of Readings*, 4th edn. New York and London.

Costouros, G. J. (1976): 'Early Greek accounting on estates', Working Paper No. 21 in *Working Paper Series Vol. II* (E. N. Coffman, ed.), 1–6 Acad. of Accounting Historians, Richmond, Va. 1979.

Cvetler, J. (1935a): 'Daneion und chresis' *Zeitschrift der Savigny-Stiftung für Rechtsgeschichte* (Roman. Abt.) 55: 275–7.

Cvetler, J. (1935b): 'Daneion et prêt de consommation dans le droit de l'Egypte ptolémaïque', *Chronique d'Egypte* 10: 129–32.

Dareste, R. (1882a): 'Le ΧΡΕΩΦΥΛΑΚΙΟΝ dans les villes grecques', *Bulletin de correspondance hellénique* 6: 241–5, (reprinted in shortened form in Dareste 1902: 105–8).

    (1882b): 'Les Testaments des philosophes grecs', *Annuaire de l'association pour l'encouragement des études grecques* 16: 1–21.

    (1902): *Nouvelles études d'histoire du droit*. Paris.

Darling, M. (1947): *The Punjab Peasant in Prosperity and Debt*, Bombay, (cited from the reprint edited by C. J. Dewey, Manohar 1977).

David, E. (1984): *Aristophanes and Athenian Society of the Early Fourth Century B.C.* Leiden.

Davies, J. K. (1981): *Wealth and the Power of Wealth in Classical Athens.* New York.

Day, J. (1942): *An Economic History of Athens under Roman Domination*, New York, (reprinted New York 1973).

Day, J. and M. H. Chambers (1962): *Aristotle's History of Athenian Democracy.* Berkeley and Los Angeles, Calif.

Delebecque, E. (1983): *Mélanges Edouard Delebecque.* Aix-en-Provence.

den Boer, W. (1979): *Private Morality in Greece and Rome.* Leiden.

de Roover, R. (1944): 'What is dry exchange? A contribution to the study of English mercantilism' *Journal of Political Economy* 70: 250–66, (reprinted in, and cited from, de Roover 1974: 183–99).

(1948): *Money, Banking and Credit in Medieval Bruges.* Cambridge, Mass.

(1954): 'New interpretations of the history of banking', *Cahiers d'histoire mondiale* 2: 38–76, (reprinted in, and cited from, de Roover 1974: 200–38).

(1957) 'Cambium ad Venetias: contribution to the history of foreign exchange' in *Studi in onore di Armando Sapori*, Milan, 631–48 (reprinted in, and cited from, de Roover 1974: 239–59).

(1965): 'Gli antecedenti del banco Mediceo e l'azienda bancaria di Messer Vieri di Cambio de' Medici' *Archivo storico italiano* 123: 3–13 (translated as 'The antecedents of the Medici bank: the banking house of Messer Vieri di Cambio de' Medici' in de Roover 1974: 260–9).

(1974): *Business, Banking and Economic Thought in Late Medieval and Early Modern Europe. Selected Studies of Raymond de Roover*, J. Kirshner (ed.). Chicago, Ill.

de Ste Croix, G. E. M. (1953): 'Demosthenes' TIMHMA and the Athenian *eisphora* in the fourth century B.C.', *Classica et Mediaevalia* 14: 30–70.

(1956): 'Greek and Roman accounting' in Littleton and Yamey 1956: 14–74.

(1966): 'The estate of Phaenippus (ps.-Dem. xlii)' in Badian 1966: 109–14.

(1974): 'Ancient Greek and Roman maritime loans' in Edey and Yamey 1974: 41–59.

(1981): *The Class Struggle in the Ancient Greek World.* London.

de Vaux, R. (1958–60): *Les Institutions de l'Ancien Testament*, 2 vols., Paris (translated as, and cited from, *Ancient Israel. Its Life and Institutions*, 2nd edn, by J. McHugh London 1965).

Detienne, M., ed. (1988): *Les Savoirs de l'écriture en Grèce ancienne.* Lille.

de Vessilitsky, V. and M. E. Bulkley (1916–17): 'Money-lending among the London poor', *The Sociological Review* 9: 129–38.

Dewindt, E. B. (1972): *Land and People in Holywell-cum-Needingworth. Structures of Tenure and Patterns of Social Organization in an East Midlands Village 1252–1457.* Toronto.

Diamond, S. (1987): *In Search of the Primitive. A Critique of Civilization*, 3rd edn, New Brunswick, N.J., and London.
Diehl = *Anthologia Lyrica Graeca*, 3rd edn, E. Diehl (ed.). Leipzig 1949–52.
Diels, H., ed. (1909): *Theophrasti Characteres.* Oxford.
Diller, A. (1937): *Race Mixture among the Greeks before Alexander.* Urbana, Ill.
Dindorf, W., ed. (1852): *Scholia Graeca in Aeschinem et Isocratem.* Oxford.
DK = *Fragmente der Vorsokratiker*, 5th edn, H. Diels and W. Kranz (eds.), 2 vols. Berlin 1952–6.
Dobb, M. (1966): *Soviet Economic Development since 1917.* London.
Donlan, W. F. (1982): 'Reciprocities in Homer', *The Classical World* 75: 137–75.
  (1989): 'The unequal exchange between Glaucus and Diomedes in light of the Homeric gift-economy', *Phoenix* 43: 1–15.
Dover, K. J. (1951–2): Review of Ehrenberg 1951, *Cambridge Journal* 5: 636–8, (reprinted in Dover 1987: 179–82).
  ed. (1965): *Thucydides Book VI.* Oxford.
  ed. (1968a): *Aristophanes, 'Clouds'.* Oxford.
  (1968b): *Lysias and the 'Corpus Lysiacum'.* Berkeley, Calif.
  (1974): *Greek Popular Morality in the Time of Plato and Aristotle.* Oxford.
  (1987): *Greek and the Greeks.* Oxford.
Draper, J. W. (1935): 'Usury in *The Merchant of Venice*', *Modern Philology* 33: 37–47.
DS = *Dictionnaire des antiquités grecques et romaines d'après les textes et les monuments*, Ch. Daremberg and E. Saglio (eds.), 5 vols. in 9, Paris 1877–1919, (reprinted Graz 1961).
DSS = *Dictionary of the Social Sciences*, J. Gould and W. Kolb (eds.), 1964, London.
Ducrey, P. (1986): *Le Traitement des prisonniers de guerre dans la Grèce antique.* Paris.
Earp, F. R. (1929): *The Way of the Greeks.* London.
Eatwell, J., M. Milgate and P. Newman, eds. (1989): *Money*, London, (a collection of articles from Palgrave).
Edey, H. and B. S. Yamey, eds. (1974): *Essays in Honour of W. T. Baxter.* London.
Edmonds = *Lyra Graeca*, J. M. Edmonds (ed.), 3 vols. (Loeb edition), London and Cambridge, Mass. 1922–7.
Edmonds, J. M. and G. E. V. Austen, eds. (1904): *The Characters of Theophrastus.* London.
Ehrenberg, V. (1951): *The People of Aristophanes. A Sociology of Attic Comedy*, 2nd edn, Cambridge, (reprinted New York 1962).
Eisenstadt, S. N. (1956): 'Ritualized personal relations', *Man* 55: 90–5.
Eisenstadt, S. N. and L. Roniger (1984): *Patrons, Clients and Friends. Interpersonal Relations and the Structure of Trust in Society.* Cambridge.
Ellis-Jones, J. (1984–5): 'Laurion: Agrileza, 1977–83: Excavations at a silver-mine site', *Archaeological Reports* 31: 106–23.

Endenburg, P. J. T. (1937): *Koinoonia en gemeenschap van zaken bij de Grieken in den klassieken tijd.* Amsterdam.

Ennew, J. (1981): *Debt Bondage – A Survey*, Anti-Slavery Society, Human Rights Series, Report No. 4. London.

Epigraphica I = *Texts on the Economic History of the Greek World*, H. W. Pleket (ed.). Leiden 1964.

Epigraphica III = *Texts on Bankers, Banking and Credit in the Greek World*, R. Bogaert (ed.). Leiden 1976.

Epstein, D. F. (1987): *Personal Enmity in Roman Politics 218–43 B.C.* London.

Erxleben, E. (1973): 'Das Kapital der Bank des Pasion und das Privatvermögen des Trapeziten', *Klio* 55: 117–34.

    (1974): 'Die Rolle der Bevölkerungsklassen im Aussenhandel Athens im 4. Jahrhundert v.u.Z.' in Welskopf 1974: 1, 460–520.

ESS = *Encyclopaedia of the Social Sciences*, 15 vols. New York 1930–5.

Etienne, R. (1985): 'Le Capital immobilier dans les Cyclades à l'époque hellénistique' in Leveau 1985: 55–67.

Evelyn-White, H. G., trans. (1914): *Hesiod, the Homeric Hymns and Homerica*, (Loeb edition). London and Cambridge, Mass.

FAC = *The Fragments of Attic Comedy*, J. M. Edmonds (ed.), 3 vols. Leiden 1957–61.

Ferguson, W. S. (1911): *Hellenistic Athens. An Historical Essay*, London, (reprinted Chicago, Ill. 1974).

    (1944): 'The Attic *orgeones*', *Harvard Theological Review* 37: 61–140.

    (1949), 'Orgeonika', *Hesperia* Supp. 8: 130–63.

FGH = *Die Fragmente der griechischen Historiker*, F. Jacoby (ed.). Berlin and Leiden 1922–58.

Figueira, T. (1984): 'The Lipari Islanders and their system of communal property', *Classical Antiquity* 3: 179–206.

    (1985): 'The Theognidea and Megarian society' in Figueira and Nagy 1985: 112–58.

Figueira, T. and G. Nagy, eds. (1985): *Theognis of Megara. Poetry and the Polis.* Baltimore, Ma.

Fine, J. V. A. (1951): *Horoi. Studies in Mortgage, Real Security and Land Tenure in Ancient Athens*, *Hesperia* Supp. 9.

Finley, M. I. (1952): *Studies in Land and Credit in Ancient Athens, 500–200 B.C.* New Brunswick, N. J., (reprinted New York 1973; corrected reprint New Brunswick 1985, with Millett 1982 as introductory essay).

    (1953a): 'Land, debt and the man of property in classical Athens', *Political Science Quarterly* 68: 249–68 (reprinted in, and cited from, Finley 1981: 62–76).

    (1953b): 'Multiple charges on real property in Athenian law. New evidence from an agora inscription' in *Studi in onore di Vincenzo Arangio Ruiz*, Naples, III, 473–91.

    ed. (1960): *Slavery in Classical Antiquity*, Cambridge, (reprinted with supp. to bibliog. 1968).

    (1962): 'Athenian demagogues', *Past and Present* 21: 3–24 (reprinted in, and cited from, Finley 1974: 1–25; reprinted in revised form in Finley 1985c: 38–75).

(1965a): 'La Servitude pour dettes', *Revue historique de droit français et étranger* 43: 159–84 (translated as, and cited from, 'Debt-bondage and the problem of slavery' in Finley 1981: 150–66).

(1965b): Review of French 1964, *Economic Journal* 75: 849–51.

(1965c): 'Classical Greece', *Deuxième conférence internationale d'histoire économique*, Aix-en-Provence 1962 1: *Trade and Politics in the Ancient World*, Paris and The Hague, (reprinted New York 1979).

(1970): Review of van Groningen and Wartelle 1968, *Classical Review* 20: 315–19.

ed. (1973): *Problèmes de la terre en Grèce ancienne*. Paris.

ed. (1974): *Studies in Ancient Society*. London.

(1975): *The Use and Abuse of History*. London.

(1977): *The World of Odysseus* 2nd edn. London.

(1978): 'The fifth-century Athenian empire: a balance sheet' in Garnsey and Whittaker 1978: 103–26 (reprinted in, and cited from, Finley 1981: 41–61).

ed. (1979): *The Bücher–Meyer Controversy*. New York.

(1981): *Economy and Society in Ancient Greece*, B. D. Shaw and R. Saller (eds.). London.

(1982): 'Problems of slave society: some reflections on the debate', *Opus* 1: 201–11.

(1983): *Politics in the Ancient World*. Cambridge.

(1985a): *Ancient History: Evidence and Models*. London.

(1985b): *The Ancient Economy*, 2nd edn. London.

(1985c): *Democracy Ancient and Modern*, 2nd edn. London.

ed. (1987): *Classical Slavery*. London.

Firth, R. (1966): *Malay Fishermen: Their Peasant Economy*, 2nd edn. London.

Firth, R. and B. S. Yamey, eds. (1964): *Capital, Saving and Credit in Peasant Societies*. London.

Fisher, N. R. E., ed. (1976): *Social Values in Classical Athens*. London.

Foraboschi, D. and A. Gara (1982): 'L'economia dei crediti in natura (Egitto)', *Athenaeum* 70: 69–83.

Ford, J. (1988): *The Indebted Society. Credit and Default in the 1980s*. London and New York.

Fornara = *Archaic Times to the End of the Peloponnesian War: Translated Documents of Greece and Rome*, vol. I, 2nd edn. C. W. Fornara (ed.). Cambridge 1983.

Forster, E. S., trans. (1927): *Isaeus* (Loeb edition). London and Cambridge, Mass.

Fortenbaugh, W. W. (1975): 'Aristotle's analysis of friendship: function and analogy, resemblance and focal meaning', *Phronesis* 20: 51–62.

Fortes, M. (1969): *Kinship and the Social Order: The Legacy of Lewis Henry Morgan*. London.

Foster, G. M. (1967): 'The dyadic contract: a model for the social structure of a Mexican peasant village' in Potter, Diaz and Foster 1967: 213–30.

Fowler, H. N., trans. (1936): *Plutarch's 'Moralia'* (Loeb edition), vol. x. London and Cambridge, Mass.

Fox, R. (1967): *Kinship and Marriage*. London.

Fraenkel, E., ed. (1950): *Aeschylus, 'Agamemnon'*, 3 vols. Oxford.

Fraisse, J.-C. (1974): *Philia. La notion d'amitié dans la philosophie antique*. Paris.

Francotte, H. (1900): *L'Industrie dans la Grèce ancienne*, 2 vols., Paris, (reprinted New York 1979).

Frank, T., ed. (1933–40): *An Economic Survey of Ancient Rome*, 5 vols. Baltimore, Md.

Franzmann, J. W. (1972): 'The early development of the Greek concept of charis' (unpublished Ph.D. thesis). University of Wisconsin.

Frederiksen, M. (1966): 'Cicero, Caesar and the problem of debt', *Journal of Roman Studies* 56: 128–41.

(1975): 'Theory, evidence and the ancient economy' (review-article of first edition of Finley 1985b) *Journal of Roman Studies* 65: 164–71.

Freeman, K., trans. (1947): *Ancilla to the Pre-Socratic Philosophers*. Oxford.

Freese, J. H., trans. (1926): *Aristotle, 'Art' of Rhetoric* (Loeb edition). London and Cambridge, Mass.

French, A. (1964): *The Growth of the Athenian Economy*. London.

Frost, F. J. (1985): 'Towards a history of Peisistratid Athens' in Starr 1985: 57–78.

Fuks, A. (1979–80): 'Τοῖς ἀπορουμένοις κοινωνεῖν: the sharing of property by the rich with the poor in Greek theory and practice', *Scripta Classica Israelica* 5: 46–63 (reprinted in Fuks 1984: 46–63).

Fuks, A. (1984): *Social Conflict in Ancient Greece*, M. Stern and M. Amit (eds.) Jerusalem.

Fustel de Coulanges, N. D. (1864): *La Cité antique*, Paris, (translated as, and cited from, *The Ancient City*, with a new preface by Momigliano and Humphreys, Baltimore, Md.).

Gabrielsen, V. (1986): 'ΦΑΝΕΡΑ and ΑΦΑΝΗΣ ΟΥΣΙΑ in classical Athens',. *Classica et Mediaevalia* 37: 99–114..

(1989): 'The number of Athenian trierarchs after ca. 340 B.C.', *Classica et Mediaevalia* 40: 145–59.

Gallant, T. W. (1982): 'Agricultural systems, land tenure and the reforms of Solon' *Annual of the British School at Athens* 77: 111–24.

Gamoran, H. (1971): 'The biblical law against loans on interest', *Journal of Near Eastern Studies* 30: 127–34.

Garlan, Y. (1982): *Les Esclaves en Grèce ancienne*, Paris, (translated as, and cited from, *Slavery in Ancient Greece* by J. Lloyd, Ithaca, N.Y. and London).

Garlan, Y. (1987): 'War, piracy and slavery in the Greek world' in Finley 1987: 7–20.

Garland, R. (1987): *The Piraeus from the Fifth to the First Century B.C.* London.

Garnsey, P. D. A. (1985): 'Grain for Athens' in Cartledge and Harvey 1985: 62–75.

(1988): *Famine and Food Supply in the Graeco-Roman World*. Cambridge.

Garnsey, P., K. Hopkins and C. R. Whittaker, eds. (1983): *Trade in the Ancient Economy*. London.

Garnsey, P. and C. R. Whittaker, eds. (1978): *Imperialism in the Ancient World*. Cambridge.

Garnsey, P. and G. Woolf (1989): 'Patronage of the rural poor in the Roman world' in Wallace-Hadrill 1989b: 153–70.

Gauthier, A. and J. Y. Jolif, eds. (1970): *L'Ethique à Nicomaque. Introduction, traduction et commentaire*, 2nd edn, 3 vols. Louvain and Paris.

Gauthier, P. (1973): 'A propos des clérouquies athéniennes du Ve siècle' in Finley 1973: 163–78.

ed. (1976): *Un commentaire historique des 'Poroi' de Xénophon*. Geneva and Paris.

(1982): 'Les Saisies licites aux dépens des étrangers dans les cités grecques', *Revue historique de droit français et étranger* 60: 553–76.

Gehrke, H.-J. (1985): *Stasis. Untersuchungen zu den inneren Kriegen in den griechischen Staaten des 5. und 4. Jahrhunderts v. Chr.* Munich.

Germain, L. R. F. (1973): 'Antinomie entre le témoignage des *horoi* et celui des orateurs attiques' *VI. Kongress für griechische und lateinische Epigraphik*.

(1982–4): '*Une sûreté mal connue: l'apotimema attique. Etude de la troisième famille d'apotimema*' in Biscardi (1982–4) III, 445–57.

Gernet, L. (1933): 'Comment caractériser l'économie de la Grèce antique?' *Annales d'histoire économique et sociale* 2: 561–6 (reprinted in, and cited from, Gernet 1983: 193–201).

(1948–9): 'Droit et prédroit en Grèce ancienne', *L'Année sociologique*, 21–119 (translated as, and cited from, 'Law and prelaw in ancient Greece' in Gernet 1981: 143–215).

ed. (1954–60): *Démosthène, Plaidoyers civils* (Budé edition), 4 vols. Paris.

(1956): 'Choses visibles et choses invisibles', *Revue philosophique* 146: 79–86 (reprinted in Gernet 1982: 227–38: translated as, and cited from, 'Things visible and things invisible' in Gernet 1981: 343–51).

(1981): *The Anthropology of Ancient Greece*, J. Hamilton and B. Nagy (trans.). Baltimore, Md.

(1982): *Anthropologie de la Grèce antique*, 2nd edn. Paris.

(1983), *Les Grecs sans miracle*, R. di Donato (ed.). Paris.

Gernet, L. and M. Bizos, eds. (1955–9): *Lysias, Discours*, 2nd edn, (Budé edition), 2 vols. Paris.

GHI = A Selection of Greek Historical Inscriptions, M. N. Tod (ed.), 2 vols. Oxford 1946–8.

Giglioni, G. B. (1980): 'Immagini di una società. Analisi storica dei "Caratteri" di Teofrasto', *Athenaeum* 68: 73–102.

Gigon, O. (1950): *Kommentar zum ersten Buch von Xenophons Memorabilien*. Basel.

(1956): *Kommentar zum zweiten Buch von Xenophons Memorabilien*. Basel.

Bibliography

Glotz, G. (1904): *La Solidarité de la famille dans le droit criminel en Grèce*, Paris, (reprinted New York 1973).

(1920): *Le Travail dans la Grèce ancienne*, Paris, (translated as, and cited from, *Ancient Greece at Work* by M. R. Dobie, London 1926).

Glover, T. R. (1917): *From Pericles to Philip*. London.

(1942a): 'The Greek farmer' in Glover 1942b: 51–71.

(1942b): *The Challenge of the Greek*. Cambridge.

Gluckman, M. (1965): *Politics, Law and Ritual in Tribal society*. Oxford.

Gluskina, L. M. (1970): 'Some aspects of credit relations in Attica in the fourth century B.C.', *Vestnik Drevnej Istorii* 3: 17–43 (in Russian with English summary).

(1974): 'Studien zu den sozialökonomischen Verhältnissen in Attika im 4. Jh. v.u.Z.', *Eirene* 12: 111–38.

Goldhill, S. D. (1984): 'Two notes on τέλος and related words in the *Oresteia*', *Journal of Hellenic Studies* 104: 169–76.

(1986): *Reading Greek Tragedy*. Cambridge.

Gomme, A. W. (1933): *The Population of Athens in the Fifth and Fourth Centuries B.C.* Oxford.

(1937a): 'Traders and manufacturers in Greece' in Gomme 1937b: 42–66.

(1937b): *Essays in Greek History and Literature*. Oxford.

(1954): 'Two old jokes. Aristotle *Poetics* 15.1454a16ff. and Demosthenes 55 (*c. Calliclem*), 16–17' *Classical Quarterly* 4: 46–52.

Gomme, A. W. and F. H. Sandbach, eds. (1973): *Menander, A Commentary*. Oxford.

Goody, J., ed. (1974): *The Character of Kinship*. Cambridge.

(1986): *The Logic of Writing and the Organization of Society*. Cambridge.

Goody, J., J. Thirsk and E. P. Thompson, eds. (1976): *Family and Inheritance. Rural Society in Western Europe 1200–1800*. Cambridge.

Gordon, B. (1982): 'Lending at interest: some Jewish, Greek and Christian approaches 800 B.C. – A.D. 100', *History of Political Economy* 14: 406–26.

Gottschalk, H. B. (1972): 'Notes on the wills of the peripatetic scholarchs', *Hermes* 102: 314–42.

Gould, J. (1989): *Herodotus*. London.

Grant, M. and R. Kitzinger, eds. (1988): *Civilizations of the Ancient Mediterranean. Greece and Rome*, 3 vols. New York.

Gras, N. S. B. (1930): 'Stages in economic history', *Journal of Economic and Business History* 2: 395–418.

Green, P. (1959): 'A peasant on Helicon: a study of Hesiod and his society', *History Today* 9: 729–35, (reprinted in Green 1960: 36–44).

(1960): *Essays in Antiquity*. London.

Gregory, C. A. (1982): *Gifts and Commodities*. Cambridge.

Grote, G. (1846–56): *A History of Greece*, 8 vols., London, (cited from the edition of 1888, 10 vols. London).

Gulick, B., trans. (1927–41): *Athenaeus, 'The Deipnosophists'* (Loeb edition), 7 vols. London and Cambridge, Mass.

Guthrie, W. K. C. (1962–81): *A History of Greek Philosophy*, 6 vols. Cambridge.

Habib, I. (1963–4): 'Usury in medieval India', *Comparative Studies in Society and History* 6: 393–419.

Halliday, W. R., ed. (1928): *The Greek Questions of Plutarch*, Oxford, (reprinted New York 1975).

Hamilton, J. R., ed. (1969): *Plutarch, 'Alexander': A Commentary*. Oxford.

Hamburger, M. (1951): *Morals and the Law. The Growth of Aristotle's Legal Theory*. New Haven, Conn.

Hamp, E. P. (1982): 'Philos', *Bulletin de la société de liguistique de Paris* 77: 252–62.

Handley, E. W., ed. (1965): *The 'Dyscolus' of Menander*. London.

(1975): 'Some new fragments of Greek comedy', *Proceedings of the XIV International Congress of Papyrologists*, London.

(1985): 'Aristophanes and the real world', *Proceedings of the Classical Association* 82: 7–16.

Hands, A. R. (1968): *Charities and Social Aid in Greece and Rome*. London.

Hansen, M. H. (1982): '*Atimia* in consequence of private debts?' *Symposion* 1977: 114–20.

(1983): 'The Athenian politicians 403–322 B.C.', *Greek, Roman and Byzantine Studies* 24: 35–56 (reprinted in Hansen 1989).

(1985): *Demography and Democracy. The Number of Athenian Citizens in the Fourth Century B.C.* Herning.

(1987): *The Athenian Assembly in the Age of Demosthenes*. Oxford.

(1988): *Three Studies in Demography*. Copenhagen.

(1989): *The Athenian Ecclesia II. A Collection of Articles 1983–89.* Copenhagen.

Hansen, M. V. (1984): 'Athenian maritime trade in the fourth century B.C. Operation and finance', *Classica et Mediaevalia* 35: 71–92.

Hanson, V. D. (1983): *Warfare and Agriculture in Classical Greece*. Pisa.

Hardie, W. F. R. (1980): *Aristotle's Ethical Theory*, 2nd edn. Oxford.

Harding = *From the End of the Peloponnesian War to the Battle of Ipsus: Translated Documents of Greece and Rome*, vol. II, P. Harding (ed.). Cambridge 1985.

Harmatta, J., ed. (1984): *Proceedings of the VIIth Congress of the International Federation of the Societies of Classical Studies*, 2 vols. Budapest.

Harper, E. B. (1961): 'Moneylending in the village economy of the Malnad', *Economic Weekly Journal*: 169–77.

Harris, E. M. (1988a): 'When is a sale not a sale? The riddle of Athenian terminology for real security revisited', *Classical Quarterly*, 38: 39–41.

(1988b): 'The date of Apollodorus' speech against Timotheus and its implications for Athenian history and legal procedure', *American Journal of Philology* 109: 44–52.

Harrison, A. R. W. (1954): Review of Finley 1952, *Classical Review* 4: 39–41.

(1968–71): *The Law of Athens*, 2 vols. Oxford.

Harvey, F. D. (1976): 'The maritime loan in Eupolis' *Marikas*', *Zeitschrift für Papyrologie und Epigraphik* 23: 231–3.

(1985): '*Dona Ferentes*: some aspects of bribery in Greek politics' in Cartledge and Harvey 1985: 76–117.

Hasebroek, J. (1920): 'Zum griechischen Bankwesen der klassischen Zeit', *Hermes* 55: 113–73.

(1923): 'Zum Giroverkehr im IV. Jahrhundert', *Klio* 18: 375–8.

(1928): *Staat und Handel im alten Griechenland*, Tübingen (translated as, and cited from, *Trade and Politics in Ancient Greece* by L. M. Fraser and D. C. MacGregor. London 1933).

Havelock, E. (1966): 'Thoughtful Hesiod', *Yale Classical Studies* 20: 61–72 (reprinted in, and cited from, Havelock 1982: 208–19).

(1982): *The Literate Revolution in Greece and its Consequences*. Princeton, N.J.

Healey, J., trans. (1616): *Theophrastus, His Morall Characters*. London.

Heath, M. (1987): *Political Comedy in Aristophanes*. Göttingen.

Hedrick, C. W. (1988): 'The Thymaitian phratry', *Hesperia* 57: 81–5.

Heichelheim, F. M. (1930): *Wirtschaftliche Schwankungen der Zeit von Alexander bis Augustus*, Jena, (reprinted New York 1979).

(1938): *Wirtschaftsgeschichte des Altertums, vom Paläolithikum bis zur Völkerwanderung der Germanen, Sklaven, und Araber*, 2 vols., Leiden, (translated as, and cited from, *An Ancient Economic History from the Palaeolithic Age to the Migration of the Germanic, Slavic and Arabic Nations* by J. Stevens, 3 vols. Leiden 1958–70).

Hemelrijk, J. (1982): Πενία en Πλοῦτος. Utrecht.

Henderson, J., ed. (1987): *Aristophanes, 'Lysistrata'*. Oxford.

Hennig, D. (1987): 'Kaufverträge über Häuser und Ländereien aus der Chalkidike und Amphipolis', *Chiron* 17: 143–70.

Herman, G. (1987): *Ritualised Friendship and the Greek City*. Cambridge.

Herrmann, J. (1975): 'Verfügungsermächtigungen als Gestaltungselemente verschiedener griechischer Geschäftstypen', *Symposion 1971*: 321–32.

Hewitt, J. W. (1927): 'The terminology of "gratitude" in Greek', *Classical Philology* 22: 142–61.

Hicks, J. (1969): *A Theory of Economic History*. Oxford.

Hicks, R. D., trans. (1925): *Diogenes Laertius, 'Lives of Eminent Philosophers'* (Loeb edition), 2 vols. (vol. I, revised reprint 1972). London and Cambridge, Mass.

Hill, P. (1986): *Development Economics on Trial. The Anthropological Case for a Prosecution*. Cambridge.

Hodkinson, S. (1988): 'Animal husbandry in the Greek polis' in Whittaker 1988: 35–74.

Holderness, B. A. (1976): 'Credit in rural society before the nineteenth century', *Agricultural History Review* 24: 97–109.

Holladay, J. (1977): 'The followers of Peisistratus', *Greece and Rome* 24: 40–56.

Homer, S. (1977): *A History of Interest Rates*, 2nd edn. New Brunswick, N.J.
Hommel, H. (1964): Review of Mannzmann 1962, *Gnomon* 36: 614–21.
Hooker, J. T. (1974): 'χάρις and ἀρετή in Thucydides', *Hermes* 102: 164–9.
    (1987): 'Homeric φίλος', *Glotta* 65: 44–65.
    (1989): 'Gifts in Homer', *Bulletin of the Institute of Classical Studies* 36: 79–90.
Hopkins, M. K. (1978): *Conquerors and Slaves*. Cambridge.
Hopper, R. J. (1961): '"Plain", "Shore", and "Hill" in early Athens', *Annual of the British School at Athens* 56: 189–219.
    (1979): *Trade and Industry in Classical Greece*. London.
Hudson, K. (1982): *Pawnbroking, an Aspect of British Social History*. London.
Hume, D. (1752): *Political Discourses*, Edinburgh (selected essays reprinted in, and cited from, David Hume, *Writings on Economics*, E. Rotwein (ed.). London 1955).
Humphreys, S. C. (1970): 'Economy and society in classical Athens', *Annali della scuola normale superiore di Pisa* 39: 1–26 (reprinted in, and cited from, Humphreys 1978: 136–58).
    (1974): 'The social structure of the ancient city', *Annali della scuola normale superiore di Pisa* 4: 329–67 (reprinted in, and cited from, Humphreys 1978: 192–208).
    (1977/8): 'Public and private interests in classical Athens', *Classical Journal* 73: 97–104 (reprinted in, and cited from, Humphreys 1983a: 22–32).
    (1978): *Anthropology and the Greeks*. London.
    (1980): 'Family tombs and tomb cult in Ancient Athens' *Journal of Hellenic Studies* 100: 96–126 (reprinted in, and cited from, Humphreys 1983a: 79–130).
    (1983a): *The Family, Women and Death*. London.
    (1983b): 'The family in classical Athens: search for a perspective' in Humphreys 1983a: 58–78.
    (1985): 'Social relations on stage: witnesses in classical Athens' *History and Anthropology* 1: 313–69.
    (1986): 'Kinship patterns in the Athenian courts', *Greek, Roman and Byzantine Studies* 27: 59–61.
Husselman, E. M. (1961): 'Pawnbrokers' accounts from Roman Egypt', *Transactions and Proceedings of the American Philological Association* 92: 251–66.
Hutter, H. (1978): *Politics as Friendship. The Origins of Classical Notions of Politics in the Theory and Practice of Friendship*. Waterloo.
Huxley, G. (1979): *On Aristotle and Greek Society*. Belfast.
IC = Inscriptiones Creticae, M. Guarducci (ed.), 4 vols., Rome 1935–50.
IESS = International Encyclopaedia of the Social Sciences, 18 vols. London and New York.
IG = Inscriptiones Graecae (details of individual volumes in Woodhead 1981: 163–7).
IJG = Recueil des inscriptions juridiques grecques, R. Dareste, B. Haussoullier

and Th. Reinach (eds.), 2 vols., Paris 1891–1904, (reprinted Rome 1964).

Inschr. v. Priene = Inschriften von Priene, H. von Gaertingen (ed.). Berlin 1906.

Irwin, T., trans. (1985): *Aristotle, 'Nicomachean Ethics'*. Indianapolis, Ind.

Isager, S. I. and M. H. Hansen (1975): *Aspects of Athenian Society in the Fourth Century B.C.* Odense.

Isnardi, M. (1954): 'Sugli apocrifi platonici "Demodoco" e "Sisifo"', *Parola del Passato* 9: 425–31.

Jackson, D. F. and G. O. Rowe, eds. (1969): 'Demosthenes 1915–1965', *Lustrum* 14.

Jameson, M. H. (1977–8): 'Agriculture and slavery in classical Athens', *Classical Journal* 73: 122–45.

Jardé, A. (1925): *Les Céréales dans l'antiquité grecque*, Paris, (reprinted Paris 1979).

Jebb, R. C., ed. (1909): Θεόφραστου Χαρακτῆρες. *The Characters of Theophrastus* (revised edition by J. E. Sandys). London.

Johnson, P. (1985): *Saving and Spending. The Working-Class Economy in Britain 1870–1939*. Oxford.

Johnson, T. and C. Dandeker (1898): 'Patronage: relation and system' in Wallace-Hadrill 1989b: 219–38.

Jones, A. H. M. (1956): 'Slavery in the Ancient World', *Economic History Review* 9: 185–99 (reprinted in, and cited from, Finley 1960: 1–16).

(1957): *Athenian Democracy*. Oxford.

Jordan, D. R. (1985): 'A survey of Greek defixiones not included in the special corpora', *Greek, Roman and Byzantine Studies* 26: 151–97.

Kamps, W. (1937): 'Les Origines de la fondation cultuelle dans la Grèce ancienne', *Archives d'histoire du droit oriental* 1: 145–79.

(1938): 'Une affaire de fraude successorale à Athènes', *Annuaire de l'Institut de philologie et d'histoire orientales et slaves* 6: 15–27.

Karkal, G. L. (1967): *Unorganized Money Markets in India*. Bombay.

Kelly, J. M. (1970): 'A hypothesis on the origin of *mutuum*', *The Irish Jurist* 5: 156–63.

Kelly, T. (1985): 'The Spartan scytale' in Starr 1985: 141–69.

Kennedy, G. (1963): *The Art of Persuasion in Greece*. Princeton, N.J.

Kenny, A. (1978): *The Aristotelian Ethics. A Study of the Relationship between the 'Eudemian' and the 'Nicomachean' Ethics of Aristotle*. Oxford.

Kerferd, G. B. (1981): *The Sophistic Movement*. Cambridge.

Keynes, J. M. (1936): *The General Theory of Employment, Interest and Money*. London.

(1937): 'Alternative theories of the rate of interest', *The Economic Journal* 47: 241–52.

Kindstrand, J. F., ed. (1976): *Bion of Borysthenes. A Collection of the Fragments with an Introduction and Commentary*, Studia Graeca Upsaliensia 11. Stockholm.

Kirk, G. S., J. E. Raven and M. Schofield, eds. (1983): *The Presocratic Philosophers* (new edition) Cambridge.

Klingenberg, E. (1982): 'Das Zinsrecht in Platos *Nomoi*', *Symposion 1977*: 99–112.

Knorringa, H. (1926): *Emporos. Data on Trade and Traders in Greek Literature from Homer to Aristotle*, Amsterdam, (reprinted Amsterdam 1961).

Körte = *Menandri quae supersunt*, 2nd edn, A. Körte (ed.), 2 vols. Leipzig 1959.

Körte, A. (1941): 'Literarische Texte mit Ausschluss der christlichen', *Archiv für Papyrusforschung* 14: 103–50.

Korver, J. (1934): *De terminologie van het crediet-wezen en het Grieksch*, Amsterdam, (reprinted New York 1979).

(1942): 'Demosthenes gegen Aphobus', *Mnemosyne* 10: 8–22.

Kränzlein, A. (1975): 'Die attischen Aufzeichnungen über die Einlieferung von φιάλαι ἐξελευθερικαί', *Symposion 1971*: 255–64.

Kreissig, H. (1982): 'Versuch einer Konzeption der hellenistischen Epoche', *Jahrbuch für Wirtschaftsgeschichte*, 153–60.

Kuper, A. (1988): *The Invention of Primitive Society: Transformation of an Illusion*. London and New York.

Lacey, A. R. (1971): 'Our knowledge of Socrates' in Vlastos 1971: 22–49.

Lacey, W. K. (1968): *The Family in Classical Greece*, London, (reprinted, Auckland 1980).

Lancaster, L. (1962): 'Crédit, épargne et investissement dans une économie "non-monétaire"', *Archives européennes de sociologie* 3: 149–64 (translated as 'Some aspects of credit, saving and investment in a "non-monetary" economy (Rossel Island)' in Firth and Yamey 1964: 35–52).

Landfester, M. (1966): *Das griechische Nomen 'philos' und seine Abteilung*. Hildesheim.

Lane Fox, R. (1985): 'Aspects of inheritance in the Greek world' in Cartledge and Harvey 1985: 208–32.

Langholm, O. (1983): *Wealth and Money in the Aristotelian Tradition*. Oslo.

(1984): *The Aristotelian Analysis of Usury*. Oslo.

Larsen, J. A. O. (1938): 'Roman Greece' in Frank 1933–40: IV, 259–498.

Laslett, P. (1983): *The World We Have Lost – Further Explored*, 3rd edn. London.

Lattimore, R., ed. (1962): *Themes in Greek and Roman Epitaphs*. Urbana, Ill.

Lauffer, S. (1974): 'Die Liturgien in der Krisenperiode Athens' in Welskopf 1974: I, 147–59.

(1979): *Die Bergwerkssklaven von Laureion*, 2nd edn. Wiesbaden.

Laum, B. (1914): *Stiftungen in der griechischen und römischen Antike*, 2 vols. Berlin.

(1922): 'Kein Giroverkehr bei athenischen Banken', *Philologische Wochenschrift* 41: 427–32.

Leach, E. (1982): *Social Anthropology*. London.

Lebel, M. (1980): *Mélanges d'études anciennes offerts à Maurice Lebel*, J.-B. Caron, M. Fortin and G. Maloney (eds.). Quebec.

332 Bibliography

Leemans, W. F. (1950): 'The rate of interest in Old Babylonian times', *Revue internationale des droits de l'antiquité* 5: 7–34.

Legon, R. P. (1981): *Megara. The Political History of a Greek City State to 336 B.C.* Ithaca, N.Y.

Lejeune, M. and J. Pouilloux (1988): 'Une Transaction commerciale ionienne avant vᵉ siècle à Pech-Maho', *Académie des inscriptions et belles-lettres*, 526–36.

Le Roy Ladurie, E. (1966): *Les Paysans de Languedoc*, 2 vols., Paris, (translated as, and cited from, *The Peasants of Languedoc* by J. Day. Urbana, Chicago and London 1974).

(1975): *Montaillou, village occitan de 1294 à 1324*, 2 vols., Paris, (translated as, and cited from, *Montaillou, Cathars and Catholics in a French Village 1294–1324* by B. Bray. London 1978).

Leveau, P., ed. (1985): *L'origine des richesses dépensées dans la vie antique.* Aix-en-Provence.

Lévi-Strauss, C. (1949): 'Le Principe de réciprocité' in *Les Structures élémentaires de la parenté* (translated and abridged by R. L. Coser and G. Frazer in *Sociological Theory. A Book of Readings*, 4th edn, R. L. Coser and B. Rosenberg (eds.). New York and London 1976, 161–70).

Lévy-Leboyer, M. (1968): 'Le Rôle historique de la monnaie de banque', *Annales ESC* 23: 1–8.

Lewis, D. M. (1959): 'Attic manumissions', *Hesperia* 28: 208–38.

(1966): 'After the Profanation of the Mysteries' in Badian 1966: 177–91.

(1968): 'Dedications of *phialai* at Athens', *Hesperia* 37: 368–80.

(1973): 'The Athenian *Rationes Centesimarum*' in Finley 1973: 187–214.

Lewis, I. M. (1985): *Social Anthropology in Perspective*, 2nd edn. Cambridge.

Leyton, E., ed. (1974): *The Compact. Selected Dimensions of Friendship.* Newfoundland.

Lintott, A. (1982): *Violence, Civil Strife and Revolution in the Classical City.* London.

Lipsius, J. H. (1905–15): *Das attische Recht und Rechtsverfahren*, 3 vols. in 1, Leipzig, (reprinted Hildesheim 1984).

Littleton, A. C. and B. S. Yamey, eds. (1956): *Studies in the History of Accounting.* London.

Littman, R. J. (1979): 'Kinship in Athens', *Ancient Society* 10: 5–31.

Lloyd, G. E. R. (1968): *Aristotle: The Growth and Structure of his Thought.* Cambridge.

Loew, R. (1908): χάρις. Marburg.

Lofberg, J. O. (1932): 'The speakers in the case of Chrysippus v. Phormio', *Classical Philology* 27: 329–35.

Lombardo, M. (1988): 'Marchands, économie et techniques d'écriture' in Detienne 1988: 159–87.

Longo, O. (1985): 'Eranos' in Delebecque 1983: 247–58.

Lowry, S. T. (1987): *The Archaeology of Economic Ideas. The Classical Greek Tradition.* Durham, N.C.

LSJ⁹ = *Greek–English Lexicon*, 9th edn, H. G. Liddell, R. Scott and H. S. Jones (eds.). Oxford.

McCartney, F. J. (1931): 'On the Cnossian custom of snatching money from lenders', *Transactions and Proceedings of the American Philological Association* 62: 26–39.

MacDowell, D. M., ed. (1962): *Andokides, 'On the Mysteries'*. Oxford.
  (1963): *Athenian Homicide Law in the Age of the Orators*. Manchester.
  (1978): *The Law in Classical Athens*. London.
  (1986a): 'The law of Periandros about symmories', *Classical Quarterly* 36: 438–49.
  (1986b): *Spartan Law*. Edinburgh.
  ed. (1990): *Demosthenes Against Meidias (Oration 21)*. Oxford.

Macherel, C. (1983): 'Don et réciprocité en Europe', *Archives européennes de sociologie* 24: 151–66.

McKechnie, P. (1989): *Outsiders in the Greek Cities in the Fourth Century B.C.* London.

McKechnie, P. and S. Kern, eds. (1988): *Hellenica Oxyrhynchia*. Warminster.

Macleod, C. (1982): 'Politics and the *Oresteia*', *Journal of Hellenic Studies* 102: 124–44 (reprinted in Macleod 1983: 20–40).
  (1983): *Collected Essays*, O. Taplin (ed.). Oxford.

Macve, R. (1985): 'Some glosses on Ste Croix's "Greek and Roman accounting"' in Cartledge and Harvey 1985: 233–64.

Maidment, K. J. trans. (1941): *Minor Attic Orators I* (Loeb edition). London and Cambridge, Mass.

Maier, G. (1961): *Eranos als Kreditinstitut*. Erlangen.

Maine, H. (1861): *Ancient Law. Its Connexion with the Early History of Society, and its Relation to Modern Ideas*, London, (reprinted Tucson, Ariz. 1986).

Mair, L. (1972): *An Introduction to Social Anthropology*, 2nd edn, Oxford.

Mair, A. W. and G. R. Mair, trans (1955): *Callimachus: Hymns and Epigrams, Lycophron and Aratus*, 2nd edn, (Loeb edition) London and Cambridge, Mass.

Maloney, R. P. (1971): 'Usury in Greek, Roman and Rabbinic thought', *Traditio* 27: 79–109.

Manfredini, M. and L. Piccirilli, eds. (1977): *Plutarco, La vita di Solone*. Rome.

Mannzmann, A. (1962): *Griechische Stiftungsurkunden. Studie zu Inhalt und Rechtsform*. Münster.

Mansion, S., ed. (1961): *Aristote et les problèmes de méthode*. Louvain.

Marchant, E. C., trans. (1923): *Xenophon, 'Memorabilia' and 'Oeconomicus'* (Loeb edition). London and Cambridge, Mass.

Markle III, M. M. (1985): 'Jury pay and assembly pay at Athens' in Cartledge and Harvey 1985: 265–97.

Marshall, A. (1890): *The Principles of Economics*. London.

Marx, K. (1857–8): *Grundrisse der Kritik der politischen Ökonomie* (cited from the translation by M. Nicolaus. London 1973).
  (1867–94), *Das Kapital*, 3 vols. (translated as, and cited from, *Capital*. London 1954–9).

Mathias, P. (1983): *The First Industrial Nation. An Economic History of Britain 1700–1914*, 2nd edn, London and New York.

Mathieu, G. and E. Brémond (1924–62): *Isocrate, 'Discours'* (Budé edition), 4 vols. Paris.

Mauss, M. (1921): 'Une forme ancienne de contrat chez les Thraces', *Revue des études grecques* 34: 388–97.

   (1925): *Essai sur le don*, Paris (translated as, and cited from, *The Gift. Forms and Functions of Exchange in Archaic Societies* by I. Cunnison. London 1954).

Meiggs, R. (1972): *The Athenian Empire*. Oxford.

Meikle, S. (1979): 'Aristotle and the political economy of the *polis*', *Journal of Hellenic Studies* 99: 57–73.

   (1989): 'Et in Arcadia Chicago', (review-article of Lowry 1986), *Polis* 8: 25–34.

Meislin, B. J. and M. L. Cohen (1963–4): 'Backgrounds of the biblical law against usury', *Comparative Studies in Society and History* 6: 250–67.

Meritt, B. D. (1952): 'Greek inscriptions', *Hesperia* 21: 355–9.

Messina, A. (1948): 'Di alcuni frammenti della orazioni di Lisia I', *Emerita* 16: 235–53.

   (1949): 'Di alcuni frammenti della orazioni di Lisia II' *Emerita* 17: 42–71.

Meyer, Ed. (1895): 'Die wirtschaftliche Entwicklung des Altertums' *Jahrbücher für Nationalökonomie und Statistik* 9 (64): 1–70, (reprinted in, and cited from, *Kleine Schriften zur Geschichtstheorie und zur wirtschaftlichen und politischen Geschichte des Altertums*, 2nd edn, Halle 1924; also in Finley 1979).

Michell, H. (1953): Review of Finley 1952, *Canadian Journal of Economics and Political Science* 19: 246–8.

   (1957): *Economics of Ancient Greece*, 2nd edn, Cambridge.

Mickwitz, G. (1937): 'Economic rationalism in Greco-Roman agriculture', *English Historical Review* 52: 577–89.

   (1939): 'Zum Problem der Betriebsführung in der antiken Wirtschaft', *Vierteljahrschrift für Sozial- und Wirtschaftsgeschichte* 32: 1–25.

Migeotte = *L'Emprunt public dans les cités grecques*, L. Migeotte (ed.). Quebec and Paris.

Migeotte, L. (1980a): 'Note sur l'embloie de *prodaneizein*', *Phoenix* 34: 219–28.

   (1980b): 'Engagement et saisie de biens publics dans les cités grecques' in Lebel 1980: 161–71.

Mikalson, J. (1983): *Athenian Popular Religion*, Chapel Hill, N.C. and London.

Miles, J. (1951a): 'The marriage of Plangon (Dolly)', *Hermathena* 77: 38–46.

   (1951b): 'Some observations on Demosthenes' speech against Pantaenetus', *Hermathena* 78: 50–66.

   (1952): 'The case of Leochares (Dem. *Or.* 44)', *Hermathena* 80: 48–57.

   (1955): 'On Demosthenes, *contra Spudiam*', *Hermathena* 88: 45–9.

Mill, J. S. (1848): *Principles of Political Economy*, London, (cited from the *Collected Works of John Stuart Mill*, vols. II–III. London and Toronto 1965).

Miller, M. (1953): 'Greek kinship terminology', *Journal of Hellenic Studies* 73: 46–52.

(1968): 'Solon's timetable', *Arethusa* 1: 62–81.

Millett, P. C. (1980): 'Note on a Greek text relating to credit transactions', *Proceedings of the Cambridge Philological Society* 26: 67–9.

(1982): 'The Attic *horoi* reconsidered in the light of recent discoveries', *Opus* 1: 219–49, (reprinted with corrections and minor additions as introductory essay to the 1985 reprint of Finley 1952; references in the text are to this version).

(1983): 'Maritime loans and the structure of credit in fourth-century Athens' in Garnsey, Hopkins and Whittaker 1983: 36–52.

(1984a): 'Hesiod and his world', *Proceedings of the Cambridge Philological Society* 30: 84–115.

(1984b): Review of Roberts 1983, *Times Higher Education Supplement*, 17 August 1984, 17.

(1989a): 'Patronage and its avoidance in classical Athens' in Wallace-Hadrill 1989b: 15–48.

(1989b): Review of Ober 1989, *Times Literary Supplement*, 29 December 1989, 1449.

(1990): 'Sale, credit and exchange in Athenian law and society' in Cartledge, Millett and Todd 1990: 167–94.

(forthcoming): 'Note on a text relating to credit transactions (Athen. XIII.612c)'.

Minkes, A. L. (1953): 'The decline of pawnbroking', *Economica* 20: 10–23.

Mitchel, F. (1964): 'Derkylos of Hagnous and the date of *IG* II² 1187' *Hesperia* 33: 337–51.

Mitchell, B. and P. Deane (1962): *Abstract of British Historical Statistics*. Cambridge.

Montgomery, H. (1986): '"Merchants fond of corn." Citizens and foreigners in the Athenian grain trade', *Symbolae Osloenses* 61: 43–61.

Morris, I. (1986): 'Gift and commodity in archaic Greece', *Man* 21: 1–17.

(1987): *Burial and Ancient Society. The Rise of the Greek City-State*. Cambridge.

Mossé, C. (1962): *La Fin de la démocratie athénienne. Aspects sociaux et politiqes du déclin de la cité grecque au IVe siècle avant J.-C.*, Paris, (reprinted with Mossé 1972 New York 1979).

(1970): 'A propos de la loi d'Eucratès sur la tyrannie', *Eirene* 8: 71–8.

(1972): 'La Vie économique d'Athènes au ive siècle: crise ou renouveau?' *Praelectiones Patavinae*, F. Sartori (ed.), Rome, (reprinted as appendix to reprint of Mossé 1962, New York 1979).

(1973): 'Le Statut des paysans en Attique au IVe siècle' in Finley 1973: 179–86.

Mulgan, R. G. (1977): *Aristotle's Political Theory*, Oxford.

Mullett, M. E. (1988): 'Byzantium: a friendly society?', *Past and Present* 118: 3–24.

Murray, A. T., trans. (1936–9): *Demosthenes, Private Orations* (Loeb edition), 3 vols. London and Cambridge, Mass.

Needham, R., ed. (1971a): *Rethinking Kinship and Marriage*. London.

(1971b): 'Introduction' to Needham 1971a: xiii–cxvii.

Needham, R. (1971c): 'Remarks on the analysis of kinship and marriage' in Needham 1971a: 1–34.

Nelson, B. N. (1969): *The Idea of Usury. From Tribal Brotherhood to Universal Otherhood*, 2nd edn, Chicago and London.

Neufeld, E. (1955): 'The prohibitions against loans at interest in ancient Hebrew laws', *Hebrew Union College Annual* 26: 355–412.

New English Bible (1970): Oxford and Cambridge.

Nippel, W. (1982): 'Die Heimkehr der Argonauten aus der Südsee. Ökonomische Anthropologie und die Theorie der griechischen Gesellschaft in klassischer Zeit', *Chiron* 12: 1–39.

Nisbet, C. (1967): 'Interest rates and imperfect competition in the internal credit market of rural Chile', *Economic Development and Cultural Change* 16: 73–90.

Noonan, J. T. (1957): *The Scholastic Analysis of Usury*. Cambridge, Mass.

Norlin, G. and L. Van Hook (1928–45): *Isocrates* (Loeb edition), 3 vols. London and Cambridge, Mass.

Ober, J. (1989): *Mass and Elite in Democratic Athens: Rhetoric, Ideology and the Power of the People*. Princeton, N.J.

OCD² = *Oxford Classical Dictionary*, 2nd edn, N.G.L. Hammond and H. H. Scullard (eds.). Oxford 1970.

Oertel, F. (1930): 'Zur Frage der attischen Grossindustrie', *Rheinisches Museum* 79: 230–52.

OGIS = *Orientis Graeci Inscriptiones Selectae*, W. Dittenberger (ed.), 2 vols. Leipzig 1903–5.

Oliver, J. H. (1960): *Demokratia, the Gods and the Free World*. Baltimore, Md.

Oost, S. I. (1973): 'The Megara of Theagenes and Theognis', *Classical Philology* 68: 186–96.

Osborne, R. G. (1985a): *Demos: The Discovery of Classical Attika*. Cambridge.

(1985b): 'Law in action in classical Athens', *Journal of Hellenic Studies* 105: 40–58.

(1987): *Classical Landscape with Figures. The Ancient Greek City and its Countryside*. London.

(1988): 'Social and economic implications of leasing land and property in classical and hellenistic Greece', *Chiron* 18: 279–323.

Ostwald, M. (1955): 'The Athenian legislation against tyranny and subversion' *Transactions and Proceedings of the American Philological Association* 86: 102–28.

Owen, G. E. L. (1961): '*Tithenai ta phainomena*' in Mansion 1961: 83–103 (reprinted in, and cited from, Barnes, Schofield and Sorabji 1975–9: I, 113–26).

PA = *Prosopographia Attica*, J. Kirchner (ed.), 2 vols. Berlin 1901–3.

Paley, F. A., ed. (1861): *The Epics of Hesiod*. London.
Paley, F. A. and J. E. Sandys, eds. (1910): *Demosthenes, Select Private Orations*, 4th edn, 2 vols. Cambridge.
Palgrave = *The New Palgrave. A Dictionary of Economics*, J. Eatwell, M. Milgate and P. Newman (eds.), 4 vols. London 1987.
Partsch, J. (1909): *Griechisches Bürgschaftsrecht*. Leipzig and Berlin.
Pearson, A. C., ed. (1917): *The Fragments of Sophocles*. Cambridge.
Pearson, H. W. (1957): 'The secular debate on economic primitivism' in Polanyi, Arensberg and Pearson 1957: 3–11.
Pearson, L. (1966): 'Apollodorus, the eleventh Attic Orator' in Wallach 1966: 347–59.
   (1969): 'Demosthenes (or pseudo-Demosthenes) XLV', *Antichthon* 3: 18–26.
   ed. (1972): *Demosthenes. Six Private Speeches*. Norman, Okla.
Pečírka, J. (1966): *The Formula for the Grant of Enktesis in Attic Inscriptions*. Prague.
   (1976): 'The crisis of the Athenian *polis*', *Eirene* 14: 5–30.
Pendrick, G. (1987): 'Once more Antiphon the Sophist and Antiphon of Rhamnus', *Hermes* 115: 5–30.
Percival, G., ed. (1940): *Aristotle on Friendship*. Cambridge.
Perlman, S. (1958): 'A note on the political implications of *proxenia* in the fourth century B.C.', *Classical Quarterly* 8: 185–91.
   (1965): 'Menander, *Dyscolus* 13–20. A note on the veracity of Menander's portrayal of contemporary society', *Rivista di filologia* 98: 271–7.
Pestman, P. (1971): 'Loans bearing no interest', *Journal of Juristic Papyri* 16: 7–29.
Petrie, A., ed. (1922): *Lycurgus, the speech 'Against Leocrates'*. Cambridge.
P. Hib. = *The Hibeh Papyri*, B. P. Grenfell and A. S. Hunt (eds.). London 1906.
Pippin, A. (1956): 'The Demioprata of Pollux x', *Hesperia* 25: 318–28.
Pleket, H. W. (1962): Review of Vondeling 1961, *Tijdschrift voor Geschiedenis* 75: 447–80.
   (1969): 'The archaic tyrannis', *ΤΑΛΑΝΤΑ* 1: 19–61.
   (1971): Review of Bogaert 1968, *Mnemosyne* 24: 433–7.
Polanyi, K., C. M. Arensberg and H. W. Pearson, eds. (1957): *Trade and Market in the Early Empires. Economies in History and Theory*. Glencoe, Ill.
Pomeroy, S. (1982): 'Charities for Greek women', *Mnemosyne* 34: 113–35.
Potter, J. M., M. N. Diaz and G. M. Foster, eds. (1967): *Peasant Society, a Reader*. Boston, Mass.
Pouilloux, J. (1954): *La Forteresse de Rhamnonte*. Paris.
P. Oxy. = *Oxyrhynchus Papyri*, B. P. Grenfell, A. S. Hunt et al. (eds.). London 1898– .
Préaux, Cl. (1957): 'Ménandre et la société athénienne', *Chronique d'Egypte* 32: 84–100.
Preisigke, F. (1910): *Girowesen im griechischen Ägypten*, Strasburg, (reprinted Hildesheim 1971).
Price, A. W. (1989): *Love and Friendship in Plato and Aristotle*. Oxford.

Pringsheim, F. (1950): *The Greek Law of Sale*. Weimar.
  (1955): 'The transition from witnesses to written transactions in Athens'
    in *Festschrift Simonius*, 287–97, (reprinted in Pringsheim 1961: II,
    401–9).
  (1961): *Gesammelte Abhandlungen*, 2 vols. Heidelberg.
Pritchett, W. K. (1977): 'Loans of Athena in 407 B.C.', *Ancient Society* 8:
    33–47.
P. Ryl. = *Catalogue of the Greek Papyri in the John Rylands Library, Manchester*,
    A. S. Hunt et al. (eds.), 4 vols. Manchester 1911–52.
Rabinowitz, J. J. (1944): 'Evasion of usury laws in the middle ages',
    Harvard Theological Review 37: 49–59.
RAC = Realencyclopädie der classischen Altertumswissenschaft, Stuttgart 1894–
    1981.
Radermacher, L. (1918): *Beiträge zur Volkskunde aus dem Gebiet der Antike*,
    Kais. Akademie der Wissenschaften in Wien. Sitzungsberichte Philos.-hist.
    Klasse. 187, vol. III 3–17.
Rädle, H. (1970): 'Selbsthilfeorganisationen der Sklaven und Freige-
    lassenen in Delphi', *Gymnasium* 77: 1–5.
Raepsaet, G. (1971): 'Les Motivations de la natalité à Athènes', *L'Antiquité*
    classique 40: 80–110.
RE = Realencyclopädie der classischen Altertumswissenschaft. Stuttgart 1894–
    1981.
Redlich, F. (1971): *Steeped in Two Cultures*. New York.
Rhodes, P. J., ed. (1981): *A Commentary on the Aristotelian 'Athenaion Politeia'*,
    Oxford.
  (1982): 'Problems in Athenian *eisphora* and liturgies', *American Journal of*
    Ancient History 7: 1–19.
Ricardo, D. (1817): *Principles of Political Economy and Taxation*, London,
    (cited from vol. I of *The Works and Correspondence of David Ricardo*.
    Cambridge 1951–5).
Roberts, R. (1974): *The Classic Slum*. London.
Roberts, J. W. (1983): *City of Sokrates. An Introduction to Classical Athens*.
    London.
Robertson, R. N. N. (1989): Introduction to U. Bitterli, *Cultures in Conflict*.
    Cambridge, 1–19.
Robinson, J. (1951): 'The rate of interest' *Econometrica* 19: 92–111,
    (reprinted in, and cited from, *The Generalisation of the General Theory and*
    Other Essays, London 1979, 137–64).
  (1971): *Economic Heresies. Some Old-fashioned Questions in Economic Theory*.
    London.
Robinson, J. and J. Eatwell (1974): *An Introduction to Modern Economics*, 2nd
    edn, London.
Robinson, T. M., ed. (1979): *Contrasting Arguments. An Edition of the*
    'Dissoi Logoi'. New York.
Rocchi, M. (1979): 'Contributi allo studio delle Charites (I)' *Studii classice*
    18: 5–16.

(1980): 'Contributi allo studio delle Charites (II)' *Studii classice* 19: 19–28.

Rorty, A. O., ed. (1980): *Essays on Aristotle's Ethics*. Berkeley, Los Angeles and London.

Rose, H. J. (1938): Review of Endenburg 1937, *Classical Review* 52: 30.

Ross, W. D., ed. (1925): *Aristotle, 'Ethica Nicomachea'*. Oxford.

(1945): *Aristotle*, 5th edn, Oxford.

Rostovtzeff, M. (1941): *Economic and Social History of the Hellenistic World*, 3 vols., Oxford (cited from the corrected reprint of 1953).

Roussel, D. (1976): *Tribu et cité: études sur les groupes sociaux dans les cités grecques aux époques archaïque et classique*. Paris.

Rowe, C. J. (1971): *The Eudemian and Nicomachean Ethics: A Study in the Development of Aristotle's Thought*, Proceedings of the Cambridge Philological Society Supp. no. 3.

Roy, J. (1988): 'Demosthenes 55 as evidence for isolated farmsteads in classical Attica', *Liverpool Classical Monthly* 13: 57–9.

Royer, J. P. (1967): 'Le Problème des dettes à la fin de la république romaine', *Revue historique de droit français et étranger* 45: 193–240, 407–50.

Rubin, M. (1987): *Charity and Community in Medieval Cambridge*. Cambridge.

Rupprecht, H. A. (1967): *Untersuchungen zum Darlehen im Recht der gräko-ägyptischen Papyri der Ptolemäerzeit*. Munich.

Russell, D. A. F. M. (1973): 'Remarks on Plutarch's *De Vitando Aere Alieno*', *Journal of Hellenic Studies* 93: 163–72.

Sahlins, M. (1965): 'On the sociology of primitive exchange' in *The Relevance of Models for Social Anthropology*, M. Banton (ed.), London 139–236, (reprinted in, and cited from, Sahlins 1974: 185–276).

(1968): 'La Première société d'abondance' *Les Temps Modernes* 268: 641–80 (translated as, and cited from, 'The original affluent society' in Sahlins 1974: 1–39).

(1974): *Stone Age Economics*. London.

Sakellariou, M. (1979): 'Discussion' in Welskopf 1979: 99–113.

Salmasius, Claudius (1639): *De modo usurarum*. Leiden.

(1640): *Dissertatio de foenore trapezitico*. Leiden.

Salmon, J. B. (1984): *Wealthy Corinth. A History of the City to 339 B.C.* Oxford.

Samuelson, P. A. (1970): *Economics*, 11th edn, New York.

Sandbach = *Menandri Reliquiae Selectae*, F. H. Sandbach (ed.). Oxford 1972.

Sandbach, F. H. (1975): *The Stoics*. London.

Sanmarti, E. and R. A. Santiago (1987): 'Une Lettre grecque sur plombe trouvée à Emporion', *Zeitschrift fur Papyrologie und Epigraphik* 68: 119–27.

(1988): 'Notes additionnelles sur la lettre sur plombe d'Emporion', *Zeitschrift für Papyrologie und Epigraphik* 72: 100–2.

Sayers, R. S. (1967): *Modern Banking*, 7th edn, Oxford.

Schäfer, A. (1858): *Demosthenes und seine Zeit*, Leipzig (Beilagen, III.2 not included in second edition).

Schaps, D. (1979): *Economic Rights of Women in Ancient Greece*. Edinburgh.
Schuller, W., ed. (1982): *Korruption im Altertum*. Munich.
Schuller, W., W. Hoepfner and E. L. Schwandner, eds. (1989): *Demokratie und Architektur. Der hippodamische Städtebau und die Entstehung der Demokratie*. Munich.
Schwahn, W. (1929): *Demosthenes gegen Aphobus. Ein Beitrag zur Geschichte der griechischen Wirtschaft*. Leipzig.
Scott, M. (1983): '*Charis* in Homer and the Homeric Hymns', *Acta Classica* 26: 1–13.
Seager, R. (1967): Review of Bogaert 1966, *Classical Review* 17: 378–9.
SEG = *Supplementum Epigraphicum Graecum*. Leiden and Germantown, Md. 1923– .
SGHI² = *A Selection of Greek Historical Inscriptions*, rev. edn, R. Meiggs and D. M. Lewis (eds.). Oxford 1988.
Sharma, R. S. (1965–6): 'Usury in early medieval India', *Comparative Studies in Society and History* 8: 56–77.
Sherwin-White, A. N., ed. (1966): *The Letters of Pliny. A Historical and Social Commentary*. Oxford.
SIG³ = *Sylloge Inscriptionum Graecarum*, 3rd edn, W. Dittenberger (ed.), 4 vols. Leipzig 1915–24.
Simon, D. (1965): 'Quasi-ΠΑΡΑΚΑΤΑΘΗΚΗ, zugleich ein Beitrag zur Morphologie griechisch-hellenistischer Schuldrechtstatbestände', *Zeitschrift der Savigny-Stiftung für Rechtsgeschichte* (Roman. Abt.) 82: 39–66.
Skydsgaard, J. E. (1988): 'Transhumance in ancient Greece', in Whittaker 1988: 75–86.
Smeed, J. W. (1985): *The Theophrastan 'Character'. The History of a Literary Genre*. Oxford.
Smith, A. (1776): *An Inquiry into the Nature and Causes of the Wealth of Nations*, 2 vols. London (cited from the Glasgow edition of Smith's works, R. H. Campbell, A. S. Skinner and W. B. Todd (eds.), 2 vols. Oxford 1976).
Smith, R. C. (1985): 'The clans of Athens and the historiography of the archaic period', *Classical Views* 29: 51–62.
Souilhé, J., ed. (1930): *Platon, Dialogues apocryphes*, (Budé edition), vol. XIII, pt. III. Paris.
Spufford, M. (1974): *Contrasting Communities. English Villages in the Sixteenth and Seventeenth Centuries*. Cambridge.
(1976): 'Peasant inheritance customs and land distribution in Cambridgeshire from the sixteenth to the eighteenth centuries' in Goody, Thirsk and Thompson 1976: 156–76.
Spufford, P., ed. (1986): *Handbook of Medieval Exchange*. London.
Starr, C. G. (1977): *The Economic and Social Growth of Early Greece 800–500 B.C.* New York and Oxford.
(1985): *The Craft of the Ancient Historian. Essays in Honour of Chester G. Starr*, J. W. Eadie and J. Ober (eds.). New York.

Stedman Jones, G. (1984): *Outcast London. A Study in the Relationship Between Classes in Victorian Society*, 2nd edn. London.

Stein, S. (1952): 'The laws on interest in the Old Testament', *Journal of Theological Studies* 3: 161–70.

Steinmetz, P., ed. (1960–2): *Theophrast, 'Charaktere'*, 2 vols. Munich.

Stocks, J. L. (1936): 'ΣΧΟΛΗ', *Classical Quarterly* 30: 177–87.

Stonex, A. B. (1916): 'The usurer in Elizabethan drama', *Publications of the Modern Language Association of America* 31: 190–210.

(1923): 'Money lending and money lenders in England during the sixteenth and seventeenth centuries' in *Schelling Anniversary Papers*. New York, 263–85.

Storey, P., trans. (1930–5): *Plato, 'The Republic'* (Loeb edition), 2 vols. London and Cambridge, Mass.

Strauss, B. S. (1986): *Athens after the Peloponnesian War. Class, Faction and Policy 403–386 B.C.* London.

Stroud, R. S. (1974): 'An Athenian law on silver coinage', *Hesperia* 43: 157–85.

Szegedy-Maszak, A., ed. (1981): *The Nomoi of Theophrastus*. New York.

Taillardat, J. (1982): 'ΦΙΛΟΤΗΣ, ΠΙΣΤΙΣ et FOEDUS', *Revue des études grecques* 91: 1–14.

Talamanca, M. (1971): 'L'oggetto dell'azione di Apollodoro contro Formione. Contributo allo studio di Demostene Or. 36 e 45' in *Scritti dedicati ad Alessandro Raselli*, Milan, vol. II.

Tarn, W. and G. T. Griffith (1952): *Hellenistic Civilization*, 3rd edn. London.

Tawney, R. H. (1926): *Religion and the Rise of Capitalism*. London.

Taylor, G. V. (1964): 'Types of capitalism in eighteenth-century France', *English Historical Review* 79: 478–97.

Tebbutt, M. (1983): *Making Ends Meet. Pawnbroking and Working-Class Credit*. Leicester and New York.

Thalheim = *Lysias*, T. Thalheim (ed.). Leipzig 1901.

Theophrast (1897): *Charactere*, (Herausgegeben, erklärt und übersetzt von der Philologischen Gesellschaft zu Leipzig). Leipzig.

Thomas, R. (1989): *Oral Tradition and Written Record in Athens*. Cambridge.

Thompson, F. (1939): *Lark Rise*. Oxford (reprinted as, and cited from, *Lark Rise to Candelford*. London 1973).

Thompson, M., O. Mørkholm and C. M. Kraay (1973): *An Inventory of Greek Coin Hoards*. New York.

Thompson, W. E. (1976): *De Hagniae Hereditate. An Athenian Inheritance Case*. Leiden.

(1978): 'The Athenian investor', *Rivista di Studi Classici* 36: 402–23.

(1979a): 'A view of Athenian banking', *Museum Helveticum* 36: 224–41.

(1979b): 'An aspect of Athenian public finance', *Acta Classica* 22: 149–53.

(1980): 'An Athenian commercial case: Demosthenes 34', *Tijdschrift voor Rechtgeschiedenis* 48: 137–49.

(1981): 'Apollodorus v. Phormion: the computation of the damages', *Revue internationale des droits de l'antiquité* 28: 83–94.

(1982): 'The Athenian entrepreneur', *L'Antiquité classique* 51: 53–85.

(1988): 'Banking and insurance' in Grant and Kitzinger 1988: 1, 829–36.

Thorburn, S. S. (1886): *Musalmans and Money-Lenders in the Punjab*. Edinburgh.

Thür, G. (1975): 'Komplexe Prozessführung, dargestellt am Beispiel des Trapezitikos (Isocr. 17)', *Symposion 1971*: 157–88.

(1989): 'Wo wohnen die Metöken?' in Schuller, Hoepfner and Schwander 1989: 117–21.

Todd, S. C. (1990a): 'Use and abuse of the Attic Orators', *Greece and Rome* 37: 159–78.

(1990b): 'Lady Chatterley's Lover and the Attic Orators', *Journal of Hellenic Studies* 110: 146–73.

Todd, S. C. and P. C. Millett (1990): 'Law, society and Athens' in Cartledge, Millett and Todd 1990: 1–18.

Tredennick, H., trans. (1970): *Xenophon, Memoirs of Socrates and the Symposium*. Harmondsworth.

Treu, K. (1984): 'Traditional elements in Menandrean society' in Harmatta 1984: 1, 261–2.

Trittle, L. A. (1988): *Phocion the Good*. London.

Tscherikower, V. and F. M. Heichelheim (1942): 'Jewish religious influence in the Adler Papryi?', *Harvard Theological Review* 35: 35–44.

Turner, E. (1984): 'Menander and the new society' in Harmatta 1984: 1, 243–59.

Usher, A. P. (1943): *The Early History of Deposit Banking in Mediterranean Europe*, vol. 1. Cambridge, Mass.

Ussher, R. G., ed. (1960): *The Characters of Theophrastus*. London.

U Tun Wai (1957–8): 'Interest rates outside the organized money markets of underdeveloped countries', *International Monetary Fund Staff Papers* 6: 80–125.

Vanderpool, E. (1966): 'Some Attic inscriptions', *Hesperia* 35: 274–83.

(1971): 'Hoplon, an Athenian archon of the third century B.C.' *Hesperia* 40: 109–11.

Van Groningen, B. A., ed. (1933): *Aristote, le second livre de l'Economique*, Leiden, (reprinted New York 1979).

Van Groningen, B. A. and A. Wartelle, eds. (1968): *Aristote, Economique* (Budé edition). Paris.

Van Houtte, J. A. (1936): 'Les Courtiers au moyen âge', *Revue historique de droit français et étranger* 15: 105–41.

Vélissaropoulos, J. (1980): 'Les Symbola d'affaires. Remarques sur les tablettes archaïques de l'île de Corfu' *Panteios* 93–104, (reprinted in *Symposion 1977* 1982: 71–83; texts reproduced in *SEG* xxx 519–26).

Vellacott, P., trans. (1973): *Theophrastus, 'The Characters'; Menander, Plays and Fragments*, 2nd edn. Harmondsworth.

Verdenius, W. J., ed. (1985): *A Commentary on Hesiod's 'Works and Days'*. Leiden.

Veyne, P. (1976): *Le Pain et le cirque. Sociologie historique d'un pluralisme politique*, Paris (translated and abridged as *Bread and Circuses. Historical Sociology and Political Pluralism*, by B. Pearce. Harmondsworth 1990).

Vial, C. (1984): *Délos indépendente (314–167 avant J.-C.)*. Paris.

Vickers, M. (1984): 'Demus's gold phiale', *American Journal of Ancient History* 9: 48–53.

Vince, J. H., trans. (1926–35): *Demosthenes, Public Orations* (Loeb edition), 3 vols. London and Cambridge, Mass.

Vinogradoff, J. (1981): *Olbia. Geschichte einer altgriechischen Stadt am Schwarzen Meer*. Constance.

Vlastos, G., ed. (1971): *The Philosophy of Socrates. A Collection of Critical Essays*. New York.

Volterra, E. (1971): *Studi in onore di Eduardo Volterra*, 6 vols. Milan.

Von Below, G. (1901): 'Über Theorien der wirtschaftlichen Entwicklung der Völker', *Historische Zeitschrift* 86: 1–77.

Vondeling, J. (1961): *Eranos*. Groningen.

Von Pöhlmann, R. (1925): *Geschichte der sozialen Frage und des Sozialismus in der antiken Welt*, 3rd edn, F. Oertel (ed.), 2 vols. Munich.

Von Reden, S. (1987): 'Der Piräus im 5. und frühen 4. Jahrhundert: Eine Hafenstadt in einer Agrargesellschaft' (unpublished dissertation). Berlin.

Wade-Gery, H. T. (1930): 'A note on Kleon's finance' *Classical Review* 44: 163–5.

Wallace-Hadrill, A. (1989a): 'Patronage in Roman society: from Republic to Empire' in Wallace-Hadrill 1989b: 63–88.

  ed. (1989b): *Patronage in Ancient Society*. London.

Wallach, L., ed. (1966): *The Classical Tradition*. New York.

Wankel, H. (1982): 'Die Korruption in der rednerischen Topik und in der Realität des klassischen Athen' in Schuller 1982: 29–47.

Weber, M. (1904–5): 'Die protestantische Ethik und der Geist des Kapitalismus', *Archiv für Sozialwissenschaft und Sozialpolitik*, 20–1 (reprinted in *Gesammelte Aufsätze zur Religionssoziologie* I Tübingen 1922–3; translated as, and cited from, *The Protestant Ethic and the Spirit of Capitalism*, 2nd edn, by T. Parsons. London 1976).

  (1909): 'Agrarverhältnisse im Altertum' in *Handwörterbuch der Staatswissenschaft* I, 52–188 (reprinted in *Gesammelte Aufsätze zur Sozial- und Wirtschaftsgeschichte*, Tübingen 1924: 1–288; translated as, and cited from, *The Agrarian Sociology of Ancient Civilizations* by R. I. Frank. London 1976).

  (1921): 'Die Stadt', *Archiv für Sozialwissenschaft und Sozialpolitik* 47: 621–773 (translated as, and cited from, *The City*, by D. Martindale and G. Neuwirth. Chicago, Ill. 1958).

Weiss, B. (1986): *The Hell of the English. Bankruptcy and the Victorian Novel*. London and Toronto.

Welcker, U. (1834): 'Unechtheit der Rede des Lysias gegen den Sokratiker Aeschines' *Rheinisches Museum* 2: 391–410 (reprinted in, and cited from, Welcker 1844–50: I, 412–30).

(1844–50): *Kleine Schriften*, 3 vols. Bonn.

Welles = *Royal Correspondence in the Hellenistic Period*, C. B. Welles (ed.). London 1934.

Welskopf, E. C., ed. (1974): *Hellenische Poleis: Krise, Wirkung, Wandlung*, 4 vols. Berlin.

ed. (1979): *Terre et paysans dépendants dans les sociétés antiques*. Paris.

West, M. L., ed. (1978): *Hesiod, 'Works and Days'*. Oxford.

Westermann, W. L. (1930): 'Warehouse and trapezite banking in antiquity', *Journal of Economic and Business History* 3: 30–54.

Wevers, R. F. (1969): *Isaeus: Chronology, Prosopography and Social History*. The Hague.

Whitehead, D. (1977): *The Ideology of the Athenian Metic*, Proceedings of the Cambridge Philological Society Supp. no. 4.

(1983): 'Competitive outlay and community profit: φιλοτιμία in democratic Athens', *Classica et Mediaevalia* 34: 55–74.

(1986): *The Demes of Attica 508/7-ca. 250 B.C. A Political and Social Study*. Princeton, N.J.

Whittaker, C. R., ed. (1988): *Pastoral Economies in Classical Antiquity*, Proceedings of the Cambridge Philological Society Supp. no. 14.

Wilcken, U. (1939): 'Urkunden-Referat', *Archiv für Papyrusforschung* 30: 214–43.

Wilhelm, A. (1904): 'Der älteste griechische Brief', *Jahreshefte des Österreichischen Archäologischen Instituts* 7: 94–105.

(1909): 'Der Brief des Artikon', *Jahreshefte des Österreichischen Archäologischen Instituts* 12: 118–26.

Wiles, D. (1984): 'Menander's *Dyscolos* and Demetrios of Phaleron's dilemma', *Greece and Rome* 31: 170–80.

Will, Ed. (1954): 'Trois quarts de siècle de recherches sur l'économie grecque antique', *Annales ESC* 9: 7–22.

(1965): 'Archaic Greece', *Deuxième conférence internationale d'histoire économique*, Aix-en-Provence 1962; I: *Trade and Politics in the Ancient World*, Paris and the Hague, (reprinted New York 1979).

(1969): 'Soloniana. Notes critiques sur des hypothèses récentes', *Revue des études grecques* 78: 542–56.

Will, E., C. Mossé and P. Goukowsky (1985): *Le Monde grec et l'Orient*, vol. II: *Le IVᵉ siècle et l'époque hellénistique*, 2nd edn. Paris.

Willetts, R. F. (1955): *Aristocratic Society in Ancient Crete*, London, (reprinted Westport, Conn. 1980).

ed. (1967): *The Law Code of Gortyn*. Berlin.

Wills, G. (1990): 'Shylock without usury', *New York Review of Books*, 18 January 1990, 22–5.

Wolf, E. R. (1966): 'Kinship, friendship and patron–client relations in complex societies' in Banton 1966: 1–22.

Wolff, H. J. (1943): 'The *dike blabes* in Demosthenes Or. 55', *American Journal of Philology* 63: 332–47.

(1966): *Die attische Paragraphe*. Weimar.

Wood, E. M. (1988): *Peasant-Citizen and Slave. The Foundations of Athenian Democracy*. London and New York.

Woodhead, A. G. (1981): *The Study of Greek Inscriptions*, 2nd edn, Cambridge.

Woodhouse, W. J. (1938): *Solon the Liberator. A Study of the Agrarian Problem in Attika in the Seventh Century*. London.

Wright, C. T. (1934): 'Some conventions regarding the usurer in Elizabethan literature', *Studies in Philology* 31: 179–97.

(1938): 'The usurer's sin in Elizabethan literature', *Studies in Philology* 35: 178–94.

Wrightson, K. (1982): *English Society 1580–1680*. London.

Wyse, W. (1892): 'On the use of *prodaneizein*', *Classical Review* 6: 254–7.

ed. (1904): *The Speeches of Isaeus*, Cambridge, (reprinted Hildesheim 1967).

Yang, L. S. (1952): *Money and Credit in China. A Short History*. Cambridge, Mass.

Yavetz, Z. (1963): 'The failure of Catiline's conspiracy', *Historia* 12: 485–99.

Zanker, G. (1986): 'The *Works and Days*: Hesiod's *Beggars' Opera*' *Bulletin of the Institute of Classical Studies* 33: 26–36.

Ziebarth, E. (1917): 'Delische Stiftungen', *Hermes* 52: 425–41.

Zielinski, T. (1924): 'Charis and Charites', *Classical Quarterly* 18: 158–63.

Zimmern, A. (1911): *The Greek Commonwealth*, Oxford, (cited from the fifth edition of 1931).

(1928a): 'Suggestions towards a political economy of the Greek city state' in Zimmern 1928b: 165–99.

(1928b): *Solon and Croesus, and Other Greek Essays*. London.

Indexes

INDEX OF PASSAGES CITED

GREEK

346

LATIN AND MISCELLANEOUS

INDEX OF PAPYRI

INDEX OF INSCRIPTIONS

GENERAL INDEX

NOTE: This is an index of names, places and selected subjects. Ancient authors and modern scholars are indexed only where their views are discussed in the text; anonymous and pseudonymous works are cited by title. In the notes only extended discussions of points not covered in the text have been indexed.